TRANSATLANTIC STOWE

Transatlantic Stowe

HARRIET BEECHER STOWE AND EUROPEAN CULTURE

Edited by Denise Kohn, Sarah Meer,

and Emily B. Todd

· · ·

University of Iowa Press

Iowa City

University of Iowa Press, Iowa City 52242
http://www.uiowapress.org
Printed in the United States of America

Design by Omega Clay

The University of Iowa Press is a member of Green Press Initiative and is committed to preserving natural resources.

Printed on acid-free paper

Library of Congress Cataloging-in-Publication Data
Transatlantic Stowe: Harriet Beecher Stowe and European culture / edited by Denise Kohn, Sarah Meer, and Emily B. Todd.
    p. cm.
Includes bibliographical references (p.) and index.
ISBN 10: 1-58729-473-7 / ISBN 13: 978-1-58729-473-0 (cloth)
    1. Stowe, Harriet Beecher, 1811–1896—Criticism and interpretation. 2. Stowe, Harriet Beecher, 1811–1896—Influence. 3. Stowe, Harriet Beecher, 1811–1896. Uncle Tom's cabin. 4. American literature—European influences. 5. European literature—American influences. 6. Slavery in literature. 7. United States—Intellectual life—19th century. 8. Europe—Intellectual life—19th century. I. Kohn, Denise, 1963–. II. Meer, Sarah, 1969–. III. Todd, Emily B. (Emily Bishop), 1967–.
PS2958.152T73 2006
813'.3—dc22   2006045618

06 07 08 09 10 C 5 4 3 2 1

CONTENTS

Foreword *by Joan D. Hedrick* vii

Acknowledgments ix

Reading Stowe as a Transatlantic Writer xi
Denise Kohn, Sarah Meer, and Emily B. Todd

PART ONE
BLURRING BORDERS, WRITING NATIONS

Stowe and the Byronic Heroine 3
Caroline Franklin

Uncle Tom's Cabin and the Irish National Tale 24
Clíona Ó Gallchoir

Nature, Magic, and History in Stowe and Scott 46
Monika Elbert

PART TWO
RACE, CLASS, AND LABOR IN THE ATLANTIC WORLD

The First Years of *Uncle Tom's Cabin* in Russia 67
John MacKay

Stowe, Gaskell, and the Woman Reformer 89
Whitney Womack Smith

Stowe, Eliot, and the Reform Aesthetic 111
Clare Cotugno

Sunny Memories and Serious Proposals 131
Donald Ross

PART THREE

TRANSNATIONAL WRITER

The Construction of Self in *Sunny Memories* 149
Shirley Foster

Art and the Body in *Agnes of Sorrento* 167
Gail K. Smith

Stowe and Religious Iconography 187
Carla Rineer

The Afterlife of *Dred* on the British Stage 208
Judie Newman

About the Contributors 225
Works Cited 229
Index 249

by Joan D. Hedrick

When Harriet Beecher Stowe was just married, her husband, Calvin Stowe, set off on a trip to Europe to buy books for the Lane Seminary Library. Full of trepidation about this transatlantic trip, he was buoyed by his wife, who told him, "My dear, I wish I were a man in your place; if I wouldn't have a grand time!"[1] Stowe herself would enjoy three trips to Europe, the first at the invitation of two Glasgow antislavery societies after the phenomenal success of *Uncle Tom's Cabin* in 1852. Already an American writer of some distinction, with the publication of *Uncle Tom's Cabin* Stowe became an international celebrity. Her book was translated into more than sixty-three languages and entered the canon of world literature. Adapted and replied to in many forms—theatrical, novelistic, and musical—*Uncle Tom's Cabin* has from the time of its publication traveled the globe. Controversial in the United States and embroiling Stowe in a series of debates in the British Isles about parallels between black slavery and white wage slavery, as well as the Scottish clearances, *Uncle Tom's Cabin* has been read around the world as a story of the liberation of a people.

Just as Stowe viewed the struggle over slavery as the defining national struggle of the American republic, so Europeans viewed *Uncle Tom's Cabin* as a national epic. Appearing at a time when American literature was not an established fact, Stowe's novel created national and regional types and was widely embraced in other countries for the Americanness of its material. Charles Kingsley hailed the book as "a really healthy indigenous growth, autochthonous, & free from all that hapless second & third-hand Germanism, & Italianism, & all other unreal-isms that make me sigh over almost every American book I open."[2] Raised on the Bible and the novels of Sir Walter Scott, Stowe cast her materials in the form of a national narrative. The passion for freedom that animated her characters to flee to Canada resonated with the struggles of the Hebrews against the pharoah and of peoples fighting for nation states in the nineteenth century. As George Harris fights off his pursuers, Stowe addresses the reader,

> If it had been only a Hungarian youth, now bravely defending in some mountain fastness the retreat of fugitives escaping from Austria into America, this would have been sublime heroism; but as it was a youth of African descent, defending the retreat of fugitives through America into Canada, of course we are too well instructed and patriotic to see any heroism in it; and if any of our readers do, they must do it on their own private responsibility.[3]

Seeing fugitive slaves through the lens of worldwide revolutionary struggles for self-determination is likely what led Stowe to send her characters to Liberia at the end of her novel. While this plot was much criticized for seeming to endorse the conservative, colonizationist arm of the antislavery movement, it does underscore the internationalism of Stowe's novel. Seeing Stowe in a transatlantic context is to see her in the way she viewed historical events and the way in which she was viewed in her time.

NOTES

1. Harriet Beecher Stowe to Calvin E. Stowe, [June 1836], qtd. in Hedrick, *Stowe*, 100.

2. Charles Kingsley to Harriet Beecher Stowe, 12 August 1852, qtd. in Hedrick, *Stowe*, 234.

3. Harriet Beecher Stowe, *Uncle Tom's Cabin; or, Life among the Lowly*, qtd. in Hedrick, ed., *Oxford Stowe Reader*, 224.

ACKNOWLEDGMENTS

The editors would like to thank all of our contributors for their commitment to this project. We also want to thank the following for their support and suggestions: Dorothy Baker, Bridget Bennett, Nairn Chadwick, Carole Dupont-Stonestreet, Jaime Gionet, Liam Harte, Jen Pollard, Niko Pfund, Robert Shelton, Elizabeth Starr, Michael Tilby, and Richard Todd. In addition, we appreciate the help of Prasenjit Gupta, Holly Carver, John Joerschke, and Charlotte Wright with the University of Iowa Press.

Reading Stowe as a Transatlantic Writer

DENISE KOHN, SARAH MEER, AND EMILY B. TODD

N 1864, the British burlesque publisher Thomas Hailes Lacy added a new play to his Sensation Series, parodying the melodramatic versions of *Uncle Tom's Cabin* on the London stage. As its title suggests, *The Tyrant! The Slave!! The Victim!!! & the Tar!!!!* had taken some liberties with the text, but Lacy's subtitle was telling: this was billed as a "transatlantic Sensation Drama."[1] Harriet Beecher Stowe's fiction of American slavery had become transatlantic: it had not only been removed to the British stage but had partly come to represent the process of cultural translation.

Uncle Tom's Cabin had turned Stowe into an international phenomenon, but the transatlantic element of Stowe's career was not confined to that one novel: instead, her development as a writer and her publishing career were both thoroughly implicated in wider patterns of transatlantic cultural influence and exchange.

Though recent scholarship has demonstrated the historical and cultural importance of transatlantic influences, Stowe has been understood primarily within her national boundaries as an American author writing about American issues. This is curious because the international success of *Uncle Tom's Cabin* arguably made Stowe the most internationally visible American writer of her time. Stowe's significance for transatlantic studies extends far beyond her most popular novel. Stowe's life, spanning the whole of the nineteenth century, coincided with a turn in the tide of cultural influence as American writers moved from imitation of European models to the export of new, distinctively American forms of art. In all aspects of her life and career—her early childhood reading, adult literary friendships, travel abroad as a literary celebrity, participation in international politics, involvement in literary scandals—Stowe illustrated these broad patterns of transatlantic exchange and also helped to transform them.

The omission of Stowe from recent transatlantic scholarship is symptomatic of a larger elision of American women writers from these studies.[2] Even though the new transatlantic literary scholarship moves beyond old-fashioned studies of British influence on American writers, the canon studied in these works is a familiar and largely male one. In *Transatlantic Insurrections* (2001), Paul Giles compares writers such as Richardson and Franklin; Jefferson, Sterne, and Burke; and Hawthorne and Trollope. The one chapter devoted to a woman writer is on Austen, and in his *Virtual Americas* (2002), with a part of a chapter on Sylvia Plath, American women writers are paid proportionally little attention. Robert Weisbuch's *Atlantic Double-Cross* (1986) also considers pairs of British and American male authors, such as Melville and Dickens, Whitman and Arnold, and Carlyle and Emerson; women writers are discussed only in passing.

When transatlantic scholarship has broadened in scope to consider questions of race in the Atlantic world, it has focused on African and African American figures in works such as Paul Gilroy's *Black Atlantic* (1993) and Martin Crawford and Alan Rice's collection *Liberating Sojourn: Frederick Douglass and Transatlantic Reform* (1999). Stowe clearly plays an important role in the racial history of the Atlantic world, but her part, and that of other white women writers, such as Lydia Maria Child, is still relatively neglected.

Stowe's life and career also force us to see the transatlantic in terms well outside the Anglo-American patterns to which many studies confine themselves.[3] The translation of Stowe's work into dozens of European languages; her travels in France, Switzerland, Germany, and Italy; her husband's trip, within weeks of their marriage, to Germany to study Prussian education—all demonstrate connections between the United States and Europe as a whole. Stowe's meeting Elizabeth Barrett Browning in Italy, as well as her encounters with other Britons and Americans, also points to complex relationships within Europe. So do the Russians whom John MacKay describes in his essay here, who read Stowe in French and German or made secondary translations from the French.

It is the goal then of *Transatlantic Stowe: Harriet Beecher Stowe and European Culture* not only to broaden our readings of Stowe's texts and of Stowe herself as a literary figure but also to broaden the scope of transatlantic studies. *Transatlantic Stowe* examines Stowe's literary and literal forays in Europe and the ways in which intellectual and cultural exchanges between the Old and New Worlds shaped her work and the work of other major nineteenth-century authors. The collection argues that reading Stowe within a transatlantic context is crucial to understanding her career. Just as important, however, since Stowe was one of the most famous—if not for a time *the* most famous—author of her period, understanding Stowe as a transatlantic writer also illuminates American and European literature and culture in the nineteenth century. *Transatlantic Stowe* aims to restore Stowe—the exemplary nineteenth-century American woman writer—to her preeminent position in transatlantic culture and, in the process, to provide readers with a new understanding of nineteenth-century American and European literature and culture.

...

Alongside other nineteenth-century American women writers who have gained prominence recently, Stowe has come to occupy a particularly central position in American studies in the twenty-first century. The rewriting of literary history to include women's novels in the 1980s and 1990s called for scholars to reread *Uncle Tom's Cabin*, the best-selling novel of antebellum America.

To be sure, Stowe, unlike other members of that "damn'd mob of scribbling women" as Hawthorne so infamously called popular female authors, had never fallen out of history. She had long existed in American myth as that "little woman" whom Lincoln credited with starting that "great war" and, simultaneously somehow, as the narrow-minded Christian who created the shameful, shuffling image of an Uncle Tom. She has had a complex mythic status in American consciousness: she is supposed to have single-handedly brought the abolitionist crusade against slavery to fruition yet also to have created our culture's most pernicious image of African Americans. As a result, her work has been too influential and controversial ever to be forgotten, even though for most of the twentieth century she was misunderstood and compared unfavorably to Romantics such as Hawthorne and Melville and to Modernists such as Hemingway and Faulkner.

Feminist critics such as Nina Baym, Cathy Davidson, and Jane Tompkins, however, and the women's recovery project offered a new, more complex matrix of interpretation. Redefining sentiment as a legitimate aesthetic of cultural power, they revealed a crucial context to Stowe's work and reopened some of the powerful contemporary resonances that it had lost. Stowe intertwined domestic subplots with didactic reform—and thereby made the political vividly personal for a mass audience of middle-class readers. Many popular women's novels of the period function as political critiques in their representations of young heroines denied opportunities for education, careers, independence, and even suitable choices for spouses. These novels can be seen as spanning a spectrum from politely subversive texts such as Susan Warner's *The Wide, Wide World*, Louisa May Alcott's *Work*, and Augusta Jane Evans's *St. Elmo*, to more radical books such as E. D. E. N. Southworth's *The Hidden Hand*, Elizabeth Stuart Phelps's *The Story of Avis*, and Fanny Fern's *Ruth Hall*. Stowe's most famous novels, *Uncle Tom's Cabin* and *Dred*, are unusual in their treatment of slavery and religion.[4] Her fervent sense of woman's duty and power to create a moral order is just as evident in novels such as *Oldtown Folks*, *The Pearl of Orr's Island*, and *The Minister's Wooing*, where in nostalgic New England settings, she promotes a national identity that includes society's least powerful members.

Nevertheless, although scholars have restored Stowe to the canon, her significance has been established in relation to *American* literary culture, especially her connections with other women writers and her influence on debates over slavery. It is perhaps not surprising that Stowe has been studied mainly within her American context, especially considering that the ideology of American literary studies has demanded that American authors be defined in opposition to their European counterparts, to the point that the greater the difference, the greater the claim an author has had to being American.

Yet nineteenth-century writers also saw themselves as part of an Atlantic world. An essay about slavery in the January 1853 issue of the British periodical *Blackwood's Edinburgh Magazine* notes that the "influence exercised upon each other by England and the United States is already very great" and argues that "[m]anners, customs, legislation, policy, and institutions will gradually assimilate more and more" ("Slavery" 1). The only likely obstacle to this creation of a common transatlantic culture, the essay notes, is that "the sympathies of the British people with their Transatlantic connections" may lead them to a misunderstanding of the politics of slavery ("Slavery" 1). However, any misunderstanding of the "social and moral evils" of slavery will be forestalled by "the almost universal circulation of the admirable work of Mrs. Beecher Stowe" ("Slavery" 1).

Even if in the nineteenth century Stowe was understood as a significant transatlantic writer, more recently she has been read within the tradition of American women's writing in the nineteenth century, scholarship that until now has been national in scope. As *Transatlantic Stowe* shows, however, Stowe's oeuvre ranges far beyond the "American novel." Her European travel narrative *Sunny Memories of Foreign Lands*, her exposé *Lady Byron Vindicated*, her religious and art history *Woman in Sacred History*, and her Italian novel *Agnes of Sorrento* are frequently neglected because they do not mesh with her reputation as American. These works are crucial to understanding Stowe as an author, though, for they situate her in the rich cultural exchange between Europe and the United States in the nineteenth century, and they place her alongside American writers—like Irving, Poe, Hawthorne, and later Wharton and James—who were reinventing Europe as an imaginative source. Just as important, *Transatlantic Stowe* argues that "national debate" novels such as *Uncle Tom's Cabin* and *Dred* need to be reread within the broader context of transatlantic culture.

In the nineteenth century, as we have already suggested, it would have been odd *not* to consider Stowe in relation to Europe, and she viewed herself as a transatlantic citizen. As a child, she devoured Scott's novels and Byron's poetry.[5] Walter Scott became a particular favorite; his novels were, in fact, the first ones to be welcomed into her childhood home, and the Beecher children read them hungrily. Stowe recalled that she and her brother sped through *Ivanhoe* seven times one summer and that her father challenged the children to "see who'll tell the most out of Scott's novels" (Lyman Beecher 1: 391). Stowe later returned to the Waverley novels and read them in chronological order as she composed *Uncle Tom's Cabin*,[6] and Monika Elbert's essay here shows how much Scott's influence on Stowe was a lasting one.

There were other British influences too. Charles Dickens had made the fictionalization of social ills into hugely popular texts in the 1840s; he claimed to "have been assured on reasonably good authority—Mrs. Stowe's —that she was animated to [her] task by being a reader of mine."[7] Stowe herself acknowledged in the preface to a British edition of *Uncle Tom's Cabin* that she had drawn on the representations of the British poor in the novels of Charles Kingsley and Charlotte Elizabeth Tonna as well as Dickens.[8] Like other midcentury Americans, Stowe emerged as a writer in a literary culture shaped by British books.

Recognizing this adds a great deal to our understanding of her work. While recent critics have tied Stowe to an American women's sentimental tradition, reading Stowe within the larger sphere of transatlantic culture allows us to relate this tradition to European women's didactic novels such as those of Hannah More and Maria Edgeworth. As Clíona Ó Gallchoir argues here, Edgeworth's construction of Irish character in a European context influenced an American pattern that linked Stowe and Catharine Maria Sedgwick. And Stowe's "regional" novels such as *The Minister's Wooing* and *Oldtown Folks* become transatlantic in scope, as Caroline Franklin's essay shows, when they are read as part of the didactic debate about the Byronic hero and the position of the woman writer as moral champion.

Stowe herself strengthened these links, traveling to Europe and befriending British writers. On her first trip to London, in 1853, Stowe was honored at the lord mayor's banquet, where Mr. Justice Talfourd toasted Stowe and Dickens together as having "employed fiction as a means of awakening the attentions of the respected countries to the condition of the oppressed and suffering classes" (Stowe, *Sunny Memories* vol. 1, xli).

There were also important literary friendships, of which Elizabeth Gaskell's was one of the most significant. Gaskell was also a mother, the wife of a minister, and a novelist, and like Stowe, Gaskell built on earlier women's didactic traditions to dramatize themes of labor and oppression in contemporary society. Gaskell and Stowe's literary friendship cross fertilized their major novels, as Whitney Womack Smith demonstrates in this collection, especially in their representations of the power of female agency.

The connection Stowe formed with Elizabeth Barrett Browning was so warm that in 1861 the poet confided in Stowe about "the greatest affliction of my life—the only time when I felt *despair*," and the poem it resulted in, "De Profundis," as well as writing of the comfort she found in spiritualism and of politics in Italy and France.[9]

John Ruskin, too, became a friend, protesting at Stowe's return home in a playful letter: "What a dreadful thing it is that people should have to go to America again, after coming to Europe! It seems to me an inversion of the order of nature." Ten years after the publication of the first volume of *The Stones of Venice*, he personally pressed the merits of the city upon Stowe: "So you are coming around to Venice, after all? We shall all have to come to it, depend upon it, some way or another" (Ruskin to HBS, 18 June 1861, qtd. in Stowe, Charles 354–355).[10]

Although she never met her, Stowe also developed a warm correspondence with George Eliot on literature, spiritualism, and their lives as women and writers. Both women read each other's work, and as Clare Cotugno argues here, Stowe's *Dred* and Eliot's *Daniel Deronda* share an aesthetic of reform, though the two writers diverged in their views of audience, art, and progress.

In a letter to Eliot in 1872, Stowe wrote, "I felt, when I read your letter, how glad I should be to have you here in our Florida cottage . . . Though resembling Italy in climate, it is wholly different in the appearance of nature. . . . The green tidiness and culture of England here gives way to a wild savageness of beauty" (HBS to Eliot, 11 May 1872, qtd. in Stowe, Charles 468). In this correspondence, Stowe figures herself as a citizen of a transatlantic world who imagines the scene outside her southeastern cottage not from the perspective of a New Englander but through European eyes, whose reference points are England and Italy.

. . .

The publication of *Uncle Tom's Cabin* transformed Stowe from a participant in a transatlantic community into an international celebrity, and the novel's publishing and reception history abroad highlights its status as a transatlantic text. Several British publishers issued the novel in the summer of 1852, and by the fall the book had become a phenomenal success, with ten new editions appearing during two weeks in October alone.[11] Without international copyright laws, scores of pirated British editions of *Uncle Tom's Cabin* appeared, from cheap railway issues to deluxe editions.[12] Clarke and Company registered the novel's extraordinary British success in a prefatory note to one of its illustrated editions (published with G. Routledge), noting that all three of its editions of *Uncle Tom's Cabin* were selling at an unprecedented rate, with 96,000 railway editions already sold and 25,000 of an illustrated edition in penny numbers selling weekly. "A Hundred and Fifty Thousand Copies of this Work are already in the hands of the public," the publisher continued, "while still the weekly returns of sale show no decline." Clarke and Company was right to predict the continuation of such brisk sales: sales in Great Britain in fact surpassed those in America by more than half a million copies, with some 1.5 million copies sold around Britain and its colonies (Altick 384).

The pirating and rapid reprinting of *Uncle Tom's Cabin* in Britain marked the most significant shift in cultural influence. For the first time since Sidney Smith had asked rhetorically, "Who reads an American book?" the answer was everyone. "Few are the societies in which it has not for some time past formed the staple topic of conversation," noted one British preface (Howard iii). The novel circulated widely, read by those in the "loftiest regions of . . . social life, and in the obscure cottages of hardworking and unpolished labourers and miners" (Howard iv). Stowe had become a literary giant in

Britain. In late 1852, one British observer commented that "any work of fiction is likely to appear Dwarfish, beside the colossal pedestal at present occupied by Mrs. Beecher Stowe," and in anticipation of her visit, the London publisher Richard Bentley wrote in February 1853, "Was there ever such a furore as England has made of this lady! I suppose when she arrives she will be [lionized] from John O'Groats to Lands' [sic] End."[13]

Stowe's success spread throughout Europe, and by 1853 the novel had been translated into French, Italian, Welsh, German, Portuguese, Spanish, Norwegian, and Slovenian, among other languages. Readers across Europe interpreted the story not solely as American but as a text that spoke for them; it became a book that reflected issues of oppression and reform in their own nations. In many ways, *Uncle Tom's Cabin* in its travels became a different text. There were multiple editions in several European countries, and titles differed so that in France rival publishers produced *La Cabane de l'Oncle Tom, ou La Vie des Négres en Amérique* and *La Case de l'Oncle Tom: Ou, Tableaux de l'Esclavage dans les Etats-Unis d'Amérique* in 1853.[14] Just as these titles asserted the Americanness of their subject matter, so the Parisian paper *Le Charivari* saw a special national significance in this literary import from the United States. Although many of its 1852 and 1853 references to the novel are comical or ironic (as in the cartoon of the couple who cannot sleep for "Tom Manie" [fig. 1] or the description of a man held up in Philadelphia by robbers who demand "your *Uncle Tom* or your life"), *Le Charivari* also suggested that the novel might have serious literary implications: "Le roman *réalist* dont on parle si souvent le voilà, c'est l'*Oncle Tom*. Idées, sentiments, caractères, moeurs, paysages, là dedans tout est réel" ("Here is the realist novel we have heard so much about—it is *Uncle Tom*. Ideas, feelings, characters, customs, and landscapes are all real"). Not only this, the paper speculates that this realism, which for so long France had thought its own secret, might have its most obvious home in America—"nous perdons tous les jours cet instinct qui fut longtemps notre secret, d'associer la poésie à la réalité, de mêler l'art à la vie; on dirait que la muse a émigré vers le Nouveau-Monde" ("every day we lose that instinct which for a long time was our secret, of associating poetry with reality, of mixing art with life; one could say that the muse has emigrated to the New World").[15]

European publishers also turned *Uncle Tom's Cabin* into a novel about particularly American problems. Even though the British editions retained the same text, the packaging—the title pages, covers, advertisements, prefaces, illustrations—made the novel into a different book. Like the French

1. A French couple is awakened by an order to read *Uncle Tom* as part of the "Tom Manie" sweeping Paris in this cartoon published in *Le Charivari* on 21 June 1853. Courtesy of the British Library.

publications, British editions of *Uncle Tom's Cabin* remade the novel to highlight the Americanness of its subject.[16] The subtitle of the "people's illustrated edition" of Clarke and Company was *Negro Life in the Slave States of America*; that of Ingram, Cooke and Company was *A Tale of Life among the Lowly, or Pictures of Slavery in the United States of America*; and Nathaniel Cooke's was subtitled *A Tale of Slave Life in America*.

Like the subtitles, British prefaces interpreted Stowe's novel in national terms. By the mid-nineteenth century there was a thriving discourse of British commentary on American institutions, which often stressed the contradiction of the coexistence of American ideals of freedom and liberty with slavery. Over two hundred books by British travelers in the United States were published between 1815 and 1860, and many were highly critical of American institutions.[17] The most infamous, at least among Americans, included Basil Hall's 1830 *Travels in North America*, Frances Trollope's 1832 *Domestic Manners of the Americans*, Captain Marryat's 1839 *Diary in America*, and Charles Dickens's 1842 *American Notes for General Circulation*. The prefaces to British editions of *Uncle Tom's Cabin* recalled this genre of sociopolitical commentary in their stress on what the novel could teach readers about American society. Implicitly, of course, they also made Britain, whose own slaves in the West Indies had been freed in the 1830s, look virtuous by contrast. John Cassell's preface is typical in pointing out the irony that the "land of the free" is also the land of slavery: "Strange to say, but, courteous reader, if you want to see tyranny in absolute perfection, unbridled and unrestrained,—aye and licensed by law, and blessed by an obsequious and time-serving priesthood, to oppress, ill-treat, exact, scourge, pollute, degrade, torture, murder, and destroy down-trodden humanity, you must cross the Atlantic to the vaunted land of the free!" (x).

In Routledge's sixth edition, the publishers also used their preface to *Uncle Tom's Cabin* for a critique of the United States: "It is vain to assert for the republic of the United States greatness, or any share of progress in the world. Commercial greatness we are willing to allow her; but prosperous infamy is not palliated infamy, and cruelty imbibes no virtue from purple and fine linen" (iv–v). Prefaces to British editions of *Uncle Tom's Cabin* do not linger on the novel's emotional effects or highlight Little Eva's death, the separation of slave families, or Tom's martyrdom. Instead, *Uncle Tom's Cabin* in its British context is framed by discussions of American failings and backwardness and English superiority and progress.

British reviews of *Uncle Tom's Cabin* also struck the same note. In 1853 *Blackwood's Edinburgh Magazine* imagined a reader of *Uncle Tom's Cabin* a hundred years in the future and immediately wondered about "the possible state of things then existing on the other side of the Atlantic," suggesting how racial politics would look in the aftermath of nineteenth-century slavery ("Uncle Tom's," *Blackwood's* 393–394). Perhaps an American "Empire" of "harmonious diversities" would be ruled by a black emperor and white empress; perhaps a "united republic" would be created in which all "offices, rights, and privileges" were "equally distributed" ("Uncle Tom's," *Blackwood's* 393–394); or else the future might be an ominous, indeterminate one of racial conflict. Another British reviewer, Nassau William Senior, observed that the novel would give some British readers a chance to understand slavery and the nature of black people, but he feared that the novel "gratified . . . national jealousy and national vanity. We have long been smarting under the conceit of America—we are tired of hearing her boast that she is the freest and most enlightened country that the world has ever seen." This is why, he surmises, in Britain "All parties hailed Mrs. Stowe as a revolter from the enemy" (qtd. in Gossett 240).

This pattern was repeated in British stage adaptations of *Uncle Tom's Cabin*. There were at least twenty different productions of *Uncle Tom's Cabin* on the London stage between 1852 and 1855, and they dramatized not only Stowe's novel but also popular British attitudes to slavery and the United States. "Americanness" was praised in reviews; in some productions the "star-spangled banner" was declared stained with slavery ("Metropolitan Theatres" 307).[18] Stowe's novel partly owed its success in Britain to the way that it seemed American in its setting, language, and rhetoric of rights and yet expressed deep concerns about society in the United States. It would be read and reinterpreted across Europe in relation to labor and class ideologies and the relationships between the wealthy and the poor.

Americans were acutely aware of British interpretations of Stowe's novel. The common American practice of reprinting reviews from British periodicals underscores the importance attached to transatlantic opinion, especially about a novel as incendiary as *Uncle Tom's Cabin*. British reviews were themselves treated as newsworthy: the *New York Daily Times* ran both a story about the London *Times* review and the piece itself in September 1852. Three days later, entrepreneurial printers in New York had reprinted the London *Times* review as a pamphlet, which they advertised in the *New York Daily Times*, stating they felt assured that both the book's "opponents" and "admirers" in the "American Public" would read the London evaluation ("Advertisement" 5). Two months later when the New York paper reprinted the review of *Uncle Tom's Cabin* from Charles Dickens's *Household Words*, it once again ran a story about the review itself. It is interesting that in both cases, while the newspapers referred to the articles as reviews, the main headlines for both British essays did not even mention *Uncle Tom's Cabin*. Instead, the New York paper ran the London *Times* piece under the main headline "AMERICAN SLAVERY" ("American Slavery" 6) and the Dickens article under the headline "NORTH AMERICAN SLAVERY" ("North American Slavery" 3). The word *slavery* was enough to let readers know that the topic was also *Uncle Tom's Cabin*; the two were becoming inextricable in the transatlantic discourse of 1852.

British readings of *Uncle Tom's Cabin* as a reflection on American shortcomings caused a great deal of anxiety. The *New York Herald* saw such reviews as an anti-American conspiracy: "the aristocrats of England and Europe . . . fancy they are dealing a desperate blow at our institutions by their patronage of Uncle Tom" and predicted an unexpected and dire outcome: the British poor would revolt instead, and the aristocrats would "discover when it is too late that they themselves are the Legrees and Haleys upon whom retribution must fall" ("The Effect of Uncle Tom in Europe" 69–70). This line of argument was repeated in several anti–*Uncle Tom* novels set in Britain. Lucien Chase's *English Serfdom and American Slavery* (1854), Marian Southwood's *Tit for Tat* (1856), and Ebenezer Starnes's *The Slaveholder Abroad* (1860) show British aristocrats weeping crocodile tears over American slaves while they starve, ill-treat, and brutalize the poor tenants on their estates.

Not only, then, did *Uncle Tom's Cabin* push Stowe onto the international stage, but as the many editions of *Uncle Tom's Cabin*, the plays, and the spin-offs suggest, the novel became part of a transatlantic community, influencing literary culture and entertainment in Europe and beyond. So while Stowe's success with *Uncle Tom's Cabin* raised the status of American literature abroad, the novel also became a vehicle for European critiques of the United States, exposing the hollowness of some of its most treasured ideals. Becoming a transatlantic text, then, transformed *Uncle Tom's Cabin*.

The book also embroiled its author in new political questions.[19] Like their counterparts in the United States, British abolitionists were heartened by *Uncle Tom*'s awakening of interest in slavery outside established abolitionist communities: the Uncle Tom Penny Offering amassing contributions from thousands of working-class sympathizers as well as from the Nonconformist middle classes, and the novel stoking new interest in antislavery societies, particularly among women and in Scotland and the North of England.[20]

With their longstanding traditions of correspondence and exchange, the transatlantic antislavery networks were also revitalized by *Uncle Tom*.[21] When, in 1853, Stowe visited Britain at the invitation of two antislavery societies, she helped renew and extend links between organizations in the two countries.[22] Her visit may have helped British abolitionists to suspend or to mitigate their ideological disputes; it was also extremely significant for Stowe herself (Hedrick 236). For Frederick Douglass, the lecture tour in Britain and Ireland was personally and politically formative—as a result of his visit in 1845 and 1846 Douglass secured his freedom from his former master, collected the support he needed to found his newspaper the *North Star*, and developed the political independence that led him eventually to break with his former mentor, William Lloyd Garrison.[23] As Donald Ross shows in this volume, Stowe's antislavery politics shifted during her 1853 visit too, as her perceptions changed, both of issues and institutions.

Nevertheless, the transatlantic phenomenon that was *Uncle Tom's Cabin* fractured relationships as well as forging them. As in the United States, *Uncle Tom* had its detractors in Britain, and the book's popularity abroad also served to incense proslavery American critics at home. Reports of Stowe's personal reception in Britain—greeted by rapturous crowds, sought after as a celebrity, attended by the famous and the fashionable—only compounded this resentment.[24] And the intensity of emotion aroused by the novel and its author triggered what may almost be described as an international newspaper war over the petition devised by the Earl of Shaftesbury, printed in the *Times*, and circulated by the Duchess of Sutherland, "An Affectionate and Christian Address of Many Thousands of Women of Great Britain and Ireland to Their Sisters, the Women of the United States of America."[25]

This transatlantic invocation of the common sex, culture, and religion of British and American women begged that ladies in the United States would "raise your voices to your fellow-citizens, and your prayers to God" to end slavery.[26] The "Address" was condemned in London for broaching subjects unsuitable for women, while responses from Julia Gardiner Tyler and Louisa McCord were reprinted by more than fifty newspapers in the United States.[27]

The involvement of an earl and a duchess allowed critics to cast the novel in the ideological terms—democracy and monarchy, feudalism, slavery, and capitalism—that were the subject of the new discipline of political economy. Complex and urgent social questions, including the relative merits of Britain and America (and within the United States, of the northern and southern states), even the nature of freedom, now also occupied the violent debate centered on the writing—and the person—of Harriet Beecher Stowe.

In *Uncle Tom's Cabin*, Stowe's character St. Clare considers but rejects the analogy between slaves and free laborers; for a diverse collection of thinkers in both the United States and Europe (including Carlyle, George Fitzhugh, and Louisa McCord), the comparison was an important one (Stowe, *Uncle Tom's Cabin* 199–200).[28] The conditions of slaves and the free poor had been likened since the West Indian planters fought their doomed battle to maintain slavery in the British colonies, not only among apologists for slavery in the Americas but also in the reform literature of Britain. As Catherine Gallagher has demonstrated, the debate was enshrined in the "white slave" metaphor, which had been invoked for decades as much by middle-class reformers and working-class radicals as by slaveowners. Predictably, the phrase was redeployed in criticism of Stowe: in Britain *Reynolds's Newspaper*, the *Northern Ensign*, the *Leader*, and the *Star of Freedom* all argued that "wage-slavery" or "the slavery of labour" was nearly as bad or even worse than the plight of actual slaves in America.[29] Refuting the comparison, Lord Shaftesbury and the antislavery journals insisted on the greater iniquity of the slave system, which made submission to a cruel master compulsory.[30]

Examinations of feudalism and democracy and slavery and freedom were thus as vital in Europe as in the United States, especially in the aftermath of the 1848 revolutions, and John MacKay's essay in this collection suggests how the serfdom issue endowed *Uncle Tom's Cabin* with powerful local resonances for readers in Russia. With slavery such a fraught topic in Europe in the 1850s as well as in the Americas, it is clear that *Uncle Tom's Cabin* should be considered crucial to the history of the Black Atlantic: the book's impact reverberated throughout the world envisaged by Paul Gilroy: "[t]he Atlantic as one single, complex unit of analysis . . . in discussions of the modern world" (15). Along with Stowe's other books on slavery, *The Key to Uncle Tom's Cabin* and *Dred*, *Uncle Tom* played a formative role in the transatlantic history of race relations and in the representation of black people.

After 1852, Stowe was also inevitably implicated in the real travels of African Americans in Europe. African American tourists and exiles in Britain, for instance, repeatedly found themselves understood in relation to *Uncle Tom's Cabin*, while black speakers themselves incorporated references to Stowe's novel in their arguments.[31] In addition, Stowe assumed the role of patron to the singer Elizabeth Greenfield and to Mary Webb, who gave dramatic readings in London.[32] First in her fiction and then in person, Stowe introduced Europeans to African Americans, encounters that she then reproduced for American readers in *Sunny Memories of Foreign Lands*.[33] Stowe herself, as well as her texts, played a role in creolizing and syncretizing the cultural and political conjunctions that Gilroy attributes to the Black Atlantic in the nineteenth century.

Just as the publication of *Uncle Tom's Cabin* in Britain shifted the meanings of the text onto the plane of national rivalry, Stowe's 1853 journey to Britain and the continent made Stowe herself an international phenomenon. A British woman compared Stowe to spiritualism—another American import of 1853: "the great talk now is Mrs Stowe and spirit rapping, both of which have arrived in England," while in Paris *Le Charivari* depicted the fashion for table-turning (another spiritualist manifestation) as displacing a disconsolate-looking Stowe (fig. 2).[34]

The visit also altered Stowe's sense of herself as an author. Her account of this trip in *Sunny Memories of Foreign Lands*, a text that Shirley Foster and

Donald Ross consider here, registers this change. Oddly juxtaposing accounts of Stowe's literary pilgrimages (typical of an Old World tour) and her reception in Britain (crowds gathering to greet her train), *Sunny Memories of Foreign Lands* illustrates the beginnings of a cultural shift in British and American relations. Like earlier Americans conducting an Old World tour, Stowe visited the literary shrines of Scott, Burns, and Shakespeare, but to her British hosts she was the literary celebrity. In Scotland, for example, she and her traveling companions excitedly recalled details from Scott's novels but found that "our enthusiasm for Walter Scott does not apparently meet a response in the popular breast" (Stowe, *Sunny Memories* 1:69). In Britain Stowe began to eclipse the very British writers who had dominated the literary landscape of her childhood.

2. In this cartoon published 21 June 1853 in the Parisian paper *Le Charivari*, Harriet Beecher Stowe wanders forlornly, forgotten by a public now absorbed with the fashion for table-turning, a spiritualist practice. Courtesy of the British Library.

None of her later books matched *Uncle Tom's Cabin*'s effect in Britain and Europe (although, as Judie Newman shows in her essay here, *Dred* made a significant impact on the British stage). But when it came time to publish other novels, Stowe had learned from the experience of losing royalties from the British sales of *Uncle Tom's Cabin*. If *Uncle Tom's Cabin* illustrates the risks of piracy overseas, Stowe's preparations for publishing *Dred* in 1856 demonstrate her growing skills at managing her international publication. In order to register British copyright, an author needed to be in Britain at the time of publication, so Stowe traveled to Britain in the summer of 1856 to meet this condition when Sampson Low brought out *Dred*. Behind schedule, she finished *Dred* as she sailed—literally writing the book on a transatlantic passage. Like *Uncle Tom's Cabin*, it sold better in Britain than in the United States in its first year (Newman, introduction 12). *Dred* demonstrated that Stowe had come to conceive of herself as an international author writing for a global—not a national—market.

As well as learning copyright practicalities from the experience of becoming an international author, Stowe allowed her travel on the Continent to change her work itself. As Gail K. Smith and Carla Rineer argue here, encountering the art, monuments, and culture of a variety of European countries inspired in Stowe a new interest in visual art, an altered response to images of the body, and a changed relationship with Catholicism.[35] Moreover, her *Agnes of Sorrento* (1862) was born in precisely the expatriate community in Italy that inspired Hawthorne's *The Marble Faun* (1860). While Father Charles Henry Manning attempted to convert Stowe to Catholicism in Florence and instead prompted the fascination with the Renaissance that developed into *Agnes*, Hawthorne was living among the American sculptors then gathered in Florence and Rome—Thomas Crawford, William Wetmore Story, Maria Louisa Lander, Harriet Hosmer, and Hiram Powers—who inspired his novel (Monga 123).[36] Stowe also met many of these artists, and she shared literary friends with Story, including Robert and Elizabeth Browning and Elizabeth Gaskell.[37] Hawthorne had helped create an international reputation for Story's *Cleopatra* in *The Marble Faun*; Stowe's description of Sojourner Truth inspired Story's *The Libyan Sibyl*. Story's statue was itself a multiply transatlantic production: created by an American sculptor in Italy, inspired by Stowe's description (in Rome) of a former slave from New England, exhibited in London in 1862, and eventually acquired by the Metropolitan Museum in New York. When Story's creation was admired at the London exhibition, Stowe published an article in the *Atlantic Monthly* about her meeting with Truth and its transformation into the statue; the article, charting crossings between Europe and the United States, itself of course extended this creative traffic ("Sojourner Truth, the Libyan Sibyl").

While her stay in Italy did not have the impact Rome had on Margaret Fuller (another of Story's friends), Stowe's Italian novel should perhaps be read in the context of these contemporary American encounters with Italy: it both echoed those of British writers like Byron, the Shelleys, the Brownings, and Landor and partly presaged later American expatriate gatherings like those in Paris in the 1920s. Stowe's career not only exemplifies the currents of transatlantic relationships in the nineteenth century, it invites comparison with all such relationships since.

Over a decade later, in 1869 and 1870, Stowe's defense of Lady Byron placed her once again at the center of literary culture. Stowe had befriended Lady Byron during her 1856 trip to Britain and had learned from her about Byron's affair with his half-sister. Stowe had urged Lady Byron to keep the affair secret (though it was evidently an open secret by the time Stowe learned of it),[38] but Stowe herself published the story to defend Lady Byron after a public attack by Byron's mistress, Countess Guiccioli. Sympathetic to Lord Byron and disparaging about his wife, Guiccioli's memoir inspired Stowe to publish "The True Story of Lady Byron's Life" in the *Atlantic Monthly* in 1869 and *Lady Byron Vindicated* the next year. Though she had hoped to build on her past international successes with the book, it damaged her reputation. The text is nevertheless an important chapter in Stowe's transatlantic interventions. For while the exposé of Byron grew out of a desire to defend a "wronged" woman and a British friend, it also marked anxiety about Byron's pernicious influence on American readers. In the *Atlantic Monthly* piece, Stowe writes that Guiccioli's story "is going the length of this American continent, and rousing up new sympathy with the poet, and doing its best to bring the youth of America once more under the power of that brilliant, seductive genius" (295–296). Stowe's attack on Byron, as Caroline Franklin argues here, reveals a desire to overthrow the literary figure who had dominated the literary culture of her childhood—and who, she worried, risked "seducing" American readers once again.

. . .

The three sections of *Transatlantic Stowe* are designed to highlight Stowe's transatlantic connections and to suggest larger patterns of transatlantic exchange. The first section, "Blurring Borders, Writing Nations," includes essays on the influence of three early nineteenth-century British and Irish writers—Byron, Edgeworth, and Scott—on American writers in general and on Stowe in particular. The second, "Race, Class, and Labor in the Atlantic World," examines Stowe's participation in international debates about slavery and society as well as *Uncle Tom's Cabin*'s role in Russian debates on serfdom. The final section, "Transnational Writer," reveals the increasingly international perspectives her writing took after 1852. Taken together, the essays in this collection offer new interpretations of Stowe's most popular novel as well as new readings of her many other (largely neglected) works; they illuminate connections between Stowe and European writers; and they return Stowe—finally—to the larger political, historical, and literary context of nineteenth-century European culture.

NOTES

1. On Lacy and burlesques, see Baddeley.

2. A notable exception is Janet Beer and Bridget Bennett's collection *Special Relationships*, which discusses, among others, Edith Wharton, Virginia Woolf, George Eliot, Charlotte Perkins Gilman, Harriet Wilson, Sarah Grand, Gertrude Stein, and Stowe herself. Other exceptions include Lisa Surwillo's essay "Representing the Slave Trader: *Haley* and the Slave Ship; or, Spain's *Uncle Tom's Cabin*" and Jennifer Cognard-Black's *Narrative in the Professional Age*.

3. The unique connections between Scotland and American literature have also been charted, most notably by Susan Manning in *The Puritan Provincial Vision* and *Fragments of Union*, while Judie Newman's "Stowe's Sunny Memories of Highland Slavery" insists on the differences between Stowe's reception in the Scottish Highlands and elsewhere.

4. In *Woman's Fiction*, her groundbreaking discussion of nineteenth-century novels by women, Nina Baym argues that Stowe's novels are distinct from the plots of most women's fiction of the period.

5. On Stowe's reading, see Hedrick (18–21) and Wagenknecht (44).

6. On Stowe's reading of Scott, see Hedrick (20, 198) and Lyman Beecher (1: 391).

7. Dickens, letter to Mrs. Cropper, 1852, reprinted in Harry Stone, 196.

8. See the preface to T. Bosworth's 1852 edition of Stowe's *Uncle Tom's Cabin*, vii–ix.

9. Elizabeth Barrett Browning, letter to Harriet Beecher Stowe, 14 March 1861; qtd. in Charles Edward Stowe, *Life*, 356–357.

10. References to *The Life of Harriet Beecher Stowe* by Charles Edward Stowe in this essay are from the London edition. The book was published in 1889 by Houghton, Mifflin in Boston and by Sampson Low in London.

11. This detail comes from Altick 301. For more details on the publication and reception of *Uncle Tom's Cabin* in Britain, see Altick 301 and 384, Gossett 239–259, and Fisch, "Uncle Tom and Harriet Beecher Stowe in England."

12. Given the popularity of *Uncle Tom's Cabin* in Britain it is remarkable that there has not been more scholarship on British editions of the novel. See Wood, "Uncle Tom in England," and Fisch, *American Slaves in Victorian England* and "Uncle Tom and Harriet Beecher Stowe in England."

13. Letters from William Stirling and Richard Bentley to William H. Prescott, Prescott papers, Massachusetts Historical Society.

14. For a listing of translations of *Uncle Tom's Cabin* see Hildreth 24–67.

15. *Le Charivari*, 28 November 1852; Louis Huart, "Le Roman Phenomenale," *Le Charivari*, 9 November 1852; Taxile DeLord, "L'Oncle Tom," *Le Charivari*, 23 November 1852.

16. In her *American Slaves in Victorian England*, Audrey Fisch also notices this pattern in her analysis of periodical reviews of *Uncle Tom's Cabin* (see pages 11–32).

17. Whitley and Goldman 11. See also Mesick.

18. *Uncle Tom's Cabin, or the Negro Slave* was first performed at the Standard, 13 September 1852. MS. Lord Chamberlain's Collection, British Library. 2.3; John Courtney, *Uncle Tom's Cabin* was first performed at the Royal Surrey Theatre, 20 September 1852. MS. Lord Chamberlain's Collection, British Library. 2.1. On the British plays see Waters and Meer.

19. On the transatlantic dimensions of antislavery work, see Bolt, Fladeland, Blackett, and Clare Taylor.

20. There is conflicting evidence about the purpose of the Uncle Tom Penny Offering, some sources suggesting that it was collected for slaves, others to compensate Stowe for revenue lost through the piracy of British publishers. See Fladeland 356, Forrest Wilson 233, and Hedrick 246–248. Audrey Fisch describes contemporary commentators' unease at the support of Stowe's working-class readership, *American Slaves in Victorian England*, 11–32. On the novel's recruitment, see Fladeland 357, 353; Midgley 146.

21. See Bolt, Fladeland, Blackett, and Ripley, *The Black Abolitionist Papers*. Not only was the British antislavery movement, in Frank Thistlethwaite's words, "oriented towards the Atlantic," but American societies were modeled on British organizations and had invited British orators like George Thompson and Charles Stuart to make speaking tours in the United States (105). For their part, American abolitionists visited Britain regularly during the 1840s: to attend the World Anti-Slavery Convention of 1840 or, like Charles Lenox Remond, Frederick Douglass, or Moses Grandy, as antislavery lecturers.

22. On Stowe's invitation see Shepperson.

23. See McFeely 119–145, and Rice and Crawford.

24. On Stowe's celebrity in Britain see Brodhead.

25. Finlayson 343; "The Affectionate and Christian Address of Many Thousands of the Women of England to their Sisters, the Women of the United States of America," *Times* (London), 9 November 1852, 3 f.

26. The full text is quoted in Forrest Wilson 207.

27. "To the Editor of the *Times*," *Times* (London), 1 December 1852, 8c; "To the

Earl of Shaftesbury," *Times* (London), 1 December 1852, 8b; Academicus, "To the Editor of the *Times*," *Times* (London), 1 December 1852, 8b; Finlayson 344–345; "The Lady Abolitionists," *Spectator* (London), 4 December 1852, 1164; *Times* (London), 1 December 1852, 4, 8. "To the Duchess of Sutherland and the Ladies of England," *Southern Literary Messenger* 19 (February 1853): 120–126, 120. The essay was also reprinted elsewhere, including in the *New York Daily Times*, 5 February 1853. Louisa S. McCord, "British Philanthropy and American Slavery: An Affectionate Response to the Ladies of England, etc., from the Ladies of the Southern United States," *De Bow's Review*, March 1853, reprinted in *Louisa S. McCord: Political and Social Essays*, ed. Richard Lounsbury. On Tyler's and McCord's responses, see Pugh and Seager, 404–405.

28. For other contemporary comparisons see, for instance, George Fitzhugh, *Sociology for the South: or the Failure of Free Society* (1854; New York: Burt Franklin, 1971); Thomas Carlyle, *Latter Day Pamphlets*, ed. by M. K. Goldberg and J. P. Seigel (1858; n.p.: Canadian Federation for the Humanities, 1983); Louisa McCord, "Slavery and Political Economy," *De Bow's Review* 21 (October and November 1856): 331–349, 443–467, reprinted in Lounsbury, pp. 422–469; Louisa McCord, "Negro and White Slavery: Wherein Do They Differ?" *Southern Quarterly Review*, n.s. 4 (July 1851): 118–132, reprinted in Lounsbury 187–202; Louisa McCord, "Uncle Tom's Cabin," *Southern Quarterly Review*, n.s. 7 (January 1853): 81–120, reprinted in Lounsbury 245–280; "'British Philanthropy and American Slavery': An Affectionate Response to the Ladies of England, etc., from the Ladies of the Southern United States; Together with Some Remarks for the *North British Review*—by a Southern Lady," *De Bow's Review* 14 (March 1853): 258–280, reprinted in Lounsbury 281–321; "Charity Which Does Not Begin at Home," *Southern Literary Messenger* 19.4 (April 1853): 193–208, reprinted in Lounsbury, 321–349; "A Letter to the Duchess of Sutherland from Lady of South Carolina," Charleston *Mercury*, 10 August 1853, reprinted in Lounsbury 350–360.

29. *Reynolds's Newspaper* (London), 15 May 1853, 1a; George W. M. Reynolds, "Black Slavery Abroad and White Slavery at Home," *Reynolds's Newspaper* (London), 10 April 1853, 8c; *Leader* (London), 18 September 1852, 900; *Star of Freedom* (London), 24 September 1852, 105. These and other articles making the comparison are discussed in Lorimer, *Colour* 93–100, and Klingberg, "Harriet Beecher Stowe" 548.

30. "The Earl of Shaftesbury's Rejoinder," *Globe* (London), 26 January 1853, 1; Lorimer, *Colour* 100.

31. William Wells Brown, speech delivered at Manchester Town Hall, 1 August 1854, reprinted in Ripley 1: 398–406, 400; reviews in the *Critic*, the *Literary Gazette*, the *Eclectic Review*, and the *Caledonian Mercury* all made mention of *Uncle Tom's Cabin*. Quoted in "Opinions of the British Press," 229–232. See Jefferson, introduction to Wells Brown, *Travels* 16. See also Winks, Ripley, 1: 458; 1: 317; 1: 367–370; 1: 465–468.

32. See Pickering 29; Trotter 66–87; Stowe, *Sunny Memories* 207, 307–10, 335. On Webb, see Lapsansky, Clark, and Eric Gardner.

33. See for instance, Stowe, *Sunny Memories passim*. Meer discusses Stowe's role in these interactions in *Uncle Tom Mania*.

34. Mary Howitt to William Howitt, cited Burton 44; *Le Charivari*, 21 June 1853.

35. Luigi Monga argues that the main importance of *Agnes of Sorrento* lies in this changed attitude to Catholicism, 123.

36. See also Earnest 170.

37. Earnest 171; Yellin, *Women and Sisters* 82; Monga 123; Uglow notes Gaskell's presence at Stowe's account of Truth, 423, London edition, 1999. On Americans in Italy, see also William W. Stowe and Dulles.

38. See McPherson. For more on the Byron–Stowe controversy, see Wolstenholme and Hedrick 366–369.

PART ONE

Blurring Borders, Writing Nations

Stowe and the Byronic Heroine

CAROLINE FRANKLIN

HE MOST POPULAR POET of the century on both sides of the Atlantic, especially among women readers, had been ostracized by the British aristocracy in 1816 when rumors of his libertinism and brutal treatment of his wife circulated in the wake of their separation.[1] In 1869—the year that saw the publication of John Stuart Mill's *The Subjection of Women*—the bestselling novelist of the century on both sides of the Atlantic reactivated the Byron scandal by revealing for the first time in print that the cause of the separation had been Byron's incest with his half-sister. "The True Story of Lady Byron's Life," published in the American *Atlantic Monthly* and British *Macmillan's Magazine*, was the "most widely discussed article dealing with a man of letters to appear in nineteenth-century England" (Lang 345) and probably America too. Harriet Beecher Stowe expanded it into a book, *Lady Byron Vindicated: A History of the Byron Controversy* (1870).

This incident is usually sidelined as an embarrassing irrelevance to Stowe's literary career. However, arguably, Byron was a seminal figure in the story of nineteenth-century women's sentimental fiction in general and was of particular significance to Stowe because of his repudiation of his Calvinist heritage. Byron's early poetry had itself been influenced by female-authored sentimental romances inculcating patriotism, the tradition that Stowe would extend. Germaine de Staël and Sydney Owenson's *Corinne, or Italy* (1807) and *Ida of Athens* (1809) were Italophile/Philhellenist romances whose themes Byron would adapt in his verse. After the separation scandal, he himself began to feature in female-authored fiction, portrayed as a Gothic villain, for example, by his ex-lover Lady Caroline Lamb and friend Mary Shelley. Byron then consciously engaged in a literary war of the sexes, satiriz-

3

ing the authoritarian agenda of didactic conservative novelists Hannah More and Maria Edgeworth in canto 1 of his self-justifying masterpiece *Don Juan* (1819–1824). More importantly, in this work he flung down the gauntlet to women readers by challenging them to deny that they were as much (or more) creatures of passion and sexual desire as were men. Further revelations about Byron's life and marriage after his death ensured that the sexual politics of Byronism continued to fascinate British and American midcentury women novelists. They needed to come to an accommodation between, on the one hand, the rationalist Puritanism of the "feminist" heritage, epitomized by Mary Wollstonecraft's *Vindication of the Rights of Woman* (1792), and Byronic Romantic individualism on the other.

The Victorian women's movement was predicated on opposition to male libertinism, of course, and for Stowe and her contemporaries the separation story illustrated the feminist case against the inequity of the marriage laws.

> Much of the beautiful patience and forgiveness of women is made possible to them by that utter *deadness to the sense of justice* which the laws, literature, and misunderstood religion of England have sought to induce in woman as a special grace and virtue.
>
> The lesson to woman in this pathetic piece of special pleading is, that man may sink himself below the brute, may wallow in filth like the swine, may turn his home into a hell, beat and torture his children, forsake the marriage-bed for foul rivals; yet all this does *not* dissolve the marriage-vow on her part, nor free his bounden serf from her obligation to honour his memory,—nay, to sacrifice to it the honour due to a kind father and mother, slandered in their silent graves. (Stowe, *Lady Byron Vindicated* 79)

Byron's disgrace symbolized the overthrow of Regency aristocratic sexual mores and marked the official endorsement of domesticity as the ideal of the forthcoming Victorian age. The union of Byron and his wife Annabella had been a meeting of two egotisms fuelled by conflicting ideologies: the surge of the male individualist's will to power against the rock of the female mission to reform the male sex through marriage.[2] Stowe was not the only woman writer to use Lady Byron as a role model for the burgeoning cult of saintly womanhood. The account of the separation in Thomas Moore's *Life of Byron* had also inspired Anne Brontë's *The Tenant of Wildfell Hall* (1848). This Christian feminist novel portrays a wife who left her debauched husband to protect her child from his influence yet returned in order to attempt (unsuccessfully) to convert him on his deathbed. Anne Brontë had been particularly struck by Lady Byron's continued hopes of reforming her husband and by Byron's determination not to give up his legal right of custody of their child (Pinion 245).

It has long been recognized that Byron was "the single greatest literary and imaginative influence on the writings of Harriet Beecher Stowe" (Crozier, "Stowe and Byron" 195–196). Her audacious defense of her English heroine and friend, Lady Byron, cannot therefore be satisfactorily written off as an anomaly: a self-publicizing attempt to regain her flagging popularity; evidence of her naive hero-worship of this lady of the European aristocracy; or even as an expression of her version of feminism, though it partook of all those elements.[3] It was in fact the culmination of Stowe's lifelong "anxiety of influence" regarding the British poet that, this essay hopes to show, was not merely productive of a few clichéd characterizations of predatory high-class villains in her fiction but was a major inspiration behind the womanist attack on patriarchal religion and capitalism in her best work and in her representation of heroines who save or grieve for lost souls.

Charles H. Foster has described how Stowe had been introduced to *The Corsair* at the age of seven by her aunt Esther and, indeed, how the whole family avidly followed the story of the poet's separation from his wife in 1816 and his untimely death in 1824 (219–220). Byron's poetry—because he explored the theme of damnation—attracted intense interest in religious households such as that of the Reverend Brontë and his literary children[4] and that of Lyman Beecher, whose sermons on the tortures of hell had reputedly caused students at the Litchfield Female Academy to lose their reason. Beecher fantasized about saving the poet's soul: "Oh if Byron could only have talked with Taylor and me, it might have got him out of his troubles."[5] (Nathaniel Taylor, 1786–1858, was the Yale professor of theology.) On the day of Byron's death Beecher preached a sermon on the text "The name of the just is as brightness, but the memory of the wicked shall rot." Byron was idolized by the young Stowe, whose earliest writings replicated her father's fantasy of converting such a magnificently sinful soul: a theme to become central to the cult of womanhood she elaborated as an adult.[6] Her denunciation of the poet in 1869 may obviously be seen as an exorcism of her own adolescent hero-worship of him, but I will go on to show that it was also a way of defining for herself the limits of her own apostasy against her Puritan heritage.[7]

To religious readers such as Stowe, Byron's protagonists were primarily libertines in the original sense of the word—freethinkers or skeptics. His fallen heroes ranged from the arch-skeptic Childe Harold, who "through Sin's long labyrinth had run" (1, 4) to the Giaour who refuses to participate in the monks' Christian rites (lines 814–815); Lara, who smiles scornfully on the proffered cross on his death bed (2, 477–481); Alp, who fights for Islam against the Christians; and Manfred, who refuses the abbot's exhortation to repent.[8] The poet's stress on the remorse, yet refusal to repent, of Byronic heroes, his placing of them in situations where they discuss their spiritual state with abbots or mythological beings just before their imminent demise, focused all the reader's fear on the state of their souls. This preoccupation, particularly in the earlier poetry, was calculated to appeal to pious women who wanted—like Dr. Beecher—to save the poet's own soul. Annabella Milbanke, Byron's future wife, was typical of many young readers of *Childe Harold* 1 and 2 in identifying the author with his protagonists: "His poem sufficiently proves that he can feel nobly, but he has discouraged his own goodness" (Elwin 106).[9] Byron had artfully manipulated such female readers. His membership in an aristocratic family notorious for its libertinism for three generations had meant he could not only recreate but even seem to inhabit the persona of a sentimentalized version of the Richardsonian aristocratic seducer who needed to be saved by the virtue of the middle-class heroine.

But when Byron was attacked as a libertine in 1816 he changed tack. His greatest work was forged in the heat of an ideological battle with Stowe's forebears, an earlier generation of conservative novelists who disapproved of liberals glamorizing the transgressive individual and who preferred to focus on the collective nature of society and the importance of social duty. *Don Juan* went on the attack by deconstructing Don Juanism as a myth that it was necessary for women to perpetuate in order to sustain the ideology of pure womanhood. In canto 1 the hypocritical Inez (a satiric portrait of Lady Byron) gains power over men by projecting a saintly image of motherhood artificially constructed from texts. Stanza 16 targets the moralistic women writers Maria Edgeworth, Hannah More, and Sarah Trimmer, of whom the two latter used fiction only to propagandize on behalf of the Evangelical wing of the National Church.[10]

> In short, she was a walking calculation,
> Miss Edgeworth's novels stepping from their covers,
> Or Mrs. Trimmer's books on education,
> Or 'Coelebs' Wife' set out in search of lovers,

Morality's prim personification,
In which not Envy's self a flaw discovers,
To others' share let "female errors fall,"
For she had not even one—the worst of all.

Later satire of Inez again links her with Evangelicals like More and Trimmer who set up Sunday Schools to discipline poor children (2, 10). Hannah More was, of course, the premier inspiration behind Harriet's sister Catharine Beecher's *A Treatise on Domestic Economy* (1841), which would be revised with the aid of Harriet and republished in the same year as "The True Story of Lady Byron's Life." It was "probably the single most influential statement of domesticity" (Romero 23), the ideology that conceded that woman's power be confined to influence over men but eventually succeeded in so far extending the domestic agenda of health, education, and morality that it engaged the centers of power and concomitantly professionalized women's pseudomaternal roles in society.

This literary war of the sexes, in which we have seen Stowe's *Lady Byron Vindicated* was but one late (and lost) battle, was not a straightforward dualism, for both Byron and the female novelists were locked into a mutual attraction to as well as repulsion from each other's ideology. Byronic skepticism functioned as a lightning rod for Puritan women writers whose fiction was itself a sign of the secularization of their social vision.[11] George Eliot and Harriet Martineau made the whole journey from guilt and predestination to atheism and sociological determinism while retaining their moralism. Both distanced themselves from the skeptic poet in print: we find pejorative references to the deleterious effects of Byron's poetry in *Felix Holt*, while Martineau's earlier defense of Lady Byron in the *Atlantic* was cited by Stowe. But for those still struggling to throw off their Calvinist heritage, Byron's poetry articulated the outright rebellion that religious writers such as the Brontë sisters and Stowe most feared within themselves. *Don Juan* was saturated with imagery of the fall, yet Byron refused to send the Don off to hell as in the original myth. The doctrine of eternal damnation was also challenged in *The Vision of Judgment*; in the depiction of an authoritarian God in *Cain*; and in the humanist protest against the Calvinist doctrine of predestination of the majority to hell in the apocalyptic drama of Noah's flood, *Heaven and Earth*.[12] Although his protagonists are heroic in their defiance and repudiation of Calvinist doctrine, Byron places them in a metaphysical universe, especially in the biblical plays, in which the existence of God and the literal

B's appeal

truth of the Bible are unquestioned. The protagonist's sinfulness is fully acknowledged. Byron's preoccupation with predestined damnation as tragedy,
and tragedy unmitigated, thus particularly resonated with those like Stowe
struggling to shake off the same Calvinist mindset.

Stowe's *Lady Byron Vindicated* quoted from a letter of Lady Byron asserting that Byron was a believer in the inspiration of the Bible, and had the
gloomiest Calvinistic tenets. "To that unhappy view of the relation of the
creature to the Creator I have always ascribed the misery of his life . . . Judge,
then, how I must hate the creed that made him see God as an Avenger, but
not as a Father!" (263–264). Stowe herself asserted that Lord Byron's life
illustrated a passage from the Thirty-Nine Articles, revised by Calvin himself: "[F]or curious and carnal persons, lacking the spirit of Christ, to have
continually before their eyes the sentence of God's predestination, is a most
dangerous downfall, whereby the Devil doth thrust them either into desperation, or into recklessness of most unclean living,—no less perilous than
desperation" (164). This tells us more about these women's own religious
preoccupations than about Byron himself. We see that Stowe's representation of Byron in the *Vindication* is a culmination of her gallery of ever-dark-
ening portraits of fine men vitiated by religious despair from Augustine St.
Clare in *Uncle Tom's Cabin* to Aaron Burr in *The Minister's Wooing* and Ellery
Davenport in *Oldtown Folks*.[13]

The Byronic characteristics of these male characters have often been remarked but no attention has hitherto been paid to the equally interesting influence on Stowe of Byron's heroines and in particular *Don Juan's* Aurora
Raby. The portrait of the virginal Aurora Raby in the English Cantos (15,
43–47) demonstrates Byron's own attraction toward the virtuous heroine of
the female novelists, whom he had formerly satirized in the description of
Inez. The originality of his characterization lies in Aurora's extreme youth
and physical slightness and her grave observation of the corruption around
her (anticipating Dickens's Little Dorrit), as well as her Catholicism, which
would have been anathema to such chauvinist Protestants as Hannah More.
Moreover, the suggestion that Don Juan might meet his nemesis by marrying her is a literary joke, implying that the Byronic libertine and the heroine
of the cult of domesticity belong together, each needing the other to justify
their existence.

> Aurora Raby, a young star who shone
> O'er life, too sweet an image for such glass

A lovely being, scarcely form'd or moulded,
A rose with all its sweetest leaves yet folded;

Early in years, and yet more infantine
In figure, she had something of sublime
In eyes which sadly shone, as seraphs' shine.
All youth—but with an aspect beyond time;
Radiant and grave—as pitying man's decline;
Mournful—but mournful of another's crime,
She looked as if she sat by Eden's door,
And grieved for those who could return no more.

She gazed upon a world she scarcely knew
As seeking not to know it; silent, lone,
As grows a flower, thus quietly she grew,
And kept her heart serene within its zone.
There was an awe in the homage which she drew;
Her spirit seem'd as seated on a throne
Apart from the surrounding world, and strong
In its own strength—most strange in one so young!
(*Don Juan*, 15, 43, ll. 5–8; 15, 45; 15, 47)

This was the passage that came to haunt the work of Stowe like no other lines of Byron's poetry: "What can more express moral ideality of the highest kind than the exquisite descriptions of Aurora,—pure and high in thought and language, occurring, as they do, in a work full of the most utter vileness?" (*Lady Byron Vindicated* 265). Stowe read the character as a portrait of Byron's wife, for when recording her meeting with Annabella she quoted the passage: "When I was introduced to her [Lady Byron], I felt in a moment the words of her husband,—'There was awe in the homage that she drew;/ Her spirit seemed as seated on a throne'" (*Lady Byron Vindicated* 135).

Stowe's intertextuality with Byron epitomizes her balancing act between conservatism and radical vision. Like Byron, she wrote as a crusader bravely challenging her own society. Yet she justified her public denunciation of the evils of slavery of blacks and women by adapting the apolitical reformatory role of wife and mother to authorship, for she was writing to save the soul of the nation. At the heart of *Uncle Tom's Cabin* (1852), famously accredited by Lincoln with igniting the civil war, is the pairing we found in *Don Juan* between a holy Virgin and the Byronic fallen male. The angelic child, Eva (whose name presumably alludes to the play on Eva/Ave Maria in medieval typology), is introduced by an epigraph slightly misquoted from canto 15, stanza 43, of *Don Juan* on Aurora Raby:

> A Young star! Which shone
> O'er life—too sweet an image for such glass!
> A lovely being, scarcely formed or moulded;
> A rose with all its sweetest leaves yet folded. (226)[14]

Just as Aurora's virgin purity and naivete unwittingly showed up the corruption of the high society in Norman Abbey and in particular Don Juan's own tarnished innocence, so little Eva's innocent questioning of the unthinking cruelties perpetuated by slavery throws into relief the failure of her father, St. Clare—despite his essentially good nature—to change the system on which his lavish mansion was built. St. Clare, the most complex character in the book, is a radical visionary yet also a religious skeptic whom the pious slave Uncle Tom attempts to convert. It will not surprise us that he is described in overtly Byronic terms:

> He had one of those natures which could better and more clearly conceive of religious things from its own perceptions and instincts, than many a matter-of-fact and practical Christian. The gift to appreciate and the sense to feel the finer shades and relations of moral things, often seems an attribute of those whose whole life shows a careless disregard of them. Hence Moore, Byron, Goethe, often speak words more wisely descriptive of the true religious sentiment, than another man, whose whole life is governed by it. In such minds, disregard of religion is a more fearful treason,—a more deadly sin. (440)[15]

The child heroine represents naive and natural American religion: morally superior to her father's sophisticated, secular sensibility nourished instead by European Romanticism.

In her feminist critique of "the New England theology" as "the effect of a slow poison" (197) in *The Minister's Wooing* (1859),[16] Stowe went on to adapt the allusions to Mariology in Byron's Catholic Aurora to create a protestant mater dolorosa whose religion of love contrasts with the deathly dogma of the patriarchal priesthood.[17] Mary Scudder is explicitly related to Byron's description of Aurora Raby (*Don Juan* 15, 45) in the mind of her cousin/lover:

> Her eyes filled with tears, her face kindled with a sad earnestness, and James thought, as he looked, of a picture he had once seen in a European cathedral, where the youthful Mother of Sorrows is represented,

"Radiant and grave, as pitying man's decline;
All youth, but with an aspect beyond time;
Mournful of another's crime;
She looked as if she sat by Eden's door,
And grieved for those who should return no more." (23) [18]

Mary's spiritual opposite and potential husband is Dr. Samuel Hopkins (a fictionalization of the famous Calvinist theologian), whose stern God ordains the damnation of the greater part of the human race to demonstrate the evil nature of sin and its consequences. After James is lost at sea, Hopkins's pitiless religion is set in dramatic opposition to unconditional motherly love when, instead of comforting Mrs. Marvin, he is only concerned with whether James had experienced true conversion, for if not he must certainly be damned. Only the black servant Candace dares to contradict Hopkins's doctrines, comforting James's mother, who is in danger of losing both her faith and her reason through grief: "Honey, darlin', ye a'n't right,—dar's a dreful mistake somewhar . . . Why, de Lord a'n't like what ye tink,—He *loves* ye, honey!" (201).[19] Candace, together with Mary and her Catholic friend Virginie, as the names of the latter indicate, embody Stowe's call for a *female* ministry of New Testament maternal love: a modern protestant adaptation of the Catholic cult of the Virgin Mary. [20]

But in their contrasted reactions to the seductive Byronic male, Aaron Burr, Mary, and Virginie also reprise the roles of the pious Annabella (Mary is even given a liking for mathematics like Lady Byron [198]) and the poet's married Italian mistress, Countess Teresa Guiccioli, who had also gone straight from the convent to wed an older man.[21] Both Stowe's fictional women resist temptation—unlike their real-life counterparts. For, while Dr. Hopkins is only eventually rejected as Mary's too severely Puritan wooer, she unhesitatingly takes the lead in facing down the secular temptation of Byronism.

Aaron Burr had played an equivalently equivocal role in American history to that of Byron. The charismatic hero of the war of independence and an incorrigible womanizer, Burr was frequently fictionalized not only by Stowe but by other American writers. Born of a family described by a modern historian as the New England equivalent of royalty, the daring Burr was impervious to the restraints imposed by fearing for the loss of honor and reputation (Freeman 160).[22] Burr's motives in joining the Republican party and becoming vice president to Jefferson were mistrusted, and his enemies accused him of intriguing with the Federalists. Like Byron, because he was aristocratic yet republican, he was suspected of mere opportunism. Actually, as with Byron, he perceived himself a natural leader on account of his aristocratic heritage and free to respond to public opinion in favor of democracy. Burr fell from favor when he killed political rival Alexander Hamilton in a duel and then became "the *enfant terrible* of American politics" (Freeman 201). In 1805–1807, he and General James Wilkinson schemed with first Britain and then Spain to obtain money, apparently with the treasonable intention of liberating the West from the Union, but their secret agenda was possibly to double-cross their sponsors and conquer Mexico for the United States. Betrayed by Wilkinson, Burr was tried but acquitted of treason. Of particular psychological interest to Stowe was the fact that Burr seems to have been driven on to challenge moral boundaries by revulsion for his Puritan heritage. He was the grandson of Jonathan Edwards, the spiritual fountainhead of the Great Awakening.

When Stowe fictionalizes Burr, she unmistakably paints a portrait of Byron: "[h]is beautifully-formed head, delicate profile, fascinating sweetness of smile, and, above all, an eye which seemed to have an almost mesmeric power of attraction" (124).[23] It is made clear that, as in the case of Byron, it is not despite but actually *because* of his Calvinist upbringing that Burr, with all his capacity for deep feelings, has become a heartless seducer.[24] He is pictured deliberating over, then setting aside, his grandfather's severe "Resolutions." The spiritual despair produced by his inability to conform had left Burr "with all his beautiful capabilities, as the slave of the fleeting and the temporary, which sent him at last, a shipwrecked man, to a nameless, dishonoured grave" (159).

Like Don Juan on meeting the infantine Aurora Raby, Burr found it a "new sensation" to be calmly measured by Mary's thoughtful blue eyes (155). She reminds him of the description of his grandmother Sarah Pierpoint at the age of thirteen written by her future husband, Jonathan Edwards (155, 342). The novel makes clear that, had his Puritan heritage given more weight to the feminine religion of mercy represented by his fore*mothers* and less to the male system-makers, then Burr might have been saved and with him the new nation he helped to establish. To emphasize the point, Mary's dashing sweetheart James is *also* portrayed as a Byronic character, with his "high forehead shaded by rings of the blackest hair" (21) and his skeptical questioning of the doctrine of election. But he is a younger version—who *will* be saved through Mary's love for him and greater anxiety for his soul than her own.

"There be soul-artists, who go through this world . . . as one looks amid the dust and rubbish of old shops for hidden works of Titian and Leonardo," comments the narrator. "Such be God's real priests . . . Many such priests there be among women" (78). On the other hand, Stowe makes sure James has found his faith through reading the Bible long before Mary agrees to marry him. Mary does not repeat Annabella's mistake of wedding the Byronic hero in order to convert him, which might raise the possibility of spiritual pride in the reader's mind.

Despite this marriage-and-morals resolution of the plot, it is Virginie's eloquent defense of Burr after his death as "not so much more sinful than all the other men of his time" (331) that is given Stowe's emphatic endorsement by forming the closure of the novel. Virginie's love has repeatedly been described as "a trance of hero-worship" (135, 176), and here the European explains to her friend of New England yeoman stock the attraction of an aristocratic individualism combining defiance of all restraint with chivalric defense of the oppressed:

> Because he is a sinning man, it does not follow that he is a demon. If any should have cause to think bitterly of him, I should. He trifled inexcusably with my deepest feelings; he caused me years of conflict and anguish, such as he little knows; I was almost shipwrecked; yet I will still say to the last that what I loved in him was a better self,—something really noble and good, however concealed and perverted by pride, ambition, and self-will. Though all the world reject him, I still have faith in this better nature, and prayers that he may be led right at last. There is at least one heart that will always intercede with God for him. (331)

This could almost be Lady Byron speaking. It is significant that Virginie has told her son of her idealizing love for Burr and thus in some way handed on to the coming generation an understanding of this now-outmoded form of masculine heroism, so that in future years he pays the disgraced revolutionary the tribute of a memorial.

Ten years later in *Oldtown Folks* Stowe deepened her analysis of the soul-sickness at the heart of New England and thus of America, for New England is described in the preface as the "seed-bed of this great American Republic" (Stowe 883).[25] The inhabitants, having thrown off the British yoke, would emigrate to colonize the whole continent, ruling over the indigenous peoples and African Americans, the implication being that they thus emulated the British Empire. This is an ominous note to strike in a novel written at the time of Reconstruction, and Stowe has little time for nostalgia in her analysis of the Calvinist origin of modern materialism. The plot is similar to that of *The Minister's Wooing,* and the Byronic Aaron Burr character reappears as the dashing Ellery Davenport, again making love to a pair of contrasting women and this time succeeding with both. As in *Uncle Tom's Cabin* and *The Minister's Wooing,* the Byronic male is paired with an innocent young girl, for the suave Ellery is attracted to the flirtatious child Tina, abandoned daughter of a British officer (1173). (This alludes to the legend of Major Burr's alleged conquest of the thirteen-year-old Margaret Moncrieffe, daughter of a British major left with American friends in 1776.) However, Tina is not an Aurora figure, for Stowe moves away from the inviolable purity of the angelic heroine and toward greater psychological realism in this novel. Instead of typological characterization of New Testament Christianity based on maternal love, she looks naturalistically at the effect of theology on nurture and relates the resulting character of the adult to it. If the slavery of the African was the subject of *Uncle Tom's Cabin* and the subjection of woman under patriarchal religion was the target of *The Minister's Wooing,* then the oppression of the child is the focus of *Oldtown Folks.*

The upbringings are compared of five children: fatherless Horace Holyoke, Harry and Tina Percival, motherless Esther Avery, and orphaned Emily Rossiter. As Dorothy Berkson has commented, "The orphan tests the community's domestic principles" (249). The children's religious experiences range from the utmost rigors of Edwardsean Calvinism and its secular offspring, utilitarianism, to the modified Puritanism of the Arminian wing and beneficial influence of Episcopalianism that, while it retained the doctrine of original sin, at least deemed it worthwhile to teach a child to pray. Children's humanitarian rights are defended (1011, 1028). Stowe's chief concern is presenting the waste of those souls neglected or deformed through the effects of overaustere Calvinism. Most important of all is her analysis of the way the Calvinist upbringing of the orphaned Ellery Davenport himself produced his mocking skepticism in reaction to Edwardsean doctrine. He is stated to be an epitome of his generation. This introduces an excursion into theological history at the very heart of the novel (1230). Like Byron, Davenport was by nature intelligent and passionate. Stowe gives him humanitarian credentials and bravery when she portrays him rescuing black children from kidnappers who would sell them to slavers (1227–1228). But, though well read in theology, he has been alienated from his inherited religion by its exclusiv-

ity and the fact that its God is modeled on an absolute monarch (1244) and
not a loving mother, so his gifts are wasted.

> Well you see I was a little fellow when my parents died, and brought up under
> brother Jonathan, who was the bluest kind of blue; and he was so afraid that I
> should mistake my naturally sweet temper for religion, that he instructed me
> daily that I was a child of wrath, and couldn't, and didn't, and never should do
> one right thing till I was regenerated, and when that would happen no mortal
> knew; so I thought, as my account was going to be scored off at that time, it
> was no matter if I did run up a pretty long one; so I lied and stole whenever it
> came handy. (1186)

Stowe's novel starkly demonstrates the opposition between maternal love
and patriarchal theology, especially Augustinianism, the Pauline doctrine of
original sin augmented by the church fathers to encompass infant damnation. The narrator comments: "woman's nature has never been consulted in
theology. Theologic systems, as to the expression of their great body of ideas,
have, as yet, been the work of man alone. They have had their origin, as in
St. Augustine, with men who were utterly ignorant of moral and intellectual
companionship with woman, looking on her only in her animal nature as a
temptation and a snare" (1305). Foster has suggested that Stowe was probably influenced by her Episcopalian sister Catharine Beecher's *Religious Training of Children in the School, the Family, and the Church* (1864), which com-
mended the Episcopal Church for welcoming in children as "lambs of
Christ's fold" while targeting Jonathan Edwards as responsible for the Puritan church's inhumane exclusivity by reviving the restriction of membership
of the church to the Elect (those who were deemed to have experienced a
genuine conversion experience), leaving children outside the fold (179 [1970
ed.]). It is true that the novel dramatizes the historical importance of Anglicanism and, in the loyalism of Miss Deborah Kittery and Lady Widgery in
the Boston scenes, the fact that the War of Independence had been a civil
war. Nevertheless, Foster has perhaps overstated the novel's validation of
Episcopalianism, which is after all ironized for its snobbish Anglophilia and
lack of theological credibility. Though Ellery Davenport is a selfish seducer,
his sharp intellect gives credence to his noticeably faint praise of Episcopalianism as "a nice old motherly Church, that . . . coddles us when we are
sick" while complaining that the "the mischief of a Calvinistic education is,
it wakes up your reason, and it never will go to sleep again and you can't take

a pleasant humbug if you would" (1186–1187). Indeed, the success of the up-bringing of Tina and Harry lies in the fact that it is a hybrid: though their mother's Episcopalianism protected their infancy, in their adolescence they tested their intellects in a Puritan academy. The sensuality of an Ellery or a Tina may be expressed in a "religion of beauty" (1172): Episcopalianism has nurtured the aestheticism stunted by Puritanism, so Tina has a Byronic "ge-nius for poetry" (1270) but, like the poet, also needs the whetstone of Cal-vinist rationalism to burnish away showy sentimentalism and "school-girl platitudes" (1301).

When we look at the effect of religion on the upbringing of girls, we see that Puritanism's stress on the equality of souls has resulted in their being given an equally rational education to that of the boys even though the pro-fessions are not open to them (1289, 1374). Education complements the nat-ural feminine graces of a beauty like Tina (1298). But the most extreme Calvinist doctrines, which viewed the majority as doomed to eternal damna-tion, are portrayed as inimical to woman's maternal nature (1254). Horace's kindly grandmother "regarded the birth of an infant with a suppressed groan, and the death of one almost with satisfaction" (1238). Hypersensitive Esther Avery (possibly a self-portrait of the author) "was one of those in-tense, silent, repressed women that have been a frequent outgrowth of New England society" (1304). The melancholy of this Aurora Raby figure is thus seen with less equanimity than that of Mary Scudder. Importantly, in the portrayal of Emily Rossiter we see that Stowe is for the first time experi-menting with endowing a female character with the reactionary skepticism usually reserved for the Byronic male.

Like Ellery, whose name is similar to hers, Emily is bludgeoned by the most severe doctrines of Calvinism as a child: those of Dr. Moses Stern whose system was "calculated, like a skilful engine of torture, to produce all the mental anguish of the most perfect sense of helplessness with the most torturing sense of responsibility" (1249)[26] and whose self-appointed mission was to combat the democratic ideas of Thomas Paine. Like that of Byron himself, hers "was a nature that would break before it would bow. Nothing could have subdued her but love—and love she never heard" (1090). By the time she was fourteen "the revolt of a strong sense of justice and humanity" against the tyranny of the patriarchal God led her to lose her faith, and she was soon deep in the writings of the French Enlightenment (1258). Leaving for Europe with a French family, she experiences the French Revolution and there enters into a liaison with the "Jacobin" Davenport in which she rejects marriage as a matter of principle. "On her part, there was a full and conscientious belief that the choice of the individuals alone constituted a true marriage, and that the laws of human society upon this subject were an oppression which needed to be protected against" (1441). This very much reminds us of the trajectory of British feminist Mary Wollstonecraft, who also lived in revolutionary France with, bore a child to, and was deserted by an American radical and adventurer, Gilbert Imlay (himself involved in land speculation schemes with General Wilkinson).[27] Emily's words echo those of Julia in Byron's *Don Juan*: "I gave up all for him,—country, home, friends, name, reputation" (1440–1441).

Stowe has gone a very long way toward sympathetic presentation of this Byronic feminist, having had Tina plead on her behalf to Miss Mehitable: "Should we not make a discrimination between errors that come from a wrong belief and the mere weakness that blindly leads to passion?" (1415). After she has married Davenport and discovered he was Emily's faithless lover, Tina even adopts their child and thus enables her predecessor to be rehabilitated in society. Nevertheless, the novel depicts Emily as having been led astray by European Utopian secular ideals. Mr. Rossiter comments: "It is *man* who always takes advantage of woman in relations like these . . . Hard as marriage bonds bear in individual cases, it is for woman's interest that they should be as stringently maintained as the Lord himself has left them" (1446), though Horace feels this is too inflexible. Rather than endorsing Enlightenment feminism based on rationalism, Stowe's domestic ideology, in the words of Elizabeth Ammons, "makes the point that home and mother must not figure as sanctuaries from the world but as imperative models of its reconstitution" (160). Jacobin-turned-Federalist Davenport himself explains that "Men must have strong, positive religious beliefs to give them vigorous self-government; and republics are founded on the self-governing power of the individual" (1357). But Stowe blames the masculinist rationalism of theology and the antidemocratic image of its patriarchal God for alienating the chosen people of America. When New England lost its lifeblood of faith it would leave behind the bitter rind of the joyless work ethic of Miss Asphyxia and Old Crab Smith and the self-serving individualism of leaders like Ellery.

Stowe wrote of *Oldtown Folks*: "It is more to me than a story: it is my résumé of the whole spirit and body of New England—a country that now is exerting such an influence on the civilised world that to know it truly becomes an object" (qtd. in Forrest Wilson 312). So it was all the more galling when this novel was patronizingly denounced in the *Nation* and other reviews as mere provincial genre-painting. As Hedrick has pointed out, this attack was an opening salvo in the *Nation*'s misogynistic war on novels campaigning for civil rights for blacks and for women by Anna Dickinson, Rebecca Harding Davis, and Stowe as sentimental, didactic, and bad art (353–354). Stowe's response was to strike out against sexism in the literary world, and so it was now, thirteen years after Lady Byron had confided the incest story to her on her triumphant second trip to Europe, that she decided on her revelation. Her demonization of Byron was an attempt by Stowe to lead her sister novelists to carry the war over writing into the enemy's male canonical camp. As Susan Wolstenholme has emphasized, Stowe presents the issue precisely in terms of the woman writer's right to speak, and her mission to speak *for* those who (like slaves, women, or children) were enjoined to silence by lack of education or the coercive power of propriety (54). Of course, her brave gesture backfired. Stowe, like Lady Byron before her, was in a no-win situation. Even mentioning sexual sin like incest besmirched the Victorian woman herself, however respectable. As the *Times* dryly commented, "It would have been in better taste if Mrs. Stowe . . . had imitated the 'religious silence' the latter so much commends in the case of Lady Byron" (qtd. in Dallas 29–30). Praising Lady Byron's silence and castigating Byron's seductiveness as a writer had only reinforced the existing stereotype of man as writer and woman as muse.

The attack on Byron may seem paradoxical to the modern reader in that as a writer Stowe herself manifested Romantic traits. In her use of romance for crusading purposes, her historicism, and her validation of minority cultures, she was following Byronic precedents. Moreover, as we have seen in *Uncle Tom's Cabin, The Minister's Wooing,* and *Oldtown Folks,* she put her cult of maternity into dangerous alliance with the Byronic male. Wicked he may be, but into his skeptical mouth is often placed the sharpest critique of New England religion and its complicity in the institution of slavery, which would be too unfeminine for her saintly heroines. She consciously adopted and adapted his character of Aurora Raby to embody her cult of womanhood. Lastly, in her chivalric defense of Lady Byron, Stowe could be said to be making a bid to usurp Byron and enact the role he should have played. In other words, Stowe sought to make herself a female evangelical Byron.

The press saw it that way. The cartoon from *Fun Magazine* reprinted by Forrest Wilson shows her aggressive ambition by depicting her climbing up his statue. She is also depicted as a dirty muckraker—she has her foot in Byron's groin area—and is caught in a sexually suggestive posture. She leaves filthy footprints on Byron's white marble. Algernon Swinburne, too, scatologically satirized her as "Mrs. Bitcher Spew—author of Uncle Tom's Closet" (Lang 345).[28] Ironically, Stowe's attack on Byron had resulted in a vitriolic counterattack, particularly by the nationalistic British press, comparable to or even worse than that the poet had himself suffered in 1816. A good example is [H. Savile Clark], *Lord Byron's Defence* (London: 183 The Strand, 1869), whose cover has a picture of a handsome young Byron after Phillips with a white background and his motto, "crede Byron," superimposed on one of a haggard old Stowe in profile with a black background, her bedraggled hair hanging down under her chin, giving her the appearance of having a long beard like an old Puritan preacher (fig. 3). The satire is in ottava rima, in the style of *Don Juan,* as if written by the poet himself from Hades. This emphasis on black and white is continued throughout the poem, with imagery of dirt being predominant. Stanza 5 claims Stowe has "scatter'd lies with dirty prodigality,/And made me blacker even than reality," while stanza 8 punningly associates her pages with dirty linen: "Her publisher will pay—game worth the candle,/For sheets befoul'd with literary scandal." The racist implications of the imagery of blackness are overt in stanza 12, where "Byron" defends his sister Augusta from Stowe:

> She wished our reputations both to tar
> With the same foul brush; 'twas a worthy whim
> Of her who white-washed hosts of fetid niggers
> To take such pains to blacken both our figures.

The British public were informed by Charles Mackay in his opportunist edition of Byron's niece, and perhaps daughter, Medora Leigh's autobiography that "Lady Byron was . . . what the Americans call a nigger-worshipper" and that he deplored the "very black smoke that has been pouring forth from the funnel of Mrs. Beecher Stowe's literary engine to darken the fame of Lord Byron" (17–18, 171). "J. M.," however, explains to his British readers that Mrs. Stowe's attack must be ascribed to American men's overreverence for women, which has resulted in the latter's taking "a low view of man's manliness. . . . From this Western chivalry run mad arise those continual efforts, which we hear of ladies taking this or that position usually occupied by men; hence those 'Women's Rights conventions' and other manifestations of contempt for man in a country the most indulgent in the world towards the ladies" (8).

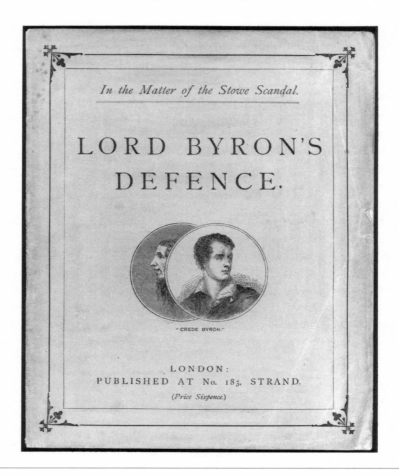

In the Matter of the Stowe Scandal.

LORD BYRON'S DEFENCE.

"CREDE BYRON."

LONDON:
PUBLISHED AT No. 183, STRAND.

(Price Sixpence.)

3. The cover of *Lord Byron's Defence* (London: 183 The Strand, 1869) shows a picture of a handsome young Byron with a white background and the motto "crede Byron" superimposed on one of a haggard Stowe in profile with her bedraggled hair hanging down under her chin, giving her the appearance of a bearded Puritan preacher. Courtesy of the Yale Collection of American Literature, Beinecke Rare Book and Manuscript Library.

Byron's depictions of the soul in torment following his own rejection of Calvinism had seemed to anticipate the spiritual crisis of New England in the throes of repudiating its Edwardsean Puritan legacy. According to Alice C. Crozier, his poems were "of vastly more importance for Americans of the first half of the nineteenth century than were Wordsworth's consolations and pieties" ("Stowe and Byron" 198).[29] So when even conservative and deeply religious writers like Harriet Beecher Stowe and Anne Brontë were to throw off a Puritan heritage of fatalism and obedience in favor of free will and practical Christianity, they stepped into Byron's shoes even as they set him up as the satanic extreme against which to measure their own apostasy. The skeptical Byron functioned for such nineteenth-century women novelists as the serpent in the Calvinist garden—tempting them to rebel against their minister-fathers and even against the father-God himself.

Notes

1. The present article is a revision and further development of the section on Stowe in my 2001 University of Nottingham Foundation lecture, "Byron and Women Novelists," which deals more broadly with the importance of Byron to the history of the nineteenth-century female-authored novel of sentiment. Quotes from *Lady Byron Vindicated* are from the 1870 London edition.

2. Stowe asserts that Lady Byron kept silent on the reasons she left him in order to facilitate Byron's repentance, in *Lady Byron Vindicated* (49).

3. Joan D. Hedrick gives a full analysis of Stowe's mixed motives (353–68).

4. The Reverend Brontë was influenced by Methodism, and though he repudiated the most extreme Calvinist doctrines of Election, his own sermons and poetry stressed hellfire more than redemption. Charlotte Brontë suffered a religious crisis in 1836, writing to Ellen Nussey, "In writing at this moment I feel an irksome disgust at the idea of using a single phrase that sounds like religious cant—I abhor myself—I despise myself—if the Doctrine of Calvin be true I am already an outcast—you cannot imagine how hard rebellious and intractable all my feelings are—When I begin to study on the subject I almost grow blasphemous, atheistical in my sentiments." See Wise and Symington 1, 143.

5. Foster, *The Rungless Ladder* (1970 ed.) 220–222; Hedrick 21–22; and Crozier 195.

6. At fourteen she began a verse drama, *Cleon*, imagining Byron being converted. See Foster 221.

7. Stowe flattered herself that her friendship with Byron's wife was a mode of relationship with the poet: "I told her that I had been from childhood powerfully influenced by him; and began to tell her how much, as a child, I had been affected by the news of his death,—giving up all my plays, and going off to a lonely hillside, where I spent the afternoon thinking of him. She interrupted me before I had quite finished, with a quick impulsive movement. 'I know all that,' she said: 'I heard it all from Mrs. ————; and it was one of the things that made me wish to *know* you. I think *you* could understand him," *Lady Byron Vindicated* 143–144; see also 171. On the intensity of her feelings for Lady Byron herself, see 168.

8. References to Byron's poetry are taken from *Lord Byron, Complete Poetical Works*,

ed. Jerome J. McGann, 7 vols. References are by canto and stanza or, in the case of *The Giaour*, by line number.

9. Stowe recounts her conversation with Lady Byron on whether Byron had repented on his deathbed and whether he had been saved. *Lady Byron Vindicated* 163.

10. Hannah More's *Coelebs in Search of a Wife* (1808) was written to refute the celebration of female genius in Madame de Staël's *Corinne* and to reaffirm the Christian domestic feminine role.

11. In the preface to an early work, *The Incarnation; or, Pictures of the Virgin and Her Son* (1849), a fictionalized biography of Christ, Stowe justified the use of "romance" in a good cause to combat the attraction for readers of "the strains of a Byron, or the glowing pictures of a Bulwer or a Sue." See Hedrick 188.

12. On Byron's anti-Calvinistic resistance to the doctrine of eternal damnation, see Hirst 87.

13. Foster attributes the darkening of these characters to Stowe's friendship with Lady Byron in 1853 and her disclosure of the cause of the separation in 1856 (222 [1970 ed.]). In "Harriet Beecher Stowe and Byron," Crozier also notes the Byronic aspects of the characters: Legree in *Uncle Tom's Cabin*, Dred in *Dred: A Tale of the Great Dismal Swamp*, James Marvin in *The Minister's Wooing*, and Harry Percival in *Oldtown Folks* (196–197).

14. Another Byron quotation is used as the epigraph for chapter 34 (524).

15. Quotes from *Uncle Tom's Cabin* are from the 1987 Penguin edition. There is an excellent discussion of the character of St. Clare and the importance of his disturbing millennial vision by Joshua D. Bellin.

16. Susan K. Harris reads the images of the novel as "a female imaginary that resisted the androcentrism not simply of Calvinism but of secular and heterosexual American life" ("Female" 98). In "Harriet Beecher Stowe's Conversation with the *Atlantic Monthly*," Dorothy Z. Baker has illustrated how the novel, serialized in the *Atlantic Monthly*, engaged in a larger discussion within the magazine's fiction and nonfiction on political, religious, and social issues.

17. Stowe hung four pictures of the Virgin Mary in her Hartford home, according to Kimbrell (73).

18. Quotes from *The Minister's Wooing* are from the 1999 Penguin edition. This passage from *Don Juan* is paraphrased again on p. 264: "Mary sat as placid and disengaged as the new moon, and listened to the chatter of old and young with the easy quietness of a young heart that has early outlived life, and looks on everything in the world from some gentle, restful eminence far on towards a better home." Mary later paraphrases the famous passage from Julia's letter (*Don Juan* 2, 194–195) when reproaching the Byronic would-be seducer Burr for his treatment of Madame de Frontignac: "You men can have everything,—ambition, wealth, power; a thousand ways are open to you: women have nothing but their heart; and when that is gone, all is gone" (275).

19. Jean Lebedun has suggested the character is based on the crusading feminist Sojourner Truth (359–363).

20. Hopkins himself is made to endorse this: "Yet if we consider that the Son of

God, as to his human nature, was made of a woman, it leads us to see that in matters of grace God sets a special honour upon it. Accordingly, there have been in the Church, in all ages, holy women who have received the Spirit and been called to a ministration in the things of God,—such as Deborah, Huldah, and Anna, the prophetess" (*The Minister's Wooing* 211).

21. Ten years later, Teresa Guiccioli would publish her *My Recollections of Lord Byron and Those of Eyewitnesses of His Life*, tr. H. E. Jerningham (London: Bentley, 1869), whose idealized portrait of the poet and justification of his conduct toward his wife prompted Stowe's *Lady Byron Vindicated*. Byron had first become acquainted with his solemn future wife while in the throes of an earlier adulterous affair with glamorous socialite Lady Caroline Lamb, so Stowe's fictionalization of the piquant situation replaces Lamb with Guiccioli. Byron, too, fictionalized these relationships in the English cantos of *Don Juan* (but replacing Caroline with Teresa). Stowe even has Burr telling all the details of the entanglement to a female confidante (159) as Byron did to Lady Melbourne—Annabella's aunt and Caroline's mother-in-law, mother of the man he was cuckolding. Byron's poem was unfinished at his death so we will never know if Aurora Raby or Lady Adeline do fall for the libertine's blandishments.

22. See also Schachner. Disappointingly, Charles J. Nolan does not deal with Stowe.

23. Burr is also associated with the arts. C. P. Wilson has commented on the paradox that Stowe herself, nevertheless, endorses romance (575). I would suggest that Stowe situates her own didactic romance as a median between the dichotomy she sets up between Byron's poetry and "Edwards on the Affections" on p. 73 of the novel.

24. On Burr as estranged from his forefather's religious doctrines, see Edward Tang (94).

25. All quotations from *Oldtown Folks* are taken from *Three Novels*, Sklar, ed.

26. Gayle Kimbrell points out that Dr. Stern is based on Nathaniel Emmons, whose harsh sermons after the death of her fiancé, who had not experienced conversion, provoked Catharine Beecher's rebellion against Calvinism (44).

27. The historical Aaron Burr was excited by *Vindication of the Rights of Woman* and based his daughter's education on it. See Nolan, *Aaron Burr and the American Literary Imagination* (10). Burr wrote to Godwin asking permission to obtain a copy of Opie's portrait of Wollstonecraft after her death.

28. On the other hand, according to Paul Baender, Mark Twain defended Stowe in six unsigned editorials in the *Buffalo Express*.

29. See also Eakin (40) and Lawrence Buell, "Calvinism Romanticized."

Uncle Tom's Cabin and the Irish National Tale

CLÍONA Ó GALLCHOIR

T THE TURN of the eighteenth century in Ireland, the novel form was successfully exploited by women as a means of commenting not only on their own relationship to society but also on the relationship between Great Britain and Ireland, two badly matched partners in a legislative union established in 1801. In fact, the novelists Maria Edgeworth and Sydney Owenson (Lady Morgan) were the most successful of all Irish writers in the first two decades of the nineteenth century, becoming closely associated with the "Irish" or "National" Tale.[1]

The influence of these Irish models on the early novel in America, particularly the novel as authored by women, is evident in the fact that one of America's earliest women writers, Catharine Maria Sedgwick, dedicated her first novel, *A New-England Tale* (1822), to Edgeworth and made numerous references to Edgeworth both in her novels and in letters and journals, describing for instance receiving a letter from Edgeworth following the publication of *A New-England Tale* as "quite an epoch in my quiet, humble life" (*Life and Letters* 1: 161).

The pioneering studies of early American women's writing acknowledged the influence of figures such as Edgeworth as significant on the development of women writers in America but gave no consideration to the specifically Irish dimension of this influence. Nina Baym, for instance, unfortunately includes Edgeworth among a list of "English women moralists" whose works formed the "childhood reading" of the first generation of American women novelists, contributing toward a literary tradition that "then developed indigenously in America" (*Woman's Fiction* 29–30). It is nonetheless increasingly evident that the distinct contribution of Irish—as opposed to English or British—women novelists to nineteenth-century American women's writing deserves special consideration. Writing before Walter Scott, Edgeworth and Owenson had already successfully challenged the definition of the novel as exclusively domestic or romantic in focus. Their concern to address the complex relations between the partners in the recently created United Kingdom also created a new space within the novel for representations of and reflections on national identity. Although politically and stylistically at odds, both Edgeworth and Owenson shared a commitment to imagining this new political community as shaped by female concerns and female agency, and as such their work constitutes an important source of influence for nineteenth-century American women's writing, including the work of Harriet Beecher Stowe.

Edgeworth has been acknowledged as an important influence on Stowe's achievements in social realism and in the observation and representation of characteristic modes of speech in particular, with Joan Hedrick remarking that Edgeworth, "whose novels were part of the literary culture into which Harriet Beecher was born," was the most significant model on which Stowe would have drawn in this regard (210). But the emphasis on Edgeworth's role as a pioneer in the field of social realism and the representation of regional speech and manners fails to take full account of the complex political intervention that her novels (like those of Owenson) were designed to make in the fractured public sphere of the United Kingdom, thus masking the extent to which these Irish novels provided a model upon which Stowe based her sensationally successful depiction of a nation divided against itself.

Critics have recently begun to address the role played by these Irish novels as a resource for American women writers whose novels also aimed to intervene in the discourse of nation-formation in the nineteenth century. This topic has, for instance, been explored in a study of the relationship between Edgeworth and Sedgwick, both of whom, according to Jenifer Elmore, are "preoccupied with modeling Union—the harmonious union of qualities within the individual, of husbands and wives, of disparate groups within larger societies, and, most importantly, of member states within larger political nations, such as Edgeworth's United Kingdom of England, Scotland, and Ireland, and Sedgwick's young United States of America" (vii). Elmore's emphasis on the desire for "harmonious" union is, however, insufficiently alert to the tensions the concept of "union" brought with it on both sides of the Atlantic, and in particular the Irish Tale's recognition of its imperfect and problematic reality. Susan Manning's discussion of "the recurrent tension between unity and fragmentation in . . . Scottish and American writing from the eighteenth and nineteenth centuries" (4) is much closer to my own sense of the Irish novelists' engagements with Union and their legacy for women writers in America. Manning's methodology, which focuses less on specific paths of influence than on "more associative and analogical models of comparison . . . derived from the structuring principles" (4) of the texts she discusses is also a very useful point of reference for the approach adopted in this essay.[2]

Briefly stated, my aim in what follows is, first, to show the striking similarity between some of Stowe's narrative structures and those employed by Edgeworth, Owenson, and Sedgwick, all of whom are concerned with the imaginative construction of a nation and whose texts sift the elements out of which this nation is to be composed. Locating Stowe's novel in the context of these earlier texts provides us with an opportunity for fresh reflection on her construction of the nation through the balancing of contrasting qualities and the exploration of the potential conflict between northern and southern values and perspectives. The potential of this approach to contribute to rereadings of Stowe is suggested by a recent essay on Stowe and regionalism by Marjorie Pryse. Pryse notes the importance of both Sedgwick and Edgeworth as influences on Stowe's achievements as a regional novelist, but she concludes that although *Uncle Tom's Cabin* displays the influence of regionalist writing it cannot be termed a regionalist novel (unlike some of Stowe's later fiction such as *The Pearl of Orr's Island*). The reason for this, according to Pryse, is that Stowe writes about the South from an outsider's perspective: "Stowe imposes a perspective on a region she did not know from lived experience" (134); "crossing sectional lines and writing a northern nationalist novel for a sectional readership, she writes a powerful but hardly regionalist novel" (135). Issues of external perspective and audience are, however, not unique to *Uncle Tom's Cabin*: they in fact form a defining characteristic of the Irish Tale as pioneered by Edgeworth and Owenson. The very obvious presence of an outsider perspective in *Uncle Tom's Cabin* therefore suggests not, or not simply, the sectional nature of Stowe's mentality, but her use of a method of representation that had originated with the Irish Tale and that had proved highly adaptable to an American context.

Another aim of my essay is to consider the ways in which Stowe departs from the tradition she inherited. The sentimentality for which Stowe became notorious in the twentieth century is often presented as an aspect of the "feminization" of American literary culture in the nineteenth century

(Fiedler, Douglas), but as I will argue here, the skeptical approach to rationality that characterizes *Uncle Tom's Cabin* is not specifically "feminine," as it represents a departure from the Enlightenment tradition of Edgeworth, Owenson, and Sedgwick, all of whom predicated their advocacy of women's agency on the basis of Enlightenment thought. Stowe's work therefore both draws from and breaks with an existing female tradition, offering (among other things) a radical critique of the limitations of Enlightenment concepts of the individual and the national community.

Leslie Fiedler proposes that "the novel and America did not come into existence at the same time by accident" (32). The same could be claimed of the emergence of the novel in Ireland, where the advent of political union focused attention on the "strange country" that had been incorporated into the United Kingdom. The newly won independence of the American colonies seems, however, to form a stark contrast with the dependent status that marked Ireland's entry into the nineteenth century, the century of nationalism. Critics of nineteenth century Irish writing have tended to focus on this apparent anomaly and argue that the literature of this period is characterized by an unhealthy concern with Irishness *in relation to* Englishness. Both Edgeworth and Owenson habitually engage in a process of comparison and contrast, defining Irish national character with reference to that of England. A number of critics including Seamus Deane have argued that the effect in Edgeworth's case is to create Irishness as an inferior and deviant quality, only and always recognizable insofar as it fails to mimic Englishness perfectly (Deane 28–36). Owenson's depiction of Ireland, particularly in her hugely popular *The Wild Irish Girl* (1806), is, if anything, even more intensely focused on representing Ireland as England's Other. The effect in her case is a difference that produces desire and renders Ireland attractively exoticized.

Joep Leerssen, however, argues that there is an inevitably "contrastive" element to *all* descriptions and definitions of national character and identity because, as he says, "The border that surrounds one group is also the border that separates it from another" (20). Leerssen suggests that "what one should look for when dealing with the concept of 'nationality' would then, seem to be a pattern of differences or differentiations" (19). Rather than being an anomaly peculiar to Irish writing under the Union, the system of representation characteristic of this period in Ireland is, following Leerssen's argument, available as a model through which other nationalities could find articulation, particularly in cases where national identity was either emergent or contested.

The external perspective evident in *Uncle Tom's Cabin*, which is highlighted by Pryse as detracting from its status as truly regional writing, can thus be regarded in another light as an extension of an existing model for the exploration of national and regional differences held in tension in the form of a political union. As Manning has argued with respect to the connections between Scottish and American writing, it is likely that the Irish model proved particularly compelling for American writers precisely because it was so clearly concerned with the union of contrasting elements, contrasts that were drawn not only between the new nation and its former colonial ruler but also between the northern and southern states. William R. Taylor's portrayal of divisions within American culture, and the growing differentiation between concepts of North and South before the war, has been qualified by historians like Michael O'Brien who have also restored a sense of the international cultural and intellectual influences on the antebellum South as well as the North. Nevertheless, O'Brien's own description of an "asymmetrical" relationship between South and North, in which "Northerners knew less about the South than Southerners did of the North" and in which "mutual suspicions and incomprehensions" (27) frequently characterized relationships between the inhabitants of the two regions, strikes a very familiar chord for those familiar with the state of British–Irish relations in the nineteenth century.

Taylor's use of the term *counterpoint*—for the way in which the perceived strengths and weaknesses of the northern and southern characters were compared and contrasted—helps to define one element that American writers may have borrowed from the Irish Tale. Taylor argues that counterpoint was used in order to come to some kind of agreed picture of the outstanding virtues of the American national character. Although contained within the notional unity of the American state, the use of counterpoint is very similar to Leerssen's contrastive model for the articulation of national characters and to the attempts of Edgeworth, Owenson, and other Irish writers to account both for the differences between Ireland and Britain and the fact of their political union.

Leerssen has coined a specific term to describe the defining quality of Irish writing after the union, labeling it *auto-exotic*. For Leerssen, auto-exoticism denotes the ways in which Irish writers told stories about Ireland from the point of view of outsiders, almost always employing English narrators or focalizers. Leerssen thus argues that "the central Irish character is de-Irishized, to a certain extent" and that "the narrative of romantic Anglo–Irish fiction will tend to marginalize its most Irish characters" (36, 37). Auto-exoticism is a pronounced feature of Owenson's *The Wild Irish Girl* and Edgeworth's *Ennui* (1809). Both novels feature Anglo–Irish protagonists brought up in England whose journeys to and encounters with Ireland are characterized by an initial sense of alienation that gives way to sympathy and understanding.

In American fiction, the same tendency to exoticize the familiar is evident in Sarah Josepha Hale's *Northwood* (1827), in which the central character, Sidney Romilly, is relocated to a southern plantation and then shifted back and forth between the North and the South until he seems to have acquired the ideal character. Taylor places great emphasis on *Northwood* as a key text in the development of an idea of American character that rested on the opposing poles of North and South. He points out that Hale was a northerner and earlier in her writing career had produced a series of sketches of characters representative of New England and the Yankee, and he asks what prompted her in her most successful fiction to oscillate between North and South. The answer to this, I argue, lies in the examples that American women writers found in the novels of their Irish counterparts.

The auto-exotic scene of encounter between different cultures is, as I have suggested, a staple of Irish writing of the early nineteenth century and is characterized by a tension between attraction and repulsion. Prior to his first journey to Ireland, Horatio, hero of *The Wild Irish Girl*, imagines the Irish "seated round their domestic fire in a state of perfect nudity" preparing "to broil an enemy" (13). The highly didactic purpose of the novel is to dismantle these prejudices and to present Ireland in a favorable light to a British audience who found themselves recently united to this backward province. This aim is pursued via a plot that borrows from the existing genre of the travel narrative as it invites the implicitly English reader to accompany Horatio on his journey to Ireland. His fears of squalor and savagery are banished almost instantly, to be replaced by appreciation of Irish landscape, Irish music, and most of all, Irish womanhood, in the form of Glorvina, the "princess of Inismore." A lingering sense of fear and repulsion is nonetheless evident in Horatio's nightmare in which the beautiful and charming Glorvina, with whom he is by now infatuated, appears to him as a hideous Gorgon (58). This dream, and other motifs such as Horatio's comparison of the Castle of Inismore to the Castle of Otranto, make Owenson's debt to the popular Gothic genre very clear. In *Ennui*, Edgeworth, who normally avoided the sensational in her fiction and was wary of the political connotations of the Gothic, also draws on its associations with otherness and fear, albeit partly to undermine them, when recording the reaction of the Earl of Glenthorn on his arrival in his dilapidated Irish estate: "The state tower, in which, after reiterated entreaties, I was at last left alone to repose, was hung with magnificent but ancient tapestry. It was so like a room in a haunted castle, that if I had not been too much fatigued to think of anything, I should certainly have thought of Mrs Radcliffe" (191). The dismissal of the potential for Gothic horror is an important feature of these optimistic and progressive texts and is also indicative of the dual perspective they present. The outsider's perspective is either almost immediately challenged with realities that shatter his prejudices or is insistently ironized and thus revealed to the reader as unreliable—a strategy that we shall see at work in *Uncle Tom's Cabin*.

Edgeworth's Glenthorn finds that his encounter with a culture that he initially finds alien and exotic, alternately attractive and dismaying, has a powerfully transformative effect on his character, and he eventually abandons his exoticizing perspective, embracing Ireland as "home." Like Hale's Sidney Romilly, he moves from England to Ireland, then back to England, and finally back to Ireland before the transformation is finally complete. It is only by leaving England, returning, and leaving again to return to Ireland that he can acquire all the qualities that are necessary to make him an Irish landlord like none other: educated, progressive, and most importantly, committed both by reason and sentiment to the people and the land. The repeated journeys to and from highly contrasted locations, which Taylor highlights as a peculiarity of Hale's *Northwood*, are therefore a crucial feature of these earlier works.

Very similar structures are found in Sedgwick's *Redwood*. In this novel Caroline Redwood and her father, Henry, who originate from the Southern states, experience a challenge to their ways of thinking during a period of time spent in New England. Sedgwick thus exoticizes New England by presenting it from the point of view of Caroline, who has been brought up in Charleston, South Carolina, by her maternal grandmother.[3] She is described as being, at eighteen, "the idol of the fashionable world, and as completely *au fait* in all its arts and mysteries, as a veteran belle of five and twenty" (1: 79). Caroline's appalled reaction to the New England way of life is vividly conveyed in a letter in which she expresses her disgust and boredom:

> I cannot imagine how papa can feel any interest in this Lenox family: they are common vulgar farmers. There is one oddity among them, who they call an "old girl" [Debby]; a hideous monster—a giantess: I suspect a descendant of

the New England witches; and I verily believe, if the truth were known, she has spellbound papa. The wretch is really quite fond of him; for him she wrings the necks of her fattest fowls, and I hear her at this moment bawling to one of the boys, to kill the black-eared pig—for him, no doubt. (1: 123)

In Sedgwick's description of the faithful family servant, Debby, who in many respects exemplifies the Yankee or New England character, we see the traces of a potentially threatening "otherness" that have attached themselves to her character: she is an "oddity," a "hideous monster," a "giantess," and may well be a descendant of the witches of New England. Moreover, in the references to the wringing of the necks of the fowl and the slaughtering of the black-eared pig, we have also, in comic form, the overtones of violence and threat that form part of the representation of what is "other."

Uncle Tom's Cabin, like the work of Sedgwick and Hale, shows distinct traces of the contrastive structure that originated with the Irish Tale. Its reliance on the mutually defining opposition between North and South has, however, been overwhelmed by the novel's reputed role in igniting the hostility between northern and southern states. Contemporary criticism of the novel from within the American South repeatedly drew attention to the fact that Stowe, as a northerner, could not be relied upon for accurate and fair representations of life in the South (Hedrick 219, 230).[4] However, as Taylor has pointed out, the novel is in fact carefully balanced so as to emphasize positive as well as negative aspects of southern life. Moreover, the autobiographical sketch that Augustine St. Clare provides to his cousin Ophelia draws attention to a dualistic pattern that repeats itself across generations: "My father, you know, came first from New England; and he was just such another man as your father—a regular old Roman,—upright, energetic, noble-minded, with an iron will. Your father settled down in New England, to rule over rocks and stones, and to force an existence out of Nature; and mine settled in Louisiana, to rule over men and women, and force existence out of them" (194–195).[5] Beneath the contrast, St. Clare insists on a likeness between these two apparently opposed types, the southern, slaveholding plantation owner, and the hardworking, independent New England farmer: "The fact is, though he has fallen on hard times, and embraced a democratic theory, [Ophelia's father] is to the heart an aristocrat, as much as my father, who ruled over five or six hundred slaves" (198). A similar compound of likeness and difference characterizes St. Clare and his brother: "My brother and I were twins; and they say, you know, that twins ought to resemble each other; but we were in all points a contrast. He had black, fiery eyes, coal-black hair, a strong, fine, Roman profile, and a rich brown complexion. I had blue eyes, golden hair, a Greek outline, and fair complexion. . . . he was my father's pet, and I my mother's" (195). St. Clare emphasizes the extent of the contrasts between himself and his brother, and yet the fact remains that they are *twins*, thus bound together in a profound way that cuts across these physical and spiritual contrasts: "a mysterious tie seemed to unite them in a closer friendship than ordinary . . . the very contrariety seemed to unite them, like the attraction between opposite poles of a magnet" (230). There are here echoes of the foster-brothers in Edgeworth's *Ennui*, one an earl brought up to believe himself a peasant, and the other the peasant child brought up as a wealthy nobleman. They are, like the St. Clare twins, "in all points a contrast," and yet each provides for the other a kind of mirror of alternative possibilities. St. Clare's life-story is, in fact, rather like the plot summary of an Edgeworthian novel, interpolated into Stowe's text. Partic-ularly characteristic is the reference to the failure of his marriage. His first love was "a high-minded and beautiful woman [from] one of the Northern states" (132), but parental opposition and deception prevents their marriage. In his distraught state St. Clare engages himself to a southern belle and "be[comes] the husband of a fine figure, a pair of bright dark eyes, and a hundred thousand dollars" (132–133). Compare this to *Ennui*'s Glenthorn, who chooses his bride "by the numeration table: Units, tens, hundreds, thousands, tens of thousands, hundreds of thousands" (*Ennui* 167).

Uncle Tom's Cabin also provides its own version of the auto-exotic cultural encounter in scenes where the representative northerner and New Englan-der, Miss Ophelia, confronts the domestic chaos in the St. Clare household. Viewed in one way, the scenes in which Miss Ophelia reacts with horror to southern ways (which are almost exclusively associated with the behavior and habits of black slaves) could be regarded as merely an exoticized and pa-tronizing representation of the black household servants from a northern perspective clouded by convictions of cultural superiority. The famous pas-sage about Dinah's kitchen, for instance, clearly valorizes Miss Ophelia's ideas of system and order over Dinah's adherence to impulse and random-ness, as Gillian Brown has pointed out:

> Miss Ophelia, after passing on her reformatory tour through all the other parts of the establishment, now entered the kitchen. . . .
> When St. Clare had first returned from the North, impressed with the sys-

tem and order of his uncle's kitchen arrangements, he had largely provided his own with an array of cupboards, drawers, and various apparatus, to induce systematic regulation, under the sanguine illusion that it would be of any possible assistance to Dinah in her arrangements. He might as well have provided them for a squirrel or a magpie. The more drawers and closets there were, the more hiding-holes Dinah could make for the accommodation of old rags, hair-combs, old shoes, ribbons, cast-off artificial flowers, and other articles of *vertu*, wherein her soul delighted . . .

Miss Ophelia commenced opening a set of drawers.

"What is this drawer for, Dinah?" she said.

"It's handy for most anything, Missis," said Dinah. So it appeared to be. From the variety it contained, Miss Ophelia pulled out first a fine damask table-cloth stained with blood, having evidently been used to envelop some raw meat. (180–181)

Yet it would be a mistake to read the encounter between Miss Ophelia and Dinah as a straightforward vehicle for the authorial or narrative point of view.[6] Like Owenson's Horatio or Edgeworth's Glenthorn, Miss Ophelia cannot be accepted as a wholly reliable informant on the life that she observes. Her determination to reform Dinah's haphazard approach to house-keeping compares very closely to Glenthorn's ambitious plans to demolish his Irish peasant foster-mother's cottage and replace it with one "fitted up in the most elegant style of English cottages" (199). "Irish ways" prove intractable, but Glenthorn reflects ruefully that the faults are not all on one side: "it would have been difficult for a cool spectator to decide, whether I or my workmen were most at fault; they for their dilatory habits, or I for my impatient temper" (198).

Similarly, as a characteristic New Englander, Miss Ophelia is herself exoticized to a certain extent, as is the northern way of life she represents and is determined to replicate in New Orleans. At the point at which the narrator announces her intention to introduce the character of Miss Ophelia, she first describes a typical New England house and farm, concluding that "on such a farm, in such a house and family, Miss Ophelia had spent a quiet existence of some forty-five years" (136). "Typical" modes of life are described with sympathy but also with a degree of distance, in that the insularity and self-conscious respectability of Miss Ophelia's community form part of the description. The largely ignorant assumptions of the townspeople concerning the South are portrayed, and their speculations on Miss Ophelia's journey are as much concerned with the imagined expense of her new wardrobe as with the prospect of "doing good." The short list of books that, according to the narrator, are to be found in the typical New England farmhouse parlor is limited and suggestive of a Puritan narrow-mindedness (Milton and Bunyan feature prominently) rather than a commitment to intellectual inquiry. Miss Ophelia herself is described as "the absolute bond-slave of the *ought*" (144), and her incessant activity around the house is as provoking as it is admirable: "it really was a labour to see her" (206), concludes the wry narrator.

The use of contrastive patterns and the significance of the auto-exotic scene of encounter in *Uncle Tom's Cabin* clearly place it in the transatlantic tradition of Owenson, Edgeworth, Sedgwick, and indeed, Hale, and suggest that one of Stowe's aims was simultaneously to highlight the gulf that divided North and South and to suggest the possibility of overcoming it. What distinguishes *Uncle Tom's Cabin* from these earlier texts, however, is that Stowe's vision was not simply of a unified nation but of a (unified) "anti-slavery nation" (Pryse 134). Like those of her predecessors, Stowe's novel has a clear educative function, and its intent to educate or change the minds of its readers is mirrored in the text in a variety of scenes of education, but the education of readers toward membership and participation in an antislavery nation requires a type of education radically different from that which we find in the works of Sedgwick and Edgeworth. Miss Ophelia's northern virtues, on their own, are clearly insufficient as the foundation for such a nation, a failure signalled in her unsuccessful efforts to educate and "civilize" Topsy. It is, of course, Eva who reveals Miss Ophelia's shortcomings to her: observing the way in which Eva touches the source of Topsy's misery and comforts her, Miss Ophelia exclaims, "I wish I were like her. She might teach me a lesson" (246). Augustine's response articulates the seemingly paradoxical nature of this education: "It wouldn't be the first time a little child had been used to instruct an old disciple" (246).

The Irish national tale, particularly as practiced by Maria Edgeworth, was deeply enmeshed in an Enlightenment discourse of education. Edgeworth was well-known in her time as an educational writer as well as a writer of fiction for both children and adults, and her activity in this area reflected her deeply rooted conviction that education was the medium whereby society would advance and improve. The theme of a young woman's education and entry into the world is, of course, one of the archetypal plots of women's fiction, but Edgeworth did not endorse the rigid separation of female and male, private and public concerns.[7] Government was for Edgeworth like domestic education on a large scale: laws and economic policies could either "teach" people to be lazy and dishonest, if those laws were unfair and opaque, or productive and content, if the laws allowed them to prosper and encouraged effort. This belief underlay her insistence on treating public as well as private issues in her novels.

Edgeworth's emphasis on education as a matter of national, public importance also enabled her to position women as central to national life. A number of her young male heroes owe their eventual achievement of morally legitimate leadership to the intervention of intelligent and powerful women. In the case of *Ennui*'s Lord Glenthorn, it is his attraction to Lady Geraldine that prompts his first efforts at self-improvement and, ultimately, his love for Cecilia Delamere that inspires him to engage in a long and arduous process that amounts to self-creation and culminates in his return to his Irish estates. *Ormond*'s Harry Ormond receives no moral guidance from his guardian, Sir Ulick O'Shane, and is certainly the moral superior of his beloved Uncle Corny but is deeply influenced by the moral influence of Lady Annaly and the distant prospect of being considered as a suitor for her daughter, Florence.

Edgeworth's belief in the contribution that educated women could make to society and its improvement underlies these highly artificial plots, and they provide an example of how a novel could challenge the limits of women's perceived competence while avoiding overtly radical sympathies. This clearly provided inspiration for other women writers, not least Sedgwick. In Sedgwick's *The Linwoods; or, "Sixty Years Since" in America* (1835), Isabella Linwood begins the novel as a monarchist but finds that her allegiance gradually shifts: "I am beginning to think that if I had been a man, I should not have forgotten that I was an American" (2: 10). In much the same way that Lady Geraldine, Cecilia Delamere, and Lady Annaly recall Edgeworth's heroes to their duties as Irish men by being instrumental in their decisions to remain in Ireland and work for its improvement, Isabella Linwood succeeds in winning over her monarchist father to the cause of the American nation.

Sedgwick clearly wishes to explore the possibilities of female power without overtly challenging the status quo: Nina Baym's description of the novel as "offering a liberal . . . understanding of women's place in the Revolution" (*American Women Writers* 170) thus seems accurate. The basic plot common to those novels designated by Baym as liberal is as follows:

> The protagonist first detaches herself from allegiance to the Tory side as it is personified in her father, in favour of the rebel cause as it is personified in a pa-

triot suitor. . . . this story of a daughter who reconciles a monarchical father to a republican husband . . . should be thought of as the basic narrative through which the female national identity was conveyed.

Before the daughter carries out the traditional womanly role of peacemaker, she carries out acts of untraditional resistance to paternal authority. The explanation for this behaviour is her nascent nationality. . . . The plot unites the private with the public story: the truly important achievement of the republican daughter is securing her father's allegiance to the nation. (170)

Both Edgeworth and Sedgwick portray women as active agents in the creation of enlightened authority and leadership. Female agency is, thus, for both writers, implicated in an Enlightenment position that assumes the achievement of intellectual maturity via an educative process.

The narrative structures and strategies developed in the early nineteenth century in the Irish Tale thus have a transatlantic reach, but the limitations of this model for Stowe's antislavery, abolitionist purposes become evident when we consider how slavery is positioned in the American novels that are a part of this tradition. Sedgwick's *Redwood* has been identified as the earliest novel to treat slavery in the United States (Karcher 205), but in both *Redwood* and *The Linwoods*, slaves and slave owners appear either as peripheral characters or marginal references or as characters whose function is ultimately to underline the moral chasm between North and South. Caroline Redwood, for instance, is accompanied to New England by her slave, Lily, and her unthinking endorsement of slavery is one of the many moral defects that stand in the way of her marriage to the idealized Charles Westall. Westall is, like Hale's Sidney Romilly, the son of a southern plantation owner who has been educated in the northern states. Significantly, however, his inheritance is considerably reduced because of his father's decision to free all his slaves. Caroline responds to this information with disbelief: "there is no living without slaves . . . everybody allows, that all our danger is from freed slaves" (1: 183).

The idealized national community that the novel constructs has no place for Caroline and, thus, no place for her indifference to the injustice of slavery. At the novel's conclusion she repents of and is forgiven for her malicious behavior toward her half-sister, Ellen Bruce, the secret of whose identity she has tried to conceal in order to advance her own marriage designs, but her moral flaws are apparently beyond redemption. In the scene in which Ellen forgives Caroline, the latter is described as kneeling and stretching out her arms "with an almost oriental abjectness" (2: 269). The use of the word *ori-*

ental signals very clearly that Caroline's character is out of place in the imagined nation. The further reference to her premature death and her consignment of her child to Ellen's care firmly underline her position outside the novel's moral community.

The contrastive pattern whereby Sedgwick identifies national female virtues thus involves the exclusion of a particular female type, that of the southern woman of fashion, as represented by Caroline Redwood. But more troublingly, the slaves upon whom this fashionable lifestyle depends are also, implicitly, banished from the national community.[8] The novel's conclusion upholds what are presented as northern values, but it emerges that there is no place within this nation for the freed slave, who is implicated by the narrator in the moral bankruptcy of the South and of fashionable southern femininity in particular. The narrator informs us of Lily's escape from slavery, a consequence of the "intimate . . . acquaintance with 'the mountain nymph, sweet liberty'" formed during her "northern summer" (2: 270). This escape is, however, represented in a curiously unsympathetic way as being prompted as much by "a snug love affair of her own," carried on "in imitation of her mistress" (2: 270) as by Lily's acquaintance with the "spirit of liberty."

Thus in spite of its continuities with an earlier transatlantic strand of women's writing, Stowe's vision of a truly unified antislavery nation required some radical revision of both the principles and the narrative structures she inherited from novelists such as Edgeworth and Sedgwick. Several of the characters in *Uncle Tom's Cabin*, most notably those of Miss Ophelia, Augustine St. Clare, and Marie St. Clare are recognizable from earlier works by both Irish and American women authors (Marie is, for instance, a recognizable type in the tradition of Caroline Redwood). The novel's two most significant characters, Eva and Tom, however, are without precedent in earlier works. They form the novel's moral and spiritual core and provide the novel with its originality, emotional impact, and political charge, but they have also been the focus of a good deal of the controversy and criticism the novel has received, in the twentieth century in particular.

Eva's saintliness is insisted upon by the narrator, in what for some critics is a particularly overblown (in Ann Douglas's word, "camp") example of the Victorian sentimentalization of the child, a being untainted by worldly corruption and self-interest (4). The fact that she dies while still a child could be interpreted as an evasion: her message of Christian love is safely contained, never associated with adult agency and thus tested against the compromises of the "real world."

The lack of agency that characterizes Eva's position as a child is reflected in the powerlessness of Tom's position as a slave. This powerlessness is magnified by Tom's submission to his fate, a submission that shocks some readers and enrages others. He is intelligent, responsible, honest, loyal, generous—"all the moral and Christian values bound in black morocco, complete," as Augustine St. Clare flippantly remarks of the man who has saved his daughter's life (129). And yet, he appears to accept his inferior and oppressed status and never asserts a sense of equality or a right to even the most basic freedom. Ultimately, Tom dies a horrific death, utterly alone, apparently abandoned by all those who professed attachment to him and who possessed the power to save him. Stowe's investment in Christianity and the repeated comparisons between Tom's suffering and Christ's (Steele 87–89) could be regarded as a quiescent position that focuses on the moral superiority of the passively suffering character rather than on the condemnation of the social, legal, and political institutions that are the cause of the suffering, misery, and death.

Jane Tompkins has defended these aspects of the novel in terms of "sentimental power," and they are of a piece with the novel's general attribution of spiritual strength and a superior moral sense to the marginalized and "the lowly," in Stowe's own phrase. The essence of sentimentality, I suggest, lies in the stark contrast between virtue and agency or power, with the highest form of virtue thus displayed (perversely and disturbingly for some readers) in the submissive, passive suffering and death of a guiltless person. It is my contention here that, given the continuities between *Uncle Tom's Cabin* and the Enlightenment tradition of earlier women writers, Stowe was fully conscious of the challenge that her novel offered to Enlightenment thought on the individual and society and that she actively sought to expose as a delusion the Enlightenment construction of the adult individual as an autonomous agent.[9] Within the institution of slavery it is not only slaves who are deprived of agency: Stowe's novel reveals the extent to which apparently omnipotent slaveholders themselves sacrifice real autonomy for the tainted privileges of institutionalized superiority. A central feature of Enlightenment thought, the idea that there is a standard of intellectual and moral maturity toward which an individual progresses via a process of education, is therefore repeatedly undermined in *Uncle Tom's Cabin* in scenes in which the authority of adult males is called into question. Stowe's awareness that culturally and socially endorsed notions of civilization and progress were used as rationalizations of injustice also leads her to portray the educational process as effectively co-opted by the ideology of slavery. The answer, according to the text, is not to abandon education as a means of social progress and reform but to envision a radical education that does not reinforce oppressive hierarchies.

The novel features a number of male figures who in theory exercise considerable power, including the landowners and slave owners Mr. Shelby and Augustine St. Clare and the governmental representative Senator Bird. These men are not portrayed primarily as abusing power or exercising it unjustly: their power and authority is represented as limited and circumscribed. Having decided to sell Tom and Harry, Mr. Shelby repeatedly represents himself as powerless: "I can't help myself" (28), he protests; Haley "had it in his power to ruin us all" (30); he finds it so difficult to confront his own decision that he arranges to be absent when the slave trader ultimately takes possession of Tom. The set-piece conversation between Senator Bird and his wife on the subject of the Fugitive Slave Act revolves, interestingly, on the issue of action versus inaction. The senator, the representative of national, public authority, defends the justness of literally doing nothing, while his wife insists on *doing* what is manifestly right: "I can read my Bible; and there I see that I must feed the hungry, clothe the naked, and comfort the desolate" (69). When Mrs. Bird utters what appears to be one of the classic statements of sentimental philosophy—"I hate reasoning, John"—it is easy to conclude that the novel advocates an analytically impoverished, impossibly simplified alternative, a depoliticized (and feminized) philosophy of individual feeling and "Christian love." The statement, however, could also be read as reflecting the real failure of an Enlightenment-based culture to address profound injustice.

Mrs. Bird's hatred of reasoning echoes an essay written by the seventeen-year-old Harriet Beecher, described by Hedrick as an "incisive critique of obscurantist language and the posturing of 'great men'" ("Modern Uses" 23). In it, Stowe refers to Locke, Berkeley, Thomas Reid, and Dugald Stewart, all important figures in the British and Irish Enlightenment, complaining of the tendency of philosophers to remain trapped in a circular discussion of one another's ideas and asking her readers, "have you never experienced this power of a great mind to utterly puzzle and confound you?" ("Modern Uses" 25). By the time she had come to write *Uncle Tom's Cabin*, this suspicion of philosophic obscurantism was reinforced by the fact that slavery and cruelty were routinely defended and given intellectual justification using apparently sophisticated arguments. With "proper effort and cultivation," as the narrator remarks, one could overcome "every human weakness and prejudice" (112). It is in this context that the characters of both Tom and Eva emerge as an alternative to the bankruptcy of a society that uses education as a means to defend the indefensible. Tom is repeatedly described as "unlearned" and "ignorant" in an ironic tone that suggests the self-delusion of many educated people. The narrator pours scorn on "the enlightened, cultivated, educated man" who imagines that he is morally distinct from the loathsome slave trader (115). The injection of such bitter irony into the words "enlightened, cultivated, educated" suggests that Stowe was fully conscious of the nature of the critique that she offered through the moral elevation of the "pre-Enlightened," the child and the barely literate slave.

The inability of the Enlightenment nation to recognize and confront the injustice of slavery is underlined by the repeated representation of the failure of the conventional educational process. Augustine St. Clare's life, by his own account, is a story of the wastage of talent and the betrayal of principle. Observing his nephew Henrique irrationally abusing a young slave, Augustine, "with his usual sarcastic carelessness" (232), remarks to his twin brother, "I suppose that's what we may call republican education, Alfred?" (233). The "casual sarcasm" with which St. Clare refers to the concept of republican education represents a significant challenge to contemporary faith in the power of universal education to help create a united and successful nation. Alfred is, if possible, even less concerned than Augustine with the education of the young: "there's no doubt that our system is a difficult one to train children under. It gives too free scope to the passions altogether" (235). His proposed solution is to send Henrique to the North, "where obedience is more fashionable" (235). Augustine remarks, with an echo of apparently worn-out philosophy, "since training children is the staple work of the human race . . . I should think it something of a consideration that our system does not work well there" (235). The conversation concludes very shortly afterward with a friendly game of backgammon and Augustine's defensive claim that "one man can do nothing, against the whole action of a community" (235).

Scenes such as these make it clear that what she saw as the failure of the educative process was a matter of deep concern for Stowe. The portrayal of Eva and Tom as the educators of their community thus assumes tremendous significance. Aside from her function as a Christ-like exemplar, Eva is an educator in a literal sense, and her determination to teach is in contrast to the failure of adults and guardians who have squandered their resources and advantages. She is acutely aware of the deprivation of slaves who are not taught to read and write, and finding that her mother is utterly indifferent to this, she determines to teach Mammy to read. Eva's questions about the education of slaves reveal that the sentimental power that she embodies is accompanied by a desire for agency and the power to enact her ideals. Fingering her mother's diamond earrings, she asks whether they are very expensive. When Marie replies that they are "worth a small fortune" (230), she declares that she wished they were hers to do with as she pleased: "I'd sell them, and buy a place in the free states, and take all our people there and teach them to read and write" (230). In the face of her mother's ridicule, she maintains that slaves should be able to read the Bible, "and write their own letters, and read letters that are written to them . . . I know mamma, it does come very hard on them, that they can't do these things" (230).

Eva's translation of the value of the earrings contrasts starkly with Maria Edgeworth's portrayal of the unworldly innocent Virginia in her novel *Belinda*. Virginia has been brought up in total seclusion from the world in order to protect her from the designs of men. For this reason also she has been forbidden to read and write. When the novel's hero, Clarence Hervey, comes upon her by chance, he decides that she offers him the opportunity of "creating" a wife who will not be corrupted by the usual feminine vices of worldliness and vanity. Needless to say, he soon realizes that in attempting to shape a being free of the faults of the world, he has ended up with a young woman so ignorant as to be utterly unsuitable as a wife. While still in the throes of experimental enthusiasm, he presents Virginia with a pair of diamond earrings and a rosebud in order to see which she prefers. He is enraptured when she chooses the flower and dismisses the precious stones. He soon comes to realize, however, that this choice does not indicate uncorrupted tastes but an ignorance of social values that is to be deplored rather than celebrated. Eva, by contrast, may be not of this world in terms of her boundless love and goodness, but her consideration of the value of the earrings and her estimation of how this value can be converted to practical projects (what she describes is, after all, not a fantasy) shows a firm grasp on the fundamentals of the society in which she lives.

The portrayal of Tom as an educator is particularly powerful and poignant, given the fact that the scene in which he is introduced to the reader centers on his attempts to learn to write, tutored rather inexpertly by George Shelby. It is notable that here, as in the St. Clare household, children become the means of instruction in the apparent absence of adult will.[10] Unlike Eva, however, George embraces the role of teacher partly because he en-

joys the superiority it confers on him. He "appear[s] fully to realise the dignity of his position of instructor" (18). He corrects Tom's mistakes "briskly"
and somewhat over emphatically, "flourishingly scrawl[ing] *q*'s and *g*'s innu-
merable for his edification." Tom regards this "with a respectful and admir-
ing air" (18). Aunt Chloe's reaction, "How easy white folks al'us does things!"
(18) is uncomfortably double-edged. The target audience of the novel, sympathetic white readers, would be aware that the ease with which George
Shelby could read and write does not reflect an extraordinary, racially determined intelligence and that his position as tutor to an adult reflects the
abuses of the system of slavery.

This system, under which children perceive themselves as more powerful
than adults, leads George Shelby to imagine that he is more powerful than
he really is. "I'll knock that old fellow down!" (86) he exclaims of Haley.
George imagines falsely that all that prevents him from having the power of
life and death over Tom is his position as a child: "if I was a man, they
shouldn't do it" (86). He later adds, "I'll build your house all over, and you
shall have a room for a parlour with a carpet on it, when I'm a man" (88). At
the same time, he refers to Tom's situation in terms of childish pranks: "I'll
come down after you, and bring you back. . . . I'll see to it, and I'll tease father's life out, if he don't do it" (87). As we have seen, there is no guarantee
that when he is a man George will have the kind of autonomy and power he
confidently envisages. Tom's response to George is, effectively, to remind
him that he is a child. He tells him that it is wrong to speak disrespectfully
of his parents and expresses the hope that he will grow up to be "a great,
learned, good man" (87). The text does not, therefore, construct virtue and
vice in terms of simple oppositions between children and adults, innocence
and experience. Tom's faith in the possibility of a child's becoming "a great,
learned, good man" signals continuing belief in education as an ideal, but it
is clear that education in actuality has become intricately implicated in the
institution of slavery. Tragically, therefore, George's promises to Tom remain
unfulfilled. He reappears at the end of the novel, now an adult man, but the
only service he can offer Tom is to bury him. George returns to Kentucky to
free all the slaves on the Shelby estate, an act that he represents as a tribute to
the sufferings of Uncle Tom. Like that of Christ, Tom's death redeems his
people.

The text directs us toward this reading, but what I wish to emphasize is
that Tom's role is not limited to that of a passively suffering example of
Christ-like virtue. Like Eva, he too is a teacher—a far more effective teacher

than George Shelby, for instance—and he teaches not only through his flaw-less example. His literacy is limited: "Having learned late in life, Tom was but a slow reader, and passed on laboriously from verse to verse," but this does not prevent him from being an inspiring preacher and "Christian teacher" (84). At the weekly meetings that are held at his house, he preaches and leads the congregation in prayer. This ability is presented as having little to do with formally acquired knowledge: "It was in prayer that he especially excelled. Nothing could exceed the touching simplicity, the child-like earnestness, of his prayer, enriched with the language of Scripture, which seemed so entirely to have wrought itself into his being, as to have become a part of himself, and to drop from his lips unconsciously" (26). There are a number of ways in which one could read this description. The narrator's suggestion that Tom's use of scripture is unconscious might suggest a diminution of his agency, an attempt to undermine the intellectual gifts with which he has just been credited. Additionally, this could be read as an-other instance of the narrator's identification of Tom with Christ: the words of the Bible "have wrought [themselves] into his being." I would also like to suggest that the description attempts to convey the idea of a power that does not derive solely from formal knowledge. This is crucial to Stowe's project because it reinforces the limitations of formal knowledge and it allows that those in an "unenlightened" state can have access to insight and power. Op-ponents of the sentimental may read this characterization of African Ameri-cans as simply a patronizing imposition of otherness, but its radical chal-lenge to the definition of knowledge suggests that the alternative is to insist that the standards of a racist and oppressive society are the standards to which the oppressed should themselves aspire.

The representation of otherness is one of the key features of these nine-teenth-century fictions of the nation in both Ireland and America. As sug-gested above, the tendency to associate otherness and the Gothic is evident in Edgeworth, Owenson, and Sedgwick. In all three cases, references to the Gothic are, broadly speaking, comic in tone. The emotional climax of *Uncle Tom's Cabin*, however, the death of Tom on Simon Legree's plantation, indi-cates once again that Stowe's work is a response to this trope and at the same time a powerful revision of many of its received assumptions. Legree's plan-tation is a location of pure horror: an undeniably Gothic site characterized by darkness and danger. The Gothic castle is no longer merely a fanciful idea or a bad dream from which the sleeper wakes: it is real. The road to the plan-tation is described as follows: "It was a wild, forsaken road, now winding through dreary pine barrens, where the wind whispered mournfully, and now over log causeways, through long cypress swamps, the doleful trees rising out of the slimy, spongy ground, hung with long wreaths of funereal black moss, while ever and anon the loathsome form of the moccasin snake might be seen sliding among broken stumps and shattered branches that lay here and there, rotting in the water" (296). It is here, however, in this horror story made real, that Tom achieves a kind of immortality. Whereas the fictions of Edgeworth, Owenson, and Sedgwick raise the idea of the Gothic only to debunk it, Stowe affirms the existence of such darkness within the society and culture she describes. Her reference to "One whose suffering changed an instrument of torture, degradation and shame, into a symbol of glory, honor, and immortal life" (358) is one of a series of asides that liken Tom to Christ, but it also reflects the paradox of her own novel, which locates virtue and greatness "among the lowly."

In conclusion, I would like to suggest that Stowe's techniques, aims, and strategies are inflected by an older, Enlightenment tradition of women's writing even as they mark the radical new ethos of the sentimental. What Owenson, Edgeworth, and Sedgwick had in common, aside from their gender, was an endorsement of the philosophy of the Enlightenment nation and a conviction that women had an important role to play in such a political community. Stowe's work differs from theirs, I argue, most importantly in terms of its rejection of the certainties of the Enlightenment, certainties upon which the American nation itself had been founded.

NOTES

I would like to thank Sarah Meer, whose interest in this topic encouraged me to pursue it and whose advice has been invaluable. I would also like to acknowledge the Faculty of Arts at University College Cork, whose award of a research grant enabled me to carry out the initial research for this paper in the libraries of Harvard University. Thanks also to Leah Price for her hospitality and friendship.

1. For recent discussions of Edgeworth and Owenson in the context of the National Tale see Connolly, Ferris, and Trumpener.

2. See also Lee Jenkins, who draws attention to the existence of a "common vocabulary between the abolitionist rhetoric of [Frederick] Douglass and the liberation rhetoric of mid-nineteenth century Ireland" (82).

3. Carolyn Karcher has noted Sedgwick's development of "sophisticated narrative strategies. By allowing her characters to narrate parts of the story through interpolated letters, she opened her novels to multiple voices and points of view" (212). Karcher identifies this as an important influence on Stowe.

4. For an example of the hostile southern response see George F. Holmes's review of *Uncle Tom's Cabin*, in which he positions himself explicitly as a Southerner and accuses Stowe of "misrepresentations." Ammons, ed., *Uncle Tom's Cabin*, 469.

5. Quotes from *Uncle Tom's Cabin* are from the 1994 Norton edition.

6. In this I differ from Brown, who identifies Ophelia's values with those of Catharine Beecher's *Treatise of Domestic Economy* and, by extension, with the narrative point of view: "Getting in the Kitchen with Dinah: Domestic Politics in *Uncle Tom's Cabin.*"

7. See Clíona Ó Gallchoir, "'The Whole Fabric Must Be Perfect': Maria Edgeworth's *Literary Ladies* and the Representation of Ireland," and Ó Gallchoir, *Maria Edgeworth*, chapter 1.

8. In *The Linwoods*, slave characters function peripherally as part of fashionable New York life, which is unfavorably contrasted with rural New England.

9. Jane Tompkins initiated the critical revision of the sentimental novel, and I agree with her claim that "the sentimental novel [is] a political enterprise, halfway between sermon and social theory, that both codifies and attempts to mold the values of its time" ("Sentimental" 84–85). My own aim in this article is more specific and more modest: to place *Uncle Tom's Cabin* in relation to an earlier women's tradition and thereby to emphasize Stowe's place in and departure from that tradition.

10. It is implied that Mrs. Shelby has taught Eliza to read, but this is not referred to directly.

Nature, Magic, and History in Stowe and Scott

MONIKA ELBERT

ALTER SCOTT's influence on Harriet Beecher Stowe was undeniable; her father's custom was to read the family all of Scott's novels, and she continued to read them to her own children.[1] Scott's legacy to Stowe appears in her transformation of the New England landscape into a supernatural world in which the boundaries between magic and nature become indistinct and in which national histories are rendered familial and personal through an oracular vision of humankind. I am most concerned here with Stowe's *The Pearl of Orr's Island* (1862) as it pertains to Scott's *The Bride of Lammermoor* (1819). There are many parallels between the characters, the plot, and the conflict as they relate to a revisionist feminist history. For example, Stowe borrows some of Scott's Gothic elements, especially in her rendering of the feminine realm: the preternatural woman who either dies, goes mad, or becomes deathly ill as a result of an unhappy love affair or aborted marriage; a family curse based on a social hierarchy that prevents female protagonists from finding happiness; the gypsy or magical women; and the association of nature with the supernatural/feminine realm.[2]

If Stowe adopted the conventions of the domestic novel from the contemporary school of sentimental women writers, Scott taught her how to make sense of the "unutterable" and the irrational that has come to typify the Gothic novel. And almost paradoxically, he taught her how to appropriate the use of history and of regionalism, which she wove into her own brand of realism, in contradistinction to the drawing room realism of the quotidian prevalent in American women's domestic novels. Scott was the

46

mediating force between inner and outer landscapes, between the realm of the mystical and the realm of the real.

In the pivotal central chapter (16) of *Pearl*, "The Natural and the Spiritual," Stowe shows that the basis of her local color is not simply geographical or physical but rather a spiritual yearning, which, I would argue, is more Old World than New in that her narrator's attitude toward the landscape and its people is far too mystical to be of Calvinist New England. At the end of this chapter, the narrator speaks about the promise of a seeress or prophetess. Some sensitive souls are destined to be the "priests and prophetesses of the spiritual life"; they are "beings born into the world in whom from childhood the spiritual and the reflective predominate over the physical" (166). She suggests that such "types" are usually women and that they are "ordained of God to keep the balance between the rude but absolute necessities of physical life and the higher sphere to which that must at length give place" (167). Such a savior figure is not Margaret Fuller's or Elizabeth Cady Stanton's notion of the political or active woman but rather a clairvoyant, Romantic type in touch with nature.

But I do not simply want to point out technical similarities in the framework of the two historical novels.[3] I am more interested in showing how both authors imbue local color with mysticism, thus raising it to the level of a personal history that becomes a national psychology. For both Scott and Stowe, the colorful and panoramic vision of a given people (Scottish, New England) depends upon individual yearnings and desires. In both of these authors' works, the boundaries between national and personal, public and private, are forever shifting. Though the novels seem to promise a historical inquiry into a sheltered and idyllic landscape, the authors are finally interested in the history, or development, of the soul. In a most telling passage at the end of chapter 32, Stowe shows her remarkable tendency to make the psychological natural and the historical spiritual. At the point when Mara is most enlightened, "for the first time in her life" she had "broken the *reserve* which was her very *nature*, and spoken of that which was the intimate and *hidden history* of her *soul*" (327, emphasis mine).[4]

From Scott, Stowe learns that to forge a national identity or history she must first uncover the spiritual dimension of a people (as reflected in its Nature/nature) and then fathom the feminine principle as the arbiter between the natural and supernatural realms. The evolution of a soul is far more important than the making of a "great man" in history. Thus, she imbues the landscape, as later did Sarah Orne Jewett (another writer who admired and borrowed from Scott and who appreciated Stowe's local color in *The Pearl of Orr's Island*),[5] with the mysticism unheard of in the New England of her time and especially foreign to the Congregationalist household in which she was raised. Her oracular approach to national history through an analysis of the personal realm can be traced through her other novels, most notably in *Uncle Tom's Cabin*.

The notion of personal prophecy, as it relates to a family or community destiny, is of utmost importance to both Stowe and Scott. Though the notion of prophecy had its precedents in New England, through the religious prophecies of the Great Awakening, Stowe's use of prophecy is much more metaphysical (and similar to Emerson's Transcendentalist view of the prophet). Indeed, for Stowe, a national history cannot be comprehended without an analysis of local superstitions and of regional personality types. It would be folly to understand the magnitude of a national history without analyzing the mundane familial (and often clannish) aspects of local history as well as the spiritual aspects that are embodied in the preternatural women of the community.

This blending of the mundane and the spiritual is derived from Scott's sense of the romance. Even though Stowe professes that *The Pearl of Orr's Island* is not a romance in the typical love-marriage conflict or Byronic sense of the term,[6] it is a romance in the broader sense of Scott's definition of the romance as partaking of the marvelous. Both Scott's and Stowe's historical romances do not deny the historicity of magical or divine intercession, and both share in a conflation of the magical and the mundane in which a unique regional history is unraveled. And this historical panorama has ultimately more to do with the spiritual state of the individual than with the collective consciousness of the nation, though the two are intertwined to create a regional New England history, in Stowe's case, or a Scottish history, in Scott's case.

Interestingly, in *Pearl*, unlike her other historical novels *The Minister's Wooing* or *Oldtown Folks*, Stowe does not go back to the Puritan beginnings to show the current state of New England. Instead, she invests her history with magical qualities, which may have been anathema to her stern Calvinist father but which are in accordance with seventeenth-century Puritan superstitions and folklore.[7] She attributes these mystical traits to a female influence.

There are two types of oracular women in Stowe's *The Pearl* and Scott's

The Bride: the wise, gossiping women who measure time in terms of personal history and who intuitively know what the future holds; and the younger, naïve and Romantic woman who is happier in a kind of timeless realm in Nature than in a socially sanctioned relationship, such as marriage. It is interesting that the latter type of pure woman is finally seen as the driving force behind the action, as manifest in the titles, Stowe's "Pearl" in the shape of Mara Lincoln, and Scott's equally pure pearl, "The Bride of Lammermoor," Lucy. These are not exactly depictions of the moral mothers or the angels of the house for which Stowe is so well known (in *The Pearl,* for example, there are two such women, in the shape of Sally and her mother, Mrs. Kittridge).[8] Indeed, by their spinster or widow status (in terms of the gossips) or their untimely deaths just before an impending marriage (the deaths that keep them virgins), the magical type women resist or escape the conventional paradigm for a good woman.[9] Though both types of wise women (the old crone type and the young mystical women) do not ostensibly effect social change, their presence in the novels is gripping and haunting, and they seem to be able to impart curses as well as blessings on the men around them. This is not to say that Stowe or Scott felt that history was centered on females but that the woman, in her connection to a higher realm of Nature and spirituality, had more sway over men than sea captains (in Stowe's case) or feudal lords (in Scott's case). The mythology of the sea might be enticing (in *The Pearl*), or the medieval legends of yore (in *The Bride*) might be compelling, but it is only the women who can circumnavigate in the uncharted territory of the wilderness in Nature and in the psyche. They act as more than guides to the men; like the imaginary and mystical landscape they inhabit, they become allied with the prophetic and the divine, erasing any possibility that life is haphazard and random. Not actually Fates, but knowledgeable about the workings of fate, they inspire men to move from action to introspection, from the world of politics to the realm of the divine. In Emersonian terms, they allow the men to transcend to a higher level of meaning, becoming Transcendentalist sybils or oracles.[10]

Emerson's discussion of history and fate is a possible context for Stowe that relates intriguingly well with Julia Kristeva's notion of feminine time. In Emerson's "History," he writes about his reading of *The Bride of Lammermoor* and comments on the writing of history:

> I read the Bride of Lammermoor [sic]. Sir William Ashton is a mask for a vulgar temptation, Ravenswood Castle a fine name for proud poverty, and the for-

eign mission of state only a Bunyan disguise for honest industry. We may all shoot a wild bull that would toss the good and beautiful, by fighting down the unjust and sensual. Lucy Ashton is another name for fidelity, which is always beautiful and always liable to calamity in this world.

. . . what does history yet record of the metaphysical annals of man? . . . Yet every history should be written in a wisdom which divined the range of our affinities and looked at facts as symbols. I am ashamed to see what a shallow village tale our so-called History is. (127, 129)

These two passages show the profound impact that Scott had on American Romantics like Emerson and Stowe but also indicate the similarity between the Transcendentalist view of a nonlinear sense of history and Stowe's own sense of nonlinear historical time. In "History," Emerson shows how states of mind are congruous with historical epochs and how individual perceptions are in tune with a larger time frame, which he allies with the Natural. As he expresses it, "along with the civil and metaphysical history of man, another history goes daily forward,—that of the external world,—in which he is not less strictly implicated. He is the compend of time; he is also the correlative of nature. His power consists in the multitude of his affinities, in the fact that his life is intertwined with the whole chain of organic and inorganic being" (127). In connecting man's history with the oversoul of nature, Emerson universalizes the historical experience of mankind by personalizing it.

Significantly, Emerson uses the example of his reading the historical romance *The Bride of Lammermoor* as an excursion into the interpretative dynamics involved with history making and historical analysis. He essentializes and allegorizes notions of good and evil so that they seem like personal manifestations of one's own life; thus, William, Lucy's treacherous father, can be viewed as "vulgar temptation," the castle he seizes "proud poverty," and his daughter, "fidelity." Emerson explains the plot quickly by emphasizing the commonality that we can share. Just as Edgar Ravenswood, hero of the narrative, can save Lucy from being gouged to death by a wild bull, so too, can we the common reader win the battle over the sensory and the material: "We may all shoot a wild bull that would toss the good and beautiful, by fighting down the unjust and sensual" ("History" 127). By rendering the national and collective personal and individual, Emerson is able to universalize the historical experience of seemingly disparate regions and countries. However, Emerson concludes his essay by saying that some people have more affinities with nature and intuition and, thus, have a broader view of history: "The idiot, the Indian, the child, and unschooled farmer's boy stand nearer to the

light by which nature is to be read, than the dissector of the antiquary" (130).
Although he does not include women here, I would claim that the intuitive
woman in touch with nature also has this propensity to view history accurately within the framework of much Romantic philosophy.[11] Certainly, in
Scott as for Stowe, deviant women are the profound readers of nature and
the interpreters of history.

Although such a connection might seem unlikely, French feminist Julia
Kristeva's notion of "women's time" echoes the breadth and spiritual dimension of Emerson's notion of history. Kristeva stresses the fluid, ever-shifting,
but also eternally static or universal quality of history as meaningful to the
individual in its relation to nature.

> As for time, female subjectivity would seem to provide a specific measure that
> essentially retains *repetition* and *eternity* from among the multiple modalities of
> time known through the history of civilizations. On the one hand, there are cy-
> cles, gestation, the eternal recurrence of a biological rhythm which conforms to
> that of nature and imposes a temporality whose stereotyping may shock, but
> whose regularity and unison with what is experienced as extra-subjective time,
> cosmic time, occasion vertiginous visions and unnameable *jouissance*. On the
> other hand, and perhaps as a consequence, there is the massive presence of
> temporality, without cleavage or escape, which has so little to do with linear
> time (which passes) that the very word 'temporality' hardly fits: all-encompass-
> ing and infinite like imaginary space. (191)

Kristeva allies "female subjectivity" with "intuition" to render a historical
continuum of timelessness (192). Though Kristeva's point of departure is to
recover the marginal history of women, this passage would apply equally
to "scapegoat" women in Scott and Stowe, the hags/gossips or the haunted
visionaries, who seem grotesque and otherworldly because they see with
prophetesses' eyes.[12] These visions of history are ultimately seen as more valid than those of the male participants, who, so engrossed in their action, re-
fuse to see the symbols for the facts. As Emerson would express it, such men
are inept readers of history; he calls for man to be "the priest of Pan" who
will "collect into a focus the rays of nature" and no longer see history as "a
dull book" (129).

Scott's prototypical visionary woman in touch with personal and natural
history is exemplified in Lucy Lammermoor. Like Mara in *The Pearl of Orr's
Island*, she has a romantic disposition and loves to read tales of chivalry and
of the supernatural. Indeed, like Mara, she imagines herself in the Miranda

role of Shakespeare's *Tempest* (40). Like Mara, as we shall see shortly, she is as much at home in her imagination as she is in nature. Early in the novel, Lucy leads her father, Sir William Ashton, into the forest to pay a visit to her wise friend, the gypsy/hag, "old Alice." The father, who is totally ignorant of the land and of the people that surround him, is astounded that his daughter should know her way so well in the wilderness. Ashton, who has recently become the Lord Keeper of Ravenswood after illegally seizing the land from the Ravenswood family, is also surprised at his daughter's familiarity with the people. After encountering a hunter named Norman in the woods, Ashton asks Lucy about the hunter's allegiance: "Has this fellow . . . ever served the Ravenswood people, that he seems so interested in them?" . . . "I suppose you know, Lucy, for you make it a point of conscience to record the special history of every boor about the castle" (45). Lucy in her modesty answers in the negative, "I am not quite so faithful a chronicler, my dear father; but I believe that Norman once served here while a boy" (45). She adds that if her father wants to know the whole history of the Ravenswood family "old Alice is the best authority" (45). Ashton shows disdain for Lucy's concern with the populace: "And who is old Alice? I think you know all the old women in the country" (45). Lucy admits her allegiance to the old women of the country by asserting "how could I help the old creatures when they are in hard times?" (45). She also mythologizes, especially Alice: "she is the very empress of old women, and queen of gossips, so far as legendary lore is concerned. She is blind, poor old soul, but when she speaks to you, you would think she has some way of looking into your very heart" (45).

As James Reed has pointed out, this is "a land evoked in local tradition and legend, mediated largely through Blind Alice to the eager imagination of Lucy" (125). This is not to say that the women's imaginations are fed with the fantastic, for it is their prophecies and forebodings that finally instruct the men, who think they are creating history but who are rushing to their own doom. Significantly, both Ashton and Ravenswood pay visits to Alice after Lucy prods them, but the men cannot understand Alice's prophecies because they are both too interested in material things: Ashton is concerned with political intrigue; Ravenswood, with gold. Alice tells them that she is not interested in the world of politics or the world of money. Even when Edgar Ravenswood, in the latter part of the book, has dreams that show a clearer understanding of his fate, he seeks to dismiss them as childish: "My destiny, thought Ravenswood, seems to lead me to scenes of fate and of death; but these are childish thoughts and shall not master me" (244).

Ravenswood intuitively knows that old Alice's prophecy about his undoing (and Lucy's death) is correct, and he also believes in her because of his deceased mother's wisdom, which taught him that Alice should be trusted for her "sense, acuteness, and fidelity" (194). Ravenswood is forever second-guessing the deeper intuitive reality that mystical women present to him until the quicksand mysteriously devours him.

Alice aptly predicts the demise of the Ashton household. She warns Lord Ashton: "[T]ake care what you do; you are on the brink of a precipice" (51). Though this may seem like magical foresight on Alice's part, she has a better understanding than Ashton has of the populace's allegiance to the old Ravenswood family and the importance of local history, having lived on his land for sixty years. The Ravenswood family heir, Edgar Ravenswood, respectfully sees her as an "old sibyl" who has accurately forecast his future of ruination and dishonor for his father's house (235). Also, Alice becomes a kind of folk historian, which allies her with the three other mysterious women of the text, the hags, or "gossips." The narrator often alludes to the presence of the marvellous in Scottish history: "this could not be called a Scottish story, unless it manifested a tinge of Scottish superstition" (235). Though the three gossips, or "reverend sibyls" (239), who help bury Alice can be construed as witchlike figures, they also have the ability to understand life as a cycle of birth, marriage, and death and rightfully intuit all endings and beginnings as part of that same cycle. Dame Gourlay, one of the sibyls, predicts Lucy's bridal day will bring her death: "I tell ye . . . her winding sheet is up as high as her throat already, believe it wha list" (319).

In a strange way, Edgar Ravenswood wants to belong to the people and believe in their stories even though "he despised most of the ordinary prejudices about witchcraft, omens, and vaticination, to which his age and country still gave such implicit credit, that to express a doubt of them, was accounted a crime equal to the unbelief of Jews or Saracens" (242). Indeed, his encounter with a maddened Lucy (a madness that allies her with Alice) renders him more ghostlike than alive: "Ravenswood had more the appearance of one returned from the dead, than of a living visitor" (307). And the haunted feeling wrought by Alice's mysterious death accompanies him as he witnesses the deterioration of his affianced, Lucy, and finally as he himself is given up to a strange, mysterious death.

The ruined seaside tower that Ravenswood inhabits, Wolf's Crag, like the spell that haunts the Ravenswood clan, is more surreal than real, but it typifies the historical landscape that Scott paints. There is a ruined fountain, the

Mermaiden's Well, within the wilderness, which is said in an old legend to spell the doom of the Ravenswood. The reader discovers that one of the ancient Lords of Ravenswood, Raymond of Ravenswood, had fallen in love with a nymph at this site and had lost her when he became suspicious of her origins and had the local priest try to ascertain whether she was demonic in nature. Through the priest's trickery and Ravenswood's suspicion, the nymph bleeds to an untimely death and discolors the water: "From this period the house of Ravenswood was supposed to have dated its decay" (58). Some suggest instead that Ravenswood had slain his girlfriend, "a beautiful maid of plebeian rank," in a fit of jealousy (58). Still others feel that one had to delve into "ancient heathen mythology" to understand the legend, but all consider the spot ominous, and it is here that young Master Edgar Ravenswood saves Lucy Ashton from the attack of a wild bull. Later Lucy is compared to "the murdered Nymph of the Fountain" (197), when the site of the fountain becomes their trysting place. And it is here that the identities of Lucy and Alice merge in Ravenswood's mind: at the instant where Ravenswood sees the apparition of the just-deceased Alice at the fountain, he mistakenly thinks it is his Lucy. Caleb, Ravenswood's trusty servant and one of the native Scotsmen given to superstitions, tells Edgar the prophecy: "When the last Laird of Ravenswood to Ravenswood shall ride,/And woo a dead maiden to be his bride,/He shall stable his steed in the Kelpie's flow,/And his name shall be lost for evermoe!" (178). Though Ravenswood does not want to believe the old prophecy, Alice has predicted the same fate, and though Lucy wants to deny it, both finally succumb to the folk beliefs of the people. Death seems preordained for both, and they cannot avoid their fate.

From Scott, Stowe learns how to weave the notion of fate and local history into the lives of the Maine settlers, who seem simultaneously as provincial and as wise as the native inhabitants of Scott's Ravenswood. In Stowe, too, the element of prophecy—and its relation to the unraveling of history —is best understood in the context of the female characters. The strongest women in the text are the sisters, Miss Roxy, who seems to have connections to the spirit world, and Miss Ruey, who has a type of practical wisdom of bygone ages. Though our first glimpse of these women is in Naomi Lincoln's sickroom, where their appearance seems grotesquely mundane ("Two gossips are sitting in earnest, whispering conversation" [7]), their presence takes on greater mythical proportions. The narrator describes them as belonging to "that class of females who might be denominated, in the Old Testament language, 'cunning women,'—that is, gifted with an infinite diversity of practical 'faculty,' which make them an essential requisite in every family for miles and miles" (20). Like the gossip/hags in Scott, these women know the history of the landscape and can predict the future. Like the Scott witches, these women know mysterious cures and participate in the solemn occasions of life: "Many a woman being had been ushered into life under their auspices . . . watched by them in the last sickness, and finally arrayed for the long repose by their hands" (20). It is even rumored that they are "infallible medical oracles" (20). Like the three women likened in Scott to the witches in *Macbeth*, Aunt Roxy and Aunt Ruey are called "the weird sisters." Larger than life, these women take on the mysterious qualities of the sprawling landscape that they inhabit, and their personal identity seems universal. Like the Scott hags, these sisters seem to belong to everyone: "They are nobody's aunts in particular, but aunts to human nature in general" (20). Indeed, they seem preternatural, for no one can guess their ages, but like the rugged landscape from which they originate, they seem tough and eternal. Stowe's description of Orr's Island and Scott's description of the Scottish highlands seem similar, almost interchangeable, and in both there is a connection between land and inhabitants. We seem to be in a timeless realm where the dramatic scope of history does not matter but where the natural cycle of life does. In Stowe's words, "In that cold, clear, severe climate of the North, the roots of human existence are hard to strike; but, if once people do take to living, they come in time to a place where they seem never to grow any older" (21). Miss Ruey, endowed with less power than Miss Roxy, can still spout words of guidance from the Old Testament or from poetry in the manner of a prophetess. When she herself cannot prophesy, she recounts the story of how "a weakly girl" with "the janders" had the ability to see spirits because she was born with a veil over her face (46).[13]

Miss Roxy, the more gifted of the sisters, is truly perceived as a seeress: "Was she not a sort of priestess and sibyl in all the most awful straits and mysteries of life? . . . And amid weeping or rejoicing, was not Miss Roxy still the master-spirit?—consulted, referred to by all?—was not her word law and precedent?" (21). Like the old dames in Scott who contemplate the subtle connection between bridal and funereal ceremonies, Aunt Roxy intuits the parallels and can matter-of-factly announce when Naomi Pennel/Lincoln dies (giving birth to the preternatural child, Mara) that "She'll make a beautiful corpse" (8). Later, too, Aunt Roxy is the one who knows that Mara is not long for this world, as she prophesies, "I hain't never had but just one mind about Mara Lincoln's weddin',—it's to be,—but it won't be the way people think. . . . I can see beyond what most folks can,—her weddin' garments is bought and paid for, and she'll wear 'em, but she won't be Moses Pennel's wife,—now you see" (343). Aunt Roxy knows before anyone that Mara is ill, and when Mara visits their magical cottage (much like old Alice's hut in Scott) to ask them about her weakening health, Aunt Roxy seems to know immediately that Mara is suffering from consumption. Indeed, she predicts a quick end as she confides to Sally, Mara's best friend, "They're going to take her over to Portland to see Dr. Wilson—it won't do no harm, and it won't do no good" (364). She defends herself against Sally's accusations that she is "determined" to see Mara die by pointing to her intuitive knowledge of life cycles: "Is it I that determines that the maple leaves shall fall next October? Yet I know they will—folks can't help knowin' what they know, and shuttin' one's eyes won't alter one's road" (364). These old wise women of Stowe's Maine are the same type as those in Scott's forest landscape.

Mara herself, like Lucy in Scott's narrative, seems to have a direct bond to the witchlike women because of her ethereal nature, which connects her to the divinity. Indeed, like Lucy and Ravenswood, she sees visions of the dead and intimations of her destiny. Her life itself seems to be tied with the supernatural—the sea swallows up her father, a tragedy that causes her mother's premature death. Ironically, Mara is haunted by the apparition of her beloved Moses's mother, who also drowned. The night before the shipwrecked Moses and his dead mother are found, Mara dreams of them:

Suddenly, there stood before them a woman, dressed in a long white garment. She was very pale, with sweet, serious dark eyes, and she led by the hand a black-eyed boy, who seemed to be crying and looking about as for something lost, and the woman came toward her, looking at her with sweet, sad eyes. . . . The woman laid her hand on her head as if in a blessing, and then put the boy's hand in hers, and said, 'Take him, Mara, he is a playmate for you;' and with that the little boy's face flushed into a merry laugh. The woman faded away. (50)

Mara has this premonition that she is destined to be with Moses, but she also knows intuitively that her fate is intertwined with the spirit world, which Moses's mother represents. Indeed, she is not like her best friend, Sally Kittridge, who can sew, knit, cook, and carry out all the domestic duties expected of a woman preparing for marriage in the nineteenth century. She does not prepare properly to be the angel of the house, for she is to be a different type of angel. She is a dreamy sort, like Lucy Lammermoor: "one of those sensitive, excitable natures on which every external influence acts with immediate power" (36). More than that, she seems linked to a type of Transcendentalist oversoul, and this becomes most apparent when Moses sets sail in his own boat and she realizes that she is connected to the spirit world:

> But there are souls sent into this world who seem to have always mysterious affinities for the invisible and the unknown—who see the face of everything beautiful through a thick veil of mystery and sadness. The Germans call this yearning of spirit homesickness—the dim remembrance of a spirit once affiliated to some higher sphere. . . . As Mara looked pensively into the water, it seemed to her that every incident of life came up out of its depths to meet her. Her own face reflected in a wavering image, sometimes shaped itself to her gaze in the likeness of the pale lady of her childhood, who seemed to look up at her from the waters with dark, mysterious eyes of tender longing. (300)

Here Mara, like Lucy Lammermoor, is linked to the spirit realm, and like Lucy, she has as her mentor a mysterious and ghostlike figure—in Mara's case, the deceased pale lady and, in Lucy's case, another type of mother figure, Alice. Another more earthly but nonetheless spiritual mother exists for Mara in the shape of Aunt Roxy; as Mara confesses, "No mother could be kinder" (366). It is also interesting that for Mara, as for Lucy, the object of meditation, which allows them to transcend to the other realm, is water—the fountain in *The Bride of Lammermoor* and the ocean in *The Pearl*. Water offers the women a phantasmagoric vision of life that seems more real than the visible and the known.

Moreover, both Lucy and Mara have been tantalized by the great story of shipwreck and the magical island in *The Tempest*, and both imagine themselves as Miranda, reconciling images and symbols from the secular and spiritual worlds.[14] Mara is variously perceived as a "witch," a "sprite," an "angel," and an "apocalyptic" prophetess. She defies conventional definitions of Christian womanhood and like Lucy celebrates a type of heathen magic that typifies Ariel. Fictional reality becomes as good as historical in a process that Emerson would have appreciated. As a voraciously reading child, Mara would not have been surprised to encounter "an angel in the woods, or to have formed an intimacy with some talking wolf or bear" (135). Reading *The Tempest*, she similarly merges personal history, fiction, and nature:

> Mara would lie for hours stretched out on the pebbly beach, with the broad open ocean before her and the whispering pines and hemlocks behind her, and

pore over this poem, from which she collected dim, delightful images of a
lonely island, an old enchanter, a beautiful girl, and a spirit not quite like those
in the Bible, but a very probable one to her mode of thinking. As for old Cal-
iban, she fancied him with a face much more like that of a huge skate-fish she
had once seen drawn ashore in one of her grandfather's nets; and then there was
the beautiful young Prince Ferdinand, much like what Moses would be when
he was grown up. (135)

Mara understands intuitively the workings of nature and of man; she con-
flates her physical landscape with her inner landscape, literary characters
with the people she knows. And she is fixated on the sea mystery that brings
her Moses, which she equates with the mysteries that the gossips talk about:
"Mara vividly remembered the scene on the sea-beach, the finding of little
Moses and his mother, the dream of the pale lady that seemed to bring him
to her; and not one of the conversations that has transpired before her
among different gossips had been lost on her quiet, listening little ears"
(137). Though initially Mara is afraid to share her imaginative stories with
others, she opens up to Moses, and finally, she transcends the child's imagination to reach an understanding of the divine. Moses, initially like the un-
derdeveloped Materialist in Emerson's "The Transcendentalist," cannot understand her superior mind, the mind of the Idealist, as he is tied to earthly
matters with his too concrete dreams of conquest. The narrator characterizes
him as stuck in the early stage of being: "'Howbeit, that is not first which is
spiritual, but that which is natural.' Moses is the type of the first unreflecting
stage of development, in which are only the out-reachings of active faculties,
the aspirations that tend toward manly accomplishments" (166). But the
narrator is hopeful that the feminine rule will triumph, that "the saucy boy
. . . so proudly in virtue of his physical strength and daring, will learn to
tremble at the golden measuring-rod held in the hand of a woman" (166).
Mara is seen as possessing the apocalyptic vision: "Mara . . . belonged to
the race of those spirits to whom is deputed the office of the angel in the
Apocalypse, to whom was given the golden rod which measured the New
Jerusalem" (166).[15]

What unites Mara and Lucy with the gossips/witches is their ability to
connect viscerally with the land and then to transcend the boundaries of the
real. We hear that Mara, besides reading, likes to pass her time, in the manner of the best Transcendentalist, in "wild forest rambles" (201) and "her
solitary life had made every woodland thing dear and familiar to her" (203).
Even the cove surroundings of her grandfather's cottage are conducive to a

preternatural existence, as the physical landscape seems Gothic, imbued with the majesty of a primeval spirit world. For example, there are "wide-winged hemlocks, hundreds of years old, and with long, swaying, gray beards of moss, looking white and ghostly under the deep shadows of their boughs" and "creeping round trunk and matting over stones, were many and many of those wild, beautiful things which embellish the shadows of these northern forests" (32). Though Mara's and Lucy's connection to nature, to the sea, and to their respective northern forests, is deep, they are not just isolated Romantics or Transcendentalists but social creatures. Their forte lies in exposing another realm to the men with their materialist visions of history, time, and change.

In *Bride*, Ravenswood is finally converted to a different sense of history; through Lucy's influence, he gives up his vindictive character, and he begins to believe in the realm represented by Alice, whom he has come to respect through his allegiance to Lucy. In essence, he has been feminized by the prophetic nature of the spirit world.

Like Ravenswood, Moses and Captain Zephaniah Pennel (Mara's grandfather) are also initially too much of this world, though ironically, both appear to be like Old Testament prophets, as their names suggest. However, Mara challenges their strict patriarchal demeanor. Like Ravenswood, who must give up the feudal history of his forefathers, Moses and Zephaniah learn a new way of seeing before they can understand a greater universal design. The retired Captain Zephaniah is described as "a Hebrew of the Hebrews," and though Moses was discovered in an Old Testament fashion as a baby in the water, he is described in a secular patriarchal fashion, as he imagines himself a "Sir Francis Drake" or "Christopher Columbus" (110). Zephaniah has more chance to understand Mara's nature, for he "had read many wide leaves of God's great book of Nature" (11). Little Moses, whose namesake should have made him understand the world of signs and portents, seems to have little connection to the spirit world, partly because the sins of his fathers have marked him. Moses's own father, Don Guzman, who perpetuated the evils of slavery in Cuba, bequeathed arrogance and self-centeredness to Moses, so that he does not appreciate the suffering of others (much in the way Ravenswood was blinded to the suffering of his people). Finally, though, the stern and patriarchal men seem less able to leave their mark on history than the women whose spirit seems indomitable. Indeed, the key for Moses to understanding "his people" is to fathom the secrets of old Miss Roxy as well as the love he takes for granted in Mara.

Moses is at first as repelled by Miss Roxy as Ravenswood had been by Alice. Moses declares, "I can't bear her . . . I always think of sick-rooms and coffins and a stifling smell of camphor when I see her. I never could endure her" (378). He is finally reconciled to the realm of death and the entire circle of life when he discovers the effect Mara has had on his development. Initially, the possibility of Mara's death terrifies him because he is so grounded in the material realm: "He had all that constitutional horror of death and the spiritual world which is an attribute of some particularly strong and well-endowed physical natures" (385). As Mara lies on her deathbed, Moses finally does confess that she has been his better angel who has led him to a more introspective way of thinking. "She seemed like one of the sweet friendly angels one reads of in the Old Testament, so lovingly companionable, walking and talking . . . with mortals, yet ready at any unknown moment to ascend with the flame of some sacrifice and be gone" (400).

Though this vision of woman as savior could be construed as belonging to the rhetoric of the Cult of True Womanhood, Mara does not belong to this type of domestic woman, for she is so other-worldly that she could not maintain a household. She is more intellectually developed than Moses, who does not enjoy reading histories half as much as she does, and much more sibyllike than her friend Sally, who marries Moses herself. Though Mara dies of consumption, it is almost as if it is a self-willed disease, the kind of psychosomatic disease that eats away at Lucy Lammermoor's mind and heart and finally allows her to escape marriage.

These too-pure women seem prophetic, even apocalyptic, and Mara herself takes on the grandeur of an Old Testament prophetess at the end of the narrative, seeming "like one of the sweet friendly angels one reads of in the Old Testament" (400). Her passing affects everyone who has known her; even her commonsensical grandfather dreams after her death that he has lost his "pearl of great price" and sees a shadowy Mara on the beach before the ghostlike apparition turns out to be Jesus. Having raised the consciousness of the all-too-grounded inhabitants of Orr's Island, Mara can now return to the spirit world for which she has longed throughout her earthly journey. In her mind, the two realms are inseparable, for to her "the spiritual world was a reality; God an ever-present consciousness; and the line of this present life seemed so to melt and lose itself in the anticipation of a future and brighter one" (337). Mara, in effect, lives in the same timeless realm as the gossips and witches of Stowe's and Scott's local color landscapes.

Though the theme of Christian salvation is typical of Stowe's other novels, *The Pearl of Orr's Island* seems far more indebted to Scott for the merging of pagan with spiritual elements; it is less dogmatic and doctrinaire than Stowe's other New England historical novels. Mara is, after all, not the conventional sentimental spokeswoman for Christianity and quite unlike other Stowe heroines; indeed, Mara's notion of a feminine God is alien to Stowe's Calvinist background—and even blasphemous.[16] Mara confesses to Moses that "God has always been to me not so much like a father as like a dear and tender mother" (326). She seeks to take the patriarchal elements out of religion and out of history. Both Scott in *The Bride of Lammermoor* and Stowe in *The Pearl of Orr's Island* reflect upon a vision of feminine history that is personal and attached to natural cycles and that eclipses a more chronological vision of masculine history that thrives on conquest. Women are endowed with a fecund spiritual imagination; men, bereft of their wits, need women to access this realm; women create a history that men don't understand. Both Mara and Lucy regenerate the men they love by showing them the folly of their ego and ambitions.

It is telling that both Scott and Stowe use the image of the nymph Egeria to show the power of Lucy and of Mara (and indirectly of woman) to effect change or to alter the course of history. Egeria was the nymph at the fountain who allowed King Numa, the second king of Rome, to outwit Jupiter and to avoid defeat by his enemy. In the legend of the fall of Ravenswood, we hear that "A beautiful young lady met one of the Lords of Ravenswood while hunting near this spot, and like a second Egeria, had captivated the affections of the feudal Numa" (56). The new Egeria, Lucy, captivates Edgar Ravenswood at the same spot. The reference to Egeria is even more pronounced in *The Pearl of Orr's Island*: "When Moses was full of Romulus and Numa, Mara pondered the story of the nymph Egeria" (125). When Mara is being tutored by the minister, Mr. Sewell, she is perturbed by the paucity of historical records about women and questions why no great woman is included in *Plutarch's Lives*.[17] Stowe's book itself strives to challenge the reader to rethink male-based notions of history. Mara's early pronouncement that "girls and women" count, that they create men's history, resonates throughout the text: "There was Deborah was [sic] a prophetess, and judged Israel; and there was Egeria,—she taught Numa Pompilius all his wisdom" (150). Mara sees the wisdom of the Ages driven by women, and ultimately the Maras, and not the Moseses, are the true prophets.[18] Both Scott and Stowe evoke Egeria to show how women have access to a supernatural realm, to which men can come only through their relationship with women; in both, women's behind-the-scenes influence reaches far into the destiny of men.

NOTES

A shorter version of this essay appeared as "Nature, Magic, and History: Forging a National Identity in Stowe," in *Women's Writing* 12.1 (2005): 99–114.

1. For Scott's influence on Stowe, see Joan Hedrick (7, 20, 198) and Forrest Wilson (243, 347). Alice Crozier asserts that Stowe was most indebted to Byron but concedes that she was "in very considerable debt to Scott" as well ("Stowe and Byron" 196). Karen Halttunen suggests that Stowe draws in her use of Gothic "landscape and setting" from the "tradition of Anne Radcliffe" ("Gothic" 119), but it seems just as plausible that she draws this landscape from Scott.

2. Here I disagree with the recent assessment by Judith Fetterley and Marjorie Pryse that *The Pearl of Orr's Island* is not a fully realized regionalist novel (160, 171).

3. Various critics have debated the role of history in Stowe's and in Scott's novels (though never together, to my knowledge). See Edward Tang, Lawrence Buell (*New England Literary Culture*), Marlon Ross, James Reed, Cairns Craig, Fiona Robertson. Obviously, my essay implicitly refutes Carlyle's notion of an understanding of Scott's history as male-centered in its experience.

4. In a Transcendentalist sense, the workings between Nature and the individual are used even in descriptions of characters in the Stowe text. For example, Mara is an angel, but she is also given to folding "all her feelings and thoughts inward, as some insects with fine gauzy wings, draw them under a coat of horny concealment" (150).

5. For Jewett's response to *The Pearl of Orr's Island*, see the letter to Annie Fields, in which she praises the start of the novel, with its "noble key of simplicity and harmony" (212). She also views it as "classical—historical—anything you like to say, if you can give it high praise enough" (212). See Sarah Way Sherman's comparison of Stowe's *Pearl* to Jewett's *The Country of the Pointed Firs* (27–45).

6. Judith Fetterley discusses Stowe's apology in the preface to *The Pearl of Orr's Island* that there is "no great romance" but "only a short story pale and colorless as real life, and sad as truth" (188).

7. See, for example, Dorothy Z. Baker, who examines how Stowe is influenced by the theme and framework of the providence tales of Cotton Mather in his *Magnalia Christi Americana* (1702); Stowe shared with Mather the Calvinist concept of human spiritual perfectibility. From "Wonders of the Spirit World," Baker in "Puritan Providences" maintains, Stowe borrowed the idea of godly messages and divine manifestations in the realm of the supernatural. For a discussion of the supernatural elements in early New England, see David D. Hall.

In the 1860s, which also mark the publication of *The Pearl of Orr's Island*, Stowe "converted to Anglicanism, a return to the church of her mother Roxanna Foote" (Crumpacker 94). Thus, Mara may mirror Stowe's own desire for a more feminized church. As Crumpacker asserts, "Stowe's move to the Anglican church was accompanied by an intensification of her belief in the importance of a female ministry and by her need for a more feminized divinity" (Crumpacker 94). See also John Gatta, who feels that Stowe's maternal Anglican heritage gave her a "feminized theology of divine love" illustrated in her later fiction ("Anglican Aspect" 433).

For more on the Puritan influence, and Stowe's ambivalence, see endnote 16. It is obvious that for Stowe's creative vision the folk elements of Puritanism were more compelling than the strict religious tenets. Note, for example, Mather's exploration of possession and hysteria in *Wonders of the Invisible World* (1692) and Scott's account of witchcraft and demonism in *Letters on Demonology and Witchcraft* (1830).

8. Mrs. Kittridge, who represents the strong housewife type, an exemplar of Catharine Beecher's and Harriet Beecher Stowe's Cult of True Womanhood, complains about the Pennel women, saying that they have been too otherwordly and unfit for motherhood.

9. Another example of this mystical antitype of the domestic woman is Cassy in *Uncle Tom's Cabin*. See Karen Halttunen, who argues that Cassy "exercises demonic powers" and that she is "an antitype of true womanhood"—"blasphemous," "diabolical," "fallen," "maddened," "defiant and dangerous" ("Gothic" 122).

10. Women would mediate between the real and the ideal, between the historical present (with its distorted connection to the past) and the spiritual continuity, in which time is eternal. This gets to Emerson's sense of the eternal circle in "The Over-Soul," as well as his sense of historical continuity in "History" and "Fate." In his essay "Woman," Emerson agrees that women have power in both the private and public arenas.

11. Romantics, such as Rousseau, down through the scientists, such as Darwin, often grouped women and children together with primitive beings, perhaps more in touch with nature, but less civilized.

12. Sherman and Baker ("Puritan Providences") point to Aunt Roxy's divine or ministerial qualities.

13. Aunt Cerinthy's vision of the dead woman (who lost her baby at sea) standing over the cradle of her sister's child is similar to Mara's vision of the pale lady who turns out to be Moses's drowned mother. This is a narrative of mothers who drown and mothers who lose their children and of women who fathom the pain of the dead mother.

14. Miranda was also a pivotal and liberating figure for Margaret Fuller in *Woman in the Nineteenth Century*. Perhaps Stowe is also indebted to Fuller for her ideas about gender balance.

15. Mara is a woman in tune with Nature and with the miraculous.

16. That Stowe was disenchanted with her father's religion is nothing new, even though early critics, like Vernon Louis Parrington, saw her as a true daughter of Puritanism (with its rationalism and sense of feudal order [214]). Some recent critics say her reaction to her father's cold sense of Calvinism is especially evident in *The Minister's Wooing*. See, for example, John Gatta's excellent essay, which shows how Stowe ultimately favored the warmth of Anglicanism to "austere Calvinism" (417). Dorothy

Berkson suggests that Stowe's vision in the New England novels is more utopian than "historically accurate" (248) and that she looks forward to a millennial society based upon "the domestic, feminine sphere, and shared by the 'feminine' Christ of the New Testament" (245). Sherman asserts that Mara embodies and preaches the maternal side of God: "As the daughter, priestess, and possibly even the earthly embodiment of this maternal aspect of the Godhead, Mara is appointed to reveal her truth and to 'balance' human wisdom" (32).

I would suggest that Mara does predict a type of feminine future, but she already lives it in her historical present. Moreover, she so embodies pagan with Christian that one cannot label her as a traditional spokeswoman for Christianity. See also Tang's view of the woman at the hearth as the redeeming image in three of Stowe's novels dealing with New England history.

17. Ironically, though Mara and Mr. Sewell discuss the need to write a type of *Plutarch's Lives* for women, it is actually Stowe who writes a compendium of famous women in her *Woman in Sacred History: A Series of Sketches Drawn from Scriptural, Historical, and Legendary Sources* (1873).

18. Citing Frazer's *Golden Bough*, Sherman also discusses the association of Egeria with birthing, as both she and Diana inhabit the sacred grove at Nemi (32).

PART TWO

Race, Class, and Labor in the Atlantic World

The First Years of *Uncle Tom's Cabin* in Russia

JOHN MACKAY

ARRIET BEECHER STOWE's *Uncle Tom's Cabin* (in Russian, *Khízhina diádi Tóma*) has been, since at least the late nineteenth century, one of the best-known works of American literature in Russia. The novel was published in at least sixty-seven different editions in Russia between 1857 and 1917; well over seventy separate editions in at least twenty-one different languages appeared in the Soviet Union between 1918 and 1991.[1] By the early twentieth century it had become a classic of world literature for Russians and was a ubiquitous feature (usually in variously cut or otherwise altered versions)[2] of the childhood reading of Soviet citizens, especially in the post–World War II period, during which time around three million copies rolled off presses in the USSR.

The present essay, however, focuses on what might be called *Uncle Tom's* prehistory in Russia: the response to the book in the years immediately following its initial American publication (1852), culminating in its first Russian appearance (in three separate venues) at the beginning of 1858—three years, that is, prior to the statutory abolition of serfdom. Although *Uncle Tom's Cabin* predictably lost its sharp topicality after the emancipation (when it become a pedagogic novel of "Christian example" with Uncle Tom presented as a model of piety, peacefulness, and calm strength of conviction), the novel was widely read in the 1850s (despite all efforts by the authorities) as an allegorical attack on and description of Russia's own serfdom-based society. I hope to show how *Uncle Tom's Cabin* forced the early Russian intelligentsia to engage in a fascinating comparative reflection upon their own society and that of the distant United States through the prism of bondage. Encountering Stowe's novel in an atmosphere of constraint (the book was banned in Russia until late 1857), Russian intellectuals at home and abroad nonetheless responded to it in remarkably diverse ways that reflected the full range of Russian views on politics and literature, the elite and the peasantry, Russia and its "others."

Strictly speaking, of course, Russian bondage does not belong in any obvious sense to the Atlantic world that has quite properly constituted the central field for research into the links between slavery and culture. Russian imperialism (with which the institution of serfdom had a complex dialectical relationship) was basically landlocked and continental rather than nautical and global in character; the oceanic rims of greatest relevance for Russia are those of the Pacific and the Black and Baltic Seas. Yet in the wake of Russia's defeat of Napoleonic France after 1812, over the course of intensifying interimperialist conflicts along Russia's southern edge (culminating in the Crimean War of the early 1850s), and as Russian cultural production (especially in literature) began to attract wide attention, the Russian educated classes were drawn fully, if idiosyncratically, into the Atlantic discursive and polemical matrix, even as European writers (like Tocqueville and Humboldt) found their own ways to consider the Atlantic and Russian situations in tandem. And it turns out that *Uncle Tom's Cabin*, which by virtue of its grand popular success can count as the first (the only?) "global" slavery novel, performed an especially complex function for Russian writers trying to think about their own long-isolated and unevenly developed country in global terms. Stowe's novel offered Russian thinkers the opportunity to disagree about the very comparability of their society to any other, with conservatives (like the Slavophile Alexei Khomyakov) arguing strongly for national specificity and radicals (like Alexander Herzen) insisting on the relevance of Stowe's novel to Russian conditions. At the same time, and paradoxically, some of those who sought analogies between their own Russia and Stowe's South feared that the overwhelming affective force of *Uncle Tom's Cabin* would draw world attention away from the scandal of Russian bondage rather than generating the required global abolitionism. These early readers, as we will see, are continually trying to reconcile the book's analytical strength—its critical exposure of the structure of master-slave relations, whether in Russia or in the Atlantic world—with its "sentimental power" and to unite those energies in a way that could be applied to the Russian predicament.

Tsar Alexander II officially abolished serfdom in Russia on 19 February 1861, thus freeing circa 22 million men, women, and children (or over 35 percent of the entire population of the country) from the approximately 100,000 nobles who owned them. Although historians have argued that the actual abolition process began long before and ended long after this date,[3] we can for convenience's sake take it as the pivotal moment in the history of the disappearance of this form of chattel slavery.[4] In the years leading up to the proclamation there was, of course, no sectional journalistic polemic in Russia of the type that helped give birth to *Uncle Tom's Cabin*: no North from which to launch abolitionist attacks upon bondage, no South where proslavery thought might be nurtured and propagated. Under conditions of absolute monarchy, the degree of government interference with the press (in the form of censorship) was markedly greater in Russia than in the United States, and the number of actual journalistic organs considerably smaller. The "peasant question" had been a topic of concern, however, since the late eighteenth century, with salons, government committee meetings, private oral or epistolary exchanges, and secret societies as the main settings for debate. And some writing openly or obliquely critical of serfdom did appear even before Alexander's accession to the throne in 1855, after which time a certain softening in restrictions on the press is detectable, though hardly a full-scale relaxation.[5] What is clear (from a comparative angle) is that the amount of Russian print devoted from whatever perspective to the question of bondage was, by U.S. standards, very small indeed.[6]

Already by 1857, *Uncle Tom's Cabin* had appeared in Armenian (1854; published in Venice), Czech (1854), Danish (1853), Dutch (1853), Finnish (1856), Flemish (1852), French (at least five different editions, 1852–1853), German (at least 10 editions, appearing from 1852–1854), Hungarian (thrice: 1853, 1856, 1857), Italian (1853), Polish (1853), Portuguese (a Parisian edition from 1853), Slovenian (1853), Spanish (six 1853 editions, published in Mexico, Bogotá, and Madrid), Rumanian (1853), and Welsh (1853).[7] This dissemination, extraordinary by any standards, helped to make the novel a point of reference for discussions of bondage internationally in the 1850s. But *Uncle Tom's Cabin* had to wait until very late in 1857 to appear in Russian, although it was (as we will see later) already familiar to many in liberal intellectual circles, usually in French or German translation. The relative lateness of the Russian version (given the rapid early proliferation of translations) has led some to guess that the book's publication had hitherto been banned. Although we have no actual written record of an official prohibition, there is indeed some evidence, negative and positive, of suppression.

Journals of all political stripes made it a practice in the 1850s to do overviews of the literary/cultural scene in Western Europe, and particularly those in Paris and London. Yet neither Stowe nor *Uncle Tom's Cabin* is mentioned, as far as I can tell, in any Russian journal until May 1856, although there are numerous occasions when it might well have been. George Sand, an international celebrity at the time, got a great deal of journalistic attention during this period (the left-liberal Petersburg journal the *Contemporary* ran a series on her life), yet we look in vain for any allusion to her role as one of the great early promoters of Stowe's book. Perhaps the most revealing silence occurs in an article in the *Contemporary* in 1854 on the state of American publishing. Hawthorne, Cooper, and Irving are all discussed, along with statistics on readership and sales, but there's nary a word about the foremost publishing sensation of the period. Earlier commentators are almost certainly correct in thinking that these absences, in a journalistic atmosphere intensely preoccupied with what was "hot" in the West, point to some wider, unspoken ban.[8]

More direct evidence is provided by an 1858 report on the currently burning topics preoccupying Russia's highest circles of power sent by Francis Claxton, American consul in Moscow, to Secretary of State Lewis Cass. The novel was in fact just making its way into print in Russia at the time Claxton was finishing up his communiqué (1 January 1858), and the report can be taken to describe the climate of government opinion in the period immediately prior to the publication. The government's intention to abolish serfdom effectively became public knowledge in November 1857 (Moon 68), but there was, as Claxton indicates, considerable anxiety that the revelation would provoke uprisings among peasants impatient for change:

> The fear is freely expressed and appears to be generally entertained that serious trouble may arise and blood may be shed; as an indication of this feeling, remonstrances have been made that a translation into Russ [sic] of *Uncle Tom's Cabin* now in press should not be permitted to be published, for as a French translation has for a long time been in the hands of the educated classes, the issue of the one in question is looked upon as purposely incendiary and calculated to mislead the peasantry into the idea that they are no better circumstanced and treated than the slaves in America. (qtd. in Saul 302–303)

We have (to my knowledge) no more explicit indication of the tsarist government's attitudes toward *Uncle Tom's Cabin*, although other broad hints at a prohibition are found in letters and diary entries, some of which I'll discuss below.[9] Apart from their eyewitness value, Claxton's comments raise the broader question of just how incendiary the novel was felt to be in the 1850s, especially in still-existing slave societies like Brazil, Romania, and Cuba. (About the U.S. South's attitude, of course, we know considerably more.[10])

The Russian government, though perhaps unduly paranoid about possible uprisings (not to mention the chances of Stowe's novel's finding a significant readership among Russian serfs), was certainly correct in its sense of *Uncle Tom's Cabin*'s notoriety among the educated classes. Russians living abroad, particularly exiled liberals, apparently read the book as soon as it appeared, most often in translation. Already on 8 December 1852 Alexander Herzen (1812–1870), foundational figure for the later liberal/radical intelligentsia and at that time in exile in London, received a letter from his (then) friend Vladimir Aristovich Engel'son in Paris: "Have you read *Uncle Tom's Cabin* [title written in English]? I'm reading it in the feuilleton Presse and every day I recall our homeland" (qtd. in Orlova 67). But Herzen already had his own copy and two months later (3 February 1853) wrote in turn to his old friend and fellow-exile Maria Kasparovna Reikhel': "Have you read *Uncle Tom's Cabin* [title written in Russian]? Read it for God's sake, I'm simply reveling over it (I couldn't manage it in English, though, so I got a [French] translation)" (qtd. in Orlova 67). Stowe's novel made it into Russia as well, of course: Ivan Turgenev (1818–1883) read it in 1853, apparently in French (Orlova 77), and the diaries of Leo Tolstoy (1828–1910) from the Crimean War period reveal that he bought *Onkel Toms Hütte* on 28 August 1854 and read it through over the next few days (Tol'stoi 24). And on 9 September 1854, I. I. Pushchin (1789–1859), in Siberian exile since 1825 for his participation in the Decembrist revolt of that year, informed his fellow rebel P. N. Svistunov (1803–1889) that "L'Oncle Tom," apparently peregrinating through Siberia, had made it all the way to Irkutsk on Lake Baikal (Pushchin 99).[11]

Responses of a more detailed kind are predictably hard to come by, but those we do have find, with Vladimir Engel'son, many points of similarity between the world of *Uncle Tom's Cabin* and that of 1850s Russia. Indeed, in the same letter to Herzen, Engel'son offers a whole series of correspondences: Tom is reminiscent of a Russian Old Believer, Miss Ophelia of a German (and therefore Lutheran) from the Baltic region, and St. Clare is quite simply "an educated Russian landowner of our own time" (qtd. in Orlova 79).

> Everything about him is Russian: his simple nobility, self-centeredness, elegance, indecisiveness (or laziness), and most of all a lack of all lust for power or money. . . . He's too proud to covet wealth or position, and has too much of a

sense of his own worth . . . to be pushy or a scoundrel. . . . And everything in the St. Clare house is Russian: his children love the servants, the servants love the children, and are wasteful and disorderly to boot; the spoilt valet [Adolph] can't distinguish his master's property from his own. (qtd. in Orlova 79–80)

The less appealing Marie St. Clare, in the meantime, is nonetheless a "genuine 'Princess Trubetskaia,'" who calls [her husband] a slob and an oaf" (qtd. in Orlova 80). The connections extend to literary parallels: Legree recalls the ursine landowner Sobakevich from Gogol's *Dead Souls* (1842), while Cassy, notes Engel'son, is very much like the brutalized peasant actress of Herzen's own antiserfdom tale "The Thieving Magpie" (1848). But when he wonders why there is so much similarity, Engel'son can only say that "there aren't many ideas or characters that are unique [to a single place or time]" (qtd. in Orlova 80). Other readers, as we shall see, tried to give more elaborate social-historical explanations for what they saw as "Russian" in Stowe's novel.

On the one hand, the few extant extended reactions from early Russian readers are overwhelmingly enthusiastic about Stowe's achievement, with some more critical undertones perceptible as well; on the other, the Russian readers apprehend the novel in quite varied ways, stressing in turn its political effectiveness in the abolitionist cause, its "sentimental power," or its value as a sober and convincing structural analysis of the contradictions of bondage. A strong example of this last emphasis is to be found in a remarkable letter written by yet another Decembrist, Nikolai Ivanovich Turgenev (1789–1871; a distant relative of the novelist). Turgenev, who had been a member of the Imperial Council of State before the events of 1825, published *La Russie et les Russes*, a three-volume account of contemporary Russia with a focus on the serfdom question, in Paris in 1847. The abolitionist Maria Weston Chapman (1806–1885), a friend of Stowe, read or heard about Turgenev's work and sent him (she wrote) "certain copies of the *Liberator*, and *Standard*, and *Uncle Tom's Cabin*," to which he responded with a letter in French that Chapman published in the abolitionist journal the *Liberty Bell* in 1853 (Turgenev, "Russia" 210–225).[12]

The letter is both a gesture of support from abroad and a reflection on the drastically different possibilities for antislavery activism in Russia and the United States. Momentarily questioning (for rhetorical purposes) the value of a "free press" that enables the expression of "ridiculous" and "odious" proslavery views (218–219) and concluding that such views effectively refute themselves once aired, Turgenev identifies one especially positive result of America's atmosphere of "free discussion": "Above all, this is no time to doubt the benefits of free discussion, now that we have seen the appearance of that masterpiece of art, of spirit, of sentiment and eloquence, which will bring honor to your nation and to your sex, Madame; *Uncle Tom's Cabin*, that admirable volume, which I read shedding tears, not all of which were of pain and sadness" (218). Later, he goes on to explain the different kinds of tears he shed:

> [W]hen reading *Uncle Tom's Cabin*, I was more than once sadly struck by the applicability of Mrs. Stowe's accounts to what I know about similar horrors, and not only through reports but through actual cases which passed through my hands [as a member of] the Imperial Council. Many of the scenes described in the book seem like an exact depiction of equally frightful scenes in Russia. When considering the comical aspects of the novel, too, there is not one where I have not recognized some comparable moment in Russian comedies. That delicate lady, the wife of the foolish St. Clare, who regrets that the weakness of her health prevents her from beating her slaves with a [cowhide], reminds me of another lady in a Russian comedy, who reprimands her chambermaid for the sadness she felt when administering her corporal punishment.[13] The human being is the same everywhere; if you remove from him the restraint of the law, he becomes worse than a ferocious beast. (223–224)

The "applicability of Mrs. Stowe's accounts" to the faraway Russian situation pertains, on Turgenev's reading as on Engel'son's, not only to the brutal realities of serfdom as such but to more progressive literary treatments of Russian bondage as well: both "actual cases" and "Russian comedies," represented world and mode of representation, harmonize with Stowe's materials and manner. To explain this thoroughgoing similarity, Turgenev, a strong advocate of constitutional monarchy and juridical reform, offers a classic Enlightenment "constitutionalist" argument, one based on pessimism about human nature and optimism about the law.[14] Only legal limits on landowner caprice (and presumably legal protection of peasant rights as well) can prevent the appearance of barbarities on the estates and deprive the satirists of matter for the stage; because this is true "everywhere," slaves and planters are indeed serfs and *pomeshchiki* (lords) despite all cultural and geographical distance, and *Uncle Tom's Cabin* is a "Russian" book. Thus Turgenev marks the beginning of a line of readers (one that includes Chernyshevsky and Tolstoy) who read Stowe's novel analytically, as a book that not only recounts particular horrors but also reveals the larger structure (here, an absence of law) that makes the horrors possible.

Something like the opposite emphasis can be found in the more complex response, contained in a letter of 14 March 1855 to Baroness A. D. Bludova, of Alexei Stepanovich Khomyakov (1804–1860). Khomyakov is well known as perhaps the greatest of the Slavophile thinkers, a small, informal but in-fluential group that waged polemical war against the rationalistic Westerniz-ing impulse introduced into Russia in the eighteenth century in favor of a conscious return to what was specifically Russian, particularly (in the Slavo-philes' view) the rootedness of the nation in the supposedly harmonious collectivities of the village and of the Orthodox Church. With his fellow Slavophiles, Khomyakov denounced the "foulness" of serfdom, although, unlike Nikolai Turgenev, he never freed his own peasants (he owned at least 2,000), contenting himself instead with transferring them from corvée, or day-labor, obligations (*barshchina*) to the less onerous "quit-rent" (*obrok*) payments (Semevskii 397–401).

Famously erudite and, indeed, cosmopolitan in his interests, by 1855 Khomyakov had read *Uncle Tom's Cabin* as well. Apparently Baroness Blu-dova had mentioned Stowe's novel in a previous letter, but we will need to read Khomyakov's response in light of his broader views on bondage and on Russia itself. For like Turgenev, he cannot but read the book as a comment on the "local" situation:

> What shall I say to you about Uncle Tom? They're weeping zealously over him [in Moscow], just like you no doubt wept in St. Petersburg; and just as you do there, here much is found in the book that's familiar to us, although not quite in such a black form as in America—even forty years or so ago, when members of families were sold apart from one another, the American forms of bondage were still somewhat worse than ours. . . . Having dispassionately studied our own problem, I understand well the difference between the condition of the serfs and slavery in the strict sense, although of course I in no way approve of the former. The ethical foundation [of serfdom] is different, and it follows that all of its manifestations are different as well, despite an apparent similarity in many specific instances, up to and including appalling cruelty or the display of a still more appalling indifference to humanity. (393)

Khomyakov was of the belief that Russian serfdom, in contrast to the more "criminal" sorts of bondage found in Germanic-controlled lands, found its beginning in sheer "ignorance" and as "a crude policing measure generated by the needs of the state"[15] (Semevskii 390). Crucial to his thoughts on emancipation was an insistence both that the peasants be freed with land (partially in order to prevent the creation of an English-style proletariat) and that the traditional village community, or *mir*, with its grounding in communal land tenure, be preserved through all change. It was the mir, which Khomyakov regarded as an organically self-sustaining and self-correcting social body, that gave Russians, serfs and nobles alike, a moral, social, and religious center that (he argued) long predated serfdom as such.[16]

This is the different "ethical foundation" to which he refers here and which he intends to contrast with the purely profit-driven transport of sub–Saharan Africans to the United States and their enslavement there. Although, of course, the rise of serfdom is intimately connected with the expansion of the Russian state from the sixteenth century onward (and thus never nearly as different from the colonial American situation as Khomyakov would like to think),[17] the Slavophile points nonetheless, through all the idealization, to an important fact. Serfs were enslaved gradually and on their "home turf," with the result that "the role of tradition in limiting the total control of masters over the lives of their bondsmen was greater in Russia than in the United States" (Kolchin 45). Still, "much is familiar" in Stowe's novel, and Khomyakov finds himself in the comparative historian's predicament of trying to understand strikingly similar phenomena across wide historical/cultural differences.

His solution—that the similarities are epiphenomenal merely—is a facile one, contradicted above all by his own fascinated comparison of *Uncle Tom's Cabin* with Russian scenes, a comparison he now extends into an appreciation of a single character: not Tom (who's "perhaps a bit overdone") or Little Eva ("merely a gracious and graceful sister of Paul Dombey"), but (once again) St. Clare: "He is like all of us in his elegant refinement, his artistic nature, the softness and gentleness of his disposition, his slothful philanthropy, his sybaritic egotism, the weakness of his ethical convictions and un-Christian indifference to the general good, which he skillfully justifies with deft sophisms. In his soul he casts judgment on evil, after all; and what more should he do? He is right before God and before himself" (Khomyakov 393). Russian serfs, bound together by the peasant community, are fundamentally incomparable to other bondsmen, but nobles are equally refined (read: "Europeanized") everywhere, and thus Khomyakov can find in St. Clare a satiric (if also lovable) mirror for his own mind and milieu. (*Oblomov* was to appear in 1859—had that novel existed, Khomyakov might well have alluded to it.) Yet Khomyakov concludes his comment on Stowe with a reflection that moves beyond questions of comparability back to the issue of the novel's effect—that "zealous weeping" he mentions at the outset: "I am certain that Mrs. Stowe's novel will give a significant push to the question of black slavery. Social improvement is more dependent upon the heart than people think—more dependent on the heart, perhaps, than on the mind. For this reason, in my view, women are equal to men as great actors in history, although their role is less visible" (Khomyakov 393). Behind the old banal dualism—one that by no means can account for all the intellectual critical work that Stowe's novel performs—is, I think, both a quite uncondescending acknowledgement of the book's power and a strong insight into (as we would say today) how that power is gendered.[18] The admission is striking, coming from the famously intellectual Khomyakov, and strains somewhat against the grain of his own argument and comparisons. For if *Uncle Tom's Cabin* affects the "heart" above all, the details of what links or distinguishes slavery and serfdom may not be all that important, and the novel might give "a significant push" to the question of serfdom as well.

The first mention of *Uncle Tom's Cabin* in the domestic Russian press—in a fascinating anonymous article on "The Internal Parties in the United States" in the (at that time) center-liberal Moscow journal *Russian Messenger* from May 1856—already records the novel's political effect as a fact, and comes close to identifying it with its popular success:

> Besides [demonstrations], the abolitionist uses another, at once more peaceful and noble and more universal method to oppose the barbarism of the crude defenders of bondage. This method is literature: the abolitionists press it into service for the exposure before the whole world of those scandalous injustices about which the fanatics of slavery are unashamed, and in order to protest against them within the circle of civilized peoples. The wounds inflicted by this weapon are perhaps far more tolerable than some others, but they are finally cured only by curing the vice itself, which they serve to oppose. . . . We saw a stunning example of this in the effect wrought by Mrs. Stowe on the entire educated world with her *Uncle Tom*. They read it in America, devoured it greedily all through Europe—if we're not mistaken, it sold an incredible 200,000 copies. In the opinion of many enlightened readers, a disgraceful stain has been left on the American nation, a stain that darkens even its best aspects, those that constitute its pride and adornment, in a most unpleasant way. ("Vnutrennie partii" 12)

The comment's diction stresses the enormous span of *Uncle Tom's Cabin*'s impact (with language like "universal," "the whole world," "the circle of civilized peoples," "entire educated world," "in America [and] all through Europe") but refrains from offering any theory as to why the novel has proven so irresistible to readers—that is, whether it appeals primarily to the heart or to the mind. Rather, it is the mode in which the book is written, its very status as literature, that makes it such a universal platform for critique and protest. Literature, in this classical "intelligentsia" account, creates a far wider community of sensibility than other oppositional methods can ever do and thus fashions a context in which wholly new, internationalized forces of political pressure can be brought to bear upon specific injustices, over the heads of local power.

Of course, this view presumes a certain dialectical interaction of writing with a public sphere: the book's appeal is necessarily to an already existent educated populace, which it in turn "enlightens" in new ways and which critically incorporates the book into its own discourse. An optimistic picture to be sure—but is the book's moral/political effect really directly measurable in terms of its vast popularity? This last question can be said to underlie Alexander Herzen's longest comment on the novel, contained in his well-known essay on "Russian Serfdom." Dated 20 December 1852 and written in French (but first published in English in three parts in November 1853 in the *London Leader*), the article presents Herzen's condensed history of serfdom, much fiery polemic against Russian rulers from Ivan III to the present, and what is probably the first published response to *Uncle Tom's Cabin* by a Russian.

One way to get around the censors was to publish abroad, of course; Herzen was to have a great career in this kind of publishing, and here he uses a relatively early opportunity both to rain fire upon the Russian government and subtly to chastise Europeans for their apparent indifference to conditions in Russia. Significantly, his argument is framed, beginning and end, with provocative references to *Uncle Tom's Cabin*, which (as his letter to Reikhel' indicates) he was reading even while writing the serfdom article[19]: "At the moment when all England was displaying a profound and active sympathy for the slaves in the Southern States of North America, incited thereto by the great work of Mrs. Beecher Stowe, no one seemed to remember that nearer to England, across the Baltic, is an entire population the legal property of a batch of seigneurs; a population not of 3,000,000 but of 20,000,000!"[20] (qtd. in Gertsen 7). Stowe's novel is "great," Herzen acknowledges, but he questions whether the "sympathy" it incites manages to radiate beyond a specific perimeter, whether (although this is stretching his point somewhat) the novel's very strength as a weapon in the U.S. abolitionist cause also generates a certain forgetfulness. This argument takes a different turn at the end of his article when, after outlining the enormities of serfdom, he writes:

> Surely from time to time it is well that a free voice should be lifted up to denounce these degrading institutions, this foul complicity of a government that talks of its strength, with a noblesse that boasts of its enlightenment. The mask must be torn from these slaveholders of the North [i.e., Russian serf-owners], who go lounging and lisping over Europe, mingling with your affairs, assuming the rank of civilized beings,—nay, of liberal-minded men, who read *Uncle Tom's Cabin* with horror, and shudder when they read of sellers of black flesh. Why, these same brilliant spies of the salons are the very men who on their return to their domains rob, flay, sell the white slave, and are served at table by their living property. (qtd. in Gertsen 33)

Having already become an antislavery ensign, *Uncle Tom's Cabin* (or the reading of it) can be used as sentimental wrapping, as another moral "mask" behind which the "slaveholders of the North" can conceal their iniquities even from themselves. These two types of reading—the kind that neglects the larger reality of bondage and the kind that substitutes "sympathy" for (self-) critical analysis of institutions—work together; Herzen sees both as betrayals of the novel's radical promise.

In this respect his comments, though clearly laudatory, presage later suspicions about making easy correlations between the book's moral power and its affective impact. An early example can be found in a devastating piece by one "P. E." called "Landowners and Peasants" from an 1859 number of the *Russian Messenger*. After a series of terrible descriptions of starvation and misery in the Vitebsk area (scenes he compares with what he has read of similar horrors in Ireland) the author writes that ·

> [W]e are used to seeing our serfs as tools, as laboring machines. We demand that these laboring machines be useful to us, and worry very little about the conditions or means through which this result is achieved. Indeed, we are used to their poverty, we are used to attributing it to sloth and negligence; and many of us, endowed with very good souls, are more likely to help an occasional petitioner than to get bothered about the daily needs of our peasants. How many women have I seen weeping inconsolably over *Uncle Tom's Cabin*, but who are never struck by the real misery and poverty so often encountered in our villages. Yet it's not only in America that one finds Uncle Toms.[21] (225)

"Landowners and Peasants" has a confessional aspect, inasmuch as "P. E." is writing as a nobleman deeply frustrated with the course of reform in Russia and thus with his own milieu. But he is also writing, like Herzen, as one of the international "liberal-minded"; he hopes precisely to perform one of those broader comparative applications that, Herzen implies, Stowe's book deserves. Thus the comments of both Herzen and "P. E." are true interventions, not straightforward celebrations of the power of literature.

A possible next or alternative step would be to actually appropriate Stowe's model with an eye to more direct application to the Russian problem, and indeed Herzen's article contains a disguised reference to just such a project. He mentions at the beginning that "a friend of [his] proposed to publish a pamphlet to remind English charity of [the fact of serfdom]," but that "his pamphlet was never published" (Gertsen 7). It seems certain that the friend was fellow émigré Ivan Gavrilovich Golovin (b. 1816), peripatetic hack author of works on political economy, sketches of Russian life, memoirs, a volume of "American impressions" called *Stars and Stripes* (1856), and what seems to have been a novel-length imitation of Stowe about a "Russian Tom," in French[22] (Gertsen 509). Apparently the manuscript was purchased by one Nelson from Edinburgh (Golovin, like Herzen, spent some time in Britain) but was never published[23] (Lemke 39).

Alas, as it turns out, we do not know of any full-scale transpositions of *Uncle Tom's Cabin* into the serf context (although some post-1870 adaptations certainly add "Russifying" touches). What is really fascinating, however, is that Golovin seems to have recycled his reading of Stowe's novel for a slightly later work on slavery. His three-act play *Rovira*, "on the life of slaves in Cuba," was published in Russian in Leipzig in 1858. Dedicated to Alexander von Humboldt (with whose "book in hand," Golovin claims, he traveled through Cuba),[24] *Rovira* tells the story of the handsome mulatto Rodrigo Rovira, owner-operator of a coffeehouse in Havana and beloved of the wealthy Antoinetta Lorenzo. Antoinetta's racist father is opposed to their union and, upon discovering that the Rovira family is descended from slaves, exposes their origins and attempts to return them to bondage. His plans are foiled, however, and at the end he is reconciled with both daughter and (now) son-in-law.

It turns out that Rodrigo Rovira is also an inventor—shades of George Harris—and the play finds a happy resolution in part because of his sale of his main invention, a machine for extracting sugar with steam, to a slave trader from Georgia (U.S.A.) named Brown. (The sale turns out to have ambiguously "beneficial" modernizing effects on the slavery front as well, for [as Brown puts it] "one machine like that" can replace "a thousand loads of Negroes.") It is the personage of the American Brown, however, that suggests Golovin's debt to *Uncle Tom's Cabin* most strongly; for this character seems to be an amalgam of all of Stowe's nasty slave-trader types, with aspects of Haley, Tom Loker, and even Simon Legree perceptible in the representation. Here is his first entrance (act 2, scene 1):

> (An American with a beard, chewing tobacco, dressed in nankeen, knocks
> on the door and enters.)
> Brown: Señor Rovira?
> Rovira: At your service.
> Brown (sitting down, puts both his feet up on the table and spits on the
> floor): I've got some business to discuss with you. I'm Mr. Brown from
> Georgia—traveling around doing some trading.
> Rovira: What's your business, exactly?
> Brown: Why hide the truth? I'm involved in the black slave trade. (Rovira
> pushes away a chair in disgust.) A few days ago we brought in a cargo of
> blacks, dressed up like sailors—if things turn out, we'll take some of them
> to New Orleans. (31)

Like Stowe's ruffians, Brown also makes a point of consuming alcohol and chooses to down some rum instead of a draught of "pineapple syrup with water" offered him by Rovira. *Othello*, it is not—but Golovin's play does strongly suggest that the issue of slavery worldwide was coming to be imagined through the tropes and types of *Uncle Tom's Cabin*. For while Brown comes from Georgia and the play itself is set in Cuba, Golovin's dedication to Humboldt and Humboldt's response (both published in French as a frontispiece to the play itself) touch less on Cuban slavery and more on the question of Russian bondage and Russian involvement in slavery-related issues. Golovin praises Alexander II as the monarch for whom "the glory of emancipating the serfs" is reserved, and Humboldt writes both of his own friendship with Wilberforce and of how he admired Alexander I's strong opposition to the slave trade as expressed at the Third Congress of Aix-la-Chapelle (1818) (Golovin 5–9).[25] Thus what is at least in part a rewriting of Stowe (and specifically the George and Eliza plot) becomes an occasion for a kind of quilting-together of different contexts of bondage and abolition, a rough attempt at "mapping the totality," if you will.

So it is clear that *Uncle Tom's Cabin* had at least a considerable reputation, if not indeed a wide readership, in Russia prior to its first domestic publication at the end of 1857/beginning of 1858. A review of *Dred* that appeared in the *Contemporary* in the first half of 1857 doesn't even mention Stowe's earlier novel, and it is difficult to tell if this omission is due to censorship or whether mentioning *Uncle Tom* would already have felt superfluous— although the fact that the anonymous reviewer never refers to Dred's fundamental role as leader of a slave revolt does imply that caution was still being taken ("Zagranichnye izvestiia" 140–142).

The publication in November 1857 of the famous imperial rescript, calling upon nobles in the Lithuanian provinces to form committees to work on laws outlining "a systematic amelioration of the way of life [of] the proprietary peasants" (Field 83), was generally taken as a signal that a real, Russia-wide emancipation process had in fact begun. Certainly, the announcement marked the beginning of a year or so of relative freedom to publish on the serfdom question, and it is within that privileged span of time that three different Russian editions of *Uncle Tom's Cabin* appeared: from December 1857 through March 1858 in the *Russian Messenger*, in 1858 (individual chapters only) in *Son of the Fatherland*, and all at once in January 1858 as a supplement to the *Contemporary*.

On 25 December 1857, Nikolai Nekrasov (1821–1878), major poet and coeditor (with Ivan Panaev) of the *Contemporary*, wrote to Ivan Turgenev in Rome about the state of the journal and upcoming plans:

> Regarding the journal, I shall tell you that its serious section is not bad, but things are in a bad way when it comes to stories! They do not exist. . . . [As a consequence] subscriptions began to fall; to increase them we have thought up a "Historical Library." This was followed by an opportunity to translate *Uncle Tom's Cabin*. I have decided to incur an unforeseen expenditure: the novel is to be offered gratis with Issue No. 1, this announcement leading to a jump in subscriptions. It is noteworthy that this has been most opportune: the question is very much in the public eye in respect of our own Negroes.[26] (Nikoljukin 213)

Nekrasov's note, brief as it is, is worthy of attention and unpacking. First of all, it provides a clear indication that Stowe's novel had indeed rather suddenly become publishable, and certainly part of the "unforeseen expenditure" included work on the translation itself, which (like the *Messenger* version, most likely) was done at great speed. The journal's expense-sheet for honoraria indicates that six translators were employed[27]; intriguingly enough, a man named P. M. Novosil'skii was not only involved in the translation of both the *Messenger* and *Contemporary* editions (Orlova 75),[28] but was also the government censor who gave the *Contemporary* permission to publish *Uncle Tom's Cabin* in the first place. Out of 731 rubles paid to the translators working for the *Contemporary*, 500 went to Novosil'skii—who translated (according to the same record of honoraria) a mere seven pages out of 476! Plainly enough, part of the unforeseen expenditure included a token of appreciation for the censor, who no doubt sped the text's passage through the committee.[29]

The note also offers insight into what we might call the book's dual instrumentality. On the one hand, the subject of *Uncle Tom's Cabin* is obviously politically timely in relation to the peasant question; on the other, the novel proves to be a popular hit even prior to publication, "leading to a jump in subscriptions." (We shouldn't miss the hint Nekrasov drops to Turgenev to send some stories along, either.) The dichotomy is a telling one, and it would reemerge in the latter half of the nineteenth century at those times when "edifying" models for literacy offered themselves in conscious struggle against mass market, or popular, kinds of writing. What was immediately important for Nekrasov, however, was that the Russian translation attracted readers straightaway, and indeed many of those who had already read the novel in some other language picked up one or another Russian version as soon as they appeared. I. I. Pushchin, now returned from exile, wrote to his wife on 14 February 1858 that he was going through the *Contemporary* translation, predicting that some of the serfholders around Moscow wouldn't be able to wait for the *Russian Messenger* installments and would have to send to Petersburg for the full version (352–353).

Pushchin adds, however, that the *Messenger* version is a superior translation, and although he doesn't go into details, his observation is undoubtedly correct, particularly in terms of actual completeness. Apparently, all Russian translations prior to 1883 were based on French or German versions,[30] thus compelling any student of those early Russian versions to examine them through the non-English intermediaries. Notwithstanding Novosil'skii's involvement in both versions, the two translations seem to derive from different French editions, with the *Contemporary* version more marked by the censor's pen. As so often with censorship, however, inconsistencies and inexplicable choices abound.

If one is searching for sections of Stowe's novel that might prove sore points for the pre-emancipation Russian censorship, the chapters "Miss Ophelia's Experiences, Continued," "Henrique," and "Reunion"—with their references to European bondage and class unrest worldwide—would seem the perfect places to begin. St. Clare's famous prediction of a "*dies irae*," for example, from "Miss Ophelia's Experiences, Continued": "One thing is certain,—that there is a mustering among the masses, the world over; and there is a *dies irae* coming on, sooner or later. The same thing is working in Europe, in England, and in this country. My mother used to tell me of a millennium that was coming, when Christ should reign, and all men should be free and happy" (240).[31] As it turns out, the *Russian Messenger* translation cuts perhaps the most inflammatory sentence ("The same thing is working in Europe . . .")—but leaves virtually all other references to class inequality in the novel intact, including this exchange between St. Clare and Miss Ophelia in "Reunion," perhaps the touchiest one of all from an East European point of view:

> "Do you suppose it possible that a nation ever will voluntarily emancipate?" said Miss Ophelia.
>
> "I don't know," said St. Clare. "This is a day of great deeds. Heroism and disinterestedness are rising up, here and there, in the earth. The Hungarian nobles set free millions of serfs, at an immense pecuniary loss; and, perhaps, among us may be found generous spirits, who do not estimate honor and justice by dollars and cents."[32] (322)

In contrast, the *Contemporary* version leaves the *dies irae* prediction untouched, while cutting or altering a number of passages touching on comparable subject matter. Sometimes the cuts are obvious, as in the omission in the "Henrique" chapter of all the talk (between St. Clare and Alfred) of Louis XVI; the French noblesse, *sans culottes*; "contemptible Hayti"; and the now dangerously dispersed superiority of Anglo-Saxon blood (276–277).[33] Other changes demand more complex evaluation, as in this version of the "Hungarian nobles" passage:

> "Do you really think that a country could agree to emancipate all of its Negroes at once?"
>
> "I don't know. But we live in an age of great events. Heroism and disinterestedness are beginning to raise their voices across the globe. Perhaps in America will be found great-spirited people, who do not measure honor and truth by the same standard as cotton and sugar." (Stowe, *Khizhina* 336)[34]

At first glance, the distortion seems quite obvious and readable: beside the simple omission of the Hungarian nobles, the decisions to replace "voluntarily emancipate" with "emancipate all of its Negroes," "among us" with "in

America," and (most brilliantly) "dollars and cents" with "cotton and sugar," have the effect of subtly "Americanizing" an exchange that in Stowe has a distinctly global field of reference. In fact, however, except for that rude purging of the Hungarian nobles, the entire section is a direct translation from the French "original," and not an example of censorial cunning[35] (Stowe, *La Cabane* 313). The effect remains the same, of course, but is largely due to a hidden, unexpected mediation.

Other changes, however, are unique to the Russian version in the *Contemporary*. We sometimes find rather straightforward substitutions used to inflect Stowe's critique back toward the American South when it strains toward a more universal application. A good example is the following section from the debate in the "Henrique" chapter:

> "For my part, I think half this republican talk sheer humbug. It is the educated, the intelligent, the wealthy, the refined, who ought to have equal rights and not the canaille."
>
> "If you can keep the canaille of that opinion," said Augustine. "They took their turn once, in France."
>
> "Of course, they must be kept down, consistently, steadily, as I should," said Alfred, setting his foot hard down, as if he were standing on somebody.
>
> "It makes a terrible slip when they get up," said Augustine,—"in St. Domingo, for instance."
>
> "Poh!" said Alfred, "we'll take care of that, in this country. We must set our face against all this educating, elevating talk, that is getting about now; the lower class must not be educated." (Stowe, *Uncle Tom's Cabin* 276)

> "For my part, I regard half of these republican phrases as a kind of bad joke. Educated, rich and enlightened people require equal rights, but not *Negroes*," [said Alfred.]
>
> "If you can make *Negroes* partake of that opinion," answered Augustine.
>
> "Of course, one has to curb *Negroes* with consistency and firmness, just as I would do," said Alfred, trampling the ground with his foot, as though it were one of his enemies.
>
> "*Negroes* wreak terrible devastation when they take it into their heads to rebel—as in San Domingo, for example."
>
> "Oh, we'll avoid all of that here. We simply have to place obstacles in the way of this desire to educate which is spreading these days. *Negroes* must not be educated." (*Contemporary* translation 288, emphasis added) [36]

Obviously enough, the substitution of *Negroes* for *canaille* is made easier by St. Clare's reference to San Domingo, but this change requires in its turn that St. Clare's reminder of the canaille having taken "their turn once, in France" be eliminated. The alteration, crude as it is, effectively respatializes Stowe's discourse and converts Alfred from a comprehensive reactionary into a merely (and safely) American racist.

At the same time, much in the book that might be thought inflammatory in the tsarist context is retained in the *Contemporary* edition—most notably St. Clare's analysis of the "root and nucleus" of slavery (Stowe 230–231) and his discussion of the limits of aristocratic sympathy (Stowe 233) in chapter 19. (Nor does Stowe's "Saxonist" racial logic seem to have raised any eyebrows.) Inconsistencies like this are hard to explain, especially in detail; probably some combination of haste, negotiation, and idiosyncrasy of judgment produced the somewhat-altered text that Nekrasov finally published. Unclear, too, are the reasons for the heavier censorship of the *Contemporary* version, although perhaps both Nekrasov's rush to publish the whole book (which would have drawn attention in itself) and the journal's more radical reputation led to harsher scrutiny—with the result that the more conservative *Russian Messenger* printed a considerably more accurate version.

The story of the first translations introduces themes that will stretch across the whole history of *Uncle Tom's* translation-reception in Russia: the ambiguous shaping force of political interest (whether governmental or not) on the text, and the way in which changes to the text often involve a revision of the book's social/geopolitical coordinates. In this respect, it is merely one part of the larger story of the novel's early reception, which also unfolds around the questions of how closely enserfed Russia and Stowe's "American other" can be mapped or drawn together (Herzen/Turgenev vs. Khomyakov), and of whether the sympathy Stowe elicits for slaves from the Atlantic world stretches to Russian peasants as well. It is a to-and-fro movement that will continue after the emancipation, when Tom becomes a model to be emulated by "the people," even as the horrors of American slavery are subtly distinguished from the world of serfdom, and again after the 1917 revolution, when Stowe's picture of slavery is read as specifically American and capitalist. *Uncle Tom's Cabin*, it might be said, houses a long, rocky marriage between Russia and the United States—within the Russian imaginary at any rate. How that relationship looks over the next 150 years of reception is, however, a topic for another essay.

NOTES

1. The first figure comes from Orlova's indispensable (if uneven) reception study, the second from the 1970 *Bol'shaia Sovetskaia Entsiklopediia*, ed. A. M. Prokhorov et al. 403. I have raised the estimated number given in the latter source (fifty-nine editions) to account for editions appearing between 1970 and 1991, which easily bring the total to beyond seventy and probably closer to one hundred (I have by no means seen all the Soviet editions in Russian).

2. Because I will be writing several times about cut/altered Russian versions of the whole or part of *Uncle Tom's Cabin*, I want to stress at the outset that such alterations are in no way peculiar to the Russian reception, the East's reputation for censorship notwithstanding. As is well known, the book had been Sambo-ed, bowdlerized, and dittified virtually from its first appearance in the United States; indeed, its susceptibility to every possible variety of *détournement* seems striking enough to constitute an interesting theoretical problem in its own right. (For a fascinating reflection on this question, see Hedrick 213–214.) Though there were (to my knowledge) no "Tom shows" in Russia, the history of Russian alterations of Stowe's novel goes back to the very first publications, and some of the most remarkable reworkings are pre-Soviet; see below.

3. See in particular David Moon's recent *The Abolition of Serfdom in Russia, 1762–1907*, which argues that the process begins with the abolition of mandatory state service for the nobility in 1762 and ends with the writing-off by Nicholas II of all the freed serfs' outstanding redemption payments in 1907 (3–4).

4. On serfdom as a form of slavery and on its differences from and similarities to American slavery, see Peter Kolchin's now classic study *Unfree Labor: American Slavery and Russian Serfdom* (41–46).

5. The most famous example (about which more below) is Ivan Turgenev's *Sketches from a Hunter's Notebook*, published in the *Contemporary* between 1847 and 1851. Daniel Field writes that although "there was a relaxation of the censorship in comparison with the last years of Nicholas's reign," "this striking contrast may obscure the continuity of censorship policy and divert attention from the restrictions that were imposed on the press with regard to the peasant reform" (149).

6. To take samples from only the two journals that later were the first to publish Stowe's novel: the center-liberal *Russian Messenger* (*Russkii Vestnik*) ran an important series of articles in 1856 by the famous liberal historian Boris Chicherin on the peasant community; an article in March 1857 by "V. Ch." on "Agriculture in Russia"; V. P. Bezobrazov's "Aristocracy and the Interests of the Nobility: Ideas and Observations on the Peasant Question" (September 1859); and a scathing antiserfdom piece by "P. E." on "Landowners and Peasants" (February 1859; see below). For its part, the left-liberal the *Contemporary* (*Sovremennik*) published a number of important pieces in 1858 (clearly the *annus mirabilis* for discussion of serfdom in the press), including a series on "The Organization of the Way of Life of Serf Peasants," "On the New Conditions of Village Life," and Evgenii Karnovich's "Notes toward a History of Serfdom in Russia." Numerous other articles appearing during this time (like the translation of Gustave de

Molinari's "On Free Labor" (*Russian Messenger*, April 1860) touch on closely affiliated issues, but the number of directly Russian serfdom-related articles is not great.

7. I derive these figures from the extensive bibliographical references (based largely on holdings in the British Museum) included in the Russian translation *Khízhina diádi Tóma*, trans. Z. N. Zhuravskaia (St. Petersburg: O. N. Popova, 1898) 521–532. Some of the translations are apparently abridgements, and the list does not claim to be comprehensive.

8. For other evidence of a ban, see Orlova (68).

9. For more direct evidence of the mood of the censorship organs in 1857–1858, see Skabichevskii, esp. 416–426.

10. It is worth noting that Secretary Lewis Cass (1782–1866), an early political ally of John C. Calhoun, was himself a moderate defender of slavery, though not a Southerner. As senator from Michigan during the secession crisis, Cass often attacked abolitionist agitators on the Senate floor, speaking in the following terms on 12 May 1856: "The world had been inundated with log cabin books about as worthy of credit as the travels of the renowned Gulliver, too often drawing their conclusions from the dictates of a wild or false heart, or of a disordered head" (qtd. in Klunder 285). Presumably, Cass would have understood some of the worries of his Russian counterparts.

11. The Decembrists (who were made up of several disparate factions in and around St. Petersburg, Moscow, and Kiev) staged an abortive revolt on 14 December 1825 through which they had hoped to overthrow the autocracy and establish either a republic or constitutional monarchy.

12. The quote from Chapman is from her brief introduction (210).

13. I have been unable to determine which Russian comedy Turgenev is referring to here, but the comment about the hypocritically "sad" noblewoman recalls a very similar description in one of the few extant serf narratives, M. E. Vasilieva's "Notes of a Serf-Woman."

14. Turgenev once compared a constitutional monarch to a god ruling with divine laws, in contrast to an autocrat, who was more like a shepherd ruling the herd with dogs. On his political/legal views, see Shebunin, esp. 50–51.

15. Semevskii notes that in fact Swedish warlords had introduced legal protections for Baltic peasants, protections removed by the Russians once they took control of the area.

16. On the question of the peasant community's antiquity, see Blum 508–515.

17. On the relation of both slavery and serfdom to "the geographic and economic expansion of Europe in the sixteenth and seventeenth centuries," see Kolchin 1–17.

18. On this question, see Tompkins, "Sentimental Power."

19. It is also worth noting that one of his main "historical sources" for the article is none other than Nikolai Turgenev's *La Russie et les Russes*, which was surely also on his desk at the time.

20. The piece was first published in the London journal the *Leader* (nos. 189–191), on 5, 12, and 19 November 1853.

21. The essay is dated December 1858, and a footnote on 225 indicates that it was published with "omissions."

22. For a highly entertaining account of Golovin's literary and political escapades, see Lemke. Lemke presents Golovin's planned "Tom" as pure opportunism, an attempt to cash in on the slavery theme.

23. From what I can gather, no trace remains of the manuscript.

24. Golovin is probably referring to the "Essai politique sur l'île de Cuba," first published in 1808 in the series *Voyages au regions équinoxiales du Nouveau Continent, fait en 1799, 1800, 1801, 1802, 1803, et 1804* (published between 1805 and 1834). Golovin's chapter "A Trip to Cuba" in his *Stars and Stripes, or American Impressions* (London and New York: W. Freeman and D. Appleton, 1856) is dated "Havannah [sic], April 1856" (228). The same book contains a whole chapter on "American Slavery and Russian Serfdom" but no mention of *Uncle Tom*.

25. Humboldt, the great geographer and naturalist of Latin America, had traveled extensively through Russia in 1829. For his antislavery views and his work on Cuba, see Diaz.

26. The letter was first published in Russian in *Vestnik Evropy* 12 (1903): 637–639. Nekrasov published a number of major American works over the course of the 1850s, including *The House of the Seven Gables*, *The Scarlet Letter*, and *The Song of Hiawatha*.

27. The six were Messrs. Tol', Novosil'skii, Kalistov, Borshchov, Pashkovskii, and Butuzov; it seems that the bulk of the work was done by the last three. See Reiser 3: 245.

28. I have not examined the *Son of the Fatherland* excerpts in detail.

29. See Reiser 3: 279–280; and Orlova 76.

30. I base this on the claim made by the publisher D. D. Fedorov in his preface to the edition he put out in 1883 (*Khízhina diádi Tóma ili zhizn' sredi rabov*, trans. E. Landini) that this was in fact the first translation based entirely on Stowe's original text. Fedorov, the son of publisher D. F. Fedorov, who had published a version of the novel based on the *Contemporary* translation in 1871 (*Khízhina diádi Tóma*, 2nd ed.), was a man of the book trade and no doubt familiar with a number of earlier editions of *Uncle Tom*.

31. Quotes from Stowe are from 1998 Oxford edition of *Uncle Tom's Cabin*.

32. Cf. "Khízhina diádi Tóma," *Russkii Vestnik* 13.2 (February 1858): 304. *Serfs* is translated properly as *krepostnye*.

33. Specifically: from "The nobles in Louis XVI's time" to Alfred's "Stuff!—nonsense!"

34. The quote is from the *Contemporary* edition, trans. Novosil'skii, et al.

35. The *Messenger* version seems to be based on another translation that I have yet to identify.

36. Trans. Novosil'skii et al. Apart from the shift from "canaille" to "Negroes," the diction of the Russian passage shows that it is based on the same Wailly/Texier French version.

Stowe, Gaskell, and the Woman Reformer

WHITNEY WOMACK SMITH

N SEPTEMBER 1853, Elizabeth Gaskell made her first trip to Haworth Parsonage to visit Charlotte Brontë. In her biography *The Life of Charlotte Brontë*, Gaskell reveals that during this meeting the two women discussed Harriet Beecher Stowe. The British public was abuzz over the publication of Stowe's novel *Uncle Tom's Cabin* as well as the American author's European tour. In 1853, the Glasgow Ladies' Anti-Slavery Society and the Glasgow Female New Association for the Abolition of Slavery invited Stowe to Great Britain to give a series of lectures on behalf of the U.S. anti-slavery movement. Gaskell had the opportunity to meet Stowe in June and described the encounter in a letter: "Oh! and I saw Mrs Stowe after all; I saw her twice; but only once to have a good long talk to her; then I was 4 or 5 hours with her, and liked her very much indeed. She is short and American in her manner, but very true & simple & thoroughly unspoiled and unspoil-able" (*Letters of Mrs. Gaskell* 237). In *Life*, Gaskell recalls that Brontë was eager to hear details about Stowe's personal appearance and pleased to learn that Stowe was "small and slight," much like Brontë herself (509).

It is fascinating to realize that two of England's most famous women novelists were caught up in the cultural phenomenon that the *Spectator* dubbed Tom-mania (Fisch, *American Slaves* 13). We know that Brontë read *Uncle Tom's Cabin* in mid 1852, just after unauthorized editions first began to appear in England. In a letter to publisher George Smith, Brontë heaped praise on the novel, claiming that "[I] voluntarily and sincerely veil my face before such a mighty subject as that handled in Mrs Beecher Stowe's work, 'Uncle Tom's Cabin.' . . . I doubt not, Mrs Stowe had felt the iron of slavery enter into her heart" (483). It is likely that Gaskell also read the novel in 1852 or, perhaps, in early 1853, given the fact that she so eagerly sought out a private audience with Stowe. The novel was widely accessible, leading the London *Times* to observe that *Uncle Tom's Cabin* seemed to be in "every railway book-stall in England, and in every third traveller's hand" (review 478). Its incredible sales in Great Britain—totaling more than one and a half million copies, three times the number sold in the United States—led the *Morning Chronicle* to proclaim that its "circulation . . . [is] a thing unparalleled in bookselling annals" (qtd. in Fisch, *American Slaves* 13). The novel's popularity spawned an early example of a merchandising tie-in; abolitionist groups and English shopkeepers sold mass-produced "Uncle Tom" goods, including almanacs, cups, picture books, card games, stationery, handkerchiefs, and dolls with likenesses of characters like Uncle Tom and Little Eva.

While we lack a record of what was said during Stowe and Gaskell's four- or five-hour conversation, certainly the two women writers had plenty to discuss, beginning with their remarkably parallel lives. Born less than a year apart, both women were the daughters and wives of ministers; both were deeply affected by the death of an infant son and turned to writing to help them through the grieving process; both juggled the demands of family and a literary career; and both had lived in regions—Manchester, England, and Cincinnati, Ohio—that made them witnesses to the human costs of oppressive laws and social policies. In addition, each woman wrote controversial novels protesting these injustices and yet managed to maintain her feminine respectability and largely avoid being labeled strong-minded, in part because of her marital status, as is clear in the frequent references in both the nineteenth and twentieth centuries to *Mrs.* Gaskell and *Mrs.* Stowe.

After this initial meeting, Stowe and Gaskell began a correspondence that lasted until at least 1860 and met in person two more times. During Stowe's 1857 European tour, the two women were the guests of the American sculptor William Wetmore Story, whose home served as a salon for visiting writers and artists.[1] Later that year Stowe was a guest at Plymouth Grove, Gaskell's Manchester home, and the two women attended the Manchester Art Treasures Exhibition together (Uglow 436). In a letter to her twin daughters, Stowe observed, "Mrs. Gaskell seems lovely at home, where besides being a writer she proves herself to be a first-class housekeeper, and performs all the duties of a minister's wife" (qtd. in Charles Stowe 312). Indeed Stowe thought so much of Gaskell and her writing that she proposed that they coauthor a travel narrative recounting their separate trips through Italy. In an 1860 letter, Stowe outlines the logistics of such a joint project; since copyright would need to be secured in England first, Gaskell would need to edit and prepare the manuscript for publication.[2] Stowe notes that if their accounts of places or events should differ, Gaskell should "let *both* be presented—there *are* two views often—both true[,] both important" (letter). We do not have a copy of a reply from Gaskell or knowledge of whether work on this project ever began; Gaskell died five years after this letter and no joint publication ever appeared. We are left with this tantalizing idea of a collaboration between two of the century's great women writers.

Mass publication and increasingly efficient transportation between England and America in the nineteenth century fostered such Anglo-American networks of literary exchange. Michael Winship observes that between 1828 and 1868 there was a "tremendous, even exponential growth in the international book trade," with British imports nearly tripling and American imports increasing by a factor of more than nine (99). Too often, though, literary and cultural critics leave unexplored the fact that the movement of literary production and influence was not only from England to the United States but also from the United States back to England, which is demonstrated and highlighted by the enormous popularity of *Uncle Tom's Cabin* in England. Paul Giles examines many examples of such "transnational convergence" and describes the Anglo-American literary relationship as one of "mirroring and twinning" (*Transatlantic Insurrections* 2). Richard Gravil even argues that studies continuing to ignore the impact of transatlanticism on both American and British literature in the nineteenth century are guilty of "offering a bowdlerized literary history" (xx).[3]

What I wish to do in this essay is examine the transatlantic relationship and literary exchange of Stowe and Gaskell, arguing that it was more significant and complex than their biographers and critics acknowledge. Scholars who have noted similarities between Stowe's and Gaskell's fiction, including Elizabeth Jean Sabiston, have worked under the assumption that the transmission went one way, that the composition of *Uncle Tom's Cabin* (1851–1852) was influenced by Gaskell's first industrial novel, *Mary Barton: A Tale of Manchester Life* (1848). I argue that we can chart a sort of fluid circulation or crossfertilization of ideas: while *Mary Barton* likely informed *Uncle Tom's Cabin*, I believe that reading *Uncle Tom's Cabin*, as well as meeting and corresponding with Stowe, may very well have shaped the way Gaskell approached the "Condition-of-England Question" in her second industrial novel, *North and South*, published serially from 1854 to 1855. Gaskell critics have long noted a major shift between *Mary Barton*, which ends without a resolution to the nation's industrial crisis, and *North and South*, which presents readers with Margaret Hale, a middle-class woman who transforms the role of Lady Bountiful charity-provider and fashions herself into a new breed of social reformer and class mediator. Many critics have examined literary and cultural factors that influenced Gaskell's decision to write a very different type of industrial novel, but they may have overlooked the possibility that *Uncle Tom's Cabin*, a text she read in the years between writing *Mary Barton* and *North and South*, may have provided her with images of middle-class women enacting the work of reform from the domestic sphere. With Margaret Hale, Gaskell takes Stowe's representation of women's reform work even further, allowing Margaret to negotiate and transcend the permeable barrier between separate spheres, extending the limits of women's political engagement. In these three novels, we witness Stowe and Gaskell engaging in a transatlantic, intertextual dialogue debating the roles that white, middle-class women can and should play in the work of social reform.

Gaskell's fiction, especially *Mary Barton*, almost certainly influenced Stowe's development as a social reform writer. Stowe was well aware of the tradition of the British industrial reform novel, which emerged in the 1820s and continued into the 1860s.[4] In 1844 she wrote the preface to the American edition of *The Works of Charlotte Elizabeth*, a three-volume collection containing Charlotte Elizabeth Tonna's industrial novels *Helen Fleetwood* and *The Wrongs of Woman*. Hedrick, in her biography of Stowe, discusses a letter Stowe wrote to Arthur Phelps in response to an article in *Fraser's Magazine* in which she explicitly compares the conditions of African chattel slaves and the "wage slaves" in industrial England, citing literary examples from works by Tonna, Dickens, and Kingsley (243). Stowe sought out introductions to a number of industrial reform writers; after meeting both Gaskell and Dickens in 1853, she arranged visits with Harriet Martineau and Charles Kingsley during her 1857 tour (264).

Stowe's attraction to the industrial reform novel tradition perhaps stemmed from the prominent roles that women played both as writers and characters. Joseph Kestner acknowledges that while the writers we have most commonly associated with this tradition—Disraeli, Kingsley, and Dickens—are men, it was in fact middle-class women writers—Frances Trollope, Martineau, Tonna, Gaskell, Brontë, and Eliot—who were the pioneering and sustaining force behind the industrial novel (3). Constance Harsh observes that both male- and female-authored industrial novels "make use of a potential source of power that Victorian society commonly ignored . . . :

women" (7). Industrial reform novels are replete with strong female characters who, despite limited and disenfranchised social positions, are empowered to speak out against social and political injustices. These characters both mirror and promote the work that scores of real-life women in both nations were doing through their membership in antislavery societies, the anti-Corn Law League, and other reform organizations.[5]

There is a pattern in industrial novels of establishing women and "women's values"—charity, empathy, compassion, and cooperation—as the antidotes to the evils of laissez-faire capitalism. Stowe employs a virtually identical strategy to address the scourge of slavery in *Uncle Tom's Cabin*. As Elizabeth Ammons explains, Stowe desired to make "the morality of women . . . the ethical and structural model for all of American life" ("Stowe's Dream" 159). This is clearly demonstrated in Stowe's essay "An Appeal to the Women of the Free States of America, on the Present Crisis in Our Country" (1854), in which she claims that to avoid the destruction of the nation, woman must "thoroughly understand the subject, and to feel that as a mother, wife, sister, or member of society, she is bound to give her influence to the right side." She concludes her appeal with a call to action: "let every woman of America now do her duty" (1).

Dickens was perhaps the first person to comment explicitly on the textual links between Gaskell's *Mary Barton* and Stowe's *Uncle Tom's Cabin*. In an 1852 letter, he expresses his admiration for the novel but notes that Stowe is "a leetle [sic] unscrupulous in the appropriation way. . . . I descry the Ghost of Mary Barton" (Dickens 808). *Mary Barton* was available, in an authorized edition published by Harper's and in countless unauthorized editions, in the United States as early as 1849, when a positive review appeared in the *Christian Examiner* (Easson 131). Indeed Gaskell was so well received by American audiences that when she died in 1865 the *Nation* published a moving obituary by their English correspondent Edward Dicey: "The ranks of our English novelists have sustained a heavy loss by the death of Mrs. Gaskell. . . . On your side [of] the Atlantic she must have numbered thousands of readers, as I have seen her novels in book-stalls all over the union" (qtd. in Easson 518). In an 1856 letter to Gaskell, Stowe notes that her twin daughters had recently finished reading *North and South* and reflects on her own reading of *Mary Barton*, writing "You made me cry very unfairly over Mary Barton when I bought the book to amuse myself with on a journey—but I bear no malice for that" (Waller 65–66). Stowe's remarks establish that she had read Gaskell's first novel sometime in the past, though we cannot determine with absolute certainty whether this was before or after the composition of *Uncle Tom's Cabin*.

Twentieth-century critics have continued to note parallels between these novels. Robyn Warhol compares Gaskell's and Stowe's shared use of the "engaging narrator," a rhetorical device in which the narrator speaks directly to readers ("you"), compelling them into sympathetic identification with working-class or enslaved characters, with the intention that these emotional appeals will move readers to tears and motivate them to engage in social action (103). In *Mary Barton*, for example, Gaskell urges her middle-class readership to stop ignoring the oppressed workers they pass on the street: "You may push against one, humble and unnoticed, the last upon earth, who in Heaven will for ever be in the immediate light of God's countenance" (101–102). Stowe, in turn, repeatedly appeals to the "mothers of America" to identify with the plight of slave mothers. She writes her most passionate entreaty in the final chapter of *Uncle Tom's Cabin*:

> And you, mothers of America—you who have learned, by the cradles of your own children, to love and feel for all mankind . . . —I beseech you, pity the mother who has all your affections, and not one legal right to protect, guide, or educate the child of her bosom! By the sick hour of your child; by those dying eyes, which you can never forget; by those last cries, that wrung your heart when you could neither help nor salve; by the desolation of that empty cradle, that silent nursery,—I beseech you, pity those mothers that are constantly made childless by the American slave-trade! And say, mothers of America, is this a thing to be defended, sympathized with, passed over in silence? (384)

Catherine O'Connell explains that Stowe had faith that she could effect a "sentimental transformation" in her readers, believing that "anyone who truly undergoes a change of heart will necessarily act on his or her beliefs" (17). Importantly, both Gaskell and Stowe speak directly to white women readers as citizens with a stake in the nation and with the power to produce change.

Elizabeth Jean Sabiston makes additional textual connections between the novels, showing the similarities between the Mary-Jem subplot in *Mary Barton* and the Eliza-George subplot in *Uncle Tom's Cabin*. In both novels the couple escapes their oppressive circumstances by emigrating to Canada, presented as a land of freedom and opportunity, without the race and class prejudices inherent in American and British culture. In addition, Sabiston argues that both novels highlight the destructive effects of slavery and industrial capitalism on the lives of women, particularly the ways these systems separate and destroy family life and proper domesticity. We need only think of Susan having her daughter Emmeline ripped from her bosom and sold to Simon Legree in "The Slave Warehouse" chapter of *Uncle Tom's Cabin* or Mrs. Davenport forced to watch her children die of typhus because she can't afford a doctor in *Mary Barton*. These wrenching scenes challenge middle-class female readers—many of whom, like Gaskell and Stowe, knew first-hand the pain of losing a child—to identify and empathize with the enslaved and working-class women in the texts.

While the title character of *Mary Barton* is an active, strong-minded, and resilient young woman who acts as the caretaker of her family and community, Gaskell suggests that her working-class status makes it impossible for her to be an agent of social reform, arguing instead that middle-class women are the ones who should embody this role. Both Gaskell and Stowe believe that middle-class women should possess a heightened morality and sympathy for the oppressed people around them. In *Mary Barton*, Gaskell castigates middle-class women for not stepping forward and helping Manchester's workers. John Barton describes this type of woman as a "do-nothing lady, worrying shopmen all morning, and screeching at her pianny all afternoon, and going to bed without having done a good turn to any one of God's creatures but herself" (44). She paints a vivid portrait of the middle-class Mrs. Carson and her daughters, who live in a state of "mental and bodily idleness," drowsily sitting around the drawing-room wasting the hours until tea-time, in sharp contrast to the punishing lives of women working in the factories (254). In a poignant scene, John Barton stares at the "haunches of venison" and "Stilton cheeses" in a shop window and contemplates stealing them in order to feed his hungry family (61). At that moment, Mrs. Hunter, the wife of the mill owner who had recently laid off Barton and hundreds of other workers, breezes out of the shop loaded down with purchases for a party, completely oblivious to the suffering man standing before her. As Pamela Corpron Parker explains, "Mrs. Hunter's quick retreat into the privacy of her carriage represents the broader abdication of social responsibility by the wealthy industrialists and the specific failure of feminine duty" ("Fictional Philanthropy" 326). When middle-class women abandon their social duties, Gaskell argues, there is no hope of reforming society; the novel ends with Mary and Jem escaping the industrial world. Raymond Williams declares that there cannot be "a more devastating conclusion" to this novel since Gaskell seems to write off Manchester as a lost cause, a world beyond redemption (91).

Stowe responds to Gaskell's call for middle-class women to take action, and in *Uncle Tom's Cabin* presents readers with multiple examples of middle-class, white women who will not ignore the pain and suffering of others and who are willing to undermine patriarchal authority, break the law, and even sacrifice their own bodies in order to end chattel slavery. Jean Fagan Yellin explains that the central issue of the novel is "the moral dilemma of *white* Americans who must decide how to act in the face of the 1850 Fugitive Slave Law. . . . Repeatedly the free white individuals faced with these moral dilemmas are women" ("Doing It Herself" 85). According to Clare Midgley, Stowe promotes the rather problematic idea that white women possess the "philanthropic and missionary power to bring freedom and Christianity to grateful black slaves" (146). While Stowe envisions a powerful place for women in the abolitionist debate, it is one that is largely restricted to the private sphere and the work of influence. In this respect, Stowe echoes the reality of many real-life women abolitionists in both America and Great Britain who, as Charlotte Sussman explains, did much of their work in parlors and drawing rooms and justified their political activities as "sanctioned by a morality emanating from the 'private' sphere of domesticity" (131). Jane Tompkins argues that Stowe uses this rhetoric of domesticity as a direct challenge to the traditional hierarchies of patriarchal society: "Stowe relocates the center of power in American life, placing it not on the government, nor in courts of law, nor in the factories, nor in the marketplace, but in the kitchen" (*Sensational Designs* 145). Similarly, Gillian Brown asserts that Stowe imagines "the replacement of the market economy by a matriarchal domestic economy" (*Domestic Individualism* 24). In *The American Woman's Home* (1869), coauthored by Stowe and Catharine Beecher, women are imagined to possess an almost divine power within the domestic sphere: "[t]he family state then, is the aptest earthly illustration of the heavenly kingdom, and in it woman is its chief minister" (19).[6]

Uncle Tom's Cabin opens with one such "minister," Emily Shelby, the compassionate wife of a Kentucky plantation owner who abhors the peculiar institution and refuses to ignore injustices, in contrast to the middle-class women in *Mary Barton*. A pious woman, Mrs. Shelby has brought up all of her slaves as Christians, despite Mr. Shelby's belief that religious notions are "extremely unfitted for people in that condition" (220). She even arranges for a Christian wedding ceremony for Eliza and George, although slave marriages were not sanctioned by law (220). Mrs. Shelby is heartbroken when she learns her husband's plan to sell Tom and Harry, as if she were being separated from her own kin, and laments her own part in perpetuating the institution of slavery: "I was a fool to think I could make anything good out of such a deadly evil. It is a sin to hold a slave under laws like ours,—I always felt it was,—I always thought so when I was a girl,—I thought so still more after I joined the church; but I thought I could gild it over,—I thought, by kindness, and care, and instruction, I could make the condition of mine better than freedom—fool that I was!" (29). When Mr. Shelby accuses his wife of sounding like a Yankee abolitionist, she retorts: "Abolitionist! if they know all I know about slavery they *might* talk! We don't need them to tell us; you know I never thought that slavery was right—never felt willing to own slaves" (29–30). Because her family has a vested financial interest in slavery and because of her disenfranchisement, the benevolent Mrs. Shelby is at a loss; she has no means by which to prevent the sale of Harry and Tom. She does, however, prevent the heartless Haley from catching up to Eliza and Harry by covert means. Using "every female artifice," she prolongs the slave trader Mr. Haley's dinner and encourages her slaves not to ride the horses too quickly, thus slowing down the search party by several hours, allowing Eliza and Harry to cross the Ohio River and begin their long journey to freedom in Canada (49).

Stowe also introduces us to Mrs. Bird, a middle-class Northern woman who employs feminine "entreaty and persuasion" in order to reform the views of her husband, the senator, who stands as a representative of the all-male legislature (68). Throughout the novel Stowe uses domestic conditions as a sort of barometer to measure the character and morality of the inhabitants of the home.[7] Chapter nine, "In Which It Appears that a Senator Is but a Man," opens with an idealized domestic tableau:

> The light of the cheerful fire shone on the rug and carpet of a cosey parlor, and glittered on the sides of the tea-cups and well-brimmed tea-pot, as Senator Bird was drawing off his boots, preparatory to inserting his feet in a pair of new handsome slippers, which his wife had been working for him while away on his senatorial tour. Mrs. Bird, looking the very picture of delight, was superintending the arrangements of the table, ever and anon mingling admonitory remarks to a number of frolicsome juveniles. (67)

The warm, inviting home the domestic Mrs. Bird has created stands in stark contrast to the cold, calculating, masculine "house of the State," from which

Senator Bird has just returned. When Mrs. Bird learns that her husband has voted in favor of the Fugitive Slave Act, she lets him know that she is not willing to obey what she believes is a "shameful, wicked, abominable law" (77). The senator teases Mrs. Bird about her position and belittles her by calling her a "fair politician," but she insists that, whatever the consequences, she will engage in civil disobedience if she is ever in the position to help a runaway slave. She pledges her allegiance not to man-made laws, but instead to a higher law:

> "Now, John, I don't know anything about politics, but I can read my Bible; and there I see that I must feed the hungry, clothe the naked, and comfort the desolate; and that Bible I mean to follow."
> "But in cases where your doing so would involve a great public evil—"
> "Obeying God never brings on public evils. I know it can't. It's always safest all around to do as He bids us." (69)

Such appeals to Christianity and higher authority were commonly made by women abolitionists; as Sussman explains, "in order for antislavery feelings to conform with 'propriety' and 'feminine modesty,' they had to be coded as part of the feminine realm of religion and morality, rather than as part of the masculine sphere of politics" (138).

It is just after this conversation that the fugitives Eliza and Harry appear at the Birds' door seeking asylum, which challenges Mrs. Bird to put her words into actions and act as benefactress. Eliza appeals to Mrs. Bird's maternal sympathies, asking "have you ever lost a child?" (72). She speaks to Mrs. Bird as one mother to another, not as a black slave to a white lady, emphasizing the common bonds of womanhood that cut across racial divides. The Birds, who have only recently buried a child, are all affected by Eliza's speech; even the senator has to gulp back tears. This sentimental scene provides a critical test for the senator, who only the week before had been "spurring up the legislature of his native state to pass more stringent resolutions against escaping fugitives, their harborers and abettors" (76–77). Catherine O'Connell argues that the conversion of Senator Bird, a man with "public responsibilities and allegiance to an unemotional or even antiemotional epistemology," proves the power of his wife's arguments and Eliza's sentimental appeals (16). In the end, the senator violates the very law he helped to pass, becoming a "political sinner" by giving Harry his dead son's clothes and Eliza ten dollars and risking his reputation and freedom by driving them to a safehouse. We see Stowe's vision of how women's moral suasion from within the domestic circle can influence men and ultimately effect social reforms.

Stowe also imagines a white female child, Eva St. Clare, in the role of domestic benefactress and savior figure. Eva is the daughter of a heartless and cruel plantation mistress who, Stowe implies, should be working to help slaves rather than adding to their misery and exploitation. Marie St. Clare is a bad housekeeper, a bad Christian, and a bad mother, the antithesis of proper, domestic women reformers like Emily Shelby and Mary Bird and Rachel Halliday. Her daughter, however, has an emotional and spiritual tie to the slaves on their plantation and can feel their pain and suffering; she tells Uncle Tom that "these things sink into my heart" (204). Although only a child, Eva acts as a sort of mother-figure to her family's slaves and fulfills the role of maternal benefactress. Her maternal impulses are manifested by her "adoption" of Uncle Tom after he rescues her from drowning and her desire to educate her "children." She tells her mother that she would like to establish a boarding school for the slaves: "I'd teach them to read their own Bible, and write their own letters, and read letters written to them. . . . I know, mamma, it does come very hard on them that they can't do these things" (230). Eva's emotional connection and physical displays of affection toward her "children" shocks her cousin Miss Ophelia, a New Englander and purported abolitionist: "Eva flew from one to another, shaking hands and kissing, in ways that Miss Ophelia afterwards declared fairly turned her stomach" (143).

Little Eva's inevitable death is foreshadowed when the engaging narrator of *Uncle Tom's Cabin* asks readers if there "has ever been a child like Eva?" and answers, "Yes, there have been; but their names are all on gravestones" (227). When Eva falls ill with consumption, she expresses a Christ-like willingness to sacrifice herself in the name of social change: "I've felt that I would be glad to die, if my dying could stop all this misery. I would die for them, Tom, if I could" (240). On her deathbed, she presents each slave a lock of hair, a symbol of her bodily sacrifice: "I'm going to give you a curl of my hair; and, when you look at it, think that I loved you and am gone to heaven, and that I want to see you all there" (251). As Tompkins notes, Eva's death does not lead to the sudden collapse of the slave system or even to the freedom of her beloved Uncle Tom, who is sold down the river after Mr. St. Clare's death, but it does have a lasting effect on its witnesses, initiating "a process of redemption, whose power, transmitted from heart to heart, can change the entire world" (*Sensational Designs* 130–31). Stowe's decision to create this idealized and sentimental portrait of the "little evangelist" may undercut the more realistic but less theatrical efforts of reform-minded characters like Mrs. Shelby and Mrs. Bird.

In *Uncle Tom's Cabin*, Stowe suggests that middle-class women are vital to the success of the antislavery cause, but she ultimately places limitations on them and their domestic-centered reforms. Even Eva, her idealized reformer, is only able to influence others and brighten the life of Uncle Tom; she lacks the ability to save him or end the misery of other Southern slaves. In the end it is still men, albeit men like George Shelby whose opinions have been shaped and altered by reform-minded women, who are authorized to go into the public sphere in order to make legal and political reforms. As Michael Borgstrom explains, Stowe, like her sister Catharine, implicitly believed that "the logic of separate spheres is indispensable to the abolitionist movement" (1298). Undoubtedly, these representations were also a reflection of Stowe's own reticence about female public appearance and public speaking, based in large part on her desire to "cultivate an outward posture of true womanhood" (Hedrick 239). During her European tours, for instance, Stowe's husband or brother would deliver her public addresses (or often their own lectures), while she sat by silently in the ladies' gallery, often to the dismay of the audience who had come to hear from the voice of the author herself.[8] At the same time Stowe clearly reveals that, contrary to popular belief, the "woman's sphere" is inherently politicized; there is no place in this novel that is immune to the infection of slavery. In addition, as Rosemarie Garland Thomson notes, all of the white women reformers in the novel benefit from their reform work, gaining "dignity, agency, and self-determination by acting maternally toward members of a devalued group" (563).

Both Stowe and Gaskell agree that middle-class women have social, moral, and religious responsibilities to protest against injustices. But the question remains: how far outside the domestic sphere can a woman reformer go while still retaining her moral authority and virtue? In *North and South*, Gaskell tests the physical and ideological boundaries presented in *Uncle Tom's Cabin*, foregrounding and ultimately expanding the roles that Stowe imagines for middle-class women. In the process, Gaskell negotiates the cultural and political landscape open to women reformers. According to Parker, Gaskell frequently "strained the limits of women's culturally-prescribed roles and frequently opposed male-controlled public discourses" ("Constructing Female Public Identity" 68). While there is a marked absence of middle-class women reformers in *Mary Barton*, *North and South* focuses on a single middle-class woman, Margaret Hale, whose work helps mend the class divisions in England's industrial North.

Since its publication, reviewers and critics have noted the significant shift in focus between Gaskell's two industrial reform novels. Gaskell embarked on this later project at least in part to appease contemporary critics who charged her with misrepresenting factory owners in *Mary Barton*. As Jenny Uglow explains, *Mary Barton* "sparked off furious arguments, especially, of course, in Manchester," the setting of the novel as well as Gaskell's home (214). The critic W. R. Greg, a fellow resident of Manchester and an acquaintance of the Gaskells, lambasted the novel in the *Edinburgh Review*, claiming that she exaggerated class animosities and unfairly treated factory owners, many of whom were members of William Gaskell's congregation at Cross Street Church (402–405). Because Gaskell attempts to present a more balanced, holistic view of industrial society in her latter novel, critics like Raymond Williams have asserted that *North and South* "is less interesting, because the tension is less" (91). Along with scholars like Patsy Stoneman and Pearl Brown, I argue that *North and South* is in fact in many ways a more, not less, radical novel, especially in its depiction of women's reform and its vision of a gendered reorganization of industrial society, since the female protagonist is able to attain a position of power and authority and even bring her reforms onto the public stage, something that Stowe's reformers are never able to do.

Margaret Hale's social conscience is awakened when she is transplanted from the rural South to Milton-Northern, a northern city reminiscent of Gaskell's Manchester, following her father's crisis of faith and decision to leave his position as a minister in the Church of England. The rest of the narrative focuses on Margaret's navigation and negotiation of this unfamiliar world. Gaskell sets up the industrial North of England as a sort of free zone for Margaret, where she is able to transcend the gender and class boundaries that had limited her in the South, with its set ways, and carve out a new space for herself in the public arena. During her first days in Milton-Northern, Margaret, in violation of all she has been taught, enters the public sphere alone. She goes into the town center to make housekeeping arrangements and hire a suitable servant girl, a difficult task in a mill town where girls can earn better wages working in factories. Margaret is shocked by the bold actions of working-class women and the forward comments of working men about her appearance, remarks that "made her face scarlet, and her dark eyes gather flame" (72). But Margaret soon realizes that the workers' com-

ments—such as "Your bonny face, my lass, makes the day look brighter"—
are made out of genuine kindness and a lack of understanding of the "common rules of street politeness," not out of malice or lechery (72). Ultimately,
Margaret gains confidence and a sense of independence from these encounters and comes to appreciate the flux and vitality of her new environment.

Margaret soon adopts the crucial—and at times public—role of transla-
tor and class mediator, working to bring together "masters and men" and
promote cooperation and reconciliation. When she meets the working-class
Higgins family, Margaret learns that she must rethink her old assumptions
about charitable work. After making the acquaintance of the middle-aged
weaver Nicholas Higgins and his disabled Bessy in a public space (a field on
the outskirts of Milton), Margaret asks for their address so that she can make
a Lady Bountiful–style home visit, which in the South would have "been an
understood thing" (112). As a vicar's daughter in rural Helstone, Margaret
was used to visiting the poor in her father's parish, bringing baskets of food,
moral lessons, and kind words. But Nicholas, a man of pride and dignity,
reads Margaret's inquiries as impertinence and informs her that "I'm none
too fond having strange folk in my house" (113). She is welcome only when
Nicholas extends his own invitation, which he seems to grant primarily out
of pity to the newcomer—"yo' may come if yo' like" (113). Margaret is forced
to confront the reality that a Lady Bountiful approach is, according to
Dorice Williams Elliott, "both inappropriate and ineffective in dealing with
the urban working classes" and would do little to reform a system based on
the "cash nexus" (32).

By stopping and listening to the Higginses rather than condescending to
them, Margaret learns about the conflicts between workers and the factory
owners. For instance, Margaret discovers that Bessy, who in many ways
functions as Margaret's working-class twin, is dying of a lung disease common among cotton mill workers caused by the "fluff" in the carding rooms.
Bessy explains, "I began to work in the carding-room soon after, that the
fluff got into my lungs and poisoned me. . . . Little bits, as fly off fro' the cotton when they're carding, and fill the air till it looks all fine white dust. They
say it winds round the lungs, and tightens them up. Anyhow, there's many a
one as works in the carding-room, that falls into a waste, coughing and spit-
ting blood, because they're just poisoned by fluff" (146). The masters can
prevent fluff from getting into workers' lungs by investing in a machine that
would disperse the fibers and improve ventilation, but they are unwilling to
do so because it would cost "five or six hundred pound, maybe, and bring in

no profit" (146). Ironically it is not only the masters who oppose the purchase of this machine but also many of the workers who have grown accustomed to having the fluff cut their hunger pangs: "I've heerd tell o'men who didn't like working in places where there was a wheel, because they said as how it made 'em hungry at after they'd been long used to swallowing fluff, to go without it" (146).

Because of her middle-class status, Margaret is also able to forge a relationship with factory owner John Thornton, a self-made man who has fully adopted the laissez-faire attitudes of industrial capitalists. Elliott describes the Milton section of *North and South* as a "series of debates, of contrasting scenes, of alternated speeches" (42): we see Margaret with the Higginses, then with the Thorntons, and back again, as she straddles the worlds of masters and men. From Thornton, Margaret learns the masters' positions on trade and manufacturing. Early on Margaret echoes Gaskell's preface to *Mary Barton*, remarking she is no "political economist," but she is a remarkably quick study (126).[9] By the time she attends a dinner party at the Thorntons' house (ironically held while his workers are near starvation), Margaret finds herself far more comfortable taking part in the men's conversation concerning the threat of the upcoming strike than she is sitting with the ladies, who only employ "themselves in taking notes of the dinner and criticizing each other's dresses" (215). At the same time Margaret never forgets Bessy's and Nicholas's struggles and acts as their agent and mouthpiece. She repeatedly questions and challenges Thornton's justifications of laissez-faire policies and objections to governmental or philanthropic interventions. Thornton argues that the "owners of capital"—including human capital—ought to have the absolute right to do what they like, and he resents Parliamentary meddling (164); his arguments sound much like the proslavery, anti-Congress arguments offered by Southerners in *Uncle Tom's Cabin*. Margaret's "whole soul" rises up when Thornton coldly acts "as if commerce were everything and humanity nothing" (204). Thornton justifies his "despotism" in the factory by comparing his "hands" (as he insists on calling them) to unruly children, both of whom must be governed by a wise parent with a firm hand—another clear connection to proslavery ideology (167). Margaret replies by citing a story of a forty-year-old man kept in a childlike state by an overprotective father; when the father dies, the "great old child was turned loose in the world," where he was unable to discern "good from evil" and had to be rescued from starvation (168). While Stowe's reform figures rely on appeals to emotion to persuade other characters and readers, Margaret shows she is adept at using reason and logic. Both Rosemarie Bodenheimer and Constance Harsh contend that with this dialogue Gaskell effectively undermines the paternalistic metaphor of class relations regularly employed in the Victorian era.

For the majority of the novel, Margaret's reform work takes place, as in *Uncle Tom's Cabin*, primarily in the protection of the private sphere, in the Higgins, Hale, or Thornton households. But her efforts make a shift into the public in the climactic riot scene, where a mob of angry workers who have been "turned out" surround Thornton's home and factory. Margaret boldly steps onto the public stage, asserting that middle-class, reform-minded women have a right to embody this space. When earlier in the novel Mrs. Thornton urged Margaret "to have a brave heart," Margaret replied, "I do not know whether I am brave or not till I am tried" (163); the strike, then, is Margaret's trial, the kind that Stowe's women reformers never truly face. When she arrives at the Thornton home, she learns from John's sister Fanny that hundreds of Milton workers are planning to storm the mill in protest at Thornton's decision to import "Irish starvelings" to take their places; within minutes they are at the gate and threatening the safety of the factory and the attached Thornton home (228). These men have broken ranks with the union's leadership (including Nicholas Higgins), which adamantly opposes "rioting and breaking laws" (366). Inside the barricaded house, the frightened and vulnerable women watch the spectacle unfold. Fanny reacts in a characteristically feminine way by having hysterics and then fainting, and even the strong-willed Mrs. Thornton trembles and urges the women to retreat to the upper floors. Gaskell uses the language of sexual violation in this scene, as the women attempt to escape the intrusion and penetration of animalistic working men—who are described as "wolves . . . mad for prey" (233)—into their domestic space (Harman 63).

While the Thornton women hide in the house, Margaret insists that she has the right, even the responsibility, to be in the thick of the action; we can only imagine what may have happened if Mrs. Shelby or Mrs. Bird or even Little Eva had left the domestic sphere and directly confronted slave owners or traders. Margaret urges Thornton, who is waiting for the militia to arrive, to face the striking workers:

> "Mr Thornton," said Margaret, shaking all over with her passion, "go down this instant, if you are not a coward. Go down and face them *like a man*. Save these poor strangers [the Irish], whom you have decoyed here. Speak to your

workmen as if they were human beings. Speak to them kindly. Don't let the soldiers come in and cut down poor creatures who are driven mad. I see one there who already is. If you have any courage or noble quality in you, go out and speak to them, man to man!" (232, emphasis mine)

Margaret chides Thornton to "act like a man," not to hide in the house like a coward—or a woman. When Margaret realizes that Thornton is in real danger, that the workers are armed with rocks and clogs and poised for violence, she throws off her bonnet and steps onto the public stage beside him, enacting what Elaine Hadley calls "theatricalized dissent" (2):

> The hootings rose and filled the air,—but Margaret did not hear them. Her eye was on the group of lads who had armed themselves with their clogs some time before. She saw their gesture—she knew its meaning,—she read their aim. Another moment, and Mr Thornton might be smitten down,—he whom she had urged and goaded to come to this perilous place. She only thought of how she could save him. She threw her arms around him; she made her body into a shield from the fierce people beyond. Still, with his arms folded, he shook her off.
> "Go away," said he, in his deep voice. "This is no place for you."
> "It is!" said she. (234)

Bodenheimer reads the riot scene as a "fantasy of female social rescue" in which women, by virtue of their very womanhood, are able to save society: "[Margaret's] imperious maternal instincts, a proof of Margaret's special courage, demand that we redefine women as strong protectors" (65).

At the same time that Gaskell affirms the right of middle-class women to enter the public sphere in the name of reform, she also reveals its dangers. Margaret is struck with a stone almost certainly meant for Thornton: "A sharp pebble flew by her, grazing forehead and cheek, and drawing a blinding sheet of light before her eyes. She lay like dead on Mr Thornton's shoulder" (235). The spectacle of an unconscious woman, with a "thread of dark-red blood" streaming down her face awakens the men from "their trance of passion" and causes them to retreat (235). Margaret's wounds can be seen as a bodily sacrifice, an interesting counterpoint to Little Eva's willing sacrifice of her life for the antislavery cause. Margaret puts both her body and her reputation on the line since, as Barbara Leah Harman notes, "everyone (including Thornton) reads her actions in sexual terms," equating her with another transgressive figure—the fallen woman (65–66).[10] Despite the questions about her feminine modesty, Margaret vehemently defends her actions at the riot and by extension defends the rights of women to act publicly when necessary to address social wrongs: "I would do it again. . . . If I saved one blow, one cruel angry action that might otherwise have been committed I did a woman's work. Let them insult my maiden pride as they will—I walk pure before God!" (188). Gaskell does not sugarcoat Margaret's public appearance, acknowledging its potential pitfalls as well as its benefits. As Harman explains, the incident at the mill seems to confirm what "critics of female emancipation tended to fear—that access to public life means access to potentially dangerous kinds of sexual intimacy for women" (75). Yet Gaskell ultimately does not believe the "danger of public life [is] a reason to exclude women from it," and in fact Margaret emerges as a heroic figure (75).

Margaret's "woman's work" leads to real, concrete improvements in Milton-Northern. Through her influence, Thornton discards his misguided paternalism and changes the way he runs the mill and constructs a workers' dining hall. As Catherine Gallagher notes, the dining-hall scheme is an example of how private, domestic values are used to improve the public sphere (77). In this quasi-domestic space within the factory, Thornton comes to a profound realization about the humanity of the people he once cavalierly discounted as "hands": "Once brought face to face, man to man, with an individual of the masses around him, and (take notice) *out* of the character of master and workman, in the first instance, they had begun to recognize that 'we have all of us one human heart'" (511). This one improvement, Gaskell implies, will lead to a stronger bond between management and workers:

> And thence arose that intercourse, which though it might not have the effect of preventing all future clash of opinion and action, when the occasion arose, would, at any rate, enable both master and man to look upon each other with far more charity and sympathy, and bear with each other more patiently and kindly. Besides this improvement in feeling, both Mr. Thornton and his workmen found out their ignorance as to positive matters of fact, known heretofore to one side, but not to the other. (512–513)

Soon after she initiates these reform efforts, Margaret departs Milton-Northern following the deaths of her parents, leaving her future role as a reformer in doubt. In *Mary Barton* the only solution to the industrial crisis is escape, as Mary and Jem seek a new life in Canada. In *North and South*, Gaskell has Margaret leave only to return with a renewed sense of purpose and a conviction that she can right the social wrongs of industrial capitalism. When she goes back to the South of England, she does not find it to be a preindustrial paradise; instead, during her visit to rural Helstone, she sees poverty, superstition, and stagnation among the agrarian workers and comes away disenchanted. In London with her fashionable relations, Margaret finds something wanting, feeling that she has "drifted strangely from [her] former anchorage" in Milton (496). Finding herself "wearied with the inactivity of the day" in Harley Street, Margaret seeks to continue her reform efforts by visiting the poor, though presumably without the Lady Bountiful attitude she once held. Her cousin Edith expresses fear for Margaret's safety and propriety: "I'm sure I'm always expecting to hear of her having met with something horrible among all those wretched places she pokes into. I should never dare go down some of those streets without a servant. They're not fit for ladies" (520).

When Margaret unexpectedly inherits a large fortune from her godfather, her newfound economic power enables her to reclaim her role as reformer and ultimately to move back to Milton. Her first step is to save Thornton's factory, which has fallen on hard times due to downturns in trade with the United States; here Gaskell makes an overt reference to the interconnections of the British and American economies. Significantly, Margaret demonstrates her business savvy by arranging with an attorney to lend Thornton the money, ensuring that "the principal advantage would be on her side" in this arrangement (529). With the loan, Margaret saves Thornton, recreating her role as rescuer at the workers' riot, and allows him to continue his "experiments" with the workers at Marlborough Mills. Parker correctly points out that according to Victorian laws, "Margaret's marriage vows will transfer all legal control of her property and capital to Thornton" ("Fictional Philanthropy" 330). But the legal contract protects Margaret's interests (at least the £18,057 she lends him) and serves in effect as a sort of "prenuptial agreement" (330). Critics read very differently the conclusion of the novel, which fulfills the marriage plot as Thornton proposes to Margaret in the final scene. Some imagine marriage as the inevitable end of Margaret's reform efforts and public role, as an effort to silence her public speech and push her back into the private sphere (Lenard 132). Others envision Margaret continuing her work as a sort of "evangelist of reconciliation," functioning as a model of the philanthropic capitalist (Krueger 206–207).

In either case, Margaret's public appearances cannot be taken back or forgotten. We can apply Susan K. Harris's theory of the "subversive middles" in American women's writing (*Nineteenth-Century*); although *North and South* may begin and end conventionally, it is actually the middle of the text where

Gaskell posits her more radical views about women's reform work. Importantly, we have a real sense of social change and reconciliation that is largely absent from both *Mary Barton* and even from *Uncle Tom's Cabin*; Mary and Jem are compelled to emigrate to Canada to start a new life while Eliza and George Harris emigrate to Liberia to escape the prejudices they find in all of North America. But in *North and South*, no one is forced to leave; with Margaret's help, Nicholas can remain in Milton and build a better life (though, of course, Bessy dies before Margaret's reforms are enacted). In fact, the only one to leave, briefly, is Margaret after the death of her parents, though her wedding to Thornton will bring her back to Milton-Northern. Arguably, though, Margaret Hale's activism ameliorates the conditions of middle-class women like herself as much, or more, than it helps the working classes.

Over the course of these three novels, we witness how Gaskell and Stowe write women into the larger narrative of social reform and chart the evolution of the figure of the middle-class woman reformer in mid-nineteenth-century Anglo-American literature and culture. Gaskell and Stowe grant their female characters increasing voice, agency, and self-determination, imagining them righting the social wrongs of England and the United States and, in the process, widening women's spheres of influence and activity. Indeed, it can be argued that all three novels are as much about gender, the nineteenth-century "Woman Question," as they are about slavery or industrial capitalism. Gaskell and Stowe's personal relationship compels us to consider the reciprocal influences between these two authors, especially the ways in which *Uncle Tom's Cabin* may have provided Gaskell with ideas for her model of the female social reformer in *North and South*. The transnational intertextuality of these novels also challenges us to rethink our assumptions about the literary and cultural boundaries dividing England and America in the nineteenth century, as well as the national boundaries that continue to divide contemporary literary scholarship. In this context, Stowe can be understood, to borrow Benedict Anderson's term, as part of an "imagined community" of writers and social activists influenced by and influencing women writers in Europe as well as the United States.

Notes

1. Quotes from *Uncle Tom's Cabin* in this essay are from the 1994 Norton edition; quotes from *American Woman's Home* are from the 1971 Arno edition; and quotes from Uglow are from the New York 1993 edition. Both Jenny Uglow's *Elizabeth Gaskell: A*

Habit of Stories and Joan Hedrick's *Harriet Beecher Stowe: A Life* recount this meeting in Italy, where Stowe entertained guests at Story's salon with her imitation, in dialect, of the abolitionist Sojourner Truth who had recently visited Stowe at Stone Cabin. According to Charles Edward Norton, the American community in Italy, especially the Southerners among them, were not particularly welcoming of Stowe: "The American Eagle is ruffled here a good deal by Mrs. Stowe's presence" (qtd. in Uglow 423).

2. Michael Winship provides an overview of the complexities of international copyright laws in his article "The Transatlantic Book Trade and Anglo-American Literary Culture in the Nineteenth Century" (101–102).

3. Transatlantic studies has developed into a significant field in the last decade, strengthened by the creation of two major journals, *Symbiosis: A Journal of Anglo-American Literary Relations* and the *Journal of Transatlantic Studies*. Among the important recent studies in the field are Gravil's *Romantic Dialogues: Anglo-American Continuities, 1776–1862*, Giles's *Transatlantic Insurrections: British Culture and the Formation of American Literature (1730–1860)*, and Will Kaufman and Heidi Macpherson's collection *Transatlantic Studies*.

4. Among the important studies of this subgenre are Catherine Gallagher's *The Industrial Reformation of English Fiction*, Joseph Kestner's *Protest and Reform: The British Social Narrative by Women*, Barbara Leah Harman's *The Feminine Political Novel*, and Constance Harsh's *Subversive Heroines: Feminist Resolutions of Social Crisis in the Condition-of-England Novel*. None of these studies, however, examine the industrial reform novel in a transatlantic or transnational context.

5. There are many excellent histories of mid-nineteenth-century women's reform work, including Claire Midgley's *Women Against Slavery: The British Campaigns, 1780–1870*; Kathryn Gleadle and Sarah Richardson's *Women in British Politics, 1760–1860: The Power of the Petticoat*; Charlotte Sussman's *Consuming Anxieties: Consumer Protest, Gender, and British Slavery, 1713–1833*; Susan Zaeske's *Signatures of Citizenship: Petitioning, Antislavery, and Women's Political Identity*; Jean Fagan Yellin and John C. Van Horne's collection *The Abolitionist Sisterhood: Women's Political Culture in Antebellum America*; and Lori D. Ginzberg's *Women and the Work of Benevolence: Morality, Politics, and Class in the Nineteenth-Century United States*.

6. Catharine Beecher was a crucial figure in the debate surrounding women's roles in the abolitionist movement. In response to Angelina Grimké's influential tract *An Appeal to the Christian Women of the South* (1836), in which Grimké advocates women's leadership in the cause, Beecher published *An Essay on Slavery and Abolition, with Reference to the Duty of American Females, Addressed to A. E. Grimké* (1836), asserting women should limit their expression to the domestic sphere and avoid unfeminine tasks like petitioning or public speaking.

7. In contrast to the proper domesticity found in the Bird and Halliday households, and even in Uncle Tom and Aunt Chloe's poor but neatly kept cabin, Stowe presents Simon Legree's plantation, which represents the complete bastardization of the domestic household. Legree violates all of the basic tenets of domesticity: he has no wife to organize and manage his household; he does not have a kitchen, the very "heart" of a

home; and he does not separate his home from the world of commerce and profit-making, defacing the wallpaper of his home with "chalk memorandums, and long sums footed up" (320). The disrepair of Legree's house is the physical manifestation of his corrupt moral character.

8. While Stowe was much beloved in England, her husband Calvin was not a popular figure. He was lampooned by the British press for his speeches and eventually cut short his trip, allowing Harriet and the rest of the party to go on to the Continent without him. The abolitionist women who were entertaining Harriet expressed their pleasure in the fact that her "bungling husband" was out of the way (Hedrick 242).

9. In her preface to *Mary Barton*, Gaskell writes "I know nothing of Political Economy, or the theories of trade" (38). Josephine Guy describes this statement as the "best-known confession of ignorance in literary history" (73). The novel itself, with its astute discussions of Chartism, trade unions, and workers' strikes, refutes this statement. But the disclaimer was perhaps meant to deflect a certain amount of gender-based criticism by maintaining the ruse that the author is not a strong-minded woman.

10. This connection to sexual impropriety is made at another of Margaret's public appearances, when she accompanies her fugitive brother to the train station. Thornton and other observers assume that she lies about her whereabouts in order to protect a secret lover.

Stowe, Eliot, and the Reform Aesthetic

CLARE COTUGNO

I N HER VERY FIRST LETTER to George Eliot, written 15 April 1869, Harriet Beecher Stowe confided that it was "with fear & trembling" that she was "giving to the English world" her latest novel, *Oldtown Folks*. "It is so intensely American that I fear it may not out of my country be understood," Stowe explained, "but I cast it like a waif on the waters."[1] Writing back to Stowe a few weeks later, Eliot offered a different perspective on the matter:

> I have good hope that your fears are groundless as to the obstacles your new book may find here from its thoroughly American character. Most readers who are likely to be really influenced by writing above the common order will find that special aspect an added reason for interest and study, and I dare say you have long seen, as I am beginning to see with new clearness, that if a book which has any sort of exquisiteness happens also to be a popular widely circulated book, its power over the social mind, for any good, is after all due to its reception by a few appreciative natures, and is the slow result of radiation from that narrow circle. I mean, that you can affect a few souls, and that each of these in turn may affect a few more, but that no exquisite book tells properly and directly on a multitude however largely it may be spread by type and paper. . . . Both travelling abroad and staying home among our English sights and reports, one must continually feel how slowly the centuries work toward the moral good of men. (Haight 5: 30–31)

By suggesting that Stowe reconfigure her sense of audience, from British and American readers to those who either possess or lack "appreciative natures," Eliot found for the two writers a common ground that could not be divided by the Atlantic. However, her words of comfort to Stowe actually provide for

twenty-first-century readers a rare, succinct account of one of the few irrec-
oncilable differences between these two writers who shared so much in common personally and professionally. While there is no record of Stowe's direct
response to Eliot's comments above, throughout their correspondence there
are ample demonstrations that Stowe's convictions about social and literary
reform were, in some senses, directly opposed to those of Eliot. Despite
Eliot's gentle assertions, Stowe had decidedly not "long seen" that her fiction
could affect only a "narrow circle," nor would she ever be convinced that
moral progress was inevitably the work of "centuries."

right

This fundamental difference between the two authors emerged with their
first exchange of letters, and yet the two wrote on, forming a lasting bond
that endured for eleven years and ended only with Eliot's death in 1880.
They exchanged a total of twenty-five letters; Stowe wrote fourteen and
Eliot eleven. While their correspondence began in 1869, I mark the beginning of their dialogue as October 1856, when, in her *Westminster Review* article "Silly Novels by Lady Novelists," George Eliot held up Stowe as an exemplary novelist. Noting Stowe's realistic portrayals of American slaves,
Eliot demanded of her British audience, "Why can we not have pictures of
religious life among the industrial classes in England, as interesting as Mrs.
Stowe's pictures of religious life among the negroes?" (252). In this article, as
well as in her review of Stowe's *Dred: A Tale of the Great Dismal Swamp*
(1856), Eliot praised Stowe's work in terms much in keeping with the reform
aesthetic. Twenty years after the publication of *Dred*, and seven years into
their correspondence, Eliot published *Daniel Deronda*, and in her letters to
Eliot, Stowe offered a lengthy critique of the novel. Their correspondence is
not only a testament to transatlantic bonding but also a mine of insights
that, combined with a consideration of their published writing, brings readers into the complicated intersection of factors that inform their ideal of reform through literature.

Dred and *Daniel Deronda* provide an excellent venue to study a transatlantic dialogue; in Eliot's reviews of Stowe's work and in Stowe's letters to
Eliot, each author's impressions of the other's fiction are preserved. More
than this, *Dred* and *Daniel Deronda*, and the women's discussions around
these texts, contribute significantly to my consideration of what I am calling
the "reform aesthetic."[2] That is, a modification of the novelistic technique of
Walter Scott so that it emphasizes current, rather than past, historical moments and promotes the reform of nations practicing injustices as much as it
forms a national identity on the world stage. Both novels exemplify the im-

peratives articulated by Harriet Martineau in her review essay "The Achievements of the Genius of Scott." As an antislavery novel and as a novel protesting anti-Semitism in Britain, *Dred* and *Daniel Deronda* are deeply concerned with the problems of their divided nations as well as with their
nations' positions in the world. Growing out of these similar motivations,
however, are two novels that are formally quite different. Thus, while the
concept of the reform aesthetic will generate productive new readings of
these texts, the readings themselves will demonstrate the flexibility of the
aesthetic, which could be deployed to express both Stowe's radical and populist vision of reform and Eliot's more gradual and conservative sense of social evolution.

When, in 1832, Harriet Martineau called for a "new novelist" to take on
"the birth of political principle . . . [and] the transition state in which society
now is," she was asking potential novelists to engage current political questions in a reforming spirit that would confront the issue that "one class is in a
state of privilege, and another in a state of subjugation, and that these things
ought not to be" (54, 45). Pointing out that Scott's fiction had, through its
delineation of aristocratic life, successfully bred good will by demystifying
and ennobling the upper classes for a wide readership, Martineau asked that
contemporary novelists build on Scott's model by addressing the "humbler
ranks" of the present in a similarly detailed, respectful and "kindly" way (43).
Attending especially to women and the classes usually neglected in literature
was the only way, Martineau thought, to offer the necessary "long-sighted
views respecting the permanent improvement of society" (44). Martineau
claimed that new novels developing Scott's model would constitute acts of
true patriotism that would consider "the interests of an entire nation" and yet
also do a great service to an international audience (44).

Martineau's proposition suggests that, by carefully considering the current circumstances of neglected groups within the national culture, an author would be confronting the condition not just of that group but of the
entire nation, and indeed, this is precisely what both *Dred* and *Daniel
Deronda* do. Setting out to engage the particular plights of slaves and Jews,
respectively, each novel can only achieve this end by first contextualizing the
oppressed group within a survey of life among a variety of its nation's classes
and then contextualizing the entire nation internationally. Moreover, by re-
sponding specifically to the terms of the slavery "question" in America and
the Jewish "question" in Britain, each novel gets at much more ambitious issues. How should a nation define itself—by its populace or by its institu-

tions? What constitutes national "progress," and how can this progress be fostered by writers and readers? Stowe and Eliot, while both seeming to answer Martineau's call quite scrupulously, produce novels that suggest contradictory responses. Some of the reasons for their different approaches are rooted in their opposing attitudes toward popular culture. In their letters, the two women's differing philosophies emerge both in their consideration of their respective national cultures and in their discussions of each other's writing.

A persistent point of contention between Stowe and Eliot was the current fascination with spiritualism in both Britain and America. Stowe was quite curious about the movement, and she framed her investigation of it as part of her moral and patriotic duty as an author. In May 1869, she wrote to Eliot: "We have had a war that has put almost every family into mourning. . . . there is scarce a house where there is not one dead—& hence this sudden increase of spiritualism. . . . [it] should be dealt with reverently & sympathetically not brutally. In this, as every other vox populi there is a vox dei, *if* we only can find out what it is" (Stowe's emphasis; 25 May 1869). To Stowe, the interest in spiritualism was a symptom of the needs of her popular audience. Whether there was any truth or value in spiritualism was irrelevant to Stowe, for she believed that authors had a duty to discern God's voice in the people's. For Stowe, the people's voice not only demanded her attention but was also the source of her power as a novelist. Thus, while Eliot continued to dismiss spiritualism as "the painful form of the lowest charlatanerie" and an "impudent imposture" practiced for profit upon "semi-idiots" and "the idle rich," Stowe saw the subject as "intensely a practical question" (Haight 5: 253; 23 September 1872). The terms in which they debated the subject bring to the fore the distance each saw fit to maintain between herself and her readers. Casting herself as "pastor & confessor of hundreds" Stowe explained to Eliot that she received desperate mail from grieving strangers who wanted Stowe to tell them if they could contact their war dead through spiritualism (23 September 1872). Stowe embraced both direct communication with her audience—she insisted that she would "have no power" to help those seeking advice if she "had not patiently & sympathetically explored" spiritualism (23 September 1872). Eliot, however, believed that to follow the lead of her audience in the case of spiritualism would be to practice "a melancholy misguidance of men's minds from the true sources of high and pure emotion," thus distracting them from more important subjects to which she felt compelled to draw their attention

(Haight 5: 281). Stowe and Eliot's different positions on audience colored the way they implemented the reform aesthetic.

Stowe was continually suspicious of the wisdom of Eliot's approach, as was demonstrated by her repeated doubts about the accessibility of Eliot's *Middlemarch*. Reading the novel as it came out in serial, Stowe wondered how many people it could possibly reach. In April of 1872, she told Eliot *Middlemarch* "is above the lives of ordinary thinking . . . It addresses the interest & the artistic senses more than the heart. . . . As *art* it is perfect—but perfect art as an *end*—not instrument—has little interest to me" (Stowe's emphasis; 20 April 1872). Five months later, Stowe recounted in vivid detail the passionate response both she and Annie Fields were having to the serialized novel, yet she nonetheless observed: "Your story is for the thoughtful—for the artist for the few—when it is all out I shall try and interpret it to the many. Generally you live & speak in a surge of thought above the average of society" (23 September 1872). Stowe explicitly recognized that her audience and her sense of mission were different from Eliot's. Eliot would address the few; Stowe would "interpret" for "the many."

Stowe's comments in the correspondence provide a fairly detailed understanding of her own literary philosophy, and we can see that her desire to promote emotional healing for a popular audience is in keeping with the reform aesthetic. Eliot's letters, generally more reserved and always eager to avoid outright conflict with Stowe, were less forthcoming, and they leave gaps in her literary philosophy. However, in 1856, in her essay "The Natural History of German Life," Eliot spelled out the literary reform credo that she would adhere to throughout her career. Although Eliot grew more disenchanted with the popular audience over her career, her principles of novel writing remained virtually unchanged.

"German Life" is a review of the work of Wilhelm Riehl, a German historian whose method might "serve as a model for some future or actual student of our people" (Eliot, "German Life" 31). Eliot likes Riehl's work because it carefully considers how the German classes came to be and it emphasizes that any change in German society will occur slowly. Crucial to Riehl's method is a realistic, detailed consideration of "the people as they are" (39). Unlike English portraits of the poor, which Eliot sees as nostalgic and sentimental and which erroneously imbue the lower classes with altruism, cheerfulness, and generosity, Riehl's study acknowledges the limitations of the German peasants. Societal change must happen in its own good time, and it must happen differently in different places.

Eliot argues that Riehl's philosophy is important to artists because she believes that fiction is highly influential in the formation of social and political policy. Artists, therefore, have immense power and responsibility:

> When . . . Kingsley shows us Alton Locke gazing yearningly over the gate which leads from the highway into the first wood he ever saw . . . more is done towards linking the higher classes with the lower, towards obliterating the vulgarity of exclusiveness, than by hundreds of sermons and philosophical dissertations. Art is the nearest thing to life; it is a mode of amplifying experience and extending our contact with our fellowmen beyond the bounds of our personal lot. All the more sacred is the task of the artist when he undertakes to paint the life of the People. Falsification here is far more pernicious than in the more artificial aspects of life. (30)

Eliot's theory is identical to Harriet Martineau's in some respects; both believe novels can promote sympathy across classes much better than any abstract theorizing can. Moreover, novelists themselves bear the burden of wielding this power for the national good, and the way they can do this is by offering realistic pictures of life. Unlike Martineau's and Stowe's, Eliot's notion of realism attends carefully to the perceived negative qualities of the lower classes—ignorance, selfishness, resistance to change. Indeed, her sole critique of Stowe's *Dred* concerned this very issue.

Dred draws its title from its eponymous character, a magnificent runaway slave who haunts the virtually impenetrable Dismal Swamp and the neighborhoods around it, evading capture and plotting the overthrow of white society. Stowe casts this character as the fictional son of a real African American revolutionary, Denmark Vesey, who, along with his co-conspirators, was executed in South Carolina in 1822. A self-declared prophet, Dred speaks in the language of the Old Testament and Revelation, and with his awesome speeches about divine retribution against the white race, Dred attempts to terrify whites and recruit other slaves to his cause. Along with Dred's story, the novel presents readers with the intertwined lives of black, white, and mixed-race characters. The novel includes the unconventional courtship of the young plantation owners, Edward Clayton, an effeminate, disenchanted lawyer who is educating his slaves for eventual emancipation, and the flighty Nina Gordon, who has recently returned from boarding school in the North to take over sole proprietorship of her family plantation. As these two mature into more realistic, socially conscious adults, readers meet the characters that people their lives, including both poor and rich whites who espouse a variety of pro- and antislavery positions. The novel also presents a range of people of color: Nina's well-educated slave and half-brother, Harry, torn between his rage at the slave system and his devotion to his half-sister; the loyal slave Uncle Tiff, who is foster "mother" to poor white children; the evangelical Christian slave woman Milly, a fictionalized version of Sojourner Truth. True to its title, *Dred* offers a grim message to its readers; well before the novel's end the characters Dred and Nina are dead, and by the end of the novel, all the remaining noble black and white characters have fled to the North, where they can at last lead productive and progressive lives. Demonstrating that even gradual reform is impossible in the South, *Dred* brings readers to the brink of an inevitable civil war.

Although *Dred* met with popular success, the critical response was cool. Reviewers in both Britain and America found the novel confusing and disappointing. They did not know what to make of the title character and his fearsome revolutionary rhetoric, the multiple plots, or the bleak ending, all of which amounted to a much less satisfying novel than *Uncle Tom* had been. Comparing *Dred* to *Uncle Tom's Cabin* and the work of another literary reformer, Charles Dickens, one *Blackwood's* reviewer sums up the contemporary response: "by the time we have approached the end of the book, have we abandoned all interest in such of the characters as have not died and suddenly or been unexpectedly killed, that in place of the feeling of regret with which we have usually laid down a tale of Mr Dickens . . . it is one of satisfaction even to exhilaration, that we close the volume [of Dred]" ("Dred" 695).

Twentieth-century critics have been for the most part unimpressed. With the exception of Robert S. Levine, the few critics who have paid attention to *Dred* find it to be fatally flawed. Noting the bleak ending, Joan Hedrick argues that the "failure of [Stowe's] plot reflected a failure of her political imagination" (Hedrick 260–261). Similarly, Ellen Moers comes to the conclusion that the novel demonstrates Stowe's "failure to suspect that civil war lay ahead" (25). These critics, past and present, miss the point of *Dred* because they remained fixed on the plot as the index of the successful novel and because they did not understand *Dred* as a very specific response to the political events of 1856.

Dred is a direct participant in the escalation of the slavery debate that took place between 1852, when *Uncle Tom's Cabin* was published, and 1856, when *Dred* was first released.[3] In *Uncle Tom's Cabin*, Stowe had contended that the souls of white Americans were imperiled by the existence of slavery.

By 1856, however, the sacking of Lawrence, Kansas, and the near-fatal beating of Charles Sumner proved to the author that the civil rights of white Americans and the integrity of the Senate as a national institution were under immediate attack. Thus, even as her preface to *Dred* expresses the artistic ideals of the reform aesthetic, it reveals the significant shift in her sense of the slavery question caused by these recent events: "But as mere cold art, unquickened by sympathy with the spirit of the age is nothing, the author hopes that those who now are called to struggle for all that is noble in our laws and institutions may find in this book the response of a sympathizing heart" (*Dred* 30).[4] True to Martineau's call, Stowe promises that her novel will address the "spirit of the age" and blend artistry with moral purpose. It will be infused with and promote the all-important quality of "sympathy," but here in the preface, it is a struggling white audience of abolitionists and antislavery partisans who require the "response of a sympathizing heart," for it is this group whose "noble . . . laws and institutions" are being threatened.

Stowe's shift in perceptions does not, however, compromise her sympathy for or attention to slaves. In fact, while the novel still purveys many of the pseudoscientific, racist theories and stereotypes then current, it nonetheless demonstrates a significant evolution in Stowe's thinking. Not only does it contain a broader range of African American characters than did *Uncle Tom's Cabin*, it also abandons the procolonization stance of that novel, asserting instead that liberated slaves must be accorded their rights as full citizens. Indeed, in *Dred*, people of color are depicted as African Americans, and their voices are added to the fictional chorus designed to reassert the claim that America's institutions are meant to be constituted by the voices of the people. As *Dred*'s white hero asserts, "vox populi, vox Dei"; the voice of the people is the voice of God, and this is the ideal that *Dred* is constructed to express (329).

Dred follows this imperative to great lengths. It is literally a heteroglossic text that includes a diversity of fictional voices and juxtaposes these voices with examples of institutional rhetorics that betray and overpower Stowe's sense of truly American voices and ideals. The result for many readers has been a chaotic amalgam of characters with no clearly realized plot, but given the terms of the debate as Stowe sees them, a well-realized plot is not really the point of the novel. The narrator herself, however, does provide us with the point. Intruding to prepare readers for yet another of Dred's lengthy, prophetic speeches, she states:

There is no study in human nature more interesting than the aspects of the same subject seen in the points of view of different characters. One might almost imagine that there were no such thing as absolute truth, since a change of situation or temperament is capable of changing the whole force of an argument. . . . We shall never have all the materials for absolute truth on [slavery], till we take into account, with our own views and reasonings, the views and reasonings of those who have bowed down to the yoke. . . . We all console ourselves too easily for the sorrows of others. We talk and reason coolly of that which, did we feel it ourselves, would take away all power of composure and self control. (555–556)

While this passage directly addresses the importance of listening to slaves, the principle holds true more generally in the novel. Stowe's text is concerned with presenting as many different individual and official points of view as possible because multiple points of view are necessary if there is to be any hope of arriving at the "absolute truth." The argument here indicts those who listen selectively and who are therefore able to "talk and reason coolly" about the slavery question. Forcing readers amid many voices, *Dred* removes the possibility of abstract thinking and replaces it with the "truth" that is made up of multiple voices.

Armed with this new understanding of *Dred*, we can step back and see how the seemingly problematic form of the novel constitutes Stowe's reclamation of free speech in 1856. Woven into *Dred* are multiple forms of unofficial and official discourse. As black and white characters visit mansions, slave quarters, the homes of poor whites, camp meetings, and courtrooms, we hear their personal histories, sermons, songs, poems, prayers, and letters. They quote the Constitution, the Bible, and the slave code; one courtroom scene even incorporates transcripts from the actual South Carolina State Supreme Court decision in the case of *State v. Mann*. Appended to *Dred*, we find almost the entire *Confessions of Nat Turner*, newspaper articles about the slavery question, and even the proceedings from the Presbyterian "Church Action on Slavery." *Dred* is an invitation to readers to weigh official and unofficial discourses and to draw from them both the "absolute truth" and a more genuine, feeling response to the slavery question.

Eliot's assessment of *Dred*, published in the *Westminster Review* in October 1856, locates in the novel many of the literary qualities she had called for in "German Life" and "Silly Novels." To Eliot, in principle and in subject, Stowe's *Dred* has much to tell audiences about what makes a fine novel.

Praising the text because it engages "that conflict of races . . . the great source of romantic interest," Eliot continues, "*Uncle Tom* and *Dred* will assure [Stowe] a place in that highest rank of novelists who can give us *a national life in all its phases*—popular and aristocratic, humorous and tragic, political and religious" (Eliot's emphasis, "Belles Lettres" 314). She was untroubled by the disunity that most other critics found in *Dred*, arguing that the book was one of "uncontrollable power" and that those who critique the plot as too long and disconnected "are something like men pursuing a prairie fire with desultory watering-cans" (314).

In the case of *Dred*, any potential failings were, for Eliot, overridden by the novel's ability to engage the sympathies of readers. Noting that "men, women, and children" have been "laughing and sobbing" over *Dred*, Eliot places more value on the popular emotional response than the professional, literary response, and she proudly places herself with the reading public, not her fellow critics: "*Dred* will be devoured by the million, who carry no critical talisman against the enchantments of genius. We confess ourselves to be among the million" (314). While Eliot's embrace of the popular over the professional response might seem uncharacteristic, we must remember that *Dred* follows the principles of fiction that Eliot endorsed so heartily in her essay "German Life" and also that it was only over time that Eliot became convinced that attempting to address a popular readership was futile: it was twelve years later, in 1869, that she was "beginning to see with new clearness" that popularity did not ensure a wide social influence for a novelist.

The only "artistic defect" Eliot can find in the novel is the lack of unsympathetic or corrupt slaves. By presenting only positive slave characters, Stowe seems to be following Martineau's theory, which calls for kindly and respectful presentations of lower-class characters. In "German Life," Eliot makes clear that overly positive representations of the lower classes are a source of faulty social theory. Eliot notes that in *Dred* the absence of any immoral slave characters inadvertently supports an argument for slavery rather than for emancipation. Her reading of *Dred*, however, significantly avoids politics: "Our admiration of the book is quite distinct from any opinions or hesitations we may have as to the terribly difficult problems of Slavery and Abolition—problems which belong to quite other than 'polite literature'" (314). Eliot's assessment comes close to a misreading of Stowe's text; Stowe's book is meant to enter the political fray and in this case engage a question that was almost as pressing to the English economy as it was to American society. To

ignore the political question that is the very reason for the text suggests a significant difference in the two writers' sense of what such a text ought to do.
It reveals Eliot's boundaries: there is a line between the political and the
artistic, or perhaps more accurately, she finds more value in the general question (national society) than the specific (particular political debates).

Eliot's theory strikes a delicate balance; fiction must be socially concerned
with particular conditions, and yet it must take on large questions; it must
show the way toward some kind of progress and yet must not prompt rash
actions or offer false hope of immediate improvement. *Daniel Deronda*,
Eliot's last completed novel, attempts to strike just this balance. Hovering
between the particular and the general, urging national and even international unity while positing only the slowest of change, *Deronda* engages issues quite similar to those in *Dred* but handles them quite differently.

Composed between 1874 and 1876, *Daniel Deronda* tells the story of its title character, a handsome, sensitive young man who, unbeknownst to himself for most of the novel, is of Jewish ancestry. In the custody of his well-to-
do "uncle" since infancy, young Deronda assumes he must be illegitimate,
and this is the source of his intense sensitivity—especially to those weaker
than himself. Deronda's superabundance of sympathy causes him to become
emotionally entangled with Gwendolen Harleth, a beautiful, intelligent, but
self-centered young woman whose mission at the beginning of the novel is
to marry well to secure her own fortunes and those of her recently bank-
rupted mother and sisters. The novel is as much Gwendolen's story as
Deronda's, for it gives equal time to unfolding the unhappy story of Gwendolen's marriage to the imperious, malicious Grandcourt, a wealthy aristocrat whom Gwendolen marries despite her knowledge that he has a mistress
and three children already. While Gwendolen bears a strong resemblance to
Stowe's Nina Gordon, her path to selflessness is not as smooth as Nina's. As
Gwendolen's life becomes increasingly hellish, she learns to treasure any
chance meeting with Deronda, fixating on him as the person who can both
sympathize with and advise her as to how to salvage her life.

Like Clayton in *Dred*, Deronda is often described as "effeminate,"[5] and
like Clayton, although filled with grand ideas, Deronda wallows in indeci-
siveness about the specific path his life should take. Completely by chance,
Deronda finds and rescues a young Jewish woman who is on the brink of
suicide, and he makes it his mission to help the virtuous and compliant Mirah Cohen track down her missing relations. With the help of the kindly,

middle-class British family, the Meyricks, who take in Mirah as one of their own, Deronda eventually finds Mirah's long lost brother, Mordecai Lapidoth, an ailing but enthusiastic proto-Zionist who lives with a working-class Jewish family, the Cohens. Mordecai is given to lengthy speeches arguing for a Jewish state, and he is obsessed with finding some young Jewish man who will carry his knowledge and his mission into the future. Despite Deronda's assertions that he is a Gentile, he begins to study with Mordecai. Thus, when Deronda at last makes contact with his dying mother, a once-renowned Jewish Italian actress, he is already well-prepared to embrace his newfound Jewish heritage and take up Mordecai's mission in earnest. Deronda and Mirah fall in love, but just before the novel closes with their wedding and departure for Palestine, Deronda endures a series of meetings with the now-widowed Gwendolen. Gwendolen may or may not have deliberately caused her husband's death in a boating accident, but either way she is confused and wracked with guilt. Deronda and Gwendolen's final parting is excruciating, but through Deronda's inspirational guidance, Gwendolen is ready to commence a selfless life lived for and with her mother and sisters.

Nineteenth-century critics were resistant to *Deronda*, and most found it to be markedly less readable than Eliot's other fiction. They were confused and put off by Mordecai's proto-Zionist rhetoric and bored by the passive Mirah. They had difficulty "sympathizing" with the subject matter and were frustrated by its philosophizing narrator. Perhaps most of all, they were deeply disappointed that Deronda's and Gwendolen's stories and fates were not more closely united; they did not like the separation maintained between the two plots throughout the novel, and unsurprisingly, they would much rather have had Deronda marry the spirited, Christian Gwendolen than the pious, Jewish Mirah. In a letter dated September 1876, Stowe offered her response to *Deronda* at length, and while her response is more kindly than that of many critics, her main observations about the text are much the same as those offered in published reviews.

Stowe deemed *Deronda* "a splendid success artistically," but given her professed lack of interest in art for art's sake, this was but qualified praise. Noting the separation of the two plots, Stowe observed, "[t]he story divides itself, as a parson might say, into two heads—English and Jewish life," and she further suggested that virtually all the readers she met were attracted either to one plot or the other but not to both (September 1876). Stowe recounts, for example, that a Jewish woman of her acquaintance perceived the book to be about Deronda and Mirah rather than Deronda and Gwendolen.

Stowe reported that the woman was "lost in admiration of George Eliot in *daring* to make her hero and heroine Jewish!" (Stowe's emphasis, September 1876). Among Gentiles, Stowe pointed out, only those specially educated could really appreciate the Jewish plot; general readers, she observed, "find the rhapsodies of Mordecai" difficult and "one lively friend of mine describes that part of her reading as 'wading through a Jewish morass'" (September 1876).

The popular readership, it seemed, were unable to consider Deronda, Mirah, and Gwendolen as a group or to experience the plots as interwoven. While Eliot might have meant Deronda's mixed heritage to link the two plots and the two groups, Jewish and Gentile, Stowe was perhaps typical in her inability to move beyond her Christian perspective. Even though she understood that the Jew, "Mordecai has more [C]hrist-like spirit" than the minister in the novel, and even though she recognized and praised Deronda's goodness, she could not understand how Deronda, raised as a Christian, could abandon his religion for Judaism so easily, leading her to the conclusion that "Christ is nothing to the average young Briton" (September 1876).

Even though Stowe herself had used mixed-race characters in *Dred* to interrogate the basis of citizenship and identity, she could not embrace Deronda's hybridity and choice to "be" Jewish as a recognizable or productive rumination on these subjects. Moreover, she found no solace in the excruciatingly slow march toward progress that *Deronda* presents. For Stowe, *Deronda*'s message was quite bleak: "[i]f this is the last result of modern culture—if it is only to [tell] helpless humanity—do your best & dont hope for comfort or help then what a mockery is our existence!" (September 1876). Stowe wanted not just a portrait of contemporary society but also some suggestion for immediate relief. Eliot might argue that both Daniel Deronda and Gwendolen Harleth find a new kind of spirituality and a new purpose in life by the novel's end, but echoing the popular readership, Stowe found little solace in their rebirth and their happiness, which lies all in the future. Deronda's vague mission to Palestine and Gwendolen's lonely, long road to a meaningful life accrued from daily devotion to others were not enough.

Eliot herself was frustrated with the popular reaction. Her explanation of the motivation for *Deronda* describes a novel that was intended to promote "sympathy" between groups. As she explained to Stowe in 1876:

I . . . felt urged to treat the Jews with such sympathy and understanding as my nature and knowledge could attain to. Moreover, not only towards the Jews, but towards all oriental peoples with whom we English come in contact, a spirit of arrogance and contemptuous dictatorialness is observable which has become a national disgrace to us. There is nothing I should care more to do, if it were possible, than to rouse the imagination of men and women to a vision of human claims in those races of their fellow-men who most differ from them in customs and beliefs. (Haight 6: 301)

The novel as Eliot described it meets the expectations of the reform aesthetic: by encouraging sympathy, it would promote respect for a group oppressed both within England and on foreign shores. Describing anti-Semitism as a "national disgrace," Eliot suggested that England's international reputation was being compromised; it seems equally important, then, that *Deronda* promote a kind of international sympathy by both elevating "all oriental peoples" and by redeeming England in the eyes of the world. Eliot's text is not merely a general response to an ongoing tradition of British anti-Semitism. It confronts a specific, contemporary debate that was dividing England in the 1870s, and thus it follows Martineau's imperative that novelists engage the contemporary "transition state" of the nation.

By the 1870s, Jews had won most of the same rights as Gentiles in England, but this, of course, did not mean that they had been welcomed into English culture or English politics. The 1870s in England saw a rekindling of anti-Semitism for several reasons. Traditionally, the Conservative party stood in the way of Jews' equal rights, and the Liberal party, with its strong Nonconformist constituency, supported the Jews. Nonconformist Christians had generally offered political support for the Jews because the Jewish cause helped them to undermine the entrenched power structures that also held Nonconformists back: the Anglican Church of England and the House of Lords that accorded power based on heredity. For Liberals and Conservatives alike, then, the "Jewish Question" was always also a discussion of class antagonism in England. Any discussion of Jewish rights was really a question of how England would be defined, either by its traditional institutions (endorsed by the Conservatives) or by some notion of the populace that included the lower classes and people of a variety of religious creeds.

All of this changed with the passage of the 1867 Reform Bill, and Jews actually lost much of the sympathy that they had once garnered from England's Liberal party. The 1867 Reform Bill increased the electorate in England by 89 percent, and shortly thereafter the number of Nonconformists in Parliament doubled (Feldman 75). The Nonconformists no longer needed to espouse the

Jewish cause. In fact, Liberals, who once argued against Conservatives that religious conviction should have little to do with defining the citizen or the nation, could now openly use their non-Anglican sense of Christianity to define the English nation, and they urged that "the state policy should be moralized and regenerated . . . by a combination of Protestantism and the people" (75). This mission made plenty of room for anti-Semitism, which, as the decade progressed, could be conveniently directed toward the Conservative prime minister, the Jewish-born Benjamin Disraeli. Although Disraeli converted to Christianity at the age of twelve, his Jewish heritage could always be invoked by the opposition when politically expedient.

Elected in a Conservative landslide in 1874, Disraeli pursued a foreign policy that particularly rankled the Liberals. When, in 1875, Christian Bosnians rose against their Muslim Turkish rulers, the Liberal *Daily News* published reports of atrocities against the Bosnian Christians. There was a public outcry for England to take an active, interventionist role in the crisis on behalf of the Christians. Disraeli, however, maintained the traditional neutral British policy in the Eastern Question. Conflating a pro-Christian stance with a patriotic, English "national feeling," the Liberals were quick to invoke Disraeli's Jewish roots and label his policy as typically "anti-Christian" because it supported the Muslim Turkish empire (Feldman 99). Drawing on Jewish stereotypes, Liberals revived the question of whether or not a Jew could really be an Englishman since all Jews, so the story went, were first and foremost loyal to their "race" and antagonistic toward Christians.

Daniel Deronda is in many ways a response to the Jewish question as it emerged in the 1870s. Most obviously, it engages the career of Disraeli, whom Eliot had disliked as a novelist in the 1840s but whom she supported as a Conservative prime minister in the 1870s. In the 1840s Eliot had called Disraeli's novels *Tancred* and *Coningsby* "detestable stuff" (Haight 1: 235). Both novels put forth Disraeli's belief in Young Englandism, a brand of Conservatism that called for radical change and, therefore, of course, jarred with Eliot's sense that change must be gradual. The novels also put forth theories of Jewish cultural and racial superiority, which Eliot felt had "not a leg to stand on" (Haight 1: 246). This assessment was in great part due to Eliot's anti-Semitism at that time, for she admitted that her "Gentile nature kicks most resolutely against any assumption of superiority in the Jews" (Haight 1: 246–247). By the 1870s, however, Eliot's anti-Semitism had diminished; for at least a decade she had been studying Jewish history and philosophy writ-

ten by German Jews. She had also become a close friend of the Jewish schol-
ar Emmanuel Deutsch, who is often cited as a model for the character Mordecai.[6] Eliot deeply sympathized with his suffering at the hands of his anti-
Semitic employer, the British Museum.

Deronda not only responds to rekindled anti-Semitism, it also exploits
the fact that the Jewish Question is always also a question of class representation and "Englishness" in England. Class issues had always been of interest to Eliot, and in *Deronda*, by confronting the Jewish question, Eliot is
able to revisit this territory in a new way.[7] Because *Deronda* pays special attention to the condition of women, it actively brings women into the discussion by testing out the ways women can or cannot fit into various definitions
of Englishness, as well as to what degree women can participate in national
"progress."

We can see, then, how Eliot's *Deronda* parallels to Stowe's *Dred*. Both engage the question of an oppressed minority as part of larger questions of national identity. Both pay special attention to the status of women in the national narrative, and both consider the nation in an international context. In
short, both illustrate the reform aesthetic. However, Eliot's political stance—
a response to her own national conditions—differs from Stowe's. *Dred's*
multivocal cry for immediate change in the United States stands in stark
contrast to Eliot's belief in gradual change guided by a strong, directive intellectual voice. Stowe's characters end their story in a kind of exile, but it is an
exile that offers the immediate realization of a productive, multiracial community in the North. Moreover, their exile is meant to emphasize to readers
the need for immediate action in the United States to rectify matters in the
South. Eliot's ultimate answer to England's Jewish Question is to send Deronda to Palestine to work toward the eventual foundation of a Jewish state.
The philosophy in *Deronda* both for individuals and for nations calls for
something much more vague and much more gradual than anything Stowe
was suggesting implicitly or explicitly. Consider the plan of action offered by
the novel's hero, Deronda:

> I shall call myself a Jew . . . [b]ut I will not say that I shall profess to believe ex-
> actly as my fathers have believed. Our fathers themselves changed the horizon
> of their belief and learned of other races. But I think I can maintain my grand-
> father's notion of *separateness with communication*. I hold that my first duty is to
> my own people, and if there is anything to be done towards restoring or perfect-
> ing their common life, I shall make that my vocation." (673, emphasis added)

Deronda himself personifies the idea of gradual assimilation. In his own person he will blend both his Jewish grandfather's philosophy and his English heritage. Significantly, though, he will not marry a Christian, nor will he live in a multiethnic England; his loyalty will not be to a mixed culture at home in England but rather to his "own people," the Jews, in Palestine. Deronda's eyes turn away from the problem of social divisions within England toward a vision that takes as its basic unit the nation. On the national level, the theory of "separateness with communication" is a succinct summation of the international politics voiced by Deronda's mentor, Mordecai, at his meeting of the working-class Philosophers Club.

In Mordecai's vision of the future, separateness is defined as the distance between nations, and communication occurs, it seems, mostly metaphorically, by one nation serving as an example to another. Mordecai presents the nation as the best means by which groups of people can establish meaningful and progressive communities. Using Jews as an example, Mordecai posits that a nation provides an "organic centre" enabling individuals to recognize their heritage and embrace their future (494). Nations "consecrate change . . . with kinship: the past becomes my parent, and the future stretches towards me the appealing arms of children" (490–491). Mordecai suggests that to move beyond nation is now premature and that a world comprised of individual nations is the surest means toward progress: "Each nation has its own work, and is a member of the world, enriched by the work of each" (492). In this philosophy, national and international progress are interdependent but not blended into an antinational paradigm.

This notion of "separateness with communication" is embodied in the form of the entire novel. Just as *Dred* structurally forces its readers into the heteroglossic America that embodies Stowe's ideal, *Deronda*'s divided plot places its reader in Eliot's ideal (if uncomfortable) position of "separateness with communication" in relation to the characters. Eliot's own dismay at readers' reactions is frequently quoted but never, it seems, interpreted to its fullest extent. She bemoaned to a friend "the laudation of readers who cut the book into scraps and talk of nothing in it but Gwendolen. I meant everything in the book to be related to everything else there" (Haight 6: 290). Eliot's statement does more than just point out the ironies of authorship and the risk of writing above readers' heads or beyond their hearts; it provides a key to understanding the complicated relationship between form and reform in *Deronda*.

"Everything . . . related to everything else" is another version of "separateness with communication"; another way to posit a slow, careful coming together between separate entities that ought to remain mostly separate for a while longer. Readers might have wanted a novel that let them get swept away in a happy Deronda-Gwendolen love story; such a plot might even have encouraged a stronger sense of sympathy between readers and Jews. But providing such an experience for readers would have run counter to many of Eliot's ideals. It would not have argued for slow change or for the temporary maintenance of necessary cultural and national divisions Eliot advocated in "German Life." It would have provided instead a quick, easy "answer" to anti-Semitism that, to Eliot, was no answer at all.

Thus far I have claimed that *Dred* and *Daniel Deronda* both enact the reform aesthetic and both formally reinforce the ideals expressed within their pages. Both authors pay special attention to oppressed groups, making the question of their status integral to a consideration of the question of national identity in an international context. However, in form and content, Stowe's novel enacts her principle that "the voice of the people is the voice of God," while Eliot's novel continually asserts a principle of progress based on "separateness with communication." Beneath the reform aesthetic's demand that the "everyday" and the "ordinary" be captured by writers, is the knowledge that visibility is a prerequisite for just representation. If the abstract notion of the "citizen" was to be extended beyond the white, male, and in Britain, upper-class person, then writers were going to have to embody the disenfranchised in their texts. By recognizing women and the disenfranchised, as well as the national and international context in which their characters lived, Stowe and Eliot were forcing a more accurate and, therefore, more productive vision of their nation upon the world.

The concept of the reform aesthetic helps us to consider American and British women writers together without entirely erasing the idea of national literatures. By recognizing a common method that not only Stowe and Eliot but also Catharine Maria Sedgwick, Mary Russell Mitford, Lydia Maria Child, and even Frances Trollope deployed with sensitivity to both national and international politics, this comparison helps to promote the recognition that these women were actively intervening not only in literature but also in politics. By contextualizing their work in the political debates of their times and by attending to the reactions of both the critical and the popular audience, I hope that my study has helped to suggest the degree to which these women were active in a public, political sphere that was shaped by transatlantic culture.

What might the reform aesthetic help us to discover about Eliot's *Romola* or Sedgwick's *Hope Leslie*, for example? The private correspondence of all these women deserves much further attention, too, for it suggests a way into further understanding the strange position between gender and nation, between public and private, that these internationally famous women occupied. Finally, the relationship between the reform writing of these women and their male counterparts needs investigation. Surely the reform aesthetic must have some bearing on Charles Kingsley, for example, whose *Alton Locke* was greatly admired by both Mitford and Stowe. The fact that the reform aesthetic has opened up many more questions than it has answered suggests that it could indeed prove to be a very useful term for literary study.

NOTES

1. Harriet Beecher Stowe, letter to George Eliot, 15 April [1869], the Henry W. and Albert A. Berg Collection of English and American Literature, the New York Public Library, Astor, Lenox, and Tilden Foundations, New York, NY. All quotations from Stowe's letters to Eliot are taken from unpublished letters housed at the Berg Collection and are cited parenthetically by date. I have retained Stowe's punctuation and emphasis throughout unless otherwise indicated.

2. In my unpublished dissertation, "Form and Reform: Transatlantic Dialogues, 1822–1876," I identify the "reform aesthetic" as a set of social values and artistic techniques shared among a transatlantic network of female reform writers who shaped national identity. I could not have developed the concept without the work of colleagues and scholars too numerous to list here. I am especially indebted to innovative studies by Benedict Anderson, Jonathan Arac, Lawrence Buell, Catherine Gallagher, Paul Gilroy, Elizabeth K. Helsinger, Carolyn L. Karcher, Sally Mitchell, Valerie Sanders, and Robert Weisbuch. Sandra Zagarell's essay "Narrrative of Community: The Identification of a Genre" was an invaluable early model as well as an inspiration.

3. Robert S. Levine has ably demonstrated that *Dred* is part of a "conversation" between Stowe and Frederick Douglass (Levine 144–176). Moreover, Paul Gilroy has pointed out that Martin Delaney's *Blake* is a response to *Uncle Tom* (27), and I would add that *Dred* participates in this conversation, too.

4. All quotes from *Dred* are from the 1999 edition edited by Judie Newman.

5. For example, noting the feminized descriptions of the male character Deronda, Elizabeth Helsinger describes Deronda as "the substitute heroine through whom a woman's frustrated desire can be fulfilled" (25).

6. Both William Baker and Bernard Semmel identify Deutsch as a model for More-

decai (Baker 131; Semmel 128). Baker identifies Eliot's concern for Deutsch when he was mistreated by the British Museum (Baker 132).

7. Deirdre David has noted that Eliot presents the lower-class Jewish characters from a safe remove. Of the Cohens, David writes, "We never enter into this life; it is rendered for us in rich textures which do not seem to invite an understanding of Jewish lower-class experience except in visual terms" (161). She also argues that Eliot deliberately displaces a critique of the lower classes onto the Cohens (153). Susan Meyer demonstrates that *Deronda* is "rife with anti-Semitism," especially as demonstrated in the presentation of the Cohens (745).

Sunny Memories and Serious Proposals

DONALD ROSS

N *Uncle Tom's Cabin,* Harriet Beecher Stowe made the novel a vehicle for opening up antislavery to broader discussion in both America and Britain. With *Sunny Memories of Foreign Lands,* she exploited an even more popular genre, the travel book, for the same goal. *Sunny Memories* is filled with moments of almost Eva-like naivete and charm—botanizing along the roadside; pages that evoke the ghosts of Walter Scott, Robert Burns, and even Shakespeare's mother; plus cathedrals and castles in the rain and at sunset. It also dramatizes the provincial American lady's first glimpse of paintings, tapestry, and sculpture by the European Masters, as Stowe works out her artistic sensitivity. All of this combined to make the book a guide for future generations of American tourists. But it is more since it also continues to address the slavery question and makes a sincere effort to outline a possible solution to the problem that defied religious and political efforts. Behind the scenes Stowe is involved in the complexity of transatlantic political issues related to slavery and other social reforms.

The front matter and opening of *Sunny Memories* are clearly those of a travel book. After the preface, we see a wistful engraving of steam- and sailboats heading off to the right and the inviting opening words, "My Dear Children:—You wish first of all to hear of the voyage." A travel book then, except that after the table of contents, we have "Introductory," sixty-five fine-print pages of antislavery speeches signed C. E. S., that is, Calvin Stowe.

Although the chapters on the Stowes' Continental travels are pure tourism with no overt political content, the British travels interweave sections on tourist destinations with political activities. The table of contents includes entries on places that would have been familiar to readers of other travel books: "The Cathedral . . . Bothwell Castle . . . Scott and Burns . . . Glamis Castle . . . Abbotsford . . . Stratford on Avon . . . Kenilworth." It also offers an overlapping set of chapters involving antislavery events at Stafford House and Exeter Hall, encounters with famous reform-minded aristocrats, and other political issues: "Antislavery Meeting . . . Public Soirée . . . Reformatory Schools of Aberdeen . . . Temperance Soirée . . . Dinner with Earl of Carlisle . . . Reception at Stafford House . . . The Sutherland Estate . . . Borough School . . . Exeter Hall—Antislavery Meeting . . . Kossuth . . . Clarkson . . . Lord Shaftesbury . . . Lodging House Act . . . Benevolent Movements . . . Schools, &c."

This essay will focus on the more significant aspect of the book, Stowe's political motives and agenda, which she deliberately weaves throughout the travel narrative. First, I outline what Stowe hoped to accomplish—to capitalize on the publicity that her trip had created in order to bring together the American and British antislavery movements and mend fences among their factions. I then place *Sunny Memories*'s message in the rhetorical context of *Uncle Tom's Cabin* and *A Key to Uncle Tom's Cabin*. Next, I suggest that Stowe's political thinking evolved from religious hope in Scotland and the north of England to an economic and political program as she reached London. Stowe could use favorable reception by the large crowds and British nobles for antislavery purposes, while British leaders used Stowe's fame to further their own reform agendas. Finally, the reviews of *Sunny Memories* suggest how the book's messages were received on both sides of the Atlantic.

Stowe had several goals in going to Great Britain. Most obviously, she wished to further the antislavery cause. By the time her party left for Liverpool, she had become accustomed to having press coverage of her activities and views expressed on both sides of the Atlantic. While she could not have anticipated the public demonstrations, she seems to have been aware of the strong support important British abolitionists such as Joseph Sturge and the Earl of Shaftesbury had given to the antislavery cause, and she knew about the Scottish National Penny Offering and the Address to the Women of America, both of which had the Duchess of Sutherland's sponsorship. Once in Britain, the Stowes learned how to sustain the press coverage and also to attend to and deflect the comments in the London *Times*. It was clear from reports on the early Glasgow meeting that Calvin Stowe's speeches would be publicized.

By using her prominence, Stowe sought to mediate between William Lloyd Garrison's faction and the New Movement of abolitionists in both countries. The "sunny memories" tone was part of her agenda of conciliation, as was her description of her meetings with Garrisonians. She also tried to make the connection between the abolition and peace movements, especially since the latter was of increasing significance in Britain as tension grew over the "Eastern Question" between Turkey and Russia, which soon led to the Crimean War.

Having been disappointed by her royalty arrangement with Jewett for *Uncle Tom* and the many British piratings of that book, Stowe was also attending to her financial interests in future publication. Thus, by being in Britain when *A Key to Uncle Tom's Cabin* was first published she likely insured British copyright,[1] and struck a useful and personal relationship with her London publisher, Sampson Low, who was interested enough to greet the Stowes when they returned from the Continent. Charles Beecher warned his family members not to publish his letters so that *Sunny Memories* would have the maximum impact when the letters were revised for publication upon their return.

The travel strand, in the British chapters at least, can be seen either as a smoke screen or sugar coating for the political strand. As with most travel books, this aspect of *Sunny Memories* is arranged episodically. Stowe came to see the physical reality behind her reading of Sir Walter Scott, William Shakespeare, and John Milton, and the castles, cathedrals, and ruins she had never seen. She also made literary contacts with such famous people as Charles Dickens and Thomas Babington Macaulay, and she learned more than would have been possible from guidebooks or engravings about art and architecture. The political strand, however, is a narrative that leads to the climactic speech at Exeter Hall.

· · ·

While *Uncle Tom's Cabin* dramatized the problem of slavery, *A Key to Uncle Tom's Cabin*[2] documented it and established the novel's credibility. Its brief, final chapter, "What Is to Be Done?" rehearses the possibilities for abolishing slavery, from ending prejudice of caste and unjust segregation laws to stopping name-calling between immediate and gradual abolitionists to having parents tell children that slavery is immoral (*Key* 250–255). *Key* is more a prayer than it is a political program. *Sunny Memories* followed *Key* with an honest and sincere effort to find a practical first step to forward the great work. It also somewhat obliquely associated Stowe with those who were calling for immediate emancipation. Comments within the text document the

Stowes' move from seeing abolition as a religious crusade with "our only re-source in prayer" (1: xv) to one involving economic and political tactics. Sev-eral of the men who introduced the Stowes at public gatherings hammered away at the issue of immediate emancipation, especially in the context of what Britain had done in the West Indies ("Introductory," 1: xxvii–xxvii, lvii, *et passim*). At the end of all this, in Calvin Stowe's speech on 25 May, he says of Joseph Sturge's exhortation: "the immediate termination of slavery would be far less dangerous and far less injurious than any system of compromise, or any attempt at gradual emancipation" (1: lix); "It is precisely the expres-sion of our own [Mrs. Stowe's and my] thoughts and feelings on the whole subject of slavery" (1: lxi).

In this new book, slavery is shown to be an international phenomenon, driven as much by British investment capital and textile mills as by Southern planters. The thematic and dramatic climax of *Sunny Memories of Foreign Lands* is the speech given at Exeter Hall on 16 May 1853, where the Stowes announced a new strategy in their efforts to end slavery—fostering the use of cotton and other commodities made only by free labor. The significance of this event, to Harriet Beecher Stowe at least, is signaled partly by the physical organization of the book that opens with "Introductory" speeches and comments.

Stowe embeds her political arguments in a series of interviews and con-tacts with key British abolitionists and groups, in contrast to the polemics of "Introductory." During the chapters set in Scotland and the Midlands (2 to 12), rather than rehearsing her conclusions, she dramatizes their develop-ment, so her readers are led along with her thinking. While she came to Eng-land with a fully formed notion of how to accomplish temperance reform (by adopting the Maine law), here she found out about some apparently practical ways to end slavery, as well as to advance other reforms that en-gaged the attention of the British, most notably the peace movement but also working-class education and housing and the amelioration of low wages for British workers. The London chapters (13 to 30) then show how the re-sults of her new thinking were put on public display at large-scale meetings and through contacts with high-profile individuals from the aristocracy, lit-erary establishment, and government.

Stowe's original invitation to visit Britain was from the Glasgow New Ladies Anti-Slavery Society and the New Association for the Abolition of Slavery. Garrison had warned Stowe about so-called new organizations like

these because they did not follow his doctrine of "no union with slaveholders" but sought political solutions instead. Stowe was not inclined to take
sides, but she had visited Garrison to hear him directly (Fladeland 353).

The speeches in "Introductory" chart the movement from evangelical appeals to end slavery to more hard-nosed political arguments, a movement
that gets progressively further from William Lloyd Garrison and closer to
Gamaliel Bailey and, not coincidentally, the Stowes' most influential English
host, Joseph Sturge.[3] In the first weeks, both Calvin and their hosts claim
that theirs is a religious crusade, not a political movement—Calvin disputes
a newspaper report that on one occasion the American flag was trampled un-
derfoot (1: xxxiv). But the American churches were unable to unite; few were
even willing to condemn ministers or congregations who supported slavery.
Frustration at not finding a solution is addressed frequently in these early
speeches and in the body of the text. Calvin Stowe points out in the speech
to the Edinburgh audience, "You had a power over the slaveholder by your
national legislature. . . . All the legislation that can in [America] be brought
to bear for the slave, is legislation by the slaveholders themselves" at the state
level (xxxi).

In the Stowes' first weeks in Britain, their hosts included leaders from
both factions. Edmund Cropper, a New Organization man, had his son
meet the party at the boat in Liverpool. The host in Edinburgh was Eliza
Wigham, a stolid Garrisonite who supported women's prominence in the
cause. By mentioning both names in her book, Stowe lets the insiders know
about her efforts to accommodate the whole movement, and by attending
"soirées" for working-class men, she refuted the charge that the antislavery
movement was only middle class (Midgley 151). Often in Calvin Stowe's
early speeches, he refuted the specious equation of American slavery and
British poverty. He also broached the free labor issue at one Liverpool meeting by pointing out, "It is probable that the cotton trade in Great Britain is
the great essential that supports slavery. . . . " Stowe notes that "One or two
gentlemen" took his remarks quite seriously (1: 37).[4] She then amplifies his
argument, noting "have we not been enthusiastic for freedom in the person
of the Greek, the Hungarian, and the Pole"; we now need to work until "we
have abolished slavery at home" (1: 39).[5]

At Birmingham, Joseph Sturge played host. Sturge was the main player in
the British and Foreign Anti-Slavery Society (BFASS), and in Stowe's terms,
"one of the most prominent and efficient of the philanthropists of modern

days" (1: 193). Amid their sightseeing tours,[6] Stowe and Sturge engaged in several intense discussions about the next steps in the American antislavery movement.

Under Sturge's tutelage, Stowe came to see the economics and (to a lesser degree) the politics of slavery and its abolition in an international and multicontinental perspective. Sturge's advantage was that his commitment for over two decades had included a wider range of practical political and economic measures and pressure tactics than Stowe or even most of her American colleagues had contemplated. It was Sturge who persuaded her to advocate the use of free-grown cotton and to encourage a boycott of slave-grown commodities, drawing on the British tradition of boycotts of slave-grown sugar from the West Indies going back to the late eighteenth century.[7]

Stowe reports on Sturge's argument against using slave-grown produce and notes that Britain "has large tracts of cotton-growing land at her disposal in India" and can produce it for less than the cost of Southern cotton. "The forces of nature go with free labor," she argues, but apparently so also do the forces of a free-market economy (1: 251).[8] At the Sturges' home Stowe was impressed that nothing in the house was slave-grown. She could not quite, however, go as far as to "admit the justness of the general proposition, that it is an actual sin to eat, drink, or wear any thing which has been the result of slave labor" (2: 26).

The Stowes envisioned importing free (nonslave) workers from Germany and China to toil in American cotton fields and ultimately to provide cheaper labor than that available from slavery. Advocating free labor was part of the ideology of British emancipation in the 1830s, and Sturge had traveled to the West Indies during the apprenticeship debate[9] to show the economic success of plantations worked by now-free Africans. In a similarly imperialist vein, Stowe joined her hosts in encouraging the development of British-run cotton agriculture in India and on the west coast of Africa.

During the carriage ride to Stratford-upon-Avon, Stowe and Sturge discussed peace, abolition, and "all the most wide-awake topics of the present day" (1: 195–196). Later, at Warwick Castle, Sturge talked about one of his recent interests, enlarging the British franchise further into the middle class. However, he assured her that the British would not threaten aristocratic privilege (1: 238). The dialogue with Sturge suggests how both he and Stowe sought nonviolent solutions to social problems in their two countries that would disrupt the social order as little as possible.

Sturge also pushed Stowe to advocate immediate, not gradual emancipation. "Mr. Sturge seemed exceedingly anxious that the American states should adopt the theory of immediate, and not gradual emancipation. I told him the great difficulty was to persuade them to think of any emancipation at all" (1:251). Sturge further pointed out that nothing affected English public opinion "until they firmly advocated the right of every innocent being to immediate and complete freedom, without any condition." After outlining the immediatist case, Stowe wrote that it "contains much good sense" (1: 252).

Sturge and his fellow Quaker reformers were now moving from abolition into other areas, most notably the peace, or Olive Branch, movement.[10] Pacifism did capture Stowe's interest, possibly in the context of Garrison's questions about whether *Uncle Tom's Cabin* advocated nonresistance only for the slave (*Liberator* 26 March 1852). Stowe welcomed the arrival of the famous American pacifist Elihu Burritt at Sturge's house.[11] *Sunny Memories* makes the case against standing armies and argues for a climate for arbitration and an international court of justice to avoid war. Then in the form of a brief dialogue, Stowe claims that moral pressure from the masses could convince the soldiers "of a despot's army" to drop their arms (1: 248–249).

Sturge had successfully encouraged Stowe to expand the range of social reforms she advocated (in public, in *Sunny Memories*), and to show how antislavery and temperance were related to other causes. Independently of their ideological merit or political efficacy, these passages in *Sunny Memories* show that Stowe articulates important and controversial economic and political issues in her own voice.

The major events in London were a series of receptions involving the Duchess and Duke of Sutherland, Earl of Carlisle, Earl of Argyle (Stowe's spelling), and Anthony Ashley Cooper, Seventh Earl of Shaftesbury. Shaftesbury had been engaged for many years in high-profile work on social problems such as children's and women's working hours, safety in mines and factories, and to a lesser degree, antislavery. His initial reaction to *Uncle Tom's Cabin* was that it was "marvellous work! What a power of Christian intellect!" (qtd. in Finlayson 343). He wrote "An Affectionate and Christian Address of the Many Thousands of Women of Great Britain and Ireland to Their Sisters, the Women of the United States of America," which the Duchess of Sutherland circulated.

Several anecdotes in the London section of the narrative are designed to indicate the support Stowe received at the highest circles of British society. Lord Chief Justice Pollack's comments on a court decision reported in *A Key to Uncle Tom's Cabin* are a sign of how seriously this leading jurist took the book: "We found that this document had produced the same response on the minds of several others present" (1: 260–261). In another example, Stowe recalls the Earl of Carlisle's trip to America, where he had attended the Boston antislavery fair and openly discussed his sentiments. He had written an introduction to *Uncle Tom's Cabin*, which was deprecated by American newspapers (1: 269). Not only are these aristocrats aware of Stowe's writing; she is aware of their past roles as antislavery colleagues.

Stowe's reports on other discussions allow her to expand the scope of her argument and further show the extent of support for the cause. For example, when talking over lunch at Stafford House on 7 May, the Marquis of Lansdowne, an ally of Clarkson and Wilberforce, leads Stowe to notice that, "for the great men of the old world," America "is a new development of society, acting every day with greater and greater power on the old world; nor is it yet clearly seen what its final results will be" (1: 292).

At a highly publicized but private Stafford House reception, the "Address," with over half a million signatures, was presented by the Earl of Shaftesbury to Mrs. Stowe.[12] This was not, Stowe points out, a personal honor but a public expression "of the feelings of the women of England" on slavery. "The most splendid of English palaces has this day opened its doors to the slave" and this important public fact proclaimed the "brotherhood of the human family, and the equal religious value of every human soul." It is false, as told in American papers, "that it was a political movement"; it was first organized in "deep religious feeling of the man [Shaftesbury] whose whole life has been devoted to the abolition of the white-labor slavery of Great Britain" (1: 298–299).

The Anti-Slavery Society meeting at Exeter Hall on 16 May was the main public event in London. There was a long line for tickets, and some 4,000 were able to witness the ceremony (Forrest Wilson 378). Stowe reported on Calvin Stowe's speech (2: 34; cf. 1: liii–lvii), then pointed out that the sentiments expressed here would likely hurt American national feelings—the "real old Saxon battle axe of Brother John, swung without fear or favor"— but hopes it will have a salutary effect (2: 34).

While the Exeter Hall meeting led to high-profile publicity for an apparently unified movement in England, at almost exactly the same time the annual "Anniversary Meetings" of American reform societies were taking place in New York, and they graphically revealed the split among the American abolitionists. On 11 May, Garrison's American Anti-Slavery Society (AASS) and the Tappans' American and Foreign Anti-Slavery Society (AFASS) met in separate halls. Frederick Douglass spoke at both; Stowe's brother Henry Ward Beecher and Lucy Stone (in bloomers) were at the AASS event. A New York *Daily Times* editorial for 12 May takes Garrison to task for deprecating political action and his "cant and unctious [sic] twang" while praising the AFASS as a "working institution, of business-like habits" that properly claims the loyalty of the "Mrs. Stowes."

Following the Exeter Hall meeting, Stowe reports on private visits where famous political figures discussed the issue. A couple of days after Exeter Hall, she visited Louis Kossuth, who had recently been attacked in the *Times* for advocating Hungarian independence while enjoying political asylum. Stowe does not echo American abolitionists' complaint that Kossuth was silent on the slavery question during his 1851–1852 American tour, but she notes his interest in the Exeter speech (2: 54). She then met privately with Lord John Russell and with Lady Russell (2: 59). She had a long visit with Clarkson's widow (letter 24), which established continuity with the revered leader of the British movement. The bulk of the letter is a sentimental biography of Clarkson in which she points out the value he placed on collecting documentary evidence to further the cause—implicitly endorsing the rhetorical strategy of *A Key* (2: 71). Later, at the urging of Sturge, she attended a meeting of Quaker women, at which she spoke on free labor: "In a few words I told them I considered myself upon that subject more a learner than a teacher, but that I was deeply interested in what I had learned upon the subject since my travelling in England" (2: 83).

Also, in an effort to close the antislavery ranks and to reconcile the factions, she had lunch with George Thompson, a high-profile Garrisonian (2: letter 20). In Paris, her hostess for over two weeks was "Mrs. C.," Maria Weston Chapman, who was Garrison's personal assistant, editor of the *Liberator* and *Liberty Bell*, and general manager of the American Anti-Slavery Society. On the day after Calvin had left for America, Stowe was presented with a silver inkstand depicting emancipation. At the event, with Lord Shaftesbury in the chair, her host, Reverend Binney, "complimented the nobility, and Lord Shaftesbury complimented the people, and all were but too kind in what they said to me—in fact, there was general good humor in the whole scene" (2: 134).

Letter 29 provides an interesting coda on the current state of reforms in Britain. In addition to the improvements discussed in previous chapters, Stowe lists and briefly comments on poor law reform, treatment of the insane, the ten-hour factory bill, child labor regulation, and public health (clean drinking water).¹³ All of the many religious sects were working together on these efforts (2: 133). Also, "Fashionable literature now arrays itself on the side of the working classes" (2: 124); this is complemented by "The use of tracts, committees, of female cooperation, of voluntary association" (2: 125).

Stowe used the adulation of aristocrats, the adoration of the working-class crowds, and testimonials from humble cottagers to further the antislavery cause. Her most vocal admirers came from a coterie of reform-minded British politicians. There was also reciprocal political exploitation by her hosts. Charles Beecher confided in a letter to his wife, Sarah, that some people invited his sister just to be publicly in her presence, not to hear her message (Beecher 38, dated 16 April). On the occasion of a lunch at Stafford House, Stowe notes that "nobody is invited with whom it is not proper that you should converse" (1: 290).

Stowe's visit focused British public attention on reform leaders and Liberal Party politicians whose names were prominent in the meeting reports and formal banquets as the worthies who introduced the Stowes. She also, apparently consciously, voiced her sentiments on behalf of the British working classes (Fladeland 356). In *Sunny Memories*, Stowe complemented her public presence by reporting anecdotes that illustrated the personal and family side of the leaders. Here was an American republican who proclaimed that aristocrats were welcoming and approachable and as much a part of the human family as was the slave.

The key aristocrats' controversial political activities are presented and at times defended at length in Stowe's book. Foremost among these was the Earl of Shaftesbury. For him, West Indies emancipation had been but a minor part of his Evangelical efforts to better the lot of the working classes and thereby to prevent the sort of popular agitation that the country saw during the Reform Bill movement in the early 1830s. He thought his position had helped diffuse the tensions that elsewhere produced the European revolutions of 1848. Shaftesbury showed Stowe his model housing and workplace projects, recognizing that the British newspapers would publicize these visits as she did in her book.

Stowe's immediate contacts were pleased with the Exeter Hall statements about free labor. The conservative reaction was predictable. For example, in a long review article in *Blackwood's*, the writer claims that all Britain was against slavery but opposed "republicanism and republican institutions" (311).¹⁴ But the left also reacted—leading Radical MPs Richard Cobden and John Bright had long thought the idea impractical. William Wells Brown and Samuel Ward, African Americans who were living and working in England complained that the presentations did not stress the hypocrisy of the American churches adequately (Fladeland 354).

Stowe also entered into the wage-slavery argument that had been a staple of proslavery circles for years. Several times in *Sunny Memories*, she refers to a widely quoted public letter from Julia Tyler, wife of the former Democratic president, in which the Virginian tried to deflect attention from slavery to the working conditions in Great Britain. One fan letter asked Stowe herself to write a book about cruelties and outrages in Scotland (1: 107). The critics' main tactic was, like Tyler's, to complain that Stowe and her hosts were not attending to the economic exploitation of British workers. In Britain at least, this complaint was often insincere because the same papers resisted most efforts to regulate manufacturers, mining, and agriculture.[15] Stowe, as geographically distant from those problems as the British were from American slavery, had written at the end of *Uncle Tom's Cabin*, "This is an age of the world when nations are trembling and convulsed. A mighty influence [Christianity or democracy] is abroad, surging and heaving the world, as with an earthquake. And is America safe? Every nation that carries in its bosom great and unredressed injustice has in it the elements of this last convolution" (455).[16]

As Calvin said in his Liverpool speech, "England repents and reforms. America refuses to repent and reform" (Stowe, *Sunny Memories* 1: xx). Stowe's popularity fit the interests of the British ruling classes (however defined). It diffused or deflected concerns about poverty in England and Ireland on to the United States. Instead of addressing the needs of Britain's poor, one could give pennies to Mrs. Stowe. Stowe remarks several times on the inclination of Christians in both countries to support foreign missions rather than attending to domestic problems.

However, Stowe also showed that ordinary Britons shared her views on reform principles. From Scotland, she reported on the crowds of working-class readers who greeted her. One working man invited her to tea and acknowledged that there was room for social improvement in Britain, but he emphasized, "we are *no slaves!*" He continues, "since the repeal of the corn laws and the passage of the factory bill, and this emigration to America and Australia, affairs have been very much altered" (1: 148). British workers' literacy was contrasted with the lot of slaves who could not read the Bible.[17] However, a drive through the London slums on the way to dinner at Stafford House evokes a temperance message about "drinking destruction":

"Mothers go to [gin shops] with babies in their arms, and take what turns the mother's milk into poison" (1: 271).

As a result of these contacts, Stowe could (with some justice) write that the conditions of English workers and poor were being ameliorated through the good works of enlightened leaders.[18] She quoted Lord Chief Justice Campbell to the effect that Britain has the laws to address social issues, but, unfortunately, they are not well enforced—however, America does not have the laws to end slavery (2: 19). Furthermore, even in the worst of times these men and women were free subjects of Her Majesty's government (1: 68).

Stowe's British trip failed to have the political impact she might have hoped for. Newspapers on both sides of the Atlantic reported regularly on the Stowes' activity but not in great detail. The *Times* of London, predictably hostile, gave extracts of several of Calvin's speeches, then responded to the Exeter-Hall meeting, "Mrs. Stowe would be wise to separate herself from 'the frantic impotence of the Exeter-Hall abolitionists'" (18 May 1853). *Frederick Douglass' Paper* had a series of brief notices from the time the party left for England (31 December 1852 through 6 May 1853); the New York *National Anti-Slavery Standard* noted their return and pointed out that their contacts had included pro- and anti-Garrisonites (24 September). On 10 June, *Douglass' Paper* reprinted William Wells Brown's reaction to the issue of free labor: Professor Stowe "evidently wishes for no agitation on the subject" and then claims that the issue of a cotton boycott does "nothing more than to divert the public from the main subject itself."

Longer review articles of *Sunny Memories* in America and England address the political issues, although the free-labor question is rarely treated seriously. The conservative *North American Review* approved of Stowe's account of Shaftesbury's reform projects such as the ragged schools and of her defense of the Duchess of Sutherland on the issue of Highland Clearances, but the whole of *Sunny Memories* is "a magnified reflection of the idiosyncrasies of the writer . . . from the broad mirror of Transatlantic scenery and society" (October 1854).[19] *Blackwood's Edinburgh Magazine* saw Stowe's embracing the Olive Branch movement as being wrong-headed since Britain had entered the Crimean War after the book was written. Stowe's attendance at the celebrated Quaker Sibyl Jones's lecture indicates that "Mrs. Stowe is something more than a passive spectator of the Transatlantic movement for establishing what are called the 'Rights of Women' . . . and the supremacy of the petticoat over the breeches" (September 1854). Depicting Stowe as a radical feminist and a pacifist is, of course, a curious way to read this book.

Nor were reviewers impressed with the travel sections. *Putnam's Monthly* commented that "Her descriptions are mostly meagre, and her remarks often commonplace." Further, as an obvious novice, she should not have tried to write about art, and her discussions of literature "are not those of an adept" (September 1854). The London *Examiner* notes that she has "wonderfully uncultivated" taste in art and literature.

After returning to America, Stowe wrote a rambling public letter to the Glasgow Ladies' New Anti-Slavery Society (dated 18 November 1853, and diligently reprinted in *Frederick Douglass' Paper* in January of the following year). In it she confirms the role of *A Key* in documenting the case made in *Uncle Tom's Cabin* and notes that none of the novel's claims have been refuted. She then anticipates the main argument that she will advance in *Sunny Memories*: in England, "our attention was turned very seriously" to the free labor issue. "Slave labor is as wasteful and unprofitable, compared with free labor, as it is immoral," as dramatized by a recent Georgia advertisement for whites to help with the harvest. Stowe concludes with an optimistic assessment of the prospects for the temperance cause and the success of the Maine prohibition law.

Stowe's title, *Sunny Memories*, was seductive and misleading since it implied that this was only a travel book. So is her three-page preface: "If the criticism be made that every thing is given *couleur de rose*, the answer is, Why not? They are the impressions, as they arose, of a most agreeable visit. . . . The object of publishing these letters is, therefore, to give to those who are true-hearted and honest the same agreeable picture of life and manners which met the writer's own eyes" (1: iii–iv).

Nevertheless, as I have argued, Stowe uses the form of an episodic travel account to create a narrative of her increasingly sophisticated politics. She tells the story of her education under the guidance of Joseph Sturge and the forward-looking aristocracy, while she helps British reformers advance their various projects—worldwide abolition, helping the poor, and pacifism. Her motives and public positions on government, power, money, and social class are clearly in the realm of "ordinary" politics. *Sunny Memories of Foreign Lands* was a vehicle in which Stowe could evade the strictures against women taking part in the public realm. She also rehearsed the case for immediate abolition. Its success in the British West Indies added metaphorical weight to her concluding sentence, "And thus, almost sadly as a child might leave its home, I left the shores of kind, strong Old England—the mother of us all" (2: 432).

NOTES

1. In fact, Stowe put the finishing touches on the book just before she left for England.

2. *Presenting the Original Facts and Documents upon Which the Story Is Founded, Together with Corroborative Statements Verifying the Truth of the Work.*

3. From 1840 Garrison led a radical faction of the American antislavery movement. Gamaliel Bailey was editor of the *National Era*, which had published *Uncle Tom's Cabin* in serial form; he was the leader with Lewis Tappan's financial backing of the American and Foreign Anti-Slavery Society (AFASS). Sturge founded a moderate counterpart, the British and Foreign Anti-Slavery Society (BFASS).

4. The so-called Committee of the Law and Order Party asks rhetorically: "Without sugar, cotton, and cheap clothing, can civilization maintain its progress? Can these be supplied without slavery?" ("The Voice of Kansas—Let the South Respond" *De-Bow's Review* 21 [August 1856]: 197).

5. I was not able to find these remarks in the newspaper reports from the Liverpool speeches. It may be that these sentiments were addressed at another meeting, or perhaps Stowe places these comments on the free-produce movement earlier in the book to build a case for consistency of their views.

6. And an apparently typical "small" dinner for about a hundred guests in a special room at Sturge's house (Tyrrell 183).

7. See Sussman and Pettinger.

8. Rohrback in "'Truth Stranger and Stronger than Fiction': Reexamining William Lloyd Garrison's *Liberator*," reproduces advertisements for "Free Labor Shoes" from Lynn, Massachusetts, and Charles Wise's Free Labor Dry Goods Store in Philadelphia, both in the 1 March 1839 *Liberator*. Near the beginning of the second volume, Stowe gives brief notes on a Quaker from Edinburgh who "had conscientious objections from receiving money from slaveholders" and a Friends' free-produce depot in Philadelphia and the idea of encouraging Germans to work on Texas cotton lands (2: 25–26).

9. The original terms of West Indies emancipation included a period of up to a dozen years when former slaves would be "apprentices" and work without pay. Sturge led a successful movement to curtail this practice.

10. Sturge had organized a National Peace Conference in January 1853 that set up lectures and promulgated tracts during the year of Stowe's visit (Tyrrell 206).

11. Lewis Tappan had introduced Burritt and Sturge, and Burritt's first trip to England in 1846 was at Sturge's expense (Fladeland 370).

12. Interestingly, when Lord Morpeth (later Earl of Carlisle) retired from his seat in Parliament in 1841, he received a farewell address from his constituents from the West Riding of Yorkshire with 257,000 signatures (Olien 240). Obviously, massive petitions were not unusual in Great Britain.

13. Earlier Stowe briefly mentioned pending air pollution legislation (1: 192).

14. The reviews cited here and on the following pages are included in the list of reviews and reactions to *Sunny Memories of Foreign Lands*; this list follows the essay. These reviews do not appear in the list of works cited at the end of the collection.

15. See the introduction to this volume, which discusses the wage-slavery debate.

16. This quotation comes from the 1981 Bantam edition of *Uncle Tom's Cabin*.

17. Cited in the "Address from the Women of England" and quoted in 1: xlii; see also 2: 85–86.

18. In a footnote, Stowe reports that, upon her return, she discovered that schools in New York and Boston did not admit the poor and Americans "can no longer congratulate ourselves on not having a degraded and miserable class in our cities" (1: 172–173).

19. The *North American Review*'s reaction to *Uncle Tom's Cabin* and *A Key* from a year earlier is remarkable for its extended defense of slavery that is fully justified on the grounds of the inferiority of the Negro race and the need to enforce the Fugitive Slave Law. This later article does not deal directly with the slavery question.

Reviews and Reactions

The reviews listed below are about *Sunny Memories of Foreign Lands*, unless otherwise noted. These reviews are not included in the Works Cited list at the end of this collection.

Bailey, Gamaliel. "Mrs. Stowe and Her New Book." *National Era*, 28 April 1853. University of Virginia, <http://www.iath.virginia.edu/utc/>. (This is a review of *A Key to Uncle Tom's Cabin*.)

Blackwood's Edinburgh Magazine 76 (September 1854): 301–317.

Brown, William W. *Frederick Douglass' Paper*. 10 June 1853; rpt. from *Liberator*. (Letter to Garrison dated 17 May). University of Virginia, <http://www.iath.virginia.edu /utc/>.

Edinburgh Review 101 (April 1854): 151–171. (This essay also reviews *Uncle Tom's Cabin* and *A Key to Uncle Tom's Cabin*.)

Fern, Fanny. "Mrs. Stowe's Uncle Tom." Boston *Olive Branch*. 28 May 1853. University of Virginia, <http://www.iath.virginia.edu/utc/>.

Frederick Douglass' Paper. "Mrs. Stowe Going to England." 31 December 1852; "Mrs. Stowe's Visit to England," 15 April 1853; "Mrs. Stowe in England." 6 May 1853, University of Virginia, <http://www.iath.virginia.edu/utc/>.

Gay, Sydney Howard. *National Anti-Slavery Standard*. 24 September 1853. University of Virginia, <http://www.iath.virginia.edu/utc/>.

Godey's Lady's Book 49 (October 1854): 370.

Littell's Living Age 42 (1854): 457–463 (from the *Examiner*), <http://cdl.library.cornell .edu/moa/index.html>.

London *Times*. "American Slavery: English Opinion of 'Uncle Tom's Cabin.'" 3 September 1852 as rpt. New York *Times*, 18 September 1852. University of Virginia, <http://www.iath.virginia.edu/utc/>.

North American Review. October 1853. 466–493. University of Virginia, <http://www
.iath.virginia.edu/utc/>. (This is a review of *Uncle Tom's Cabin* and *A Key to Uncle
Tom's Cabin*.)

North American Review. October 1854. 423–441.

Provincial Freeman [Toronto]. "Mrs. Stowe." 25 November 1854. University of Virginia, <http://www.iath.virginia.edu/utc/>.

Putnam's Monthly. "Editorial Notes; Literature; American." 4 (September 1854): 338–
342.

Putnam's Monthly. "Editorial Notes; Literature; English." 4 (1854): 671.

United States Magazine and Democratic Review. J. F. C. "Literary Lion Hunting, Coter-
ies and Petti-Coteries." 36 (1855): 31–43. Cornell University, Making of America,
<http://cdl.library.cornell.edu/moa/index.html>.

PART THREE

Transnational Writer

The Construction of Self in *Sunny Memories*

HEN HARRIET BEECHER STOWE made her first visit to Europe in 1853, she was already a well-known figure with a public persona. She was wryly aware of the need to live up to this persona. Describing her reception at one rail stop, where crowds had gathered to greet her, she comments ironically on her bungled response: "I . . . wave[d] a towel out of the window, instead of a pocket handkerchief, and commit[ed] other awkwardnesses, from not knowing how to play my part" (*Sunny Memories* 1: 49). The portraits of her that had already circulated throughout England and the Continent also testified to the fact of her created selfhood, "known" to foreigners but "other" to her own perception of herself.[1] In Europe, then, Stowe was the object not only of others' gaze but also of her own self-scrutiny. Inevitably, questions about role-playing, raised by her particular circumstances, elide with questions about textual self-representation. What are the possible positions available to her as an observer/commentator on the foreign, and what voices can she exploit within the consumerist sphere of which she is by now very much a part?

Stowe's consciousness of a multivocal, adaptable self-hood is linked both to her own personality and to her background. Caught up in the endless domestic round of childbearing and rearing, housekeeping and family commitments, she was also a producer whose literary efforts were increasingly essential to the Stowe finances. As for many other nineteenth-century writing women in America and Britain (parallels with Elizabeth Gaskell are particularly notable here), balancing the private/public, reactive/proactive dichotomies of her life heightened her own sense of a variable and adaptable individuality. This sense was compounded by her tendencies to self-examin-

149

ation, most intense in childhood and adolescence and deriving from her family's Calvinistic Protestantism, with its emphasis on conversion and soul-searching. Uncertain about her spiritual direction, she found it easiest to hide her feelings behind a mask: "If any one questions me, my first impulse is to conceal all I can" (qtd. in Charles Stowe 39–40). In 1833, she noted that "[t]hought, intense emotional thought, has been my disease" (Stowe, Charles 66). Although by young adulthood she had thrown off this habit of crippling introspection, contemporaries observed that she sometimes seemed remote and self-absorbed, in contrast to her normal socially active and outgoing behavior. How to present herself to the public world was, then, a matter of concern that predated her fame as an author.

If there were personal reasons for Stowe's particular kind of self-consciousness, her attempts to reproduce her experience of foreign travel inevitably fed into it. As recent theoretic studies have noted, the genre of travel writing is characterized by a fluid and complex narrative voice, of which the self is often a problematic element. Homi Bhabha argues that the discourse of cultural authority itself "may be ambivalent" because it is in process, not definitive, and is always engaged "in the act of 'composing' its powerful image" (3).   Other critics have pointed out that the observing "I" is frequently destabilized by confrontation with the Other, and that a dialogic relationship between observer and observed, in which the former's identity may undergo shift or slippage, is established. Dennis Porter, for example, proposing an alternative to Edward Said's Orientalist binary of Other/not Other, envisages "a dialogue that would cause subject/object relations to alternate . . . and replace the notion of a place of truth with that of a knowledge which is always relative and provisional" (153). This idea of relative or unstable knowledge links with poststructuralist notions of the textual "self," created as much by discursive and hegemonic restraints as by a conscious adoption of a subject position. In her *Discourses of Difference*, Sara Mills usefully implements Foucauldian theories of the subject "as a result of discursive forces," with the "author-function" as an alternative to fixed notions of an autobiographical textual "I" (17). Applying these ideas to travel writing by women, she argues that while some subject positions are available to them, others are not: "the self within the text is structured from a range of discursive factors or pressures which are not within the control of the writer" (37). While this challenge to intentionality may not be wholly appropriate to a consideration of Stowe—who faced textual constraints different from, and to some extent more open to negotiation than, those experienced by the colonialist women travelers on whom Mills concentrates—emphasis on the instability of the self in travel texts and on the diversity of voice contingent upon this instability provides a helpful way into a discussion of Stowe's representations of Europe.

The particular conditions and status of American travel writing about Europe in the nineteenth century are also relevant here. As has often been noted, the New World visitor to Europe at this time was inevitably affected by sets of subject/object relations that both predetermined response and foregrounded issues of self-representation. William Stowe argues that there is an essential connection between travel and the construction of identity in the nineteenth-century Euro-American context: Americans, he claims, used European travel "to help construct and claim identities variously defined by gender, class, race and nationality." Europe thus "served as a stage for independent self-definition, for establishing personal relations with culture and society that did not necessarily fit the conventional patterns prescribed by hometown and family standards" (xi, 5). For American travelers, Continental Europe raised the dilemma of response to preconceptual knowledge accessed through literature and art. If, as was often the case, concurrence with well-established cultural authority seemed naive or derivative, an alternative was to enact a deliberate subversion of orthodoxy, to defamiliarize the familiar. England presented the additional complication of the parent/child relation that, for most Americans at this time, constituted the most pervasive image of Anglo-American connectedness. This country inspired "a kind of thrill and pulsation of kindred" (*Sunny Memories* 1: 18), yet, while it invited identification, it also reminded the visitor of what America was not and challenged assumptions of New World superiority. Within these parameters, the American traveler often struggled to find an individual voice that was both nationally and personally authentic; seeking this voice raised questions not only of textual self-representation but also of the stability of individual identity in the context of the foreign.

As has already been remarked, when she came to Europe for the first time Stowe already had a known persona. According to her most recent biographer, when Stowe was honored by the lord mayor of London and by many of the English nobility, as well as by other well-known social and political figures, she applied herself "to fulfilling the expectations of her new role as antislavery activist . . . [she understood that] she was a de facto ambassador of American culture" (Hedrick 235–236). She was, indeed, always aware that she had a script to follow. Part of that script, moreover, was that her own voice should be ventriloquized: convention dictated that women could not speak in public, so at antislavery meetings either her husband read out her speech, or else he or her brother Charles made speeches of their own. Ironically, though—as she probably well knew—this overt signifying of her womanly modesty and self-effacement probably helped her cause. Coming to Europe as both a perceived radical activist and a tourist thus presented Stowe with several dilemmas. In the sociopolitical arena, she had not only to steer between the different positions taken up by the abolitionists she met, but she also had to reconcile her own democratic affiliation with more reactionary leanings toward the privileges conferred by a hierarchical social system. In the personal arena, she had to reconcile the role of the sentimental observer/commentator with that of a more subversive persona who wished to challenge conventional responses. One of the most effective ways of coming to terms with, if not completely uniting, these different selves, in her representation of her foreign experiences, was to implement a strategy of overt self-creation in which her own stereotypicality was coexistent with comic subversion of that position. Textually, she was able to preserve and articulate an individual voice by calling attention to its constructedness.

Sunny Memories of Foreign Lands (1854)—a simple and welcoming title—is written in the form of letters to various friends and family members. This epistolary mode was a common convention of eighteenth- and nineteenth-century travel literature and, together with journal entries, constituted the narrative format chosen by writers on both sides of the Atlantic—for example, Catharine Maria Sedgwick and the early Mark Twain in America, and Lady Mary Wortley Montagu and Isabella Bird in Britain. Such letters could be fictional or the real thing, and there is some doubt as to whether any of Stowe's were actually sent to their putative recipients. In her preface, Stowe herself declares that the "*Letters* were, for the most part, compiled from what was written at the time and on the spot. Some few were entirely written after the author's return" (1: v). Joan Hedrick takes them to be strategic invention, best answering Stowe's purpose of introducing Americans "to the cultural richness that awaited them on the other side of the Atlantic." The epistolary mode, as Hedrick goes on to argue, enables Stowe to engage with the realms of "high" European culture via the more "folksy" art of parlor literature with its "homely allusions" and familiarizing voice (266–267). Letter-writing was, of course, an intrinsic element of nineteenth-century social life, an activity that ranged across the public/private divide: at home, letters were often read out in front of family, friends, and servants; they were also one of the artistic forms imaginatively engaged with in the literary gatherings in Litchfield and Cincinnati that Stowe attended. Her own letters reveal her active sense of humor and her delight in the possibilities of language; as well as repositories of gossip, family news, and sermonizing, they were also vehicles for campaigning on local and national issues. Of the latter sort, her brother Charles wrote that they were not "the artless expression of spontaneous emotions. She is not in her letter [sic] pouring forth feeling merely because she feels it but planning by the combination of such and such feelings . . . to produce a given effect"[2] (qtd. in Hedrick 153).

Producing "a given effect" is a paramount consideration in the letters that make up the major part of *Sunny Memories*. Equally significantly, the issue of voice is intrinsic to the work's conception and production. When Stowe was invited to Europe, she knew that her itinerary, especially in Britain, would be arduous and time-consuming. Thus, as well as her husband, Calvin; her widowed sister-in-law, Sarah Buckingham Beecher; and Sarah's son, George, and brother, William Buckingham; she asked her younger brother, Charles Beecher, to accompany them as route organizer and secretary. Even more importantly, Charles was to keep a journal of their travels, which could be used as source material for the account she planned to publish on their return; as Charles himself notes in a letter home, "We shall get up a book, probably after we get back" (Beecher, Charles 38). Her literary task, therefore, was to some extent editorial: in the United States again, she selected and expanded on those parts of the journal that she considered most relevant for her own work. This task also inevitably demanded consideration of the narrator's subject position, as well as of self-representation. In Charles's journal, Stowe is one of the objects of his reproduction. Not only is she named as "Hatty," but she becomes a figure to whom certain traits are assigned—her enthusiasm for romantic scenery, her sense of fun, and her ability to "recall so much of the spiritual and inspiring past" (304), for instance. In her own text, Stowe has to reproduce this object-self as subject-observer, the "I" and the "eye," a self-constructed presence whose textual function is of her own choosing. Undoubtedly, this necessity alerted her to the complexities of this presence as well as to the possibilities of exploiting it.

Comparison of the journal and *Sunny Memories* reveals how these possibilities are implemented. The journal itself is used in two ways in Stowe's text. Sections of it are incorporated directly (indicated as such and acknowledged in the preface [1: v]). These sections are largely verbatim replication, except that names are usually anonymized and parts that Stowe considered irrelevant or unsuitable are omitted—the fact that they are reading novels by Charlotte Brontë, Elizabeth Gaskell, and Julia Kavanagh on their journey, or a joke about Calvin Stowe being a "dried-up old fellow" (Beecher, Charles 288), for example. A few textual alterations are made and chronology is sometimes reordered. One of the more amusing ones, made perhaps in the interests of tact, is the description of their Quaker friend Joseph Sturge: Charles's "an honest, portly, jolly old brick of a Quaker" (61) becomes Stowe's more anodyne "a cheerful, middle-aged gentleman" (1: 192–193). In the main body of Stowe's work—that is, in her own "Letters"—the journal has been used as an *aide-mémoire*. Thus incidents and places described by Charles are recounted, with changes and additions interpolated into her text.[3] The additions include accounts of visits at which Charles was not present, Stowe's own observations and meditations on what she sees, and some factual material, such as a long description of charity schools in Aberdeen and details of the antislavery meetings that she attended. The changes she made are particularly pertinent to the question of narrative voice. It is clear that Charles himself shared the Beecher delight in subversive humor, and some of *Sunny Memories'* iconoclasm may have emanated from him. Not only does he note the absurd moments on their travels, but he sometimes positions himself as the surfeited tourist, tired of endless sightseeing. He is skeptical about the merits of Old Masters' paintings; he insists that there is limit to the amount of mountain scenery to be endured—"I begin to think mountains are a bore. (I begin to think Switzerland is a humbug)" (261); and he reduces grand cathedrals to "these famous jolly old rumble-tumble things" (305). He is the one sane member of the party—that is, "uninspired and prosaic, matter-of-fact [and] unimaginative" (65).

Stowe's technique of self-reflexive irony as a means of marking her role as tourist and cultural assessor may have been partly inspired by her brother's irreverent observations. Her emendations and original contributions, however, extend the humor beyond "in" jokes for family consumption to a wider commentary on the significance of tourism in general and on how Americans in particular negotiate with Europe. With her novelist's eye, she enhances the dramatic and burlesque possibilities of absurd situations, positioning herself at the center of this iconoclastic vision. Thus Charles's version of the local Edinburgh boys' remarks on his sister's well-known abundance of hair—"Heck, there's the coorls (curls)" (44)—becomes a more ironically presented act of self-observation—"Heck," says one of them, "that's *her*; see the *coorls*" (*Sunny Memories* 1: 81). In Stratford, though Charles records their witty dialogue about the inaptly named rooms at the White Hart Inn, Stowe's text adds her (attributed) gloss that they "Can't sleep in Richard III, we should have such bad dreams" (1: 214), emphasizing her function as producer-commentator. And, as will be shown, her foregrounding of the cultural consumerism inherent in tourism is focalized through her conscious role-playing.

Through skillful implementation of voice and narrative viewpoint, then, Stowe's text becomes more than just self-expression and personal recall: the "I/eye" informs and instructs readers about Europe but also resists imbrication with previous voices and authorities and establishes an individual identity. Stowe makes full use of the possibilities of the epistolary form, using it as a means of instruction, entertainment, and personal opinion. She was already familiar with the practice of rendering foreign experience in letters, having worked up for the *Cincinnati Journal* portions of the letters that her husband had sent during his first solo trip to Europe soon after their marriage in 1836. Significantly, many of these letters contained ironic, debunking descriptions of the perceived absurdities of European life and customs, and Stowe may have thought of these when she started to cast her own experiences in literary form. Her main strategy, however, is to set herself up as an eager tourist, gullible and predictable, and then to deconstruct this position by revealing it as deliberate self-creation. Hedrick argues that this method of both valorizing and ironizing individual perception is Stowe's calculated attempt to make the European foreign accessible to her readership, challenging the codifying voices of cultural "authorities": through such a strategy, "she undercuts her pretensions to high culture and maintains her foothold in it," keeping an intimacy with her audience while she instructs them in "the intricacies and absurdities" of the foreign aesthetic (269). Hedrick is right to stress the element of calculation here, and Stowe certainly overtly exploits the canonical status and discourse of the traveler/guide who pronounces on the tourist's Europe. But Stowe's position is more complex than this suggests. In establishing, then demolishing, herself as the conventional tourist relaying facts and impressions to people back home, Stowe reveals some of her own anxieties about her role in Europe and the nature of her responses. Her slippage between various voices and narrative levels shows artful control of her material but also indicates some personal ambivalence and unease.

In negotiating between the discursive positions of cultural authority and individual observation, Stowe presents an identity that is fluid and sometimes elusive. Three textual voices or subject positions, interconnected rath-

er than discrete, seem particularly prominent in the construction of her literary persona. In one mode, Stowe is the unashamed tourist, eagerly express-
ing her enthusiasm for all that she has anticipated about the Old World. As
for so many of her generation, her trip to Europe represented a long-held
dream: she had learned French and Italian, and Sir Walter Scott, a favorite
family author, had provided an entry into the romantic history and landscape she was prepared to find. A letter to her husband on his first visit to
Europe indicates her envy and longing: "Only think of all you expect to see:
the great libraries and beautiful paintings, fine churches. . . . My dear, I wish
I were a man in your place; if I wouldn't have a grand time!" (Fields 94). Sev-
enteen years and seven children later, when she herself was finally able to
accomplish her desire, her sense of anticipation was just as strong: "If I live
till spring I shall hope to see Shakespeare's grave and Milton's mulberry tree,
and the good land of my fathers,—old, Old England! May that day come!"
(Fields 178). This enthusiasm, at last granted its object, is articulated in
Sunny Memories in the traditional discourses of eighteenth- and nineteenth-
century travel writing, drawing on the ideals of the picturesque and the poetic, and implementing familiar tropes of appreciation. At the same time,
however, Stowe is aware of the codification of such discourses, which,
through the establishment of canons of taste and aesthetic value, prevent
or restrict a genuinely individual response. Her attempt to circumvent this
problem is to develop two other voices that are both self-reflexive and defensive and that seek to accommodate her own personal vision to a wider
framework of cultural values and assumptions. One of these voices works to
justify her admiration of those aspects of Europe that, as she well knows, are
antithetical to the American principles of republicanism and democracy of
which she is the representative; the other employs comic subversion of her
own position as a tourist, both undermining the pretentiousness of cultural
posturing and engaging her readers in the process of reconstructing a more
honest approach to the foreign. In these linked approaches, Stowe's text prefigures the multivocalism of Mark Twain's *Innocents Abroad* and *A Tramp
Abroad*, especially in its use of self-reflexive irony, with both writers exploiting the relationship between a public, representative persona and a more private, individualistic observer.

The most conventional voice evident in Stowe's work is that of the sentimental tourist, a voice that she employs—not surprisingly—in the context
of well-known or prototypical sights/sites of visitor interest. At the old
bridge of Balgourie, in Aberdeen, for instance, she enthuses over the "wild,

overhanging banks, shadowy trees, and dipping wild flowers, [which] all conspire to make a romantic picture" (1: 103); at Kenilworth Castle, she indulges in melancholy meditation over the ivy-covered ruins; and on the way to Coventry she notes the charming "air of rural, picturesque quiet" encompassing the whole locale (1: 247). A particularly notable—and, again, predictable—aspect of Stowe's more conventional response is the way in which she reproduces the external environment in terms of visual or plastic art, composing its items as if they are part of a pictorial representation. In this, she draws, albeit not formally, on elements of the Picturesque, most appropriately with reference to the areas of Alpine scenery that she observes. Such scenery was considered particularly amenable to the Picturesque, a formulaic manner of viewing in which configurations of landscape were apprehended so as to suggest an ideal "framed" scene. Although Stowe does not often employ the specific term *picturesque* or, like many other nineteenth-century travelers, make reference to painters such as Claude Lorrain, Nicolas Poussin, and Salvator Rosa as evaluative models for apprehending the ideal landscape, inherent in her response is the desire to recreate an aesthetically familiarizing picture. In describing Swiss mountain scenery, for example, she participates in a system of ordering the landscape by establishing a common ground of evaluation that draws on previously authorized high status discourses, positioning herself at a "station" from which the prospect can be reconstructed so as to render it accessible.[4]

At various points in her visit to the area around Chamonix, Stowe attempts to create a picture in words, enabling her putative correspondent to visualize the scene. At Sallenches, trying to "study and sketch" a mountain seen from the hotel window, she meditates, "Let me try if words can paint it" (2: 206). The ensuing picture emphasizes different tiers or regions within the view—"of pasture, of pine, of bare, eternal sterility"—each with its own topographical features and colors. The whole is presented in such a way as to draw the eye upward, following hers, until the apex is reached: "surmounting all, straight, castellated turrets of rock, looking out of swathing bands of cloud. A narrow, dazzling line of snow crowned the summit" (2: 207). Spatial dimension is the most important element here, with evidence of humanity small and insignificant: "looking out over my head from green hollows, I saw the small cottages, so tiny, in their airy distance, that they seemed scarcely bigger than a squirrel's nut, which he might have dropped in his passage" (2: 209).

Her representation of her first magnificent sighting of Mont Blanc also positions reader with writer in the role of a spectator who "composes" the scene in order to familiarize it:

> How can I describe it? Imagine yourself standing with me on this projecting rock, overlooking a deep, piny gorge, through which flows the brawling waters of the Arve. On the other side of this rise mountains whose heaving swells of velvet green, cliffs and dark pines, are fully made out and colored; behind this mountain, rises another, whose greens are softened and shaded, and seem to be seen through a purplish veil; behind that rises another, of a decided cloud-like purple; and in the next still the purple tint changes to rosy lilac; while above all, like another world up in the sky, mingling its tints with the passing clouds, sometimes obscured by them, and then breaking out between them, lie the glacier regions. (2: 212–213)

The description, as well as emphasizing color, concentrates on the artistic and structural relationship between parts, again leading the eye up to the furthest summit. Moreover, Stowe's rendition does not focus merely on the visual: the final burst of the setting sun on this mountainous region is a "transfiguration" whose effect "was solemn and spiritual above every thing I have ever seen," a "dazzling revelation" offering her "an image of the light shed by his [God's] eternal love on the sins and sorrows of the time, and the dread abyss of eternity" (2: 214–215). The same kind of visionary experience occurs at the sight of the Rhone valley seen from Forclaz Mountain (where, defending the individualism of her response, Stowe claims ignorance that "this was one of the things put down in the guide book, that we were expected to admire" [2: 253]).

To note how Stowe uses these well-established discourses is not to deny that she was emotionally stirred by what she saw or to suggest that she could find only imitative language in which to represent it. The freedom to enjoy herself and wander unconstrained by worshipping crowds that she so appreciated in Switzerland is reflected in the elevated register and richness of her writing here.[5] But, as has been suggested, she was also aware of the dangers of secondhand response in which actual "seeing" is replaced by idealized and derivative representation. For this reason, juxtaposed with this orthodoxy of reception are the more consciously subversive voices of iconoclasm and self-mockery. One of Stowe's textual strategies is to deflate her own role as sentimental tourist by foregrounding the ironic discrepancy between expectation and actuality. In many contexts, she derides her own enthusiasm for its complicity with the constructed world of cultural artifact offered to American visitors. She presents herself, for instance, as participating in the economy of material consumerism that foreign travel has become, on several occasions referring to her cultural activities as commercial transactions between persuasive vendors and willing buyers. On the advisability of "doing" Melrose, Dryburgh, and Abbotsford all in one day, she comments, "There was no time for sentiment; it was a business affair, that must be looked in the face promptly, if we meant to get through" (1: 129). This self-reflexive strategy of both foregrounding herself as a tourist and separating herself from this role through the implementation of a "knowing" and ironic deflationary voice, prefigures—as has been mentioned—that of Twain. But, as with Twain, this confident self-authorization—confession and textual exploitation of the tourist's silliness, gullibility, or conventionality in order to valorize the writer/traveler's subject position—does not preclude ambivalence about the relation between the New World visitor and his or her New World "home." Neither Stowe nor Twain is an "innocent," however much they may construct themselves as such, but conversely, the engagement with what are essentially defensive strategies reveals an awareness of the complex and often contradictory response that Europe calls forth.

Stowe often foregrounds the puncturing of her own naive romanticizing. Ruined Martello towers off the coast of Ireland lose their glamor when they turn out to be mere custom houses, and the picturesqueness of fires burning around Glasgow—assumed to be castles in flames or beacons, in true Scott mode—is diminished when it is discovered that they are iron-works (1: 14, 50). Stowe also mocks her own readiness to believe what most accords with her preconceived ideas about the Old World, as she and her party watch for "signs of antiquity" (1: 44) from the train window and keep up "a bright lookout for ruins and old houses" (1: 47). So she delights in walking on Bothwell Bridge, immortalized by Scott in *Old Mortality*, but is "rather mortified, after we had all our associations comfortably located upon it, to be told that it was not the same bridge—it had been newly built, widened, and otherwise made more comfortable and convenient" (1: 65).[6] Stowe is acutely aware of the impact of romantic literary associations on the American mind, particularly in Scotland, where, as she observes, response to the scenery and buildings is always filtered through recall of the works of Scott and Burns. She recognizes, for example, that the romantic aura of Scott's historical settings is itself a construct that the traveler willingly transposes onto the scene before her: "One might naturally get a very different idea of a feudal castle by starving to death in the dungeon of it, than by writing sonnets at a picturesque distance" (1: 69). Only Americans, for whom feudalism has been "a thing so much of mere song and story," are completely free to enjoy its seductive ideality, she argues with self-referential irony (1: 69). At the ruined Dryburgh Abbey, the story about a mysterious female inmate who left her cell only at midnight "gives just enough superstitious chill to this beautiful ruin to help the effect of the pointed arches, the clinging wreaths of ivy, the shadowy pines, and yew trees; in short, if one had not a guide waiting, who had a bad cold, if one could stroll here at leisure by twilight or moonlight, one might get up a considerable deal of the mystic and poetic" (1: 140).

The most amusing instance of Stowe's self-referential mockery with regard to literary and romantic association occurs in her account of their visit to Melrose Abbey. The whole occasion is constructed like a fictional narrative with preliminary description, key events, and dialogue, all building up to the final absurd anticlimax. Having seen the abbey by daylight, Stowe declares her intention of making a romantic visit by moonlight, although told it is probable that Scott himself, being "a man of very regular habits . . . [who] seldom went out evenings" (1: 164), never saw it under such conditions. The piece becomes a burlesque, as they venture out into the gloomy night "with the comforting reflection that we were doing what Sir Walter would think a rather silly thing" (1: 165) and try to make out the details of the abbey in the indistinct light of a feeble moon. Ghostly rustlings turn out to be rooks, annoyed at being disturbed, and the whole escapade ends abruptly as a sudden gust of misty rain engulfs them on the ruined staircase, "whereat we all tumbled back promiscuously on to each other, and concluded we would not go up" (1: 168). Similarly self-reflexive deconstruction of her own willingness to buy into tourist mythologies occurs at Stratford. Here, having reverentially visited and meditated upon Shakespeare's house and seen his mulberry tree, they return to the hotel, "having conscientiously performed every jot and tittle of the duty of good pilgrims," only to be informed that "Shakespeare's house . . . wasn't his house, and . . . his mulberry . . . wasn't his mulberry"; Stowe, however, is "quite ready to allow the foolishness of the thing, and join the laugh at [my] own expense" (1: 214).

Deflation of the tourist response is not confined to the well-known cultural sites of Britain. In Continental Europe, too, Stowe employs her strategy of ironic reductiveness. Enthusing on the stupendous view of the Glacier de Boisson, for example, she adds "but in all these places you have to cut short your raptures at the proper season, or else what becomes of your supper?" (2: 232). The scenery itself, it is suggested, is a construct for tourists: in the mountains, a goat stands on a crag—"He knew he looked picturesque, and that is what he stood there for" (2: 242). A hilarious scene at St. Ursula's Church in Cologne, where they are shown the (supposed) bones and relics of the saint and her eleven thousand virgins, is rendered as an absurd dialogue between parroting guide and disingenuously credulous listeners; here, though, the rottenness of Romish superstition (in stoutly Protestant eyes) is as much the focus of the irony as the tourists' gullibility. More seriously, Stowe also recognizes that at well-known sites anticipation may be greater than fulfillment. Having recorded the achievement of making the mule-trip up to view Mont Blanc, she notes that on finally seeing the long-awaited mountain in its full glory, "in full possession of the whole my mind gave out like a rocket that will not go off at the critical moment" (2: 225).

Stowe's iconoclasm is articulated somewhat differently in her response to the pictorial art and the architecture she views in Europe. Here, she is self-authorizing instead of self-deflationary, resisting traditional evaluations rather than ironically acceding to them. Like other post-Grand Tour visitors to Europe, especially women, she challenges the (male) discourses of assessment, relying on her own immediacy of response. Thus, she refuses to relinquish her opinion that a Salvator Rosa picture in Warwick Castle is very ugly, even when told that her perception is at fault: "I utterly distrust this process, by which old black pictures are looked into shape; but then I have nothing to lose, being in the court of the Gentiles in these matters, and obstinately determined not to believe in any real presence in art which I cannot perceive by my senses" (1: 236). Similarly, at Dulwich Gallery, she questions why only *old* masters are thought well of, confessing that "I have some partialities towards young masters" and concluding that "I will keep some likes and dislikes of my own, and will not get up any raptures that do not arise of themselves" (1: 279). She reiterates her claim of the right to personal judgment in Frankfort: "Nobody shall impose old, black smoky Poussins and Salvator Rosas on me, and so insult my eyesight and common sense as to make me confess they are better than pictures which I can see have all the freshness and bloom of the living reality upon them" (2: 322).[7] Alongside this—perhaps a little too energetically stated—prioritization of individual response is the valid observation that artistic reputation is established as much by convention and historical forces as by individual merit. Stowe devotes the whole of letter 48 in volume 2 to a discussion of this point, arising from her sense that as "an art-pilgrim" (2: 340) she found herself frequently disappointed.

This humorous, though subversive, reliance on the individual and instinctive as judges of excellence is foregrounded most effectively in Stowe's account of her reaction to the marble monument to Princess Charlotte in St. George's Chapel, Windsor. She is moved to tears by its "poetical conception" and "pathos," but the next day she is told by "one of the [artistic] authorities" that the sculpture is in "miserable taste . . . melodramatic—terribly so!" (2: 46–47). With exaggerated mock self-abasement, Stowe declares herself "so appalled by this word, of whose meaning I had not a very clear idea, that I dropped the defence at once, and determined to reconsider my tears. To have been actually made to cry by a thing that was melodramatic, was a distressing consideration" (2: 47). Not only is her unashamed emotion here thus valorized over the pretentious critical evaluation, but as Hedrick points out, there is additional irony in the fact that Stowe deliberately exploited melodrama and emotion to great effect in *Uncle Tom's Cabin* (368).[8]

The other prominent subversive voice found in Stowe's text has a rather different resonance. It is heard when her native American republicanism has to confront those aspects of the Old World—landscape, history, and society—that rub up against those democratic principles that she holds dear and of which she is the perceived representative. This voice is heard in two main contexts: the response to sites of romantic literary or historical association, and the encounter with the world of privilege and elitism embodied in the British aristocracy. It is less self-reflexively parodic and operates more as a form of defensiveness with self-justification underpinning the surface irony. Aware that overreverence for the past is antithetical to an American progressive spirit, Stowe seeks to place her admiration for historical glories in the context of right feeling and contemporary relevance. So at Bothwell Castle, imagining "the splendid phantasmagoria of chivalry and feudalism," alongside "the indescribable sweetness, sadness, wildness of the whole scene [which makes] its voice heard in our hearts," she declares, "I have often been dissatisfied with the admiration, which a poetic education has woven into my nature, for chivalry and feudalism; but, on a closer examination, I am convinced that there is a real and proper foundation for it, and that, rightly understood, this poetic admiration is not inconsistent with the spirit of Christ" (1: 62–63). In Germany, she tries to argue that, despite the evidence of poverty and suffering, the money spent on beautiful cathedrals such as Strasbourg and Cologne, which she so much admires, is acceptable as a tribute to God's beauty. Of course, in Europe she was constantly reminded of the relative cultural impoverishment of her own country, and like all American visitors, she had to reconcile glorification of tradition with adherence to a perceived forward-looking ideology.

The note of apology—even of sophistry—is strongest in the context of social hierarchies that seem to privilege wealth and power. Again, at Bothwell Castle, in a burst of honesty, Stowe confesses her inability to explain "the nature of that sad yearning and longing with which one visits the mouldering remains of a state of society which one's reason wholly disapproves, and which one's calm sense of right would think it the greatest misfortune to have recalled" (1: 60). Her response is to lay herself open to "the wild, poetic beauty of these ruins" (1: 61) while at the same time praising the taste of the owners who have preserved them so well. Instinct and reason jostle for predominance, too, at Warwick Castle, where she argues herself into accepting the aesthetic pleasure afforded her by the splendor through philanthropic justification: "The influence of these estates on the community cannot but be in many respects beneficial, and should go some way to qualify the prejudice with which republicans are apt to contemplate anything aristocratic. . . . With such reflections the lover of the picturesque may comfort himself [sic], hoping he is not sinning against the useful in his admiration of the beautiful" (1: 239). Despite the note of self-mockery here, Stowe's commentary indicates ambivalence; her protest against a single vision coexists with her awareness of the dilemmas facing the intelligent and loyal American in Europe.

Her patriotism was most tested by her encounters with those members of the British aristocracy who were instrumental in promoting her antislavery cause. Chief of these were the Duke and Duchess of Sutherland, who entertained her on several occasions at their sumptuous London mansion, Stafford House, and invited her to their Scottish estate. Stowe clearly felt honored by the hospitality and generosity of the Sutherlands, as is indicated in the letter that she subsequently wrote to the Duchess: "Such an episode in the hitherto shady walk of my life seemed almost like a poetic dream. Many things in your surroundings which are to you matters of daily habitude are to me so new and beautiful!" (qtd. in Stowe, Charles 88). Stowe's biographer Annie Fields stresses that her subject's head was never turned by such "lionising": "[I]n spite of Mrs. Stowe's love of society, she did not become a woman of society, properly so called" (256). But there is no doubt that Stowe recognized in herself contrary impulses of instinctive admiration and more theoretic disapprobation. Importantly, she was acutely aware that the very class that most actively supported her campaigns could be—and were—

accused of creating and exploiting a protoslave class of oppressed workers. Most crucially, she had heard accounts of the way in which aristocratic Scottish landowners like the Sutherlands had turned their "tenants out into the snow, and order[ed] the cottages to be set on fire over their heads because they would not go out" (1: 302). This of course refers to the Highland clearances, a savage policy of depopulation that forced thousands of tenant farmers to leave their homeland, many emigrating to America.[9]

Stowe's championing of the Sutherlands' humanitarian schemes offended many Scots, for whom memories of the clearances were still very bitter. Before she had even visited their Scottish estate (this trip to Europe was cut short by news of her daughter's illness, so she did not in fact take up the invitation), she was anxious to defend their aristocratic benevolence. In *Sunny Memories* she devotes the whole of letter 17 to a rebuttal of "those ridiculous stories . . . which have found their way into many of the prints in America" (1: 301) and she points to all the improvements that the Sutherlands have in fact carried out for their tenants: to her mind, their efforts are "an almost sublime instance of the benevolent employment of superior wealth and power in shortening the struggles of advancing civilization, and elevating in a few years a whole community to a point of education and material prosperity, which, unassisted, they might never have obtained" (1: 313).[10] This distinctly colonialist discourse indicates Stowe's anxiety to square her democratic principles with her admiration of a section of British society that had broken down all her republican prejudice and proved so sympathetic to her cause. On her second visit to Europe, in 1856 and 1857, she did make the postponed trip to the Scottish Highlands, and what she found there in no way encouraged her to change her mind: "I see evidently happiness and prosperity all through the line of this estate. I see the duke giving his thought and time, and spending the whole income of this estate in improvements upon it. . . . I see the duke and duchess evidently beloved wherever they move. . . . I observe well-clothed people, thriving lands, healthy children, fine school-houses, and all that" (Fields 218–219). Similar justifications, ironically enough, are to be found in some of the accounts of nineteenth-century visitors to Southern United States plantations, who saw—or were shown—what they wanted to see. Stowe cannot be accused of deliberate distortion or sophistry here, but her eulogy, while it seeks to challenge simplistic idealizing or demonizing attitudes to British hierarchies and historical traditions, betrays a heightened eagerness to keep intact her vision of a beneficial social stratification led by enlightened paternalism.

In negotiating the possible roles open to her as both public visitor and private tourist in Europe, then, Stowe adopts a variety of voices that link and overlap. Both aware of the almost formulaic responses embedded in an American reading of the Old World and anxious to foreground that awareness as an act of independent authenticity, she situates herself within various sites of engagement with the foreign. Her strategy of self-reflexive irony allows her to range freely between the voices, valorizing each; by both presenting and deconstructing the figure of "the American abroad," she enables her readers to recognize and accept the complex mixture of receptivity and skepticism that characterizes her response. Ambivalence is part of this complexity, the more marked where it is not subjected to self-irony. Ultimately Stowe neither has—nor wants to have—the confidence to resist wholly the allure of Old World romance, as her final nostalgic farewell to it indicates: "thus, almost sadly as a child might leave its home, I left the shore of kind, strong Old England—the mother of us all" (2: 432).

NOTES

1. Stowe considered that such portraits made her look like a Gorgon or the Sphinx, resemblances that amused rather than annoyed her.

2. Charles Beecher to Isabella Beecher, 14 July 1839.

3. Charles and his sister obviously consulted about what should be included, and it was clearly never intended that the journal should be reproduced unedited. Charles notes that "Hatty does not want *any* of our journal published in the newspapers, and I agree" (38).

4. For a discussion of the principles of the Picturesque and their application in the eighteenth century, see Andrews.

5. The welcome chance to escape from the rigors of public visitations in Britain once they were in Continental Europe is noted by Charles: "We mean to see life, nature and art. We mean to take a kind of six-months' aesthetic dessert after a ten-years' meal of *practical* dogmatics and categorics" (150).

6. A similar strategy is employed when she describes her planned visit to the churchyard in which Gray wrote his famous "Elegy in a Country Churchyard," preparing herself to "have a little scene over it" (2: 48). Having discovered an ancient church with ivy-covered tower, "all perfect as could be," she recites the "Elegy" and gives herself up to melancholy, only to find out later that it was the wrong place. Her tongue-in-cheek accommodation to this deflating setback reinforces her ironic awareness of the absurdity of her touristic posturing: "However . . . we could . . . console ourselves with the reflection that the emotion was admirable, and wanted only the right place to make it the most appropriate in the world" (2: 49–50).

7. Her choice of painters on whom to comment here may link to her apparent reluctance to use them as models of picturesque apprehension of landscape.

8. It is interesting that one of Stowe's compatriots and near-contemporaries on a European visit, Catharine Maria Sedgwick, clearly accepted such guidebook teaching in this instance: "We went into St George's Chapel. . . . There is an elegant monument in wretched taste in one corner, to the Princess Charlotte" (*Letters* 1: 72).

9. For a discussion of this issue, see Newman, "Stowe's Sunny Memories," and Shepperson.

10. In the light of this remark, it is perhaps somewhat ironic that earlier Stowe comments on the sophistry of proslavery camps in the South who defend the institution on the grounds that it brings "an inferior race . . . under the watch and care of a superior race to be instructed in Christianity" (1: 25–26).

Art and the Body in *Agnes of Sorrento*

GAIL K. SMITH

OR HARRIET BEECHER STOWE, the first of her three European tours was a voyage of artistic discovery. After a triumphant progress through England and Scotland beginning in the spring of 1853, the celebrated "authoress" of *Uncle Tom's Cabin* left secretly with her party for Paris, where, unheralded and undisturbed, she could walk to the Louvre as often as she wished. "Think of it!" she wrote in a letter home, "to one who has starved all a life, in vain imaginings of what art might be, to know that you are within a stone's throw of a museum full of its miracles, Greek, Assyrian, Egyptian, Roman sculptures and modern painting, all there!" (qtd. in Wilson, Forrest 357). Until then, aside from a little training in painting, her scant acquaintance with art and artists had all been secondhand, gleaned from reviews and travel accounts in periodicals, and especially from the popular books of art historian Anna Jameson (*Sunny Memories* 2: 107). Now in Paris, she took very seriously her encounters with art. With her brother Charles Beecher, a poet and musician, she visited studios, cathedrals, and galleries, debating the typical genteel Protestant American tourist's topics of the day: the morality of art in churches, the proper representation of the Virgin Mary. Typical though it may have been, for Stowe the mere act of gazing on a Raphael was an interpretive revolution: this laywoman was suddenly reading the storied, sacred text of art all by herself.

On her return to the States, Stowe compiled her notes, with the help of Charles's travel journal, in *Sunny Memories of Foreign Lands* (1854). For Stowe, the book was more than the chatty guidebook it was often used for— it was a record of a conversion experience. The convert announced her new frame of reference with a new vocabulary. Suddenly her novels and sketches

allude authoritatively to paintings, statues, and artists. The first page of
Dred (1856) compares heroine Nina Gordon to sculptures of Venus. *The
Minister's Wooing* (1859) compares Mary Scudder to a sketch by Overbeck
and Virginie de Frontignac to the voluptuous women of Rembrandt, Ru-
bens, and Titian.

After a second trip in 1857, Stowe toured in Europe a third time in 1859
and 1860, and it was on a wet day in Salerno in the spring of 1860 that her
encounter with art took a new turn. She began writing in what was for her a
new genre: the international art novel. Joan Hedrick has pointed out the
departure this work constituted for Stowe and has argued that Stowe was
codifying the genre before Hawthorne published *The Marble Faun* and
before Henry James perfected the form (Hedrick 293). *Agnes of Sorrento*
(serialized in the *Atlantic Monthly* and the *Cornhill Magazine* in 1861; published in book form in 1862) was born of Stowe's encounter with Italian sacred art. She actually began the novel in her sketchbook/journal from this
trip, now in the Stowe-Day library in Hartford; the novel's pages are juxtaposed with scribbled lists of paintings she was seeing—"Church of the
Saluti—Tintorettos Marriage of Cana—Picture of the Virgin ascending the
steps" (*Sketchbook* n.p.). The novel is full of descriptions of sacred art and architecture, and its characters and its narrator frequently muse on artistic
questions. Unusually for Stowe, too, the Bible is almost completely absent
from this book. Set in Savonarola's fifteenth-century Italy, with much discussion of churchly politics, ritual, and belief, the novel nevertheless takes
seriously the illiteracy of its peasant characters and the typical nineteenth-
century Protestant American's sense of the scarcity of the Bible for pre-
Reformation laypeople. The diminished biblicism signals a shift in Stowe's
writing: this novel is preeminently about *visual* texts and their readers.

Still, *Agnes* has links to Stowe's earlier work, as critics have noted. In some
respects it recasts in a Renaissance Italian context the psychological and theological development of Mary Scudder in *The Minister's Wooing*. The book
echoes, too, many of the criticisms and commentary on art we find in *Sunny
Memories*. But *Agnes* also goes further. Seen in the context of Stowe's writing
on art from the 1850s, and the midcentury cultural debates in the United
States over sensuality in art, *Agnes's* controversies over art do more than echo
Hawthorne's *Marble Faun* or present another Madonna figure in the person
of Agnes.[1] The novel asks and attempts to answer many of the artistic questions Stowe was pondering as a now experienced transatlantic traveler. As art
fiction—with fiction's special capacity for ambiguity, nuance, and levels of

signification—the novel is Stowe's most intriguing contribution to mid-nineteenth-century American reactions to European art and especially to women in art. That the novel was serialized simultaneously in the *Atlantic* and London's *Cornhill Magazine* is significant as well. In *Agnes* Stowe seeks to work out her own mission as a Christian woman artist in the broader transatlantic art world—a world in which she was no longer just a bedazzled spectator, as she had been in 1853, but a working artist. Granted, *Agnes* features no female artists and has a heroine who is an artist's subject rather than an artist herself. Nevertheless, in this novel, through an extended study of how a patriarchy uses and misuses a woman's body as metonymy for art, Stowe meditates on art's mission and constructs her own artistic self.

Agnes as Misread Art

Art historian Bailey Van Hook has pointed out that by the mid-nineteenth century, "the characteristics that defined the feminine gender corresponded to what American artists had been taught, learned, or had come to believe that their art should be. Idealized images of women could fulfill the artists' prescriptions for art, as no other subjects could, because their flesh-and-blood female counterparts were perceived as occupying a position analogous to art itself" (7). The idealized heroine of *Agnes* quite clearly plays this role as metonymy for art. First of all, we notice that she is primarily conceived as a subject for art. Critics have often overlooked the fact that she is frequently compared not to the Virgin herself but to paintings of the Virgin, emphasizing her status as art: she is like "some choice old picture of Our Lady," "some of the Madonna faces of Fra Angelico," etc. (5, 25). And *Agnes* is put into this subject role explicitly by her uncle, the artist monk Father Antonio, who sees her while she is in a moment of prayerful rapture and tells her, "I have received a light that thou art to be the model for the 'Hail Mary!' in my Breviary." When Agnes responds with wondering humility, "with the moonlight streaming down on her young, spiritual face," we are told that "the painter thought he had never seen any human creature that looked nearer to his conception of a celestial being" (106).

As a work of art, Agnes is continually being interpreted. Father Antonio's is the first of several misreadings of her. The good monk reads her as "a celestial being," purely spiritual, just as Agnes tries to do herself. Both she and Father Antonio believe she is called to a life as a nun in the local convent of St. Agnes (for whom she is named). On the other hand, Agnes's local priest and spiritual director, Father Francesco, reads her as a sexual temptation, as

"he thought of the sex only in the light of temptation and danger" (44).
In other words, Agnes's beauty—her status as an aesthetic object—inspires
readings of her as pure spirit or as pure body: a saint or a sexpot. In the patriarchal church of the day, Agnes, in her iconic status as Art, inspires these
polarized readings, neither of which truly represents the woman herself.

By presenting and rejecting these misreadings of Agnes, Stowe begins to
define Woman, and the Art for which she stands, as both celestial and physical. *Sunny Memories* demonstrates how much Stowe had thought about
womanhood in art on her first European tour. In *Sunny Memories*, as she
goes from gallery to gallery, Stowe constantly scrutinizes artists' depictions of
women, especially of the Madonna. They nearly all disappoint her. Murillo's
Virgin and Child is very pretty, "but call it Mary and the infant Jesus, and it
is an utter failure. Not such was the Jewish princess, the inspired poetess and
priestess, the chosen of God among all women" (1: 280). Seeing her first
Raphael madonnas, she complains, "I expected a divine baptism, a celestial
mesmerism; and I found four very beautiful pictures. . . . Neither, any more
than Murillo, has he in these pictures shadowed forth, to my eye, the idea of
Mary" (1: 323). As the weeks go by, she becomes increasingly frustrated at all
the "effeminate inane representations" of the Virgin. Only a few even suggest to her "the *scriptural* idea" of Mary (2: 350). Mere physical beauty without the spirit could not depict what Stowe often called "sacred womanhood." As Stowe and her Protestant contemporaries hotly debated how
physical beauty and spiritual meaning should coexist in the work of art,
Agnes seeks to work out answers through the medium of fiction.[2]

Having introduced misreadings of Agnes as either body or spirit, Stowe
begins to disassemble these misreadings. Most obviously, the novel seeks to
liberate Agnes, and the art she stands for, from sexless spirituality, just as *The
Minister's Wooing* had done for Mary Scudder. For instance, Stowe takes
pains in *Agnes* to counter the assumption of Agnes and her church that only
cloistered women are holy. The novel makes clear that the fullest ideal of sacred womanhood is not to be found among women who have renounced
their sexual natures. While Stowe is careful to acknowledge that conventual
and monastic life could be a holy retreat from the world if done right, the
nuns at the convent of St. Agnes are rather melancholy specimens of womanhood. They recall the bloodless Van Eyck women Stowe had called "po-
tato sprouts grown in a cellar" (*Sunny Memories* 2: 162). The abbess, for instance, is "a moonlight sort of person, wanting in all those elements of warm
color and physical solidity which give the impression of a real vital human

existence" (70). When Agnes, troubled by her attraction to the handsome cavalier Agostino, consults with the abbess, the abbess is not much help since she "had never left the walls of that convent since she was ten years old. . . . Her ideas on the subject of masculine attractions were, therefore, as vague as might be the conceptions of the eyeless fishes in the Mammoth Cave of Kentucky with regard to the fruits and flowers above ground. All that portion of her womanly nature which might have throbbed lay in a dead calm" (329).

Pure spirituality for womanhood, then, leaves something to be desired. And though Agnes believes she is destined for a cloistered life, the reader is, of course, meant to see her awakening sexual nature: "The small lips had a gentle compression, which indicated a repressed strength of feeling" (8). While the passionless convent literally has her name on it, Agnes is and must be both physical and spiritual—as Art, for Stowe, must also be. As Agnes sits in the convent garden, the narrator compares her to the garden's Roman statue of a lovely nymph, "utterly without spiritual aspiration or life," a statue that was dug up from the convent's garden soil and that the sisters— oddly—have had baptized and named for St. Agnes (61–62). Agnes quite explicitly mirrors this nymph: "her head drooped into the attitude of the marble nymph, and her sweet features assumed the same expression" (73– 74). However the characters may misread Agnes, then, the narrator presents Agnes as both an icon of Mary and an early modern nymph. Agnes as Art is at once the pagan physical idea of Woman and the Christian ideal of spiri- tual, virgin purity: not an either/or but a both/and. She embodies what Anna Jameson called Christianity's "new type of womanly perfection, com- bining all the attributes of the ancient female divinities with others alto- gether new" (introduction, *Legends of the Madonna* xx).

Art as Palimpsest

Stowe continually emphasizes the blending of pagan and Christian, physical and spiritual, in the novel's insistent image of the palimpsest. Characters, places, religious practices, and art are all layered in this book, with a surface interpenetrated by something imperfectly buried beneath it. The Christian- ity of fifteenth-century Italy is a palimpsest, with Christian practices overlaid onto unexpurgated pagan traditions. Father Francesco, the local priest, is a former Lothario and a living and tormented palimpsest as a result of his vows. In quieter terms, the nuns are too. Their convent, we are told, was erected in the name of "Saint Agnes, the guardian of female purity, out of the wrecks and remains of an ancient temple of Venus, whose white pillars and graceful acanthus-leaves once crowned a portion of the precipice on which the town was built" (58). Making her convent a recycled temple of the goddess of love and sexual pleasure, Stowe suggests the nuns similarly wreck but cannot obliterate their preexisting physical natures. And Agnes emphasizes this return of the repressed herself when, in the convent garden, she not only looks like the nymph but sits down on a marble "fragment" from the old temple, "sculptured with dancing nymphs" (73).

Of course, descriptions of Italy as a palimpsest were commonplace in nineteenth-century writing, and we need look only as far as *Middlemarch* or *The Marble Faun* to see more of them. But Stowe's is more than the ordinary elegiac description. Her Italy is an active volcano continually belching forth vivid chunks of the past, and in case we miss this idea, Stowe places the steaming cone of Vesuvius in the literal landscape of the book. In *Agnes,* the pagan past cannot be kept down. Fragments of ancient marble continually emerge from the soil, and the beaches are littered with bits of mosaic cast up "from the thousands of ancient temples and palaces which have gone to wreck all around these shores" (85). And it's not at all clear that the pagan past *should* be obliterated since Stowe crafts some of her admirable characters as palimpsests too. Agnes, for instance, has facial features as "perfect as in those sculptured fragments of the antique which the soil of Italy so often gives forth to the day" (8), and both the staunch reformer Savonarola and the romantic hero Agostino are described as retaining certain noble traits of the old Romans. All three, in various ways, blend the best of the pagan world with Christian moral purity.

Once Stowe has sensitized us to the ways in which one cannot erase the substrate—as Father Francesco has tried to do in becoming a priest, for instance—we inevitably sit up and notice when Father Antonio talks of "demolish[ing]" the nymphs on a pagan frieze to reuse the marble for Christian art. The artist monk decides to build a shrine to the Virgin in Sorrento, and a local stonecutter tells him of a nearby beach which had "a heathen temple in the old days, and one can dig therefrom long pieces of fair white marble, all covered with heathen images. I know not whether your Reverence would think them fit for Christian purposes" (171). Father Antonio is delighted: "So much the better, boy! so much the better! . . . Only let the marble be fine and white, and it is as good as converting a heathen any time to baptize it to Christian uses. A few strokes of the chisel will soon demolish their naked nymphs and other such rubbish, and we can carve holy virgins, robed from head to foot in all modesty, as becometh saints" (171).

One might argue that Father Antonio's language of "baptizing" the marble recalls Stowe's positive description of the Venus de Milo as "beauty baptized, and made sacramental, as the symbol of that which alone is truly fair" (*Sunny Memories* 2: 170). But the monk's chiseling is a far cry from the nuns' gentler baptism of their convent nymph; unlike his phallic act of demolition, their baptism leaves the nymph intact, though named now for a saint. Stowe's plot in *Agnes* thus moves Father Antonio beyond this point, opening his eyes eventually to the fact that his niece—his ideal art object—is physical as well as spiritual.

Art as Sacrament

Stowe takes Father Antonio beyond his one-sided vision, beyond his phallic censorship of the female body, through a second set of both/and imagery woven throughout the book—the imagery of the sacraments. Father Antonio is both artist and sacrament-bearer as he wanders the country "on a pastoral and artistic tour" (97). As artist, he repairs local shrines and paints studies for a breviary for his convent of San Marco in Florence, where Savonarola is abbot. As priest, he takes to the far-flung country people the bread and wine, what the book always calls simply "the sacrament." It makes sense that Stowe has her artist figure conveying the sacrament since Stowe thought of art as a sacrament itself. In an 1856 letter to her artistically minded younger brother Charles, she links art to the catechism's definition of a sacrament: "The fine arts are the sign.—What Christ gives by his discipline his training & schooling is the thing signified. The fine arts were meant to be sacraments '*outward and visible signs of an inward and spiritual grace*'" (emphasis Stowe's).

Accordingly, Agnes performs art's sacramental function, as her admirer Agostino understands. He correctly reads her as a sacrament, the combination of an earthly sign and a spiritual grace. When Agostino asks for a copy of the monk's sketch of Agnes, Father Antonio inquires, "Would it be to thee an image of an earthly or a heavenly love?" "Of both, father," Agostino replies. "For that dear face has been . . . even as a sacrament to me" (179). Significantly, Agostino has fallen away from the corrupt church of his day, and "[h]e dared not approach the Sacrament" lest his disgust at the rapacious papacy of Alexander VI lead him to utter unbelief. Stowe mentions, too, the ways in which this church is abusing the sacrament by treating it solely as physical elements: Agostino "had heard priests scoff over the wafer they consecrated—he had known them to mingle poison for rivals in the sacramental wine" (121). Agostino's faith in the sacrament is shaken when its physical and spiritual natures are separated. Evidently Agostino does eventually take the sacrament offstage (352), but thematically he doesn't need it to reintegrate himself into the church: Agnes is the sacrament who brings him back to faith by the novel's end. Remaining an earthly sign and acknowledging her physical nature by marrying Agostino, Agnes still, by her earthly beauty, "draws the soul upward toward the angels" (108). Like the sacred art Stowe describes throughout the book, Agnes is "a perpetual sacrament of the eye" (291).

In *Agnes*, when an artist tries to obliterate the physical, he denies the duality of what art must be as a sacrament. The palimpsest images, too, make clear that one cannot bury the pagan or carnal and be fully human. Art, like Woman, must claim both physicality and spirituality. Baptize the nymph, perhaps—but don't chisel her away.

Nineteenth-Century Debates over the Body in Art

Both Stowe and her contemporaries were struggling with these and related issues, as European art invaded the States in traveling exhibits and as well-heeled Americans sailed across the Atlantic to view the galleries of the Old World. Like many Christian apologists for art in the mid-nineteenth century, Stowe maintained that the function of art was to signify the divine, both by its representation of an inspired artist's mind and by the beauties of its subject matter. As she explained in *Sunny Memories*, "The canvas, made vivid by the soul of an inspired artist, tells me something of God's power in creating that soul" (1: 232). And the subject matter was to present beauty that, like that of Agnes, served as "a priestess, through whom men were to gain access to the divine, invisible One" ("Old Oak" 33).

Such preaching about art had become typical of some of the most ardent promoters and collectors of art in America—the middle- or upper-class clergy (including Henry Ward Beecher), who increasingly took European tours and wrote up their impressions for the popular press (Neil Harris 134–136, 303–307; Beecher, *Star Papers*). Stowe's understanding is matched, too, by Anna Jameson's dictum, "A picture or any other work of Art, is worth nothing except in so far as it has emanated from mind, and is addressed to mind" (introduction, *Legends of the Madonna* lxviii). Hence, as Stowe

searched the European galleries for the truest Madonna, her disappoint-
ments were manifold as she encountered one after another with mere beauty
but no inspired mind. Only the combination of sacred subject matter and
the artist's inner grace would produce a sacramental art that brings the same
grace to the otherwise worldly viewer.

In *Agnes*, Stowe has Father Antonio and his hero Fra Angelico create art
in this way.[3] Father Antonio travels Italy in a "dream of bliss" (103), filling his
sketchbook with natural emblems of the divine and finally seeing Mary in
Agnes's face. And Fra Angelico's pictures, we are told, "were painted by the
simple artist on his knees, weeping and praying as he worked, and the sight
of them was accepted by like simple-hearted Christians as a perpetual sacrament of the eye, by which they received Christ into their souls" (291).[4]

If the novel's descriptions of sacred art and artists stopped there, there
would be little more to write here and the novel would be less interesting
than it is. But Stowe throws a wrench into this ideal mechanism of art and
artist by having Father Antonio introduce another vexed question of both
the fifteenth and the nineteenth centuries. As he tells Agnes,

> Could you believe it, daughter, in these times of backsliding and rebuke there
> have been found painters base enough to paint the pictures of vile, abandoned
> women in the character of our blessed Lady; yea, and princes have been found
> wicked enough to buy them and put them up in churches, so that the people
> have had the Mother of all Purity presented to them in the guise of a vile har-
> lot. Is it not dreadful? (104–105)

Father Antonio then describes for her how Savonarola urged the Florentine
artists to seek their models for Mary "among pious and holy women living a
veiled and secluded life, like that our Lady lived before the blessed annunci-
ation. 'Think you,' he said, 'that the blessed Angelico obtained the grace to
set forth our Lady in such heavenly wise by gazing about the streets on
mincing women tricked out in all the world's bravery?'" (105) In contrast,
Father Antonio tells Agnes that she, like Dante's Beatrice, has been given "a
beauty which draws the soul upward toward the angels, instead of downward to sensual things, like the beauty of worldly women" (108).

A modern reader might wonder if this discussion of harlots posing as
Mary is simply generic Protestant condemnation of the corruptions of
Alexander VI's papacy. From Jameson, Stowe most likely knew of Savonar-
ola's ire over depictions such as the Vatican fresco featuring the notorious
Giulia Farnese as Mary, with Alexander kneeling at her feet (introduction,

Legends of the Madonna xxxi). Since the reference to harlots as Mary is in the context of discussion of Agnes's suitability as a model, though, it seems Stowe wants readers to think about the relation between the artist's subject matter and the artist's model, and particularly about that relation in sacred art. In fact, moral questions of the relation of model to artist and model to artwork were hot topics at mid-century in the United States and Britain, and Stowe's *Atlantic* and *Cornhill* readers would have picked up on this passage's contemporary relevance.[5] Some familiarity with those debates will help us understand how and why *Agnes* dramatizes them.

What was the trouble with using a socially unacceptable woman as a model? As nineteenth-century Christian writers often reiterated, the artist of a holy subject needs to be in a holy frame of mind, and his subject matter modeled appropriately. Hence Stowe presents Father Antonio in a religious rapture as he taps Agnes as his model for Mary. The flip side of this right way to do art is the worldly artist, uninspired, who seeks among "abandoned women" for mere physical beauty to paint and to label "Mary, Mother of our Lord." A mismatch of model and subject, in this paradigm, thwarts the divine mission of art. The artist could not have chosen or painted this model with a holy intent; the model could not have had a holy frame of mind; and the ordinary viewer cannot look on a well-known woman of the streets and mentally translate her into Mary. As there is nothing spiritual in the creative artist's mind or in the artist's model, there is no effective sacrament for the viewer.

Such thinking on artist's models became most troubled in relation to the nude, itself a vexed subject in mid-nineteenth-century America. Nude paintings or sculptures were scarce in the United States before 1830, and live nude models even scarcer. Artists who defended the practice of using live models for nudes often moved to Europe, where the practice was more accepted and cheaper.[6] As nudes began to appear—tentatively at first—in American painting and especially neoclassical sculpture, many viewers could only see them as whores (because the sign of nakedness could only signify an inward reality of immorality), the artists serving as pimps proffering these figures to the public. So much for the priestly mission of art: one could argue (and plenty did) that artist, model, and intent were equally loathsome, and viewers were placed in the uncomfortable position of participating in the artist's voyeurism. Add to that secular concern the religious idea of art as sacrament, and you have the concern of a serious, educated, Platonic Christian art lover like Stowe.

Stowe's encounters with European art and artists in the years before *Agnes* prompted her meditations not only on woman's body as art but more particularly on the troublesome topic of nude female models. In 1856 when Charles Beecher wrote her announcing his intention of moving to Europe to be a composer, Stowe replied using the nude model as the paradigmatic example of the corrupt signification possible even in the sacred arts: "I believe that . . . Art *must* be redeemed to Jesus but when I see what it is now—what authors, & painters, & sculptors, & composers & musicians are—I say can these dry bones live. Conceive that the painters & sculptors must study from living models!—not merely at first but always for every picture & every statue!—& of course, it is conceded that the female models are women of no character." In Rome herself at the time, she goes on to recount a recent visit to a pious Protestant sculptor's studio, where she saw his sketch for a statue of "the raising of Jairus' daughter . . . a study of the body of a young girl of about 12 years entirely naked. . . . [O]ne cannot help thinking of the temptations which this sort of thing presents *on both sides*" (letter to Charles Beecher, emphasis Stowe's). Like many of her contemporaries, Stowe here locates the moral crux of artistic interpretation in the representation of the nude female in art, most especially in sacred art. If artists worshiped the body over the soul—a problem that her age identified as most probable when the male artist depicted the nude female—art became pornography. If the artist was a voyeur, the naked female model became not "beauty baptized" but simply a sexual object. Like Hawthorne's Miriam in *The Marble Faun*, Stowe also suggested the converse: that the presence of naked female models could make even well-meaning Christian male artists into voyeurs, rendering them incapable of producing true art.[7] Charles Beecher intended to be a composer, not a visual artist, but no matter. The sacramental nature of all art meant for Stowe that any misreading of that sign—the worship of the sign over what is signified, the material over the spiritual, the production of art for art's sake—was morally devastating and an indication of the decadence of the art world. The sacrament that art was supposed to be could not work.

Yet Stowe admired nudes she considered of chaste intent. She was enthralled with William Wetmore Story's bare-breasted *Cleopatra* and *Libyan Sibyl* when she visited the sculptor's Roman studio in 1857 and 1860 (Hedrick 270, Wilson, Forrest 453–454). From a friend in Paris she acquired "mathematical reductions of some of the best specimens, ancient & modern of the sculptures in the Louvre," some of them likely the Louvre's famous nudes (letter to Henry Ward Beecher). In painting, too—a tougher sell for Americans since the nudes were not chaste white marble but realistically colored—Stowe thought nudes could be perfectly acceptable. She had no problem with Batoni's painting of a reclining, bare-breasted Mary Magdalen: "though the neck and bosom are exposed, yet there is an angelic seriousness and gravity in the conception of the piece which would check an earthly thought" (*Sunny Memories* 2: 345). She had a copy at home and would include it in her *Woman in Sacred History* (1873). Because the body, rightly understood, was a divine creation, Stowe did not condemn Michelangelo for making "the study of the human figure almost a worship" (letter to Calvin E. Stowe)—and indeed, her theologian husband had already rhapsodized in 1848 over Hiram Powers's nude *The Greek Slave* (letter to Harriet Beecher Stowe). After *Agnes*, in an 1866 essay boldly titled "Bodily Religion," she declares, "The human form is indeed divine, as M. Belloc insists, and rightly, sacredly drawn, cannot offend the purest eye" (qtd. in Wagenknecht 107).

Nowhere were the difficulties of the signification of the woman's body more dramatically illustrated than in the mid-century exhibition of the sensational *Greek Slave*. After the *Slave*, which toured widely in the United States and Europe from the mid-1840s to the mid-1850s, while nudity in art "still had to be justified," "it could be done, and the *Slave* was followed by a whole rash of naked or partially naked figures, . . . endorsed by the clergy as well, if possible" (Gerdts, *American Neo-Classic* 33). The variety of discourses centering around the *Slave* make clear the varied ways in which, as Joy Kasson has pointed out, this work of art operated as a flashpoint for anxieties over Woman as both spiritual and sensual (48). Moreover, discussion of the *Slave* inevitably intertwined with cultural debates over the proper role of art and the artist in society, a discussion that will lead us back to the quandaries over artistic interpretation in *Agnes*.

From the *Slave*'s first unveiling, viewers were instructed to read away her nakedness. Powers described the figure as a modern Christian Greek, a captive of the Turks, orphaned and taken from her homeland during the recent Greek Revolution. But this captive body was to be seen as spirit: not only was she "too deeply concerned to be aware of her nakedness," Powers wrote, but "[i]t is not her person but her spirit that stands exposed and she bears it all as only Christians can" (qtd. in Dillenberger 127). American viewers read in their exhibition pamphlets the influential review by Unitarian minister Orville Dewey, declaring that Powers managed "to make the spiritual reign over the corporeal; . . . to make the appeal to the soul entirely control the appeal to sense" (qtd. in Kasson 59; see also Dillenberger 128, Gay 396–398).

Another line of argument tried to convince viewers that this nude was clothed. Dewey called her "clothed all over with sentiment; sheltered, protected by it from every profane eye. Brocade, cloth of gold, could not be a more complete protection than the vesture of holiness in which she stands" (qtd. in Kasson 58). Other commentators followed his lead (Kasson 61). Neither naked nor a body, the *Slave* was to be seen as spiritual, her pagan overtones submerged in her Christian purity.

As in *Agnes*, however, the attempted forcible separation of body and spirit, pagan and Christian, said more about the needs of interpreters to control readings of the female than it did about the actual character of this artwork. The more the contemporary cultural authorities explained away the *Slave*'s body and insisted on her chaste and spiritual meaning, the more we might suspect them of protesting too much, implying her real sensory appeal (Gay 392; Vance 1: 211, 235; Kasson 59–61). Powers and his customers who purchased copies of the *Slave* wrote to each other on the sale as one of simple physical beauty (Vance 1: 237). Powers, something of a Swedenborgian, was personally comfortable with her as a palimpsest of physical and spiritual (Franchot 125), but as a former wax-museum artist in frontier Cincinnati he also knew well how to market his work to an uncertain American public (Gardner, Albert, 29, 70). His deliberately punning title for the statue, too, cunningly links the nude to past and present: to the classical pagan Greek physicality on which it was modeled and to a modern Christian Greek's enslavement by the Turks.[8] Like the baptized nymph in the convent garden, or Agnes herself, the *Slave* could be seen as a Christian overlay on a pagan base not fully obliterated—just made safe to look at.

The tenuousness of that overlay was a point of tension for a number of American travelers who observed neoclassical nudes. They commented on the way sculptors and painters made their nudes as alluring as they could and only as afterthoughts gave classical or biblical names to excuse their nakedness. So nudes raised further problems of signification. Young painter Thomas Eakins, studying in Europe, wrote home to his parents of the many "naked women" in various postures whom artists "call Phyrnes, Venus, nymphs, hermaphrodites, Kouros and Greek proper names [sic]" (qtd. in Van Hook 17), and Hawthorne wrote of artists who "merely . . . make beautiful nudities and baptize them by classic names" (*French and Italian Notebooks* 73). But it was not simply that, as Hawthorne put it, nudes "mean nothing, and might as well bear one name as another" (*English Notebooks* 99–100). Especially worrisome to serious-minded observers was the disjunction between the model and the subject of the work—reflected in Father Antonio's horror at the harlot posing for Mary. Hawthorne avowed himself perturbed by the "old painters" in Rome who would willingly "paint a lewd and naked woman and call her Venus" (*French and Italian Notebook* III), but of even more concern, as American painter William Dunlap wrote, was the use of low women for *sacred* subjects, like "an English prostitute in the most voluptuous attitude, without a shade of covering enticing the man to sin" in a painting labeled "Adam and Eve" (qtd. in Vance 1: 217–218).

The female body, then, was a hotly contested site in the dilemma of how and what art signified. As contemporary art theorist Marcia Pointon has put it, "the representation of woman can be seen to stand as cypher for the act of representation itself. The female body in art becomes the site of the struggle for mastery over the process of mimesis" (83). Clearly, the same was true during the United States' encounter with European high art in the mid-nineteenth century. The debates in *Agnes* over representing the body of Woman in sacred art thus telescope many of the moral questions about art in Stowe's time. All of this background underpins the novel's discussion of the use of the harlot as model for the Virgin. It informs, too, the original readers' experience of Agnes's pilgrimage to Rome and her final confrontation there.

Repressing Agnes's Body

In the context of these anxieties over the meaning of woman's body, Agnes's strenuous mortification of the flesh in preparation for her pilgrimage takes on artistic and sexual meaning. Her emerging physical longing for Agostino prompts her guilty confessions to Father Francesco, who instructs her to wear around her neck what the narrator calls "one of those sharp instruments of torture which in those times were supposed to be a means of inward grace,—a cross with seven steel points for the seven sorrows of Mary" (279). When Agnes indulges in thoughts of Agostino, which she is told are sinful because he is excommunicated, "she would press the sharp cross to her breast, till a thousand stings of pain would send the blood in momentary rushes to her pale cheek" (322). Fasting, too, Agnes becomes thin, pale, less of a body—the female mystic as anorexic. While clearly the narrator disapproves of the cross in particular, an otherwise unnecessary scene—undressing Agnes and commenting on the damage the star is doing to her breasts—

takes on meaning when we read it in the light of the novel's continuous commentary on woman and art as both/and, flesh and spirit inseparable.

Captured on her pilgrimage by Agostino's Robin-Hood-style band of virtuous robbers, Agnes finds her hometown friend Giulietta in the bandits' mountain hideaway. Giulietta moves to help undress her exhausted friend for rest: "I'll unlace your bodice. . . . But, Holy Virgin! what is the matter here? Oh, Agnes, what *are* you doing to yourself?" When Agnes explains, Giulietta calls Father Francesco "a real butcher" and vouchsafes that Agostino will "forbid" his future "little wife" to continue her self-mutilating penance (341). Having registered her distaste in her earlier description of the cross, Stowe need not have introduced this undressing scene at all. But she sets up this unlacing-of-Agnes scene in ways that might well recall for readers Keats's steamy "Eve of St. Agnes," with its heroine who "[l]oosens her fragrant bodice" (26.4) on that romantic night (traditionally the night in which a maiden dreams of her future husband) as she lies down to her dream-become-reality with her hidden lover.

The book has already featured much punning on Agnes's name, including her naming for St. Agnes and all the references to her as a "little lamb" of Christ (Latin *agnus* [lamb]; St. Agnes was often painted with her traditional attendant, the lamb; see Jameson, *Sacred* 604ff.). Given the name play and Agnes's evident need to embrace her physicality, it's quite possible Stowe has Keats's poem in mind as an in joke with her readers. True, Stowe tones down the sexual implications by having Agnes's married woman friend undress her and simply comment on how the male sexual partner will not approve. But Stowe nevertheless brings up the subject of the man's viewing of the woman's body in a sexual context and depicts the first (nearly) visible, commented-upon breasts in Stowe's fiction. When Agnes is most like a "disembodied spirit" (350), she is most physically unhealthy. At this point, Stowe intervenes to undress her, reminding her of her flesh's sexual function and condemning her attempts to damage it with a sharp instrument reminiscent of Father Antonio's chisel.

With Keats's poem in mind, a reader will recall that in the only dream Agnes dreams in this book, she envisions her future husband. In the dream, Agostino, in the guise of an angel, greets her in her garden in his usual Romeo-and-Juliet-style double entendres, "The Lord hath sealed thee for his own! . . . Oh, Agnes! Agnes! little lamb of Christ, love me and lead me!" We are then told that "in her sleep it seemed to her that her heart stirred and throbbed with a strange, new movement in answer to those sad, pleading eyes, and thereafter her dream became more troubled" (124). No doubt it did. Father Antonio the next day shows the limitations of his imagination by interpreting her dream as her call to a nun's vocation. We might see rather the sexual call of another kind of "lord," like the one who in Keats's poem melts into the heroine's dream.

As Agnes tries to censor her physical self, Stowe brings it back with a vengeance. The scene becomes even more interesting when we recall that the legend of St. Agnes includes her being captured and stripped by Roman authorities who try to rape her and to force her to deny Christ and marry a Roman nobleman (Jameson, *Sacred* 600ff.). And to help the attentive reader catch the allusions, Stowe has supplied earlier a precis of St. Agnes's story as it is depicted in the frescoes at the convent of St. Agnes (60–61). This otherwise gratuitous undressing scene, then, gains meaning in the context of the novel's attention to Agnes as embodied sacred art. It also helps prepare the reader for the fullest reading of the dramatic assault on our saintly but physical Agnes when she finally arrives in Rome.

Recovering the Body as Art

Agnes, as we have seen, had been reading herself as solely spiritual, and Stowe supplies the corrective stripping to reclaim her body. When in Rome, the misreading goes the other way, with Agnes read solely as a body by the corrupt and unspiritual church of Alexander VI. Newly arrived in Rome, Agnes is in the crowd as the pope's Palm Sunday procession sweeps by and she kneels in adoring enthusiasm.

> "There is the model which our master has been looking for," said a young and handsome man in a rich dress of black velvet, who, by his costume, appeared to hold the rank of first chamberlain in the Papal suite.
>
> The young man to whom he spoke gave a bold glance at Agnes and answered,—
>
> "Pretty little rogue, how well she does the saint!"
>
> "One can see that with judicious arrangement she might make a nymph as well as a saint," said the first speaker. (384)

Soon thereafter Agnes is snatched up by the servants of the pope for nefarious purposes we are to infer from references to the Borgias' "impure den" (393). Again, we might think Stowe is simply highlighting the lustful corruption of the pope and his minions by having Agnes suffer lascivious seizure.

But if that were the case, there would be no need to introduce the idea of using her as an artist's model and, in particular, as a model for a nymph or a saint. The scene deliberately links Agnes's captivity with nineteenth-century debates over the meaning of an artist's model. Agnes here is a model about to be violated, one who is currently modeling the saint but could also "do" a nymph "with judicious arrangement"—without, one supposes, the clothing that Christianizes the nymph she also is. The pope's servants interpret Agnes in a more extreme version of Father Francesco's reading: as a sexual object, a pagan picture. Moreover, their dialogue denies her sacramental artistry, suggesting that as simply a beautiful plastic piece of flesh, Agnes means precisely nothing.

If we recall Hawthorne's and Eakins's commentary on arbitrarily titled nudes and the nervous clerical commentary on *The Greek Slave*, we can see that Agnes is taken by the corrupt church patriarchy as a nude model who is simply and only of the flesh—becoming the harlot, in effect, who may be posed as Mary or as a nymph, titled with equal arbitrariness. The assault on Agnes thus enacts the corruptions in sacred art that Stowe has been talking about all along in this novel and in her contemporaneous nonfiction. The attempt to violate Agnes is an attempt to destroy her signifying function as art, to violate a sacramental text which, in the right artist's hands, reveals Christ to the eye.

Agnes is saved from the Borgias by her best reader, Agostino, an admirer of Savonarola and significantly a "poet and artist" himself (116), who knows that Agnes is rightly read neither simply as saint nor as sexual body but as both/and. And Agnes finally learns to read herself rightly by being violently misread. Through this crisis in Rome, Stowe seeks to right the signification of woman in art. Part of that rectification happens when, like Mary Scudder in *The Minister's Wooing*, Agnes ultimately recognizes her true "vocation unto marriage" and weds Agostino, becoming a priestess in the "holy and venerable" "sacrament" of marriage (411). She chooses to be both Keats's heroine and St. Agnes, married and sexual but also a religious inspiration to Agostino and to a newly invigorated Christian Rome (412).

There is, however, another climax of the novel in the fiery martyrdom of Savonarola. In the context of the novel's discussions of the inevitable return of the repressed, it is fitting to see Savonarola return after his death, in the form of art—in Raphael's painting of apostles and martyrs in Rome (412). But his death makes one ponder, too, Stowe's take on his vigorous censorship of worldly art. Because of the running imagery of sacrament and palimpsest and their connections to Agnes as Art, I'm not convinced we are meant to cheer for Savonarola when he is described as having led the burning of all the licentious art and literature the penitent Florentines could fetch him, including (as Father Antonio puts it) "Boccaccio's romances and other defilements" (105). Savonarola is definitely an admired figure in this novel, and the narrator takes pains to show him as a patron of art at its best, a poet himself who inspires his disciples—including Fra Angelico—to heights of sacred creative artistry (98). And it's significant that Stowe pulls away from her contemporary Ruskinians with this depiction of him as artist and art lover. But his violent censorship seems along the same lines as Father Antonio's chisel. We know that Stowe requested a copy of the *Decameron* from her publisher to help her as she worked on *Agnes* (letter to James T. Fields). And it seems more than coincidental that Stowe alludes casually to Boccaccio as a text her *Atlantic* and *Cornhill* readers would know (44) and that Agostino, who alone can see Agnes's dual nature, has read Boccaccio (94). Clearly what Savonarola wished to repress has not stayed down and perhaps should not.[9]

The inevitability of the palimpsest, in this book, and the exploration of the idea of sacraments suggest that the wholesale destruction or denial of the physical is no healthier for art than it is for life. Savonarola's censoring fire, for instance, is mirrored in the fire with which a corrupt church censors him by burning him at the stake at the end of the novel. Father Antonio is undercut by his difficulties in seeing the inseparability of physical and spiritual in Agnes's womanhood. It's Stowe who, in the voice of the narrator, points out what they don't see—that Woman and Art are palimpsests and sacraments. Sacred art needs the earthly. Art needs those nymphs. Or at least it may as well acknowledge them: as in this book, they are going to emerge from the earth sooner or later.

If *Agnes* and Stowe's other writing on art are any indication, the more Stowe toured Europe and the more American attitudes changed toward art, the more her own sense of art, the body, and her own artistic mission developed. In an 1855 article on the Puritans, for instance, Stowe had defended religious censorship of beauty. The "great reformers," she wrote, must "break the shrines and temples of the physical and earthly beauty, when they seek to draw men upward to that which is high and divine" ("Old Oak" 33). Hence "[i]t was needed that these men should come, Baptist-like in the wilderness." Such a crisis, indeed, Stowe saw looming again on the American horizon in 1855. "We need such men now. Art, they tell us, is waking in America;

a love of the beautiful is beginning to unfold its wings; but what kind of art, and what kind of beauty?" ("Old Oak" 33).

Clearly Father Antonio, and especially Savonarola, fit this description of "Baptist-like" men needed in a corrupt century. But the fact that their portraits show some authorial ambivalence suggests a shift in Stowe's thinking. She had already created, in *The Minister's Wooing*, Mrs. Marvyn, whose hungry soul starves for what art might be (589); she had already lamented, in *Sunny Memories*, her native New England's "crushing out of the beautiful" (2: 392). Perhaps most importantly, Stowe's sojourn in Sorrento, where she began *Agnes*, came just a few weeks after her second visit to Story's studio, where she was feted at a celebratory dinner (Hedrick 270, Wilson, Forrest 453–454). It would be no surprise if Story's sculpted women had her pondering the moral ministry of the female body. Stowe's novel declares her position by bringing Agnes finally to sexual married womanhood as her destined Christian ministry and installing her at the center of Rome as renewer of the church (*Agnes* 412). The body of a woman—the flesh baptized, not obliterated—becomes the best minister of the sacred.

As a woman artist Stowe can depict Agnes as a physically beautiful body without the prurience she saw undercutting the sacrament of art when male artist gazed on female flesh (I am assuming heterosexuality in Stowe's depiction of herself). And as a Christian woman artist, Stowe can do the priestly work of delivering the sacrament—via the sacramental Agnes—to her lay readers. In her introduction to Charles Beecher's 1849 book *The Incarnation: or, Pictures of the Virgin and Her Son*, Stowe had written that Charles's technique of mingling the sensual arts of fiction and the sacred biblical narrative could "suggest to some fervent spirit that it may not be necessary to have recourse to the strains of a Byron, or the glowing pictures of a Bulwer or a Sue, for themes of boundless scope and unutterable brilliancy" (viii–ix). In the 1850s, Stowe's European travels brought a new medium, the visual arts, into her thinking about the art of fiction. *Agnes* shows Stowe consciously presenting her own artistic mission as devoted to this same mingling of sensual and spiritual, fiction and religion. In this novel whose heroine is the contested site of Art, we see that, over time, for Stowe the woman's body became *the* artistic subject to define and defend for sacred art. Stowe thus anticipates Pointon's argument that "[t]he female body in art becomes the site of the struggle for mastery over the process of mimesis." And in clarifying the mission of her own sacramental art, Stowe in *Agnes* defines not just Agnes, but herself as well, as an artist-minister in the body of a woman.

NOTES

I thank David Ullrich and Melissa Homestead for their helpful critiques of earlier drafts.

1. Early critics such as Foster (137–144 [1954 ed.]), Crozier (*Novels* 135–136), and Caskey (202–203) recognized *Agnes*'s importance in Stowe's work, emphasizing its role in charting Stowe's movement away from traditional Calvinism. Later work by Gardella (106–107), Vance (22–24), Gatta (*American Madonna* 68–71), Franchot (246–255), and Formichella (*passim*) has given perceptive analyses of Stowe's reconsideration of Mary in particular and Catholicism in general in the novel, emphasizing with varying levels of sympathy Stowe's efforts to appropriate elements of Catholic piety and ritual for American Protestantism or nationalism. Hedrick takes a different tack, pointing to the book's generic innovations as an early international novel (292–293). Art in *Agnes* has received relatively brief attention in Wright, Gatta, and Formichella.

Quotations in this essay from *The Minister's Wooing* are from the 1982 Library of America edition.

2. On the Protestant unease with Catholic uses of beauty in art, see Morgan.

3. We know Stowe admired Fra Angelico; she listed "Five Fra Angelico Angels" (doubtless reproductions) in her inventory of paintings she owned. The painter was an ideal figure for a group Stowe admired, the Nazarenes, a brotherhood of German painters based in Rome and dedicated to a Christian ideal in art (see Kefalas 66). Ruskin and Jameson also set up Fra Angelico as the ideal of the spiritually impassioned Christian artist (see Herbert 266–267; Jameson, *Legends of the Monastic Orders* 399).

4. Stowe echoes Jameson in her descriptions of Fra Angelico painting on his knees (introduction, *Legends of the Madonna* xxvi).

5. *Atlantic* readers of the late 1850s and early 1860s, in particular, were accustomed to articles on European and especially Italian art from American travelers' points of view.

6. Expatriate sculptor Hiram Powers, for instance, told an interviewer he could easily hire a model in Rome for eighty cents a day (qtd. in Gardner, Albert, 50).

7. Compare Miriam, in Hawthorne's *Marble Faun*: "An artist, therefore,—as you must candidly confess,—cannot sculpture nudity with a pure heart, if only because he is compelled to steal guilty glimpses at hired models. The marble inevitably loses its chastity under such circumstances" (123). For accounts and interpretations of the debates over the nude in American culture, see Dillenberger, Gerdts *American Neo-Classic* and *Great American*, Kasson, Nead, Pointon, Taft, Van Hook, and Vance. On the nude in Christian art, see Dillenberger, Miles, and Hart and Stevenson.

8. The statue was often interpreted in an abolitionist context as well, as Kasson and Yellin (*Women and Sisters*) have discussed.

9. For more positive readings of Savonarola's bonfire, see Sheets 333, Vance 2: 24.

Stowe and Religious Iconography

CARLA RINEER

OR DECADES, postmodern theorists have celebrated an almost continuous requiem for the written text. Having declared the nineteenth century the age of the novel, visual semioticians, structuralists, reader-response critics, and deconstructionists assert that the dawn of television, the Internet, and video games ushered in a strictly visual culture, a world where the meaning of the written word has become too arbitrary and slippery to communicate meaning effectively. However, regardless of the erudite and technological resonances of these declarations, pictures and texts are not mutually exclusive and have, in fact, cohabited symbiotically in print media for centuries. Far from working at cross-purposes, language and image frequently blend to champion ideas.

Often their shared advocacy affirms orthodox notions and bolsters the status quo. For example, Susan Warner's widely read 1850 novel *The Wide, Wide World*[1] employs a text and pictures that support the patriarchal notion of women as childlike, frail, weak, sickly, and passive, thereby buttressing the Cult of True Womanhood. One illustration, aptly encaptioned "Mrs. Montgomery's head sank upon the open page," shows an enervated woman draped over a book and soundly asleep (Warner 42). Similarly, "Her little daughter was now preparing tea," representing the true-womanly ideal of domesticity, and "As soon as she was set free Ellen brought her Bible," depicting the cult's exultation of piety, also demonstrate the powerful synergy between text and image (Warner 23, 245). In Warner's age of separate spheres, sometimes, even when texts are politically neutral, accompanying illustrations advance a conservative message about gender. For instance, while the caption "What's become of that 'ere rocking-cheer?" offers no cultural comment, its accompanying picture showing a demoralized and exhausted Ellen crouching on the floor, her arm hanging passively on the seat of a chair, clearly identifies submissiveness and debility as "womanly" characteristics (Warner 235).

At other times, images, with or without consonant texts, challenge orthodox notions rather than endorsing them. Such is the case with Warner's contemporary Harriet Beecher Stowe. Stowe's desire for a "new school of art based upon Protestant principles" (*Sunny Memories* 2: 351), her penchant for using illustrations, her understanding of their inherent power, and her increasingly bold and heterodox employment of them expose her unconventional concepts of women and religion and trace the saga of her transatlantic connections.[2]

In 1853, as she was being heralded throughout Europe as America's first great novelist, Stowe set sail for the first of three European tours. By then, she had already entered into a providential relationship with pictures. In fact, Stowe's liaison with images emerged two years earlier when inspiration struck on a blustery day in 1851. As Stowe sat in a pew of Brunswick, Maine's First Parish Church, a place from which icons were strictly banned, the vision of a bleeding slave came to her like a picture (Hedrick 155–156). From that experience grew Uncle Tom and his cabin. However, the inspiration of pictures and her calculated and unorthodox use of them did not halt there but grew more intense and insurgent as she traveled throughout Europe, speaking with artists and contemplating visual art in the homes of the wealthy, the naves of cathedrals, and the galleries of the world's most famous museums. Stowe returned from her journey, her mind teeming with ideas and her arms filled with reproductions of famous religious paintings and sculptures that she had seen in Europe. The images she brought home with her were destined to serve a far greater purpose than decoration.

While it may be tempting to dismiss Stowe's affinity for religious art as congruous with the religious fervor of her day, employing religious images was decidedly fractious for a woman of her time and background, for according to her father Lyman Beecher's strictly Calvinist theological convictions, doing so was tantamount to "popery" if not idolatry. In fact, Calvinism's objection to religious iconography is deep-seated and elemental to its theology. Much of the New World's reaction against the old European world sprang from Calvinism's protest against Roman Catholicism and Anglicanism. Although history frequently dates the birth of the English Reformation from the 1534 marital problems of a king, many religious historians proclaim Henry VIII's break from the Church a myth and credit John Calvin rather than the King of England with "the great divide." The use of religious icons and the position of women stood as primary emblems of the schism. Repudiating all of the pageantry, discourse, and iconography of so-called popery, the followers of John Calvin vigorously jettisoned the prayer book, the liturgies, and ceremonies of the Mass, along with "the graven image" and the Mariolatry that had come to embody their criticism of high church. To these elements, Calvinists assigned an evil, almost devilish connotation, causing faithful followers to regard them with horror. As Stowe relates in *Footsteps of the Master*, "[a]n image or a picture of [the Virgin Mary] in a Puritan home would have been considered an approach to the sin of Achan," a capital offense in biblical times (31).[3]

While Stowe was not by nature particularly rebellious against her father, several tensions turned her from wholly embracing his vision: the indisputably patriarchal and misogynistic essence of her father's Christianity and the incompatibility of nineteenth-century American Protestantism with the precepts of democracy and equality that the Constitution espoused. Stowe's inability to adopt her father's vision was compounded by the Puritan identification with the Israelites of the Old Testament.[4] The theologies of John Calvin and Lyman Beecher not only rejected the icons of Catholicism but, following in the footsteps of the ancient progenitors of Judaism, repudiated its notion of female divinity as well, leaving Stowe and her sisters without a viable paradigm of female power or divinity.

The diminution of the female divine began at the dawn of the Judeo-Christian heritage as reaction rather than action. During the wanderings of the patriarchs and the writing of the Scriptures (ca. 1900 to 110 BCE), goddess worship and gender equality surrounded the Israelites. The Jews' Egyptian captors venerated Isis; the neighboring Sumerians paid homage to Innana; Asia Minor worshiped Kybele; the Phoenicians, Philistines, and Moabites reverenced Astarte; the Babylonians adulated Ishtar; the Romans adored Magna Mater; and the Greeks glorified Demeter. Because of the exalted stature of the goddess, mortal women of these countries enjoyed elevated status and opportunity as well. Unlike Hebrew women, they chose from many occupations, including commerce, the arts, and high religious service. As humans are wont to do, the Israelites reacted by privileging the opposite. To form their own identity and establish a sense of uniqueness, they clung to a patriarchal concept of god and to the notion of the inherent depravity of women, thereby demonizing the beliefs of their matriarchal neighbors; vilifying their priestesses with stinging appellations like harlot, idolater, and whore; and excising the notion of female divinity altogether. To assure the censure of the goddess for millennia to come, the writers of the ancient scriptures constructed an inimical goddess figure of their own—Eve, the mother of the Fall—and assigned to her the symbols of the goddess, especially serpents, trees, knowledge, birds, nakedness, breasts, and flowing, uncovered tresses, symbols that Stowe eventually retrieved and revalued.

Although Roman Catholicism more or less embraced the goddess in its veneration of Mary *Theotokos*, the Mother of God, the Protestant Christianity that Stowe inherited reached across time and ocean to retrieve and apply the notions of the Israelites with considerable vigor. While Catholicism endorsed Mariolatry, the Puritans'[5] return to the Old Testament disavowed the divine aspect of women and announced a diminished, polarized vision of womanhood. Telling parallel stories of the Israelites' and their own American "errand into the wilderness," Puritans advanced a binary world view in texts like Cotton Mather's *Magnalia Christi Americana* and John Winthrop's "A Short Story," which celebrated the daring adventures of patriarchs; offered parables of obedient, submissive wives and mothers; and spun cautionary tales of female abominations who dared to be vocal, sexual, prophetic, or powerful. Hence the Roman Catholic figure of Mary as goddess, as virgin, as Madonna, and as Queen of Heaven was shrunken by American Protestant thought to a static figure upon a powerless pedestal. As the antecedent of the True Woman, the Protestant Mary merely believed, obeyed, gave birth, nurtured, stepped back, and mourned. The only other female biblical figures available to nineteenth-century Protestant women were Eve and her evil sisters—the whore, the virago, and the hag. The dichotomy left nineteenth-century women who had a passion to reform without an appropriate religious figure to emulate. To remedy the situation, Stowe and her (re)mastered religious iconography reconnected with European Catholicism and the distant, pagan past to recover lost images, to break stereotypes, and to conflate polarities by blurring the boundaries between "good" women and "bad" ones. Despite the virulence of Calvinist disavowal and the strength of Harriet Beecher Stowe's Puritan/Congregational connections, this daughter, sister, wife, and mother of nineteenth-century America's most celebrated Puritan divines reinstated, reaffirmed, and rehabilitated pictorial images of biblical women as she theologically and philosophically introduced them into America's Protestant religious landscape.

In the face of her religious tradition's virulent rejection of images, Stowe daringly (re)turned to the icon and to the mythical colossus and goddess roots of Mary. Her trek from the nexus of her idea to its fulfillment traversed time, oceans, and continents. She commenced by acknowledging the strong connection between her work and pictures and by calling upon the persuasive power of images to fortify the potency of her work and to invigorate her theological notions. She confessed, "My vocation is simply that of a painter. . . . There is no arguing with *pictures,* and everybody is impressed by them, whether they mean to be or not" (qtd. in Hedrick 208). Stowe's statement reveals both method and motive: to avoid argumentation, not by surrender, but by utilizing a device that deflects interrogation.

The story of Stowe's first-person acquaintance with classical and European art began with a mix of patriarchy and feminism in Liverpool in 1853, where she was greeted by a large, enthusiastic crowd of fans and a full roster of scheduled appearances. Stowe's English fans adored her talent and were intensely curious about her looks, but, sadly, adoration and scrutinizing were all that were available to her audiences, for she was compelled to be seen but not heard, to be a spectacle rather than a spectator. Regardless of her fame, she was restricted by St. Paul and the acculturation of his words to maintaining silence in public.[6] To assure propriety and to comply with the strictures of St. Paul, Stowe sat demurely and silently on stage while either her husband, Calvin, or her brother Charles recited speeches she, or they, had written (Hedrick 238). Yet, although publicly muted, she did not accede to the role of voiceless spectacle but found an alternative podium. For some time, Stowe had been circumventing one of the key adversities of her life—her banishment from the family "preaching business"—by, as James Russell Lowell noted, transforming "her writing-desk to be something infinitely higher than a pulpit" (qtd. in Stowe, Lyman Beecher 201). To further the transformation, she turned her eyes to the sights of Europe, becoming a spectator and, through her written discourse, a speaker of legendary proportion.

As she scoured Europe for fodder for her "silent" literary sermons, Stowe's flair for examination became almost as legendary as her writing prowess. Upon her arrival for a portrait sitting at the Paris studio of Monsieur Belloc, the artist "concluded that as other pictures had taken [Stowe] as looking at the spectator, this [one] should be taken looking away. M. Belloc remarked that . . . Hatty appeared always with the air of an observer. Was always looking around on everything. Hence [he] would take her . . . with the air of observation, but not of curiosity" (Charles Beecher 163–164). Much of what came under Stowe's astute purview that summer was the fine art that changed her life, her writing, and her theology forever. Her eye discovered the fragments from which she constructed an icon of divine, dynamic womanhood to influence American culture and theology, an image that would, eventually, recross the Atlantic to influence European art and thought.

Stowe's passionate devotion to art, especially of the Classical and Renaissance periods, was redoubled by her first tour of Europe. Records of her excursion, chronicled in *Sunny Memories of Foreign Lands* and in Charles Beecher's journal,[7] document her enthusiasm and excellent critical eye. Her brother Charles remembers that Stowe found the Louvre absolutely inebriating. As she emerged from her first visit there, "her cheek was flushed, and her eye seemed to swim. She looked like one intoxicated. 'Well, Hatty,' said [Charles], 'have you drunk deep enough this time?' 'Yes,' said she, 'I have been *satisfied* for the first time'" (Beecher 152).

But the art she saw not only enthralled her eye, but also awakened a certain intuitive and creative sense within her. Stowe anticipated a quintessentially religious experience at the Louvre, noting in a letter: "It was . . . with a thrill almost of awe that I approached the Louvre. Here, perhaps, said I to myself, I shall answer, fully, the question that has long wrought within my soul, What is art? and what can it do? Here, perhaps, these yearnings for the ideal will meet their satisfaction. (*Sunny Memories* 2: 159). Indeed, Stowe was not disappointed. As she studied paintings and statues, she found answers. She mused that the presence of the "emotions of God" infused the Bible with eternal omnipotence and that "some [paintings] preserve in them such a degree of vital force that one can never look on them with indifference" (*Sunny Memories* 2: 164).

Frequent visits with her friend M. Belloc further crystallized the connection between art, emotion, and religion for Stowe. She painted frequently during those months, and she routinely awed her brother with her memory for artistic detail and her penetrating commentary (Beecher 113). Even M. Belloc praised Stowe's acumen, exclaiming: "My confession as man and as artist—is that Madame Stowe had no equal. We have men and women of talent, of genius, or of feeling, but none in whom so many. . . [nuances] of thought and genius are combined with so much heart" (Beecher 325). For Stowe, "heart" stands at the very center of religious experience for, as she related to Belloc, "the more you enlarge a person's general capacity of feeling, the more you enlarge his capacity of suffering. . . . Christianity, by enlarging the scope of man's heart, and dignifying his nature, has deepened his sorrow" (*Sunny Memories* 2: 175). Art softens the pain, for Stowe continues, "Religion is not asceticism, but a principle of love to God that beautifies and exalts common life, and fills it with joy" (*Sunny Memories* 2: 175).

Upon her return to America, Stowe put her emerging theology into motion. She began with the center of nineteenth-century women's sphere—the home—both hers and those of other Protestant American women. Stowe hung the artistic mementos of her journey throughout her home. As a walk through the Harriet Beecher Stowe House in Hartford, Connecticut, evinces, her home became a veritable art gallery filled with icons of female divinity.[8] On a pedestal in the parlor, a statue of the Venus de Milo rests brazenly. Stowe first beheld this sculpture, discovered in 1820, a mere thirty-three years before her first European tour, in the Louvre, and she pronounced it her favorite classical sculpture. She visited Venus's new home no less than three times that summer and probably first met her marble likeness when she visited Stafford House, where several statues of Venus were displayed (Beecher 130). According to the etiquette of her day, Stowe's Victorian modesty should have been outraged by the sight of the goddess's naked torso and by the nudity and sexuality she discovered in other works housed in the museums and palatial homes of Europe. In fact, so strong was this supposition among her fellow travelers that Charles Beecher addresses it in his journal. In reference to Dannecker's Ariadne, Stowe's brother wonders:

> Why, when we gaze upon this form so perfect, so entirely revealed, does it not excite any of those emotions, either of shame or of desire, which the living reality would excite? And again, why does not the immediate contact of feminine helplessness and with the most brute ferocity excite that horror which the sight of the same in real life must awaken? Why, but because we behold under a spell in the transfigured world of art where passion ceases and where bestial instincts are felt to be bowed to the law of mind and of ideal truth. (Beecher 282)

So it must have been with Stowe, for instead of blushing and turning from images of female sexuality, she ensconced them first in her home and later in her writings. Even more so, Stowe should have been offended by the sculpture's homage to Venus or Aphrodite, the goddess of love, who originally presided over flower gardens and vines and whose worship was dictated by the Sibylline Oracles. Instead, the flower gardens and vines of the goddess proliferated, both inside and outside of Stowe's house. She should have been discomfited by the goddess's role as Genetrix, as mother of the Roman people, for it ties Venus to the Christian Eve whom Stowe's father's Christianity disdained. Instead, Stowe exalted Venus and her lore by celebrating the myr-iad of connections among the goddess, herself, and her ideal woman. Stowe saw in the Venus not an idol nor a relic of paganism, but an ideal to be ex-humed, emulated, and applied to Christianity. Stowe loved the statue's "majesty and grace in the head and face," seeing there "a union of loveliness with intellectual and moral strength, beyond any thing which [she had] ever seen," the representation of the Puritan poet "Milton's glorious picture of unfallen, perfect womanhood, in his Eve" (*Sunny Memories* 2: 170). More significantly, perhaps Stowe even appreciated the profound if subtle rebel-lion against the theology of her family that the figure of Venus of Melos and her connection with Eve incited, for the sculpture's left hand, separately pre-served, held Eve's fruit, an apple, Venus's award from Paris who judged her the most beautiful of the goddesses.

As if purposely emphasizing and concretizing the mythic connections between pagan and Christian, virtue and sin, Stowe hung altered reproduc-tions of Madonnas painted by celebrated European masters beside the naked goddess. It was her installation of her new, "Protestant" school of art (*Sunny Memories* 2: 351). Stowe scholars have long noted the strength of her emo-tional ties to Roman Catholicism's primary female icon, Mary. Stowe's at-tachment sprang and gained reinforcement from the deaths of her sons. In words, Stowe expressed her alliance with a touch of envy, noting that "[Mary] had a security . . . not accorded to other mothers. [Mary] knew that the child she adored was not to die till he had reached man's estate—she had no fear that accident, or sickness, or any of those threatening causes which give sad hours to so many mothers, would come between him and her" (*Footsteps* 31–32). In pictures, she articulated the connection by decorating the walls of her home with at least four portraits of the Madonna by the Catholic Italian Renaissance painter Raphael Sanzio. While the portraits ap-pear to uphold the Cult of Motherhood, each imbues Mary with a touch of divinity and power far beyond the limits American Protestant theology set for her. For example, for over a century Raphael's *Madonna del Gran Duca* (1504 or 1505), often viewed as the prototypical Madonna, conveyed a mixed message to Stowe's visitors. Mary's head is appropriately veiled, and the set-ting is formal and unearthly, as the Madonna and Child seem to issue from a ubiquitous darkness. Yet, although Mary's eyes are nonconfrontational and turned downward, her face is thoughtful and her smile enigmatic rather than submissive. Moreover, Mary seems to be ethereal, divine, while Jesus exudes a material, more human aura, making the overall message of the portrait decidedly inappropriate for Calvinism's patriarchal stance.

Another of Stowe's paintings, Raphael's *Madonna del Cardellino*, or *Madonna with the Goldfinch* (1506/1507), offers a similar monologue about admirable female attributes. Raphael's original portrait focuses upon an unveiled Mary in her serenity, dignity, and divinity, rather than on Jesus in his vulnerable human nakedness. St. John the Baptist and Jesus stand at Mary's feet, rather than lying in her hands, which are otherwise occupied with two symbols of the goddess—the bird and knowledge. One of Mary's hands holds the open book she has been reading, showing her participation in the masculine world of knowledge as well as in the feminine world of mothering. However, the version on Stowe's wall is cropped, excising both male figures, Jesus and John, from the picture, leaving a close up of Mary's unveiled head and flowing hair, the symbol of the goddess that St. Paul most directly addresses and forbids[9] and that Raphael's predecessor Sandro Botticelli (1445–1510) so openly exalts in *The Birth of Venus*.

The *Sistine Madonna*, particularly remarkable because Mary seems in the midst of a descent from heaven, also has a place in Stowe's home. The Madonna is accompanied by St. Sixtus, a martyred Pope, and by St. Barbara, a martyred daughter, who defied her father to become Christian. In reaction to an image of the crucifixion positioned directly opposite them in the original Sistine Chapel configuration, a sense of terror and worry dances across the faces of Mary and Jesus, implying that the two divine entities share an equivalent omniscience and recalling the sorrow of losing a child that Stowe shared with Mary.

Lest one think that Stowe admired Raphael, the painter, more than Mary, the subject, her interest in the female symbol of divinity is confirmed by the inclusion of another iconic portrait of the virgin in her collection. *Holy Family Dell Divino*, by an unknown artist, adds Joseph to the portrait but relegates him to a decidedly secondary position. An earthly father who is less important than the mother and a goddess figure that seems to share divinity with Jesus hardly conform to St. Paul's idea of the appropriate Christian family.

Stowe continues her pictorial *coup d'état* upstairs, near the fainting couch in a room reserved for indisposed women. On the wall, Madonnaesque companion pieces of Eliza and Harry and Eva and Topsy, painted in 1857 by J. A. Bingham, link the divine mother with secular women while purveying

notions that contest nineteenth-century white American culture and vali-
date Stowe's revised ideology (figs. 4 and 5). Remarkable for their resistance
of the anglicizing so common in Christian art, the portraits contribute a
feminist vision to a room steeped in patriarchal stereotype, extend the sacred
image to encompass alternative paradigms of race and gender, and demonstrate the centrality of the image of the mother and child in Stowe's fiction
and in the commercialization of *Uncle Tom's Cabin*. The portraits dispute
racism and sexism by showing people of color and disenfranchisement in
Madonna-like postures (*Harry and Eliza*), and by presenting a biracial and
totally female configuration of mother and child (*Topsy and Eva*).

4. Stowe hung this Madonnaesque portrait of Eliza and Harry along with a companion piece of Eva and Topsy, both painted by J. A. Bingham (1857), in her home in Hartford. Courtesy Harriet Beecher Stowe Center and Library, Hartford, Connecticut.

5. This portrait of Eva and Topsy, painted by J. A. Bingham (1857), was displayed in a room for female guests in Stowe's home in Hartford. The painting was hung next to a companion piece, a portrait of Eliza and Harry. Courtesy Harriet Beecher Stowe Center and Library, Hartford, Connecticut.

Eventually, Stowe's house could no longer contain the expanse of her vision, which traveled from her home to the homes of other Protestant American families. Stowe's concept perhaps first appeared to her countrywomen in 1869 when she and sister Catharine Beecher published an advice book, *American Woman's Home; Or the Principles of Domestic Science*. The increasingly popular form, variously called the literature of conduct, courtesy, and advice, first emerged as a conservative genre. Just as the myth of the bold and vigorous American pioneer unfolded, a torrent of books prescribing Ameri-

can women's behavior and offering them advice crossed the ocean from England to drench the fledgling culture during the second half of the eighteenth
century and far into the nineteenth. As American writers took hold of the
genre, most authors of conduct literature were appropriate, enfranchised
dictators of decorum—the male descendants of prestigious colonial families,
clergymen, educators, and moralists. Their predictable advice to their American sisters cautioned women to imitate the traditional behaviors of their
Puritan ancestresses (Ryan 20; Halttunen, *Confidence* 21). Hence, the ser-
mon-like and condescending tone of the first American courtesy literature
promoted the values of True Womanhood, counseled against unfeminine
qualities like vitality and spirit, and prescribed passivity as an infallible in-
ducement for potential husbands (Davidson 126).

Although the arrival of advice literature in the colonies seemed guileless,
it quickly gave rise to incongruous manifestations. While the genre advocated submission, domesticity, and piety for woman, it simultaneously empowered her and called upon her to write. Presumably acting only in selfless
"response to the domestic needs of their kin and neighbors," the earliest
female advisors did much more than teach their sisters how to behave. With
each successive offering of advice, iconoclastic American women writers presented an increasingly heterodox vision of female desirability. Subsequently,
many nineteenth-century women used the genre's potential to include wom-
en in democracy's enfranchising embrace, to incorporate them into evangel-
istic projects designed to prompt the millennium,[10] and to inaugurate temperance movements, reform societies, and the concept of female moral
superiority, which gave rise to campaigns for women's rights and suffrage.

The Beecher sisters' book contributed to this radical movement, for hidden within the volume's seemly pages lurked a revolutionary concept—the
design for a small church, schoolhouse, and home—"all united in one building," complete with steeple and pulpit, and under the direction of the
woman of the house (Catharine Beecher 456–457).[11] Traditionally, advice literature called upon women to be pious, praised their higher moral acumen,
and promised them great influence experienced vicariously as it purported,
"the hand that rocks the cradle rules the world."[12] In contrast, *American
Woman's Home* shuns the concept of women's static, silent influence and
replaces it with a dynamic, vocal one, when it transforms the home into
church and the pious helpmeet into pastor, preacher, and exhorter.

While Stowe's use of maternal images significantly challenges the theology of her father(s), up to this point it does not challenge the notions of fe-

male purity and polarized womanhood overtly. However, in 1873 Stowe did take that leap beneath the cover of an ultraconservative European and American genre. Just before Stowe's pen was stilled by the same dementia that had halted her father's millennial message decades before, she composed a legacy of feminized Christianity. Provisionally liberated from the religion of her father by her fictional emancipation proclamation, *The Minister's Wooing*; by Lyman Beecher's senility and death[13]; and by her own maturity,[14] Stowe constructed a collection of religious documents to codify the precepts of her matriarchal millennialism into a tangible gospel. In other words, Stowe openly commenced preaching. Within a span of four years, she defied the Pauline cloak of silence to speak out on religious matters in three "sacred texts" that refigure biblical women (*Woman in Sacred History* 1873), set forth a heterodox theology (*The Footsteps of the Master* 1877), and record her own struggle to speak, as a legacy for daring sister-successors (*Poganuc People: Their Lives and Loves* 1878). Stowe saw these works as her final religious "testament." Employing text and image to deconstruct the binary view of women as angelic or evil in *Woman in Sacred History*, a collection of portraits of Old and New Testament women, Stowe patterned her "hagiography" after a popular, conservative genre—biblical biography—that was especially fashionable in the middle years of the nineteenth century.

As Mary De Jong notes in "Dark-Eyed Daughters: Nineteenth-Century Popular Portrayals of Biblical Women," the genre of female scriptural biography figured prominently in the nineteenth-century literary landscape. From 1825 to the early 1860s and beyond, publishers inundated the American female reading public with biographies of biblical women printed in periodicals such as *Godey's Lady's Book* and *Graham's Magazine* and collected in beautifully bound, extravagantly illustrated gift books intended for parlor display (De Jong 2, 5). To entice buyers, each gift book strove to be more lavish than the last, offering an assortment of artistic renderings—biographical sketches, collected sermons, poems by contemporary writers, highly fictionalized narratives, and engraved portraits—all between gilded covers.

Like much of the literature of the century, biblical biographies professed to be ameliorating. In service of this ideal, the authors—generally clergymen—unabashedly confessed a sole tutorial purpose—spiritual improvement. George C. Baldwin, D.D., for example, claims that his volume is intended for "the edification of youth, in families, Sabbath schools, and Bible classes" (vii). Charles Adams trusts that his biographies will prove "profitable for doctrine, for reproof, for correction, for instruction in righteousness, that the child of God may be perfect" and hopes "[t]o attract the eyes of his fair readers more intently toward that blessed volume [the Bible], and the priceless treasures of wisdom and knowledge therein contained" (3–4). Similarly, the Rev. A. L. Stone assigns a desire to promote "diligent and careful" Bible study to Mrs. S. G. Ashton's publication (v).

Yet notwithstanding monolithic pledges of metaphysical purpose, other agendas peek out from beneath the elaborate bindings of the volumes. For instance, many scriptural biographers gathered under the banner of a familiar nineteenth-century gender concern—the deleterious influence of fiction,[15] a cause against which Stowe would have vehemently protested. Some biblical biographers openly acknowledge hostility toward fiction. These writers promise truth[16] or variety in their representations of biblical heroines and pledge to forego the stereotypical characterizations of novels in an effort to combat the "multiplicity of publications flooding the world" and the neglect of the Bible which they precipitate (Burchard vii, xi). Others imply rather than testify, relying on the might of high-flown language to disseminate the message. Adams, for example, vows to: "contemplate woman precisely as the inspired pen has represented her, so far as she has arisen to view in the divine history of God's providential and gracious dispensations to mankind, and so far as that pen may have sketched didactically her true position and duties [and] to keep [the] eye steady upon recorded facts and incidents, and . . . [to forgo] all undue license of the imagination" (3–4). Stowe, of course, does no such thing.

She does, however, join with her literary brothers in a more democratic mission and a hidden agenda. Many writers, including Stowe, imply a patriotic intention—the formulation of the ideal New Republican Woman. The Rev. H. Hastings Weld displays this intent in dedicating *The Women of the Scriptures*[17] "To the women of America." However, the paragon that emerges in these biographies is neither secular nor political but exclusively homebound and Christian.[18]

The primary purpose of these publications was neither to delight the senses nor to entertain; it was not to evangelize nor nationalize, but to instruct, indoctrinate, and persuade. The works were designed to convince a child-like audience of Sabbath school youths and women to uphold orthodoxy and the one particular patriarchal construct against which Stowe most vehemently argues—the silencing of women. As De Jong attests, these "[p]opular portraits of biblical women overtly prescribed and inadvertently revealed the dominant culture's norms of femininity . . . [and] were contributions to the project of defining women's place in American society" (1). In other words, in a peculiarly misogynistic way, the genre trumpeted the Cult of True Womanhood and obsessively affirmed and defined the pervasive paradigm of the nineteenth century, the "good" woman and her antithesis, the "bad" woman.

To do so, the writers pirated the beautiful heroine from sentimental fiction. Since, by definition, the True Woman impersonates abstract qualities, the biblical heroine's humanity had to be neutralized, and since, as Erich Auerbach points out, the pillars of meaning in the Hebrew scriptures are set far apart and are thus open to disparate interpretations, the text lent itself to manipulation. Endorsers of True Womanhood accentuated her exterior—the way she looked and acted—and underplayed her interior—the way she felt and thought. To corroborate this superficial definition, patriarchal writers advanced the notion that appearance manifests essence. Specifically, writers contended, an exemplary woman's outward loveliness reflects an equivalent inward beauty. Hiding behind this cosmetic notion, biblical biographers invariably portray women as beauties, regardless of whether or not the scriptural text attests to their comeliness.[19]

Beauty, however, was a double-edged sword, for within the genre, pulchritude often assumes a malignant countenance, being used as a vehicle for dishonorable women to get their way and injure the nation of Israel.[20] The sketches of beautiful heroines and the proverbial assumption that beauty is vanity and inspires deceit reveals a latent misogyny and poses the troublesome central question of the genre: are these women to be emulated or disdained? Of course, at its heart, the patriarchal Christianity of the Puritans answers that no women are worthy of emulation because they are the progeny of Eve.

In *Woman in Sacred History*, Stowe created a significantly different biblical biography to trumpet her antithetical message. In her introduction, she states a purpose that is at odds with that of most male biblical biographers. While male writers strove to emphasize the abstract, Stowe admits a humanizing purpose and engages in the Jewish scholarly practice of midrash. She reports, "We have been so long in the habit of hearing the Bible read in solemn, measured tones, in the hush of churches, that we are apt to forget that these men and women were really flesh and blood, of the same human nature with ourselves" (*Woman* 12). Stowe aims to rectify the oversight through words but also in pictures. While most biblical biographies feature black-and-white line drawings of biblical women who were often dressed in

the fashions of the nineteenth century, Stowe made use of a new, painstak-
ing, and expensive chromolithographic process[21] developed by artist-lithog-
rapher Jehenne to bring the characters to eye and to life. No reader of a first
edition of Stowe's biblical biography can deny the sensuality of the portraits
of women draped with brilliantly colored, lavishly textured fabrics that beg
to be touched. Ultimately, she does so to make the "good" and the "bad"
women appear identical, but unlike her male counterparts, she does not
sully the "good" women but cleanses and normalizes the "bad" ones.

Stowe accomplishes her goal through a number of clever techniques.
First, she offers readers two portraits of Mary. On the walls of her home and
in *Woman in Sacred History*, Raphael's *Sistine Madonna* depicts the divinity
of Mary and, according to Stowe, embodies "precisely that trait which Milton lacks—tenderness and sympathy" (*Sunny Memories* 2: 343). For the publication Stowe crops the painting to include only the four figures most important to herself—Mary, Jesus, and two "serene" cherubs.[22] While the baby
connects Mary with earthly motherhood and with the fertility of the goddess, the clouds, the rainbow-winged angels, and halo interject divinity. For
her book, Stowe also commissioned a second portrait of Mary, *Mary the
Mother of Jesus*, from Frederick Goodall. At first look, Goodall's Mary, mod-
estly veiled and wearing traditional blue and white garb, appears to be appropriate; however, Goodall underplays Mary's motherhood in this portrait.
Her absent son is replaced by two doves, which Mary holds effortlessly in
her hands. The substitution of birds for baby offers a surprising connection
to the bird imagery of the goddess, as well as playing to the more acceptable
lore surrounding Mary's miraculous impregnation. Perhaps most shocking
of all is the notion that the symbol of the third part of the Trinity, the Holy
Spirit, lies tiny and contented within Mary's hands.

As in her parlor and her earlier writing, the portraits of Mary leave the
emblem of female purity and polarized womanhood intact. However, other
images that Stowe employs do not. Instead, they lead readers to think upon
spiritual matters and woman's place within them. For example, Stowe continues her (re)vision with a striking omission. While most biblical biographies of women figures begin with Eve—the first temptress and initiator of
the Fall—Stowe's does not. The only echo of Eve in Stowe's universe is the
divine form of *Venus de Milo* that stands in her parlor. Having avoided the
negative figure of Eve, Stowe addresses the dichotomy between virtuous and
wicked biblical women by conflating them in the persons of more acceptable
biblical women. Stowe frequently ignores the motherhood of some famous

biblical mothers. At other times, she presents maternity as a source of false pride and evil doings while simultaneously acknowledging nonmaternal sexuality, power, and worthiness. For instance, Stowe's depiction of Sarah stands at odds with all other biblical biographies, which emphasize Sarah's longing for motherhood and the miracle of its manifestation in her old age. In contrast, although Stowe acknowledges Sarah's role as "mother of the Jewish nation," her words and illustration show a young, prematernal, powerful, and blatantly sexual beauty. Stowe, using *Sara the Princess* by Charles Brochart to portray Sarah's comeliness and sexuality, writes there is "no alarming amount of subjection or submission [to her husband Abraham] implied," and remarks that Sarah was "too wise to dispute the title [of Lord] when she possessed the sway . . . [for] it is quite apparent . . . that she expected [her husband] to use his authority in the line of her wishes" (*Woman* 25).

At other times, Stowe includes portraits of less acceptable mothers, some of whom serve as surrogate vessels for gestation and others who plot and scheme their way to notoriety and motherhood. For instance, Stowe uses a portrait of Hagar the slave and her son Ishmael commissioned from Christian Kowhler to represent Abraham's progeny rather than using the more proper Sarah the Israelite and her son Isaac. In a very Stowesque enfranchisement of the slave, Kowhler's piece shows Hagar appealing to the God of Israel for help.

Stowe also acknowledges that not all biblical women were beautiful and that the desire for motherhood, the apex of True Womanhood, may sometimes be the root of jealousies, pride, and unfair dealings. For example, in Jean François Portael's portrait of *Leah and Rachel*, Leah looks upward at the emblem of her superiority with crossed eyes rather than with beautiful, corrected ones. Looking at the portrait, one easily remembers how Leah's trickery and her fertility occasioned a life-long schism between the sister wives of Jacob.

As in the case of Sarah, many women who are generally thought of as old appear young, and women who are not mothers but do motherly things resonate with a sexuality that seems out of place. Edouard Dubufe's *The Widow's Mite* evinces a pretty woman with the generating power of her womb intact and several children in tow rather than the sere old woman usually depicted. Similarly, Frederick Goodall's *Widow of Nain* is a young woman who remains desirable and voluptuous even in her mourning. Even Moses's sister Miriam, long held as the Virgin Mary's predecessor, reveals a breast as she seductively stands guard over her baby brother in Paul Delaroche's *Miriam and Moses*.

Moreover, to be good in Stowe's constellation does not require gestation or motherly behavior or even membership in the Judeo-Christian pantheon. Stowe manipulates the images of women who have nothing at all to do with motherhood. For instance, Salome, the daughter of Herodias, usually pictured carrying the gory severed head of John the Baptist, holds only the finger cymbals that accompany her dance, while laudatory Judith, a widow and conqueror of Israel's enemies, has a decidedly unfeminine visage and clutches the head of Holofernes in her left hand. Frequently, Stowe even appropriates portraits of women from pagan mythologies to represent the noble women of Israel. The portrait of Deborah is adapted from Charles Landelle's portrait of Velleda, a great Druid prophetess of ancient Gaul. Stowe merely ordered the landscape behind the prophetess swept away and replaced by the scenery of Syria. Stowe transforms the same artist's *A Young Girl of Tangier* into *The Captive Maid*, his *Femme Fellah* into *Rebekah the Bride*, and Emil Vernet-Lecomte's *L'Amée* (*The Dancing Girl*) into *The Daughter of Herodias*.

Finally and perhaps most strikingly, women who along with Salome perennially reside in Christianity's hall of shame enjoy similar rehabilitation. Every other biblical biography that mentions the Witch of Endor compares her to the repulsive hags in Shakespeare's *Macbeth*; not so with Stowe's rendering. Her witch is fetching and sweet-faced. In her hand, she carries a rod that recalls not only the accoutrements of magic and wizardry but the flowering rod of Jesse as well. Even Mary Magdalene, whose image routinely suffers the most, enjoys rectification, for Stowe's chosen portrait of her hearkens back to the images of the Madonna as well as to those of Eve and the goddess. Pompeo Girolamo Batoni's Magdalene, like Eve, is associated with knowledge. Like Raphael's *Madonna with a Goldfinch*, Batoni's "whore" holds an open book in her hand, and like all of Stowe's Madonnas, she displays "an angelic seriousness and gravity" and is draped in the blue of the Virgin rather than Magdalene's usual purple (*Sunny Memories* 2: 345).

One may conclude that with this final portrait Stowe completes her quintessentially American task, doing what her Puritan fathers had done long before her—bringing the old from Europe and making it new—but Stowe's transatlantic connections are not yet complete. After being transformed and energized by the art of the masters, her persona once again crosses the Atlantic to mark indelibly European art, for Stowe herself became the image of Vincent Van Gogh's Holy Woman.

Van Gogh, the evangelist and the painter, loved Stowe's works, especially *Uncle Tom's Cabin*, *My Wife and I*, and *We and Our Neighbors*, but it was to

Uncle Tom's Cabin that he turned over and over for comfort, particularly in his lowest periods.[23] By 1881, Stowe's book had become for Van Gogh "a spiritual guide on a par with the Bible," and its author "his modern equivalent of the Virgin of Lourdes" (Soth 159, 162). He gave voice to his deep awe and devotion, noting that Stowe shows "how [the gospel] may be applied in our time, in this our life, by you and me. . . ." (qtd. in Soth 159).

Van Gogh, being an artist, could not resist creating a pictorial image of his (re)mastered notion of divine womanhood. Taking inspiration from his original portrait of Madame Ginoux entitled *L'Arlesienne*, he painted at least four additional portraits of her with different accessories. In the original version, the title of the top book, *Uncle Tom's Cabin*, is clearly legible. In another version, the volume lies open, reminiscent of Raphael's *Madonna of the Goldfinch* and Batoni's *Mary Magdalene*. Within Van Gogh's images, Stowe's vision finds fruition, for they confirm the availability of a new divine, female ideal to Western, and specifically Protestant, women and men. They celebrate an emblem of womanhood imbued with divinity, with power, and with knowledge, as well as with comfort, kindness, nurture, and humanity. For the first time, in Stowe's chosen pictures and in Van Gogh's reworked portraits, the sexuality associated with the goddess and Eve conjoins with the prophetic powers of Deborah, the faithfulness of Ruth, and the goodness and divinity of Mary, for in the art of *Woman in Sacred History*, the harlot Delilah is virtually indistinguishable from the bride Rebekah.

NOTES

1. Warner's novel, which went through fourteen editions in the first two years, may have rivaled the popularity of Stowe's *Uncle Tom's Cabin*. Although the two books told very different stories, Warner's protagonist, Ellen, and Stowe's Little Eva were approximately the same age.

2. While neither writer physically created the images that illustrate their words, Warner must have at the least approved them. For Stowe, the relationship with pictures was much more intense. In *Woman in Sacred History*, she spent considerable thought and energy to choose them and money to reproduce them beautifully.

3. The story of Achan, told in Josh. 7: 1–26, tells of his taking forbidden items from the destroyed city of Jerusalem. By coveting and taking the mantle of Shinar, silver, and gold, Achan brought trouble to Israel. As punishment, the Israelites stoned him to death.

4. See Bercovitch.

5. The Puritans of the seventeenth and eighteenth centuries became the Congregationalists of the nineteenth.

6. Paul bans women from speaking in public in 1 Cor. 14.34. "As in all congregations of God's people, women should keep silent at the meeting. They have no permission to talk, but should keep their place as the law directs. If there is something they want to know, they can ask their husbands at home. It is a shocking thing for a woman to talk at the meeting."

7. Charles Beecher's journal of his trip abroad with his sister Harriet was edited by Joseph S. Van Why and Earl French and published as *Harriet Beecher Stowe in Europe: The Journal of Charles Beecher* by the Stowe-Day Foundation in 1986.

8. The placement of the objects reflects a contemporary tour of the house, but the art displayed was Stowe's, and its placement is as close as possible to Stowe's own arrangement.

9. 1 Cor. 11.3–10. "I wish you to understand that, while every man has Christ for his head, a woman's head is man, as Christ's head is God. A man who keeps his head covered when he prays or prophesies brings shame on his head; but a woman brings shame on her head if she prays or prophesies bareheaded; it is as bad as if her head was shaved. . . . A man must not cover his head, because man is the image of God, and the mirror of his glory, whereas a woman reflects the glory of man."

10. Lyman Beecher and other Congregationalists maintained that the millennium could be induced by the proper behavior of the elect. The notion prompted the many female reform societies and movements that preceded the sustained campaign for women's suffrage.

11. References to *American Woman's Home* are to the New York 1869 edition.

12. This phrase was so often repeated in the masculinist writings of the nineteenth century that Stowe felt the need to address it in *Woman in Sacred History*. Of Moses's sister she writes, "like many of her sex who have watched the cradle of great men, and been their guardians in infancy and their confidential counselors in maturity, Miriam is known by *Moses* more than by herself" (82).

13. Hedrick notes that as Stowe's father's mind dimmed with age, he was "precluded [from] . . . knowing about [Stowe's and his other children's] apostasy" (302). He died in 1863 in his eighty-eighth year.

14. Stowe was sixty-four when *Woman in Sacred History*, the first of the three books advancing a feminist version of Christianity, was published.

15. Nineteenth-century clergy assumed readers of fiction to be almost exclusively female.

16. Most writers attest absolute fidelity to scripture. Burchard promises absolute fidelity and no concealment of fault. He pledges to present men as men, not gods, and "women . . . as women, with all the frailties and excellences of the sex" (x). Charles Adams takes a similar vow. See *Women of the Bible*, 3.

17. Weld's volume is a collection of sketches by "the authors best known in the sacred literature of our country" (5).

18. This exclusivity suggests another (non-gender-related) subfunction of scriptural biography—the promotion of Christianity. Although many of the biblical women included in these volumes come from Hebrew texts, the writers read and interpreted

them from a parochially Christian perspective. For example, writers often value Hebrew women (Ruth, for instance) for their position in the lineage of Jesus.

19. For a thorough, methodical analysis of representations of race and beauty in female scriptural biography, see Mary De Jong's "Dark-Eyed Daughters."

20. Delilah and Jezebel, for example.

21. In *Woman in Sacred History*, the process is explained as follows: "Each subject was produced by a series of color printings. The delicacy and difficulty of this art may be better appreciated by remembering that, while the painter always has the palette with numerous pigments and shades of color, the lithographer has to analyze the work that had been composed with infinite touches of the painter's brush, and also had to study the effects of each color in a single stone—which may have only touched the picture once. The final effect was produced by the colors and shades of colors superimposed one upon another. To detect the three or four reds, the varying yellows, blues, several shades of gray, and place them upon different stones, each in correct position and true in tone and intensity, required considerable artistic sensibility and training. When printed one upon another, with fifteen, twenty, or even thirty and forty separate stones, the original painting would be produced in all harmonies and contrasts, with subtle variations of color and shade" (247).

22. Stowe writes in *Sunny Memories* that: "Pope Sixtus is, in my eyes, a very homely man, and as I think no better of homely old men for being popes, his presence in the picture is an annoyance. St. Barbara, on the other side, has the most beautiful head and face that could be represented; but then she is kneeling on a cloud with such a judicious and coquettish arrangement of her neck, shoulders and face . . . as makes one feel that no saint . . . could ever have dropped into such a position in the abandon of holy rapture. In short, she looks like a theatrical actress; without any sympathy with the solemnity of the religious conception, who is there merely because a beautiful woman was wanted to fill up the picture" (2: 341). Stowe calls the green curtain, which she also excises, "a nuisance"(2: 341).

23. Van Gogh turned to *Uncle Tom's Cabin* after his attacks of mental illness in December 1888 and March 1889 (Soth 159, 156).

The Afterlife of *Dred* on the British Stage

JUDIE NEWMAN

HREE OCCASIONS, three encounters with Stowe. First, most painfully, as a ten-year-old on the North Coast of Scotland, banged heavily on the head with *Uncle Tom's Cabin* by an irate teacher who demanded to know why I was reading the lies of "the Stowe woman," instead of completing my ink exercise. Teacher, a Highland Scot, maintained an abiding distrust for Stowe, fostered by the local events touched upon in *Sunny Memories*. Two years later, *Uncle Tom's Cabin* suddenly came into focus again, transformed into a Siamese ballet in *The King and I*, incongruously associating Stowe in my mind with Yul Brynner and a screen filled by a whirling crinoline. Two years after that, in what was then Leningrad, it was almost unsurprising to discover that the Young Pioneer with whom I had escaped from a chaperoned dance in a gloomy palace of culture had just read *Uncle Tom's Cabin* (and was keen to discuss it with a young capitalist). Before the reader comes to the conclusion that I am about to indulge in what is currently known as "moi" criticism, let me come to the point. As the authors of the essays in the current volume demonstrate, to read Stowe intelligently is to read her through different cultural contexts.

If one figure in nineteenth-century American literature comes into sharp focus as a result of the "transnational turn" in American literary history, it is Stowe. Translated right across the globe, Stowe offers a permeable model of American cultural identity, not as solipsistically national, but as relational, involved in a worldwide dialogue with others. As Colleen Glenney Boggs has commented, "As an identity, culture is always multiple: linguistically as translation; personally, as dialogue; racially, as amalgamation; nationally as globalism" (52). Stowe is the ultimate shape-shifter. Gillian Brown has highlighted Stowe's own awareness in her works of "the radical variability of read-ing despite directing literary conventions" ("Reading" 78), and her readers have found her texts malleable and adaptable to very different purposes. This instability of interpretation is matched by the slipperiness of Stowe's images, language, and characters and has seen her successively configured and reconfigured as champion of the oppressed, benevolent paternalist, protofeminist, and out-and-out racist. As John MacKay comments in this volume, the susceptibility of *Uncle Tom's Cabin* to every form of *détourne-ment* is striking enough to constitute an interesting theoretical problem in its own right.

For Boggs, questions addressed in the nineteenth century concerning the relation between universalism and particularism are gaining fresh urgency in an era when critics are concerned to think about culture both specifically and yet globally. Cultural relations operate both within and between na-tions, and it is important to protect both national diversity and literary glob-alism from homogenizing universality. It is the mark of the essays in the present volume that this attention to the particular is maintained in creative tension with the expanded transatlantic readings of Stowe. As my opening anecdotes suggest, Stowe may be read in both micro- and macrocultural terms; as both local and global, translocal or transnational, speaking across the globe to other societies with their own oppressions or as part of a dia-logue limited to one circumscribed locality.

An additional factor remains to be considered. The editors of the present collection note the elision of American women writers from recent transat-lantic scholarship. But the absence of any sense of popular cultural forms from that scholarship is also striking. Groundbreaking transatlanticists offer readings of writers who are not just predominantly male but also firmly oc-cupy the higher ground of culture. One honorable exception is Lawrence Levine, whose argument suggests that the Atlantic current flowed both ways. For Levine, Shakespeare's plays functioned as popular *American* culture in the nineteenth century. Prominent British actors frequently visited America to perform; burlesques of Shakespeare became an American folk genre; and "Shakespearean" values (individualism, moralism, force of character) were reconfigured to coincide with America's own. In like fashion Harriet Beecher Stowe became a major part of British popular culture, her works dramati-cally adapted to fit British cultural values while simultaneously extending the audience for her antislavery message to lower-class audiences and mem-bers of the British public who were unlikely to read novels and unconverted to abolitionism. Stowe was performed as much as she was read; representations of her characters moved from the literary page to the popular stage; her themes were meshed with British national agendas dominated as much by class as race and were tailored to regional as well as national conventions. In this respect, therefore, Stowe enjoyed much more influence in Britain than in America. The story of her dramatic adaptations includes a chapter that is almost exclusively British. Although *Uncle Tom's Cabin* was widely adapted for the stage all over the world, the dramatic career of Stowe's second antislavery novel, *Dred: A Tale of the Great Dismal Swamp*, remains largely unrecorded, precisely because its extensive stage career took place on the British rather than the American boards. The American record is limited to the immediate prewar period and to four adaptations, only two of which survive in print.[1] The story in Britain is quite different with at least eighteen adaptations running from 1856 to 1882, both in London and in the provinces, many of them highly successful. Unlike their American counterparts (which tend to foreground gradual reform, education, religion, and the controlling figure of the white Northern male), the British versions feature strong female roles, onstage interracial violence, righteous black revenge, images of insurrection, and forthright condemnations of slavery. Their message was compromised in some respects by British national agendas, substituting class-based concerns for race politics; they varied in their engagement with the abolitionist cause, but their success and the size of their audiences made them enormously influential.

Adaptations of novels for the stage were very common in the nineteenth century. To the modern reader *Dred* may nonetheless not seem an ideal candidate for dramatic adaptation, and the anonymous reviewer for the *Times* was similarly doubtful. Dred "with his mouth perpetually overflowing with Scriptural phraseology, scarcely utters six lines which would be tolerable if spoken within the walls of a theatre"; the cholera was "a Nemesis that does not readily wear a picturesque form"; Nina's "lively rattle" was too garrulous; and there were insuperable difficulties to staging a camp meeting and a Presbyterian conference ("Surrey Theatre," *Times* 22 October 1856). Nonetheless adaptations were almost immediate. The novel was published on 22 August 1856 in both Britain and America. By the end of the year more than a dozen adaptations had reached the stage. H. Philip Bolton points out that in the nineteenth century the great mass of British dramatic productions were performed in the "minor" (i.e. nonpatent) theaters where the tastes of the great unwashed majority prevailed, and any play that demonstrated solidarity with the downtrodden and dispossessed tended to have enormous appeal. The most popular plays of the age all concern the fortunes of an oppressed group. Where a play concerned two or more such groups (women and Scots in *The Bride of Lammermoor*; children, women, and slaves in the case of *Uncle Tom*) it was even more likely to appeal. Audiences for the theater were very mixed in composition (Davis and Emeljanow), so that these plays reached lower-class spectators who were not necessarily readers; nor were they abolitionists, as opposed to the audiences for slave narratives. In short, the adapters were not preaching to the already converted. For one anonymous reviewer ("Britannia, Hoxton," *Era* 26 October 1856) the play version of *Dred* scored strategically over the novel on three counts, firstly because what was presented to the eye made a deeper and more lasting impression than what was merely read; secondly because vast numbers who would never read the novel would take away from the play "a vivid recollection of the atrocities of the slave trade"; and thirdly because "there can be no 'skipping' of the less agreeable passages by the sensitive reader, who would gladly pursue all the fun, and dwell spell-bound upon the love episodes, but would miss all that is horrible, and that is calculated to infuse one bitter element into his cup of sweets."

Most productions of *Dred* were essentially melodramatic, and it is important to situate the limitations of the plays within that mode. As Michael Booth has argued, melodrama favored plot at the expense of characterization, relied heavily on physical sensation, used character stereotypes, rewarded virtue and punished vice, provided plenty of violence but always ended happily. Instead of avoiding the obvious, melodrama tends to insist upon it, labeling heroes as heroes at the first entrance and making sure that comedians get a laugh as they come on. Tragic and farcical scenes often alternate in rapid succession, and characters may have special music or comic tags attached to them. Both in the original novel and in dramatizations the slaves Jim and Tomtit have tags. Tomtit repeatedly proclaims, "I'm going to glory"; Jim's phrase is "Seek and ye shall not find me." Stowe's novel offered a range of comic parts, and an amateur minstrel performance (2: chap. 4), on which adapters certainly capitalized. Comedy, however, should not be nakedly equated with minstrelsy and an implicit racism. David Grimsted has argued that melodrama always includes a comic middle with humorous characters who are allowed to show normal interest in sex, money, or aggression without being morally debased, thus constituting a center of decent egoism between disinterested virtue and horrible vice. These middle characters are not merely comic relief but suggest the creation of an everyday moral world to be encased in higher moral truth. Jacky Bratton similarly argues that in melodrama absolute morality prevails but some part of the play is always engaged with less absolute standards, low lifes, and comedy. Contrasting models of a hero may be offered, the one unambiguously heroic, the other a more pragmatic survivor. The comic character can be used to modify an audience's response to the clear-cut moral lead. Tiff functions in this fashion as a modifier to Dred—a hero still, but a comic one, and more likely to appeal to the laboring classes. As a result, the performances offered new readings of the novel, providing, in their very infidelity to Stowe's original, ways in which British working-class audiences could identify with and support black characters.

Actor-managers usually wrote their own adaptations or delegated the task to a member of the company. First in the field in Britain was the Victoria Theatre version, which foregrounded spectacle but with a clear antislavery message. In this adaptation Nina, married to Harry, is unaware of his slave origins. Both are committed opponents of slavery, and as the play opens Harry has bought an estate on free soil and plans to leave Carolina forever. When Tom Gordon overthrows his uncle's will to prevent Harry's manumission, the play ends with a courtroom drama. Faithfully repeating the main satirical points made by Stowe, the judge proclaims that "We must support the master as his power must be absolute" (94) and informs Harry that "The African race are foredoomed" (94). Harry's reply is forthright in its challenge to racial definitions. "But I am not of the African race. I am Colonel Gordon's son. Look at my hair, my eyes. I am not darker than my brother who stands there thirsting for my blood" (94). In a surprising twist, Harry is saved by Milly, who reveals herself as Tom's mother, not Harry's. In their infancy Milly, the wetnurse for both children, had swapped them in the cradle.[2] The spectacle of righteous black revenge is fully enacted on stage, as Dred shoots Tom and dies with a final speech foreseeing the inevitability of sectional conflict: "There's a storm rising in the South, a dreadful struggle will take place in the great nation. The Union will be rent, like her flag of stars and stripes. The stripes of the South may triumph for a while over the lacerated hearts of the poor Negro slave, but in their turn they will fade before the bright stars of the North" (102).

Although the play appears to be powerfully opposed to slavery, calls for freedom were inextricably linked to British political agendas. The pun on stripes (whipping) had made its appearance earlier in the play as part of a pro-British, anti-American rhetoric when Jim tells Hannibal, who has been flogged, "You allars supported de stars and de stripes and at last you get him belly full of de stars and de stripes" (35). A similar attack on American notions of liberty emerges with the criminalization of American Independence when Tom tells Clayton that "we will have niggers, 'tis our right."

> Clayton: Who gave you that right?
> Tom: Why the Constitution of the Glorious Union to be sure. The finest
>   government in the world.
> (Cue hissing and booing from the patriotic British pit.) (47)

The British delight in their naval triumphs and hence in nautical melodrama also influences the play. "Tar dramas" had made the honest sailor the archetypal popular working-class hero, a defender of both England and the oppressed. They tended toward national self-congratulation, equating England with liberty and tapping into the national memory of the valiant role of the navy in direct slave liberation during the period of the suppression of the slave trade (J. S. Bratton). Many theaters were therefore well provided with water tanks and naval props. Scene 7 opens at Magnolia Grove, now situated on the seashore with "Open Sea at back." Clayton comments (ominously since Tiff and the orphans are at sea in a small boat named the *Liberator*) that the cloud has burst and the sea is rising. The *Liberator* (named for the flagship periodical of the abolitionist cause) duly appears, is buffeted about, and sinks. The attractions of a good shipwreck scene triumph over the verbiage of the abolitionist cause.

The next adaptation, produced at Samuel Lane's Britannia Saloon, marked the beginning of a growing interest in Tiff and the "poor white" characters, a group with whom a British working-class audience could readily identify. Mrs. Denvil, the only woman to adapt the play, offered a depiction of slavery that emphasized masters as violent sexual predators. In scene 7 Dred taunts Harry for his inability to protect his wife: "Women always like the master better than the slave. I am a freeman. You are a slave. . . . No man whips me" (n.p.). In case the audience had missed the point, the following scene depicts Hark flayed alive with whips, wooden shingles, and boiling water. Both in its composition and in production the play was very much under female control—with an active role played by Sarah Lane, Samuel's wife. Her hand is evident in the instructions on the reverse of various pages of the promptbook (University of Kent, PETT MSS D72) and indicates many small changes. Cora's account of her infanticide remains untouched, however, providing a meaty female role and focusing the play on the suffering of women.

The Britannia version was also the basis of William Seaman's "Penny Pictorial," which condensed a two-volume novel into eight pages. Even a slow reader could get the gist of Stowe's novel in an evening's reading. The eye-catching cover depicts Dred shooting Tom dead as Harry draws his knife against a background of black slaves with rifles, flaming torches, and brilliantly striped red, white, and blue trousers. The truncated quality of the action is often comically bathetic. Nina expires at breakneck speed in the course of five lines of dialogue; Clayton, informed that she is dying, responds rather inadequately, "Nina dying! Oh, horrid" (5). The portrayal of Dred lends him more of the air of a villain than a hero.[3] Described as "a tall, powerful African with polished black skin, and great proportions" his initial entry is marked with a thunderclap and the rending of a pine tree, and he promptly gloats in thoroughly unchristian fashion: "Rage on ye thunder-claps! flash ye livid lightning! I like to see the elements thus at war with each other, for then I know that mischief is afloat, and that the inhabitants of the doomed city will have to mourn" (6). Unsurprisingly Lisette is decidedly chary of him and cautions Harry, "I don't like to see you in the company of that dark man, 'ere long he will make you as dismal as himself" (7). Unworried by any censor, Seaman also foregrounded sexual enslavement. Dred taunts Harry that women always like the master better than the man and expands considerably on the original: "Where a man licks his master's rod, his wife scorns him—serves him right—Take it meekly my boy—Take your master's old coat—take your wife when he has done with her" (6). Hark is murdered by Hokum for erotic reasons:

> Tom: Hark had a pretty wife. Hokum wanted her so he gladly put the
> husband to death for the sake of this wench. (6)

The play closes with Dred waving a torch on high and crying, "Shout for liberty and vengeance" (8). For a penny, the reader certainly got his dreadful money's worth in terms of violence and action undiluted by comic minstrelsy.

Not all British productions resisted the lure of minstrelsy, however. At the Queen's Theatre, W. E. Suter's play (probably the most questionable of the British adaptations) left mixed-race Harry a happy slave-owner, and made no attempt to attack slavery as an institution. By focusing on an individual legal case (Harry's rightful inheritance), the play sidestepped Stowe's own indictment of the law in general. The individual was saved from slavery without any challenge to the legality of slavery itself.[4] The play was also racist in its comedy, involving the exchange of stereotypical blackface malapropisms between the slaves Jim and Katy. Katy resents Jim's "resulting" speech and threatens to "infect" someone else, and Jim gets "seriously defended" (12). They are reconciled when he describes her as a stellar "consternation" and they look forward to a grand "sore-eye" (soiree). The pair sing duets, one of which includes the following verse from Jim:

> Him is black, oo is brown,
> Both am nobby figger,
> And no doubt, our first born
> Will be a piebald nigger. (28)

Perhaps the adaptation that was most faithful to the novel was the version performed at the Surrey Theatre, which also illustrates the nature of the censorship that *Dred* plays encountered in Britain. It was written by Frederick Phillips, who was applauded for "the comprehensive manner in which he has grasped all the leading features of a rather tiresome book" (*Era* 26 October 1856). Dred is closer to Stowe's visionary hero and makes his initial entrance leaning on his rifle and soliloquizing to the moon: "Fair moonlight, how I love you. You are free. I contemplate your beauty and am lost in wonder at your pale and shining rays. I look to earth and lovely as it is the reptile Man has blurred and blotted all" (n.p.). Ironically, this play, which involved insurrection, miscegenation, and frequent flagellation, actually faced its major problems with the censor on religious grounds. By the Theaters Act of 1843, the lord chamberlain was empowered to demand a "true copy" of any play being performed in Britain "for hire, gain or reward" fourteen days (later seven days) before the projected date of performance and had an unlimited power of veto. Scripture was considered unsuitable for the stage; all sacred invocations and any direct quotation from the Bible were banned, and it was a serious offense to bring ministers of the Christian religion into contempt, effectively preventing any actor appearing on stage as a clergyman. It is not surprising, therefore, that the British productions remove all reference to the lengthy scenes in Stowe's novel that feature clergymen. The scenes in the novel in which Tiff learns to read from the Bible, or where characters exchange different Biblical quotations to attempt to prove or disprove the rightness of slavery, and the entire camp meeting sequence were a lost cause to British adaptors.

The Surrey production is unusually religious among adaptations. Stowe left Dred's final destination uncertain, merely stating that "that splendid frame . . . was now to be resolved again into the eternal elements."[5] The Surrey had fewer doubts of his salvation and sent him straight to heaven. The *Times* noted that "We are informed by a transparency at the end of the piece that the soul of the sable hero is on its road to the realms of bliss." The censor promptly demanded large cuts. Dred was played by William Creswick, whose *Uncle Tom* play was one of the strongest in condemning slavery (and also included an insurrection on stage). The *Times* described Creswick as "sonorous of voice, graceful in attitude, lofty in bearing," and he clearly assumed a tragic and heroic character rather than playing Dred as demonic or brutal.

The part of Nina was taken by Adelaide Biddles, who had been acting professionally from the age of six and had just returned from two years on stage in Boston, where she had played Oceana, the young heroine, to Edwin Forrest's Metamora, the Indian chief. The British and American stages were well entwined at this point. Biddles's father, formerly the manager of the Bower Saloon, had married the daughter of the ringmaster at Astley's and later became an American citizen. Her sister Clara married Thomas Barry, the manager of the Boston Theater. Creswick, in partnership with Richard Shepherd, was trying to improve the Surrey from a stronghold of nautical melodrama to a more respectable theater. Importantly, *Dred* was produced to save their financial bacon. In early 1856 they had attempted to stage opera sung in Italian at double the usual ticket price. Forced to end the run after three weeks, they had an unprecedented ten-week gap before reopening with *Dred* and successfully recouping their heavy financial losses. The *Era* noted that the play was "rapturously received by a very crowded audience" and that both Dred and Uncle Tiff took curtain calls. By now the play was in preparation at the City of London Theatre and in full swing at the Britannia, but despite the competition, Phillips's play ran for forty-one nights.

The extent to which a novel about slavery could be briskly translated from race to class oppression was demonstrated at the Bower Saloon, a low Southside theater, staging a burlesque in rhyming couplets. Burlesques of a popular play might have only an indirect relation to the original adaptation, tending to be unserious spoofs, yet as H. Philip Bolton notes, "A burlesque is often the greatest testimonial to the popular appeal of the plot and characters of a published narrative" (viii). The scene opens in a miserable garret to "The Song of the Shirt," written by Thomas Hood in response to an incident in which a poor widow with two children was brought to trial for pawning clothing belonging to her employer in a clothing factory. The trial exposed the wretched pay and living conditions of factory workers and aroused the public's sympathy. Hood's poem (*Punch*, December 1843), was dramatized as *The Sempstress* by Mark Lemon and printed upon broadsides and handkerchiefs. It includes the lines

> It's O! to be a slave
> Along with the barbarous Turk
> Where woman has never a soul to save
> If this is Christian work.

In the play's opening scene, Lucy, a seamstress, laments how hard she has to work for Solomon Dred, owner of a loan office. Stowe's Messianic avenger appears to have become an anti-Semitic stereotype connected to the garment industry. Solomon Dred addresses the workers as "you infernal niggers" but there is little connection to American slavery. If anything the play probably aims its satire at Stowe, who had been criticized for buying a costume made by sweated labor. Seamstresses were often portrayed by contemporaries as the slaves of fashionable ladies (Midgley). The malleability of the play was also demonstrated in the equestrian version at Astley's Royal Amphitheatre in which every opportunity was taken to bring horses into the action. Given the number of abolition publications that criticized the comparison of slaves with horses—as in sale advertisements that paired them (Wood, *Slavery* 368) —it is interesting to speculate whether the play strengthened the racist associations or demonstrated slave superiority over the animal.

So far, so populist. With some exceptions the London adaptations do not appear to have engaged with abolitionist agendas so much as with the interests of British nationality or class. But in the regions the story was a different one, with several productions aimed squarely at a more overtly abolitionist audience. These productions highlight the fact that there are not only national and continental differences in the reception and transmission of Stowe's work but also regional. Stowe is both transnational and translocal. As in London, *Dred* enjoyed enormous popularity throughout Britain. Productions were staged in Glasgow, Bristol, Nottingham, Newcastle, Sunderland, and Sheffield in 1856; Birmingham, Dundee, and Hull in 1857; Swansea and Bath in 1858; in Wolverhampton and at the Pavilion Theatre in 1872; in Hull in 1873 and 1875; and at Beverly in 1882. Such was the popularity of the play that Kathleen Barker has argued that "versions of *Uncle Tom's Cabin* and to a lesser extent *Dred* were the mainstay of many a provincial manager, and the positive salvation of some—John Coleman in Sheffield and J. H. Chute in Bristol particularly" (360). In Nottingham (a town dependent on the textile industry and thus on Southern cotton) the play was an enormous success even though *The Nottingham Weekly Journal* (28 November 1856) condemned it as "so crowded by the incidents that no room is left for details. The consequence is that the characters are hardly worth the pains bestowed upon them by the actors, the dialogue being so trumpery as to give them no chance of making anything of their abilities."[6]

Getting the balance right between entertainment and high seriousness was often a delicate matter. Two provincial performances offer representative examples of the ways in which the regions could push an abolitionist message more directly than the London stage—though at some risk to profits. In Newcastle Upon Tyne, Edward Dean Davis staged *Dred* at the Theatre Royal and also at the Sunderland New Lyceum Theatre. Davis had a reputation for covering his costs handsomely. But *Dred* was an expensive disaster for him despite an audience sympathetic to abolition. An unusual day-to-day insight into the life of the company in December 1856 is provided in the letters of Helen Taylor, the stepdaughter of John Stuart Mill, whom Davis had taken on as a twenty-five-year-old novice (Kent). When Davis offered her a role in *Dred*, she refused disdainfully, her eyes set on playing Lady Macbeth as her first stage role. When these hopes were dashed she wrote to her mother anxiously, "If he offers me nothing but indifferent parts in trashy melodramas, do you think it would be injudicious to accept them?" (letter of 28 November, Helen Taylor to Harriet Mill). The company had high hopes of *Dred*. Davis's daughter, the business manager, told Taylor that after two weeks of opera, "they are going to bring out *Dred* which they expect will last some time" (letter of 22 November). The audience for moral drama looked promising; Taylor observed few rich people in the streets, but "the population of poor and lower middle class seems immense" and they had "a much more serious responsible air than they have about London" (letter of 24 November). The play was nonetheless costly to produce, given its sizeable cast and abundant incident. Davis had a large company by Victorian standards, thirty-one men and thirty women. On Saturday 29 November, Taylor tells her mother that Davis "talks of finding some afterpiece to act after *Dred* which he brings out on Monday. But *Dred* is very long and it would not be for several nights possible to compress it enough to admit of anything that I could act in, because as you know, serious sort of things, however trashy, are always longer than mere farces" (letter of 29 November). By Wednesday Davis's son Alfred was fetched from the New Lyceum to see if the play would do any better there. Alfred declared roundly that "*Dred* would never do for Sunderland" (letter of 2–3 December). On Thursday Taylor told her mother that "*Dred* has been a complete failure here, a more miserably empty house than that last night can scarcely be possible" (letter of 3–4 December). Later Taylor reports to her mother that the Theatre Royal will not open for the last three nights of the run, in consequence of the very poor house, and comments smugly that "it cannot be worthwhile if they persist in playing such trash" (letter of 15 December).

Despite Alfred's reluctance, *Dred* transferred to Sunderland in abridged form and made a hit. In Taylor's letter of 9 December, she encloses the play-bill for the Sunderland performance that makes much of the abolitionist elements of the play, advertised as "The New Drama *Dred*! Taken from Mrs Stowe's Favourite Work of that Name." A hefty quotation from Stowe's preface to the novel and four lines from Longfellow's "The Quadroon Girl" prefaced the cast list, which also characterized the *dramatis personae* in terms of their allegiances: Edward as "a Liberal slaveholder with his own peculiar views of that institution," Tom "a Brutal Slaveholder," Judes Jekyll (*sic*) as "an advocate of slavery as a Christian institution." Dred (played by Henry Irving, in one of his first appearances) as "The Hero and Prophet of the Dismal Swamp." The play adds a new character, Jane, a fugitive slave who foregrounds the abolitionist message. The playbill was very literary, quoting heavily from the novel and from other abolitionist works. Scene 7 ("Dred the Prophet") was introduced with eight lines from Longfellow's "The Slave in the Dismal Swamp," and the final scene was unambiguously entitled "The Warning to America! Beware!" and invoked the biblical precedent of the fall of a decadent civilization, once more quoting Longfellow ("The Warning").

> There is a poor blind Samson in your land
> Shorn of his strength and bound in bonds of steel
> Who may in some grim revel raise his hand
> And strike the pillars of your commonweal
> Till the vast temple of your liberties
> A shapeless mass of wreck and rubbish lies.

It must have been obvious that America was likely to be deaf to Sunderland's warning, but the high-flown rhetoric did much to advertise the serious moral content of the play rather than its "trashy" quality. The audience was a very good one and had been drawn by the appeal to abolitionism. Taylor noted that the gallery, which held some 500 people, was densely packed.

The moral high ground was also firmly occupied at the Theatre Royal, Birmingham, where the play was billed as the "Great Attraction for the Easter Holidays," performed from Easter Monday. Remarkably the manuscript, the prompt books, and the playbills all survive (Birmingham City Archives). The three playbills are exceptionally elaborate and shed considerable light on the ways in which the play was thought likely to appeal to audiences. Stowe's novel was credited, and extracts from it prefaced each scene description. A lengthy quotation from Lord Brougham refuting the claim that "man can hold property in man" headed the *dramatis personae*. The latter are also described in some detail: Jekyl as "a Southern Lawyer, who advocates Slavery as a Christian Institution"; Tom as "Good made Bad, and kept so by slave-owning"; Jack Dakin as "a Dealer in Flesh and Blood." The play was clearly signaled as abolitionist in intention. The women characters appear to have been a particular draw. Nina was once again billed as "a Thing of Light, of Joy, and of Goodness," and four lines of verse accompanied her name in the cast list. Cora also was featured as poetic womanhood, and Lisette's billing was accompanied with no less than eight lines emphasizing the saintly virtue of the quadroon maiden. Perhaps unsurprisingly, the other actor blessed by the Muse (Longfellow's "The Slave Singing at Midnight") was T. E. Mills playing the feminized Tiff:

> Loud he sang the Psalm of David!
> He a Negro and Enslaved
> Sung of Israel's Victory
> Sung of Zion, Bright and Free.

The fact that the play was being advertised for Easter Monday led to an emphasis on the religious quality of the characters, the worthiness of the theme, and the suitability of the event for women and children. (Babes in arms were not admitted, but children under twelve were offered half-price seats in the boxes.)

The manuscript and promptbooks reveal that the text of this adaptation was by Frederick Phillips, with some minor variations. Given the overt religious references in the Surrey production, it might well have been an obvious choice for an Easter attraction. The play lost some of its political charge as a result, however. The manager of the theater, Mercer Hampson Simpson, had initialed his special instructions in pencil on the promptbooks: "All the brutal and coarse expressions must be carefully cut out—the subject in itself being very brutal. The name of God must not be used."

The result is to increase the emphasis on resurrection and to decrease references to the Old Testament and Judgment. Mrs. Cripps expires invoking "him that they told me had a glory round his head," whereas Dred loses many of his most impassioned pleas for vengeance and almost all his biblical allusions. Milly's evangelical account of her life remains almost without alteration from the Surrey production, presumably as calculated to appeal to mothers in the audience and to the spirit of Christian forgiveness. In addition almost all direct reference to miscegenation disappeared. Harry's speech to Lisette ("I've seen many a man sold for nothing else than looking too much like his father") is crossed out. When Cora, described as a quadroon in the Surrey production, makes her entrance in Birmingham with her two children, all are described in the stage direction as "perfectly white." In London Tom was clearly established as a sexual predator who ordered his men to take Lisette "into my chamber and tie her down hand and foot." When Harry begs him to "kill her rather" he rejoins, "I mean to, afterwards." This was clearly too much for Birmingham; the production substitutes the instruction to "take her into the barn and tie her up" and cuts the exchange with Harry. Other changes suggest an attempt to cater to a more genteel audience than the predominantly working-class crowd at the Surrey. In Birmingham, instead of "falling back dead" Nina gracefully "reclines" on a chair. Harry's toil is distinctly less vulgar; "the sweat of your brow" becomes "the labour of your hands." As a result, the play found favor. Special trains were laid on from Walsall, Dudley, Wolverhampton, West Bromwich, and the surrounding area to get the respectable theatergoers to the performance for its 7:00 p.m. start and to take them home again at midnight.

Such was its popularity that the play lived on despite emancipation. Arthur Williams, a well-known comic actor, played Uncle Tiff in a version at the Pavilion Theatre in 1876, and among his papers in the University of Kent is a manuscript of another adaptation, by Harwood Cooper, in which Dred is described as "the Freeman of the Swamp and Liberator of his Race," suggesting a performance date close to or after emancipation. Even later in the century, the play was frequently revived. In the Theatre Royal, Hull, the revival of October 1873 (Suter's adaptation) included Maurice Barrymore playing Hark, shortly before he went to America and founded the Drew-Barrymore acting dynasty. Theater culture remained transatlantic.

The adaptations demonstrate, in addition to the malleability of Stowe's text, that Stowe's audiences were prepared to envisage violent solutions on stage and interracial conflict. Abolitionism *was* foregrounded in plots, characterization, and on playbills despite the implicit racism of many of the plays, and black slaves were shown as active and heroic, not as cringing "Uncle Toms." Modern scholars have tended to exalt the slave narrative as the definitive vehicle for abolitionist propaganda and as a form that offers at least a degree of documentary authenticity and black agency. But in terms of influence it is worth noting that a slave narrative might take two or three years to sell copies to as many individuals as a theater could seat in two nights. *Dred* ran at the Surrey for forty-one nights. The Victoria held a large crowd, with some 1,500–2,000 people in the gallery alone. In the 1850s the Standard had a capacity of 3,400, the Pavilion 3,500. Selling to these numbers in a successful run of a month meant that the play's influence was considerable.[7] As *Dred*'s British dramatizations suggest, the processes of transmission, translation, and exchange that Stowe's work demonstrates in such variety were as dynamic in the popular incarnations of her book as in self-consciously literary ones. Both transnational phenomenon and inflected with local concerns, *Dred*'s afterlife illuminates the paradoxes of a transatlantic career.

NOTES

I am grateful to the British Academy for funding that enabled an earlier version of part of this essay to be delivered at the American Literature Association Conference, Boston, 2003; and to Robert S. Levine for his comments as respondent to a paper delivered at a special session on *Dred* at the MLA Annual Convention, San Diego, 2003. I gratefully acknowledge the assistance of the archivists and librarians in each of the libraries and collections where evidence of adaptations has been located and the staff of the Hallward Library, University of Nottingham, and especially thank H. Philip Bolton, Barry Clarke, Sarah Meer, Michael Payne, Paul Schlicke, Michael Slater, Caroline Sloat, and Hazel Waters for invaluable advice and information.

1. On dramatic adaptations of *Uncle Tom's Cabin* see Birdoff; on *Dred* see Newman "Staging."

2. The source of Twain's version of the tale in *Pudd'nhead Wilson*. See Newman "Was Tom White?"

3. Hazel Waters argues that the black figure on the British stage was originally a fearsome, avenging figure but diminished in ferocity following the advent of T. D. Rice. Dred, while something of a return to the figure of the black avenger, could not dislodge the ubiquitous Jim Crow image. Waters also notes the brief appearance of the

mulatto female avenger in midcentury, a role that may account for the greater prominence of Cora in British adaptations.

4. See McConachie (21), who makes this point in a discussion of stage versions of *Uncle Tom's Cabin.*

5. *Dred,* 1992, 636.

6. I am grateful to Michael Payne for supplying me with a copy of this untitled review.

7. Jennifer Workman Pitcock, "Imaginary Bonds: Antislavery Dramas on the New York Stage, 1853–1861," diss. U of Kentucky, 2002, considers the Conway, Brougham, and Suter versions on the New York stage and offers comparative figures.

ADAPTATIONS

References for plays cite page numbers (where applicable) rather than act and scene. In manuscript some scenes are variously numbered, and in promptbooks, when a scene is cut, renumbering is not always consistent.

Anon. *Dred.* 27 October, 1, 3, 12, 14, 17 November 1856. Theatre Royal Sheffield. (Two playbills in Sheffield Central Library.)

Anon. *Dred: A Tale of the Dismal Swamp. An Equestrian Drama.* 15 November 1856. Astley's Royal Amphitheatre, London. BL ADD MS 52962 (U).

Anon. *Dred: A Tale of the Dismal Swamp.* 21–28 November 1856. Theatre Royal, Nottingham.

Anon. *Dred.* 1(–6?) December 1856. Theatre Royal, Newcastle Upon Tyne; and 8–10 December. New Lyceum Theatre, Sunderland.

Anon. *Dred.* 15 September 1857. Theatre Royal, Dundee.

Anon. *Dred.* 24 April 1865. Grecian, London.

Anon. *Dred, Or the Dismal Swamp.* 30–31 October and 1 November 1873. Theatre Royal, Hull.

Anon. *Dred, Or The Dismal Swamp.* 23 February 1882. Beverley.

Banks, Walter. *Dred.* 11 November 1872. Prince of Wales, Wolverhampton.

Brougham, John. *Dred: A Tale of the Dismal Swamp.* 29 September 1856. Brougham's, New York. French's American Drama. The Acting Edition, no. 145. New York, 1856.

Brushtein, Aleksandra Yakolevna. *Khizina diadi Toma.* Moskva: Gos.izd-vo "Iskusstvo," 1948. *Chicho Tomovata Kolina.* Piesa v tri deistvii. Sofia, Bulgaria: Prevela El. Kostova, 1948.

Chute, James Henry. *Dred.* 13 November 1856. Theatre Royal, Bristol; 3–4 March 1858. Swansea; and in Bath.

Conway, H. J. *Dred: A Tale of the Great Dismal Swamp.* 16 October–22 November 1856. Barnum's, New York. New York: J. W. Amerman, 1856.

Cooper, Harwood. *Dred; or, The Dismal Swamp; A Drama in Two Acts.* PETT MSS. D.73, University of Kent. n.d.

Cowell, William. *Dred! Or—The Dismal Swamp.* n.d. Boston Museum. Broadside.

John R. Hartman Center for Sales, Advertising, and Marketing History, Duke University Library.

Denvil, Mrs. *Dred: A Tale of the Dismal Swamp; Or, Poor Uncle Tiff.* 29–30 September, 5–11, 13–18, 20–25 October 1956. Britannia Saloon, Hoxton, London. BL ADD MS 52962 (H).

Green, J. K. *Dred: The Freeman of the Dismal Swamp.* London: Green's Juvenile Drama, 1856.

Phillips, Frederick Laurence and J. Colman. *Dred: A Tale of the Great Dismal Swamp.* 10–15 October, 24–29 November, 1–5 December 1856. Surrey Theatre, London. BL ADD MS 52961 (N). Also produced 20–22 April and 25 April 1857. Theatre Royal, Birmingham. Birmingham City Archives. Box 4. Nos. 104–109; 4, 12–17 January and 5 February 1857, 4 October 1875. Theatre Royal, Hull.

Seaman, William. *Dred.* London: G. Purkess, n.d. Purkess's Penny Pictorial Plays No. 26.

Suter, William E. *Dred; Or, The Freeman of the Great Dismal Swamp.* 1, 3–8, 10–15, 17–18, 20–22 November 1856, 20, 23, 26 June 1857. Queen's Theater, London; and at the Saint John Dramatic Lyceum, Canada, 20 August 1861, and the Pavilion Theatre 1876. *Dred: A Tale of the Dismal Swamp.* London: Lacy's Acting Edition of Plays, vol. 57 [1863?].

Taylor, C. W. *Dred: A Tale of the Dismal Swamp.* 22 September–25 October 1856. Purdy's National Theatre, New York; 16 February 1857. Marylebone Theatre, London; November 1858, 2 April 1860, Bowery, New York. BL ADD MS 52964 (X).

Townsend, W. *Dred: A Burlesque in One Act.* 16 October 1856. Bower Saloon, Stangate, London. BL ADD MS 52961 (P).

Webb, W. *Dred; Or, The Freeman of the Great Dismal Swamp.* Webb's Juvenile Drama. London: W. Webb, 1856.

Young, H. *Dred! A Tale of the Great Dismal Swamp.* 27 October 1856, 20, 22 October 1858. Victoria Theater, London. BL ADD MS 52962(G).

ABOUT THE CONTRIBUTORS

Clare Cotugno spent ten years teaching college writing, women's studies, and English and American literature and is currently a researcher, editor, and writer for the education initiatives of a large public charity. She has a B.A. in English from Barnard College and an M.A. and Ph.D. from Temple University. Her essay "'Stay Away from Paris!' Frances Trollope Rewrites America" appears in *Victorian Periodicals Review* 38:2 (2005).

Monika Elbert, professor of English at Montclair State University, has published extensively on Hawthorne and on gender in nineteenth-century American literature, with recent essays on Jewett and on Gilman. Her *Separate Spheres No More: Gender Convergence in American Literature, 1830–1930* appeared in 2000. She serves as associate editor of *The Nathaniel Hawthorne Review*.

Shirley Foster is former reader in English and American Literature at the University of Sheffield. She has published on Victorian women's fiction and nineteenth-century children's literature. One of her major interests is travel writing: she published *Across New Worlds: Nineteenth-Century Women Travellers and their Writings* in 1990, *American Women Travellers to Europe* in 1994, and (with Sara Mills) *An Anthology of Women's Travel Writing* in 2002. She also published *Elizabeth Gaskell: A Literary Life* in 2002, and has just finished editing that novelist's *Mary Barton*. She is currently working on nineteenth-century American visitors' responses to British cities.

Caroline Franklin is professor of English at the University of Wales, Swansea. Her publications include *Byron's Heroines* (1992), *Byron: A Literary Life* (2000), and *Mary Wollstonecraft: A Literary Life* (2004). She is currently editing *Women's Travel Writing 1750–1850*, forthcoming in 2006.

Joan D. Hedrick is Charles A. Dana Professor of History at Trinity College in Hartford, Connecticut, where she has taught since 1980 and was the founding director of the women's studies program. Her books include *Solitary Comrade: Jack London and His Work* (1982), *The Oxford Harriet Beecher Stowe Reader* (1999), and *Harriet Beecher Stowe: A Life* (1994), which won the Pulitzer Prize.

Denise Kohn is assistant professor of English at Baldwin-Wallace College. She has published articles on Stowe, Austen, and Trollope. She is currently editing an edition of *Christine: Or Woman's Trials and Triumphs* by Laura Curtis Bullard, first published in 1856.

John MacKay is associate professor of Slavic languages and literatures at Yale University. He has published on slave and serf autobiography, on poetry, and on film. His book *Inscription and Modernity: From Wordsworth to Mandelstam* will be published in 2006; his book on the life and work of Dziga Vertov is also forthcoming.

Sarah Meer is university lecturer in English at the University of Cambridge and a fellow of Selwyn College, Cambridge. She is the author of *Uncle Tom Mania: Slavery, Minstrelsy, and Transatlantic Culture in the 1850s* (2005) and has published articles on slave narratives, Charles Chesnutt, and blackface minstrelsy.

Judie Newman is currently chair of the Department of American Studies at the University of Nottingham. She is the author of *Alison Lurie: A Critical Study* (2000), *The Ballistic Bard: Postcolonial Fictions* (1995), *Nadine Gordimer* (1988), *John Updike* (1988), and *Saul Bellow and History* (1984) and the editor of Harriet Beecher Stowe, *Dred: A Tale of the Great Dismal Swamp* (1992, 1998), plus some sixty critical and scholarly essays in periodicals and collections.

Clíona Ó Gallchoir lectures in the Department of English at University College Cork. She is the author of *Maria Edgeworth: Women, Enlightenment, and Nation* (2005), and has contributed to a number of volumes in the Pickering and Chatto Novels and *Selected Works of Maria Edgeworth*.

Carla Rineer earned her Ph.D. from Temple University in 1999. Her dissertation, "Insurrection Behind the Veil: Religious Heterodoxy in Sedgwick, Child, and Stowe," uncovers the development of "American Mary," a powerful mythological figure. Her essay "Murder, Mayhem, and Myth," recently presented at

Lincoln College, Oxford University, analyzes the relationship between text and illustration in true detective magazines. Rineer teaches English and women's studies at Millersville University.

Donald Ross is professor of English at the University of Minnesota and has taught American literature and composition there since 1971. He earned his Ph.D. from Michigan in 1967. His recent publications include his editing with James Schramer of two volumes on American travel writing in the nineteenth century for the Dictionary of Literary Biography series (1997, 1998) and *American History and Culture from the Explorers to Cable TV* (2000). He is also executive secretary of the International Society for Travel Writing.

Gail K. Smith is associate professor of English at Birmingham-Southern College. She has published articles about nineteenth-century women writers in *The Cambridge Companion to Nineteenth-Century American Women's Writing*, *Arizona Quarterly*, and *American Literature*, and she is completing a book on Stowe and nineteenth-century controversies over reading and interpretation.

Emily B. Todd is associate professor of English at Westfield State College. She has published articles on Walter Scott and nineteenth-century American readers and on library history. She is working on a study of Walter Scott and the nineteenth-century American literary marketplace, and she has received Andrew W. Mellon fellowships from the Library Company of Philadelphia, the Massachusetts Historical Society, and the Virginia Historical Society to support her research.

Whitney Womack Smith is associate professor of English and an affiliate in women's studies and black world studies at Miami University, Hamilton Campus. She has published articles and biographical entries on nineteenth-century British and American women writers including Harriet Beecher Stowe, Elizabeth Gaskell, Elizabeth Siddal, and Margaret Sackville.

WORKS CITED

Academicus. "To the Editor of *The Times*." *Times* (London) 1 December 1852: 8b.

Adams, Charles. *Women of the Bible*. New York: Hunt & Eaton, 1851.

Advertisement. *New York Daily Times* 21 September 1852: 5.

"The Affectionate and Christian Address of Many Thousands of the Women of England to Their Sisters, the Women of the United States of America." *Times* (London) 9 November 1852: 3+.

"The Affectionate and Christian Address of Many Thousands of the Women of the United States of America to their Sisters, the Women of England," reprinted in *Times* (London) 13 January 1853: 3.

Altick, Richard. *The English Common Reader: A Social History of the Mass Reading Public, 1800–1900*. Chicago: U of Chicago P, 1957.

"American Slavery." *New York Daily Times*. 18 September 1852: 6.

Ammons, Elizabeth. ed. *Critical Essays on Harriet Beecher Stowe*. Boston: G. K. Hall, 1980.

———. "Heroines in *Uncle Tom's Cabin*." *Critical Essays on Harriet Beecher Stowe*. Ammons 152–165.

———. "Stowe's Dream of the Mother-Savior: *Uncle Tom's Cabin* and American Women Writers Before the 1920s." Sundquist 155–195.

Anderson, Benedict. *Imagined Communities: Reflections on the Origin and Spread of Nationalism*. London: Verso, 1991.

Andrews, Malcolm. *The Search for the Picturesque: Landscape Aesthetics and Tourism in Britain 1760–1800*. Aldershot: Scolar P, 1989.

Anon. "Britannia, Hoxton." *Era* 5 October 1856: 11.

Anon. "Surrey." *Era* 26 October 1856: 11, col. 2.

Anon. "Surrey Theatre." *Times* 22 October 1856: 7.

Ashton, Mrs. S. G. *Mothers of the Bible*. Boston: John P. Jewett, 1855.

Auerbach, Erich. "Odysseus' Scar." *Mimesis: The Representation of Reality in Western Literature*. Princeton, NJ: Princeton UP, 1953. 3–23.

Baddeley, V. C. Clinton. *The Burlesque Tradition in the English Theatre after 1660*. London: Methuen, 1952.

Baender, Paul. "Mark Twain and the Byron Scandal." *American Literature* 30.4 (1959): 467–485.

Baker, Dorothy Z. "Harriet Beecher Stowe's Conversation with the *Atlantic Monthly*: The Construction of *The Minister's Wooing*." *Studies in American Fiction* 28.1 (2000): 27–38.

———. "Puritan Providences in Stowe's *The Pearl of Orr's Island*: the Legacy of Cotton Mather." *Studies in American Fiction* 22.1 (1994): 61–79.

Baker, William. *George Eliot and Judaism*. Salzburg: Institut für Englische Sprache und Literatur, 1975.

Baldwin, Geo. C. *Representative Women: From Eve, the Wife of the First, to Mary, the Mother of the Second Adam*. Chicago: S. C. Griggs, 1856.

Barker, Kathleen M. D. "The Performing Arts in Five Provincial Towns, 1840–1870." Diss. U of Leicester, 1982.

Baym, Nina. *American Women Writers and the Work of History, 1790–1860*. New Brunswick, NJ: Rutgers UP, 1995.

———. *Woman's Fiction: A Guide to Novels by and about Women in America*. Urbana: U of Illinois P, 1993.

Beecher, Catharine. *An Essay on Slavery and Abolitionism, with Reference to the Duty of American Females, Addressed to A. E. Grimké*. Boston: I. Knapp, 1838.

Beecher, Catharine, and Harriet Beecher Stowe. *The American Woman's Home*. New York: Arno, 1971.

———. *The American Woman's Home, Or Principles of Domestic Science*. New York: J. B. Ford, 1869.

Beecher, Charles. *Harriet Beecher Stowe in Europe: The Journal of Charles Beecher*. Ed. Joseph Van Why and Earl French. Hartford, CT: Stowe-Day Foundation, 1986.

Beecher, Henry Ward. *Star Papers; or, Experiences of Art and Nature*. New York: J. C. Derby, 1855.

Beecher, Lyman. *The Autobiography of Lyman Beecher*. Ed. Barbara M. Cross. 2 vols. Cambridge, MA: Harvard UP, 1961.

Beer, Janet, and Bridget Bennett, eds. *Special Relationships: Anglo-American Affinities and Antagonisms, 1854–1936*. Manchester: Manchester UP, 2002.

Bellin, Joshua D. "Up to Heaven's Gate, Down in Earth's Dust: The Politics of Judgement in *Uncle Tom's Cabin*." *American Literature* 65.2 (1993): 275–295.

Bentley, Richard. Letter to William Hickling Prescott. 3 February 1853. Prescott Papers. Massachusetts Historical Society, Boston.

Bercovitch, Sacvan. *The Puritan Origin of the American Self*. New Haven: Yale UP, 1977.

Berkson, Dorothy. "Millennial Politics and the Feminine Fiction of Harriet Beecher Stowe." Ammons 244–258.

Bhabha, Homi K., ed. *Nation and Narration*. London: Routledge, 1990.

Birdoff, Harry. *The World's Greatest Hit: Uncle Tom's Cabin*. New York: S. F. Vanni, 1947.

Blackett, R. J. M. *Building an Antislavery Wall: Black Americans in the Atlantic Abolitionist Movement, 1830–1860*. Baton Rouge: Louisiana State UP, 1983.

Blum, Jerome. *Lord and Peasant in Russia from the Ninth to the Nineteenth Century.* New York: Atheneum, 1966.

Bodenheimer, Rosemarie. *The Politics of Story in Victorian Social Fiction.* Ithaca, NY: Cornell UP, 1988.

Boggs, Colleen Glenney. "Margaret Fuller's American Translation." *American Literature* 76.1 (March 2004): 31-58.

Bolt, Christine. *The Anti-Slavery Movement and Reconstruction: A Study of Anglo-American Co-Operation 1833–1877.* London: Oxford UP, 1969.

Bolton, H. Philip. *Women Writers Dramatized: A Calendar of Performances from Narrative Works Published in English to 1900.* London: Mansell, 2000.

Booth, Michael R. *English Melodrama.* London: Herbert Jenkins, 1965.

Borgstrom, Michael. "Passing Over: Setting the Record Straight in *Uncle Tom's Cabin*." *PMLA* 118 (2003): 1290–1304.

Bratton, J. S., *et al. Acts of Supremacy: The British Empire and the Stage, 1790–1930.* Manchester: Manchester UP, 1991.

Bratton, Jacky. "The Contending Discourses of Melodrama." Bratton, Cook, and Gledhill 38–49.

Bratton, Jacky, Jim Cook, and Christine Gledhill, eds. *Melodrama: Stage Picture Screen.* London: British Film Institute, 1994.

Brodhead, Richard. "Veiled Ladies: Toward a History of Antebellum Entertainment." *American Literary History* 1 (1989): 273–293.

Brown, Gillian. *Domestic Individualism: Imagining Self in Nineteenth-Century America.* Berkeley: U of California P, 1990.

———. "Getting in the Kitchen with Dinah: Domestic Politics in *Uncle Tom's Cabin*." *American Quarterly* 36 (1984): 503–523.

———. "Reading and Children: *Uncle Tom's Cabin* and *The Pearl of Orr's Island*." *The Cambridge Companion to Harriet Beecher Stowe.* Weinstein 77–95.

Brown, Pearl. "From Elizabeth Gaskell's *Mary Barton* to Her *North and South*: Progress or Decline for Women?" *Victorian Literature and Culture* 28 (2000): 345–358.

Buell, Lawrence. "Calvinism Romanticized: Harriet Beecher Stowe, Samuel Hopkins, and *The Minister's Wooing*." *ESQ* 24.3 (1978): 119–132.

———. *New England Literary Culture: From Revolution through Renaissance.* New York: Cambridge UP, 1986.

Burchard, Rev. S. D. *The Daughters of Zion.* New York: John S. Taylor, 1853.

Burton, Hester. *Barbara Bodichon, 1827–1891.* London: John Murray, 1949.

Byron, George Gordon Lord. *Lord Byron: Complete Poetical Works.* Ed. Jerome J. McGann. 7 vols. Oxford: Clarendon, 1980–1993.

Caskey, Marie. *Chariot of Fire: Religion and the Beecher Family.* New Haven: Yale UP, 1978.

Chase, Lucien. *English Serfdom and American Slavery.* New York: H. Long, 1854.

Clark, Susan F. "Solo Black Performance before the Civil War: Mrs. Stowe, Mrs. Webb, and 'The Christian Slave,'" *New Theatre Quarterly* 13 (November 1997): 339–348.

Cognard-Black, Jennifer. *Narrative in the Professional Age: Transatlantic Readings of Harriet Beecher Stowe, Elizabeth Stuart Phelps, and George Eliot*. New York: Routledge, 2004.

Connolly, Claire. "The Politics of Love in *The Wild Irish Girl*." Introduction. *The Wild Irish Girl*. 1806. Ed. Claire Connolly and Stephen Copley. London: Pickering and Chatto, 2000. xxv–lvi.

Cotugno, Clare. "Form and Reform: Transatlantic Dialogues, 1822–1876." Diss. Temple U, 2001.

Courtney, John. "Uncle Tom's Cabin." MS. Lord Chamberlain's Collection, British Library. 2.1.

Craig, Cairns. "Scotland and the Regional Novel." *The Regional Novel in Britain and Ireland, 1800–1990*. Ed. K. D. M. Snell. New York: Cambridge UP, 1998. 221–256.

Crozier, Alice. "Harriet Beecher Stowe and Byron." *Critical Essays on Harriet Beecher Stowe*. Ammons 190–199.

———. *The Novels of Harriet Beecher Stowe*. New York: Oxford UP, 1969.

Crumpacker, Laurie. "Four Novels of Harriet Beecher Stowe: A Study in Nineteenth-Century Androgyny." *American Novelists Revisited: Essays in Feminist Criticism*. Ed. Fritz Fleischmann. Boston: G.K. Hall, 1982. 78–106.

Dallas, E. S. *The Stowe-Byron Controversy: A Complete Resume of Public Opinion with an Impartial Review of the Merits of the Case by the Editor of Once a Week*. London: Thomas Cooper & Co., 1869.

David, Deirdre. *Fictions of Resolution in Three Victorian Novels*. New York: Columbia UP, 1981.

Davidson, Cathy N. *Revolution and the Word: The Rise of the Novel in America*. New York: Oxford UP, 1986.

Davis, Jim, and Victor Emeljanow. *Reflecting the Audience: London Theatregoing, 1840–1880*. Hatfield: U of Hertfordshire P, 2001.

De Jong, Mary. "Dark-Eyed Daughters: Nineteenth-Century Popular Portrayals of Biblical Women." *Women's Studies: An Interdisciplinary Journal* 19.2–4 (1991): 283–302.

Deane, Seamus. *Strange Country: Modernity and Nationhood in Irish Writing since 1790*. Oxford: Clarendon P, 1997.

Diaz, Carmen Cuevas. "Presencia de Alejandro de Humboldt en la Historia de Cuba." *Alexander von Humboldt und das neue Geschichtsbild von Lateinamerika*. Ed. Michael Zeuske and Bernd Schroter. Leipzig: Leipziger Unversitätsverlag, 1992. 234–247.

Dickens, Charles. *The Letters of Charles Dickens*. Ed. Madeline House and Graham Storey. Vol. 6. Oxford: Clarendon P, 1965.

Dillenberger, John. *The Visual Arts and Christianity in America: The Colonial Period through the Nineteenth Century*. Chico, CA: Scholars P, 1984.

Douglas, Ann. *The Feminization of American Culture*. New York: Knopf, 1977.

"Dred." Rev. of *Dred: A Tale of the Great Dismal Swamp*. *Blackwood's Edinburgh Magazine* 80 (1856): 693–714.

Dulles, Foster Rhea. *Americans Abroad: Two Centuries of European Travel.* Ann Arbor: U of Michigan P, 1964.

Eakin, Paul John. *The New England Girl: Cultural Ideals in Hawthorne, Stowe, Howells, and James.* Athens: U of Georgia P, 1976.

"The Earl of Shaftesbury's Rejoinder." *Globe* (London). 26 January 1853: 1.

Earnest, Ernest. *Expatriates and Patriots: American Artists, Scholars, and Writers in Europe.* Durham, NC: Duke UP, 1968.

Easson, Angus, ed. *Elizabeth Gaskell: The Critical Heritage.* London: Routledge, 1991.

Edgeworth, Maria. *The Absentee.* 1812. Ed. Heidi Van de Veire and Kim Walker, with Marilyn Butler. London: Pickering and Chatto, 1999. Vol. 5 of *The Novels and Selected Works of Maria Edgeworth.* Gen. ed. Marilyn Butler. 12 vols. 1999–2003.

———. *Belinda.* 1802. Ed. Siobhán Kilfeather. London: Pickering and Chatto, 2003. Vol. 2 of *The Novels and Selected Works of Maria Edgeworth.* Gen. ed. Marilyn Butler. 12 vols. 1999–2003.

———. *Ennui.* 1809. Ed. Jane Desmarais and Tim McLoughlin, with Marilyn Butler. London: Pickering and Chatto, 1999. Vol. 1 of *The Novels and Selected Works of Maria Edgeworth.* Gen. ed. Marilyn Butler. 12 vols. 1999–2003.

———. *Ormond.* 1817. Ed. Claire Connolly. London: Pickering and Chatto, 1999. Vol 8 of *The Novels and Selected Works of Maria Edgeworth.* Gen. ed. Marilyn Butler. 12 vols. 1999–2003.

"The Effect of Uncle Tom in Europe." *New York Herald.* Rpt. in "Uncle Tom in Europe," *New York Independent* 5 May 1852, 69–70.

Eliot, George. "Belles Lettres." *Westminster Review* 66 (October 1856): 311–319.

———. *Daniel Deronda.* 1876. New York: Oxford UP, 1984.

———. "The Natural History of German Life." *Westminster Review* 66 (July 1856): 29–44.

———. *Selected Essays, Poems, and Other Writings.* New York: Penguin, 1990.

———. "Silly Novels by Lady Novelists." *Westminster Review* 66 (October 1856): 243–254.

Elizabeth, Charlotte. *The Works of Charlotte Elizabeth.* Intro. Harriet Beecher Stowe. 2nd ed. New York: M. W. Dodd, 1845.

Elliott, Dorice Williams. "The Female Visitor and the Marriage of Classes in Gaskell's *North and South.*" *Nineteenth-Century Literature* 49 (1994): 21–49.

Elmore, Jenifer. "Sacred Unions: Catharine Sedgwick, Maria Edgeworth and Domestic-Political Fiction." Ph.D. Diss. Florida State U, 2003 Abstract. <http://etd.lib.fsu .edu/theses/available/etd-03132003-165536/> 5 August 2005.

Elwin, Malcolm. *Lord Byron's Wife.* London: Macdonald, 1962.

Emerson, Ralph Waldo. "History." *Ralph Waldo Emerson.* 1841. Ed. Richard Poirier. New York: Oxford UP, 1990. 113–130.

———. "The Over-Soul." *The Selected Writings of Ralph Waldo Emerson.* 1841. Ed. Brooks Atkinson. New York: Random House, 1968. 261–278.

Fedorov, D. D. Preface. *Khízhina diádi Tóma ili zhizn' sredi rabov.* Trans. E. Landini. St. Petersburg: D. D. Fedorov, 1883.

Fedorov, D. F. *Khízhina diádi Tóma*. 2nd ed. St. Petersburg: D. F. Fedorov, 1871.

Feldman, David. *Englishmen and Jews: Social Relations and Political Culture, 1840–1914*. New Haven: Yale UP, 1994.

Ferris, Ina. *The Romantic National Tale and the Question of Ireland*. Cambridge: Cambridge UP, 2002.

Fetterley, Judith. "Only a Story, Not a Romance: Harriet Beecher Stowe's *The Pearl of Orr's Island*." *The (Other) American Traditions: Nineteenth-Century Women Writers*. Ed. Joyce W. Warren. New Brunswick, NJ: Rutgers UP, 1993. 108–125.

Fetterley, Judith, and Marjorie Pryse. *Writing Out of Place: Regionalism, Women, and American Literary Culture*. Urbana, IL: U of Illinois P, 2003.

Fiedler, Leslie. *Love and Death in the American Novel*. 1960. Harmondsworth: Penguin, 1984.

Field, Daniel. *The End of Serfdom: Nobility and Bureaucracy in Russia, 1855–1861*. Cambridge, MA: Harvard UP, 1976.

Fields, Annie, ed. *Life and Letters of Harriet Beecher Stowe*. London: Sampson Low, Marston, 1898.

Finlayson, Geoffrey B. A. M. *The Seventh Earl of Shaftesbury, 1801–1885*. London: Eyre Methuen, 1981.

Fisch, Audrey. *American Slaves in Victorian England: Abolitionist Politics in Popular Literature and Culture*. Cambridge: Cambridge UP, 2000.

———. "Uncle Tom and Harriet Beecher Stowe in England." Weinstein 96–112.

Fladeland, Betty. *Men and Brothers: Anglo-American Antislavery Cooperation*. Urbana: U of Illinois P, 1972.

Formichella, Annamaria. "Domesticity and Nationalism in Harriet Beecher Stowe's *Agnes of Sorrento*." *Legacy* 15 (1998): 188–203.

Foster, Charles H. *The Rungless Ladder: Harriet Beecher Stowe and New England Puritanism*. Durham: Duke UP, 1954.

———. *The Rungless Ladder: Harriet Beecher Stowe and New England Puritanism*. New York: Cooper Square, 1970.

Franchot, Jenny. *Roads to Rome: The Antebellum Protestant Encounter with Catholicism*. Berkeley: U of California P, 1994.

Franklin, Caroline. *Byron and Women Novelists*. Nottingham Foundation Lecture. Nottingham: U of Nottingham P, 2001.

Freeman, Joanne B. *Affairs of Honour: National Politics in the New Republic*. New Haven: Yale UP, 2001.

Gallagher, Catherine. *The Industrial Reformation of English Fiction: Social Discourse and Narrative Form, 1832–1867*. Chicago: U of Chicago P, 1985.

Gardella, Peter. *Innocent Ecstasy: How Christianity Gave America an Ethic of Sexual Pleasure*. New York: Oxford UP, 1985.

Gardner, Albert TenEyck. *Yankee Stonecutters: The First American School of Sculpture, 1800–1850*. New York: Columbia UP, 1945.

Gardner, Eric. "Stowe Takes the Stage: Harriet Beecher Stowe's *The Christian Slave*." *Legacy* 15 (1998): 78–84.

Gaskell, Elizabeth. *Letters of Mrs. Gaskell.* Ed. J. A. V. Chapple and Arthur Pollard. Cambridge: Harvard UP, 1967.

———. *The Life of Charlotte Brontë.* 1857. New York: Penguin, 1985.

———. *Mary Barton.* 1848. New York: Penguin, 1970.

———. *North and South.* 1855. New York: Penguin, 1970.

Gatta, John. *American Madonna: Images of the Divine Woman in Literary Culture.* New York: Oxford UP, 1997.

———. "The Anglican Aspect of Harriet Beecher Stowe." *New England Quarterly* 73:3 (2000): 412–433.

Gay, Peter. *The Education of the Senses: Bourgeois Experience, Victoria to Freud.* Vol. 1. New York: Oxford UP, 1984.

Gerdts, William H. *American Neo-Classic Sculpture: The Marble Resurrection.* New York: Viking, 1973.

———. *The Great American Nude: A History in Art.* New York: Praeger, 1974.

Gertsen [Herzen], Aleksandr. "Russian Serfdom." *Sobranie sochinenii v tridtsati tomakh.* Ed. V. A. Putintsev et al. Vol. 12. Moscow: Izdatel'stvo Akademii Nauk SSSR, 1957. 7–33.

Giles, Paul. *Transatlantic Insurrections: British Culture and the Formation of American Literature, 1730–1860.* Philadelphia: U of Pennsylvania P, 2001.

———. *Virtual Americans: Transnational Fictions and the Transatlantic Imaginary.* Durham: Duke UP, 2002.

Gilroy, Paul. *The Black Atlantic: Modernity and Double Consciousness.* Cambridge, MA: Harvard UP, 1993.

Ginzberg, Lori D. *Women and the Work of Benevolence: Morality, Politics, and Class in the Nineteenth-Century United States.* New Haven: Yale UP, 1990.

Gleadle, Kathryn, and Sarah Richardson. *Women in British Politics, 1760–1860: The Power of the Petticoat.* New York: St. Martin's, 2000.

Golovin, Ivan. *Rovira: Drama v trekh deistviiakh.* Leipzig: Wolfgang Gerhard, 1858.

Gossett, Thomas F. *Uncle Tom's Cabin in American Culture.* Dallas: Southern Methodist UP, 1985.

Gravil, Richard. *Romantic Dialogues: Anglo-American Continuities, 1776–1862.* New York: St. Martin's, 2000.

Greg, W. R. [William Rathbone]. Rev. of *Mary Barton. Edinburgh Review* 89 (1849): 402–435.

Grimble, Ian. Introduction. *Gloomy Memories: The Highland Clearances of Strathnaver.* By Donald Macleod. Bettyhill: Strathnaver Museum, 1996. 24–30.

Grimké, Angelina. *An Appeal to the Christian Women of the South.* New York: American Anti-Slavery Society, 1836.

Grimsted, David. "Vigilante Chronicle: The Politics of Melodrama Brought to Life." Bratton, Cook, and Gledhill 199–213.

Guy, Josephine. *The Victorian Social-Problem Novel: The Market, the Individual, and Communal Life.* New York: St. Martin's, 1996.

Hadley, Elaine. *Melodramatic Tactics: Theatricalized Dissent in the English Marketplace.* Stanford, CA: Stanford UP, 1995.

Haight, Gordon, ed. *The George Eliot Letters.* 9 vols. New Haven: Yale UP, 1954–1978.

Hale, Sarah Josepha. *Northwood; or, Life North and South: Showing the Character of Both.* 1827. New York: H. Long, n.d.

Hall, David D. *Worlds of Wonder, Days of Judgment: Popular Religious Belief in Early New England.* New York: Knopf, 1989.

Halttunen, Karen. *Confidence Men and Painted Women: A Study of Middle-Class Culture in America.* New Haven: Yale UP, 1982.

———. "Gothic Imagination and Social Reform: The Haunted Houses of Lyman Beecher, Henry Ward Beecher, and Harriet Beecher Stowe." Sundquist 107–134.

Harman, Barbara Leah. *The Feminine Political Novel in Victorian England.* Charlottesville: UP of Virginia, 1998.

Harris, Neil. *The Artist in American Society: The Formative Years, 1790–1860.* Chicago: U of Chicago P, 1982.

Harris, Susan K. "The Female Imaginary in Harriet Beecher Stowe's *The Minister's Wooing.*" *New England Quarterly* 66.2 (1993): 179–98.

———. *Nineteenth-Century American Women's Novels: Interpretive Strategies.* Cambridge: Cambridge UP, 1990.

Harsh, Constance. *Subversive Heroines: Feminist Resolutions of Social Crisis in the Condition-of-England Novel.* Ann Arbor: U of Michigan P, 1994.

Hart, Clive, and Kay Gilliland Stevenson. *Heaven and the Flesh: Imagery of Desire from the Renaissance to the Rococo.* Cambridge: Cambridge UP, 1995.

Hawthorne, Nathaniel. *The English Notebooks, 1856–1860.* Ed. Thomas Woodson and Bill Ellis. Centenary Edition of the Works of Nathaniel Hawthorne. Vol. 22. Columbus: Ohio State UP, 1997.

———. *French and Italian Notebooks.* Ed. Thomas Woodson. Centenary Edition of the Works of Nathaniel Hawthorne. Vol. 14. Columbus: Ohio State UP, 1980.

———. *The Marble Faun.* 1860. London: Everyman, 1965.

Hedrick, Joan D. *Harriet Beecher Stowe: A Life.* Oxford: Oxford UP, 1994.

Helsinger, Elizabeth K. *Rural Scenes and National Representations: Britain, 1815–1850.* Princeton: Princeton UP, 1997.

Herbert, Robert L. *Art Criticism of John Ruskin.* Gloucester, MA: Peter Smith, 1969.

Hildreth, Margaret Holbrook. *Harriet Beecher Stowe: A Bibliography.* Hamden, CT: Archon, 1976.

Hirst, Wolf Z. "Byron's Revisionary Struggle with the Bible." *Byron, the Bible, and Religion: Essays from the Twelfth International Byron Seminar.* Ed. Wolf Z. Hirst. Newark: U of Delaware P, 1991. 77–100.

Hochman, Barbara. Introductory essay for a reprint of Harriet Beecher Stowe's introduction to Charles Beecher's *The Incarnation; or, Pictures of the Virgin and Her Son* [1849], *PMLA* 118 (2003): 1320.

Holmes, George F. Review of *Uncle Tom's Cabin.* 1852. Rpt. in *Uncle Tom's Cabin.* By Harriet Beecher Stowe. Ed. Elizabeth Ammons. New York: Norton, 1994. 467–477.

Hood, Thomas. *The Complete Poetical Works of Thomas Hood.* London: Oxford UP, 1920.

Howard, William George Frederick. Preface. *Uncle Tom's Cabin: A Tale of Life among the Lowly.* By Harriet Beecher Stowe. London: George Routledge, 1852. iii–xii.

Islely, W. H. "The Sharps Rifle Episode in Kansas History." *American Historical Review* 12.3 (1907): 546–566.

J. M. *The True Story of Lord and Lady Byron as told by Lord Macaulay etc. etc. In answer to Mrs. Beecher Stowe.* London: John Camden Hotton, n.d.

Jameson, Anna. Introduction. *Legends of the Madonna, as Represented in the Fine Arts.* 3rd ed. London: 1864.

———. *Legends of the Monastic Orders, as Represented in the Fine Arts.* 3rd ed. London: 1863.

———. *Sacred and Legendary Art.* Vol. 2. 4th ed. London: 1863.

Jefferson, Paul. Introduction. *The Travels of Williams Wells Brown.* New York: Markus Wiener, 1991. 1–20.

Jenkins, Lee. "Beyond the Pale: Frederick Douglass in Cork." *Irish Review* 24 (1999): 80–95.

Jewett, Sarah Orne. Excerpt from a letter to Mrs. Fields. Ammons 212.

Karcher, Carolyn L. "Stowe and the Literature of Social Change." *The Cambridge Companion to Harriet Beecher Stowe.* Weinstein 203–218.

Kasson, Joy. *Marble Queens and Captives: Women in Nineteenth-Century American Sculpture.* New Haven: Yale UP, 1990.

Kaufman, Will, and Heidi MacPherson, eds. *Transatlantic Studies.* Lanham, MD: UP of America, 2000.

Keats, John. "The Eve of St. Agnes." *Lamia, Isabella, and Other Poems 1820.* Vol. 3 of *The Poetical Works and Other Writings of John Keats.* Ed. H. Buxton Forman, rev. Maurice Buxton Forman. Hampstead edition. 8 vols. 1939. New York: Phaeton, 1970.

Kefalas, Carol Lynn. "The Nazarenes and the Pre-Raphaelites: A Comparative Analysis." Diss. U of Georgia, 1983. Ann Arbor: UMI, 1983.

Kent, Christopher. "Helen Taylor's 'Experimental Life' on the Stage: 1856–58." *Nineteenth Century Theatre Research* 5.1 (Spring 1977): 45–54.

Kestner, Joseph. *Protest and Reform: The British Social Narrative by Women, 1827–1862.* Madison: U of Wisconsin P, 1985.

Khomyakov, A. S. *Polnoe Sobranie Sochinenii.* Vol. 8. Moscow: Universitetskaia Tipografiia, 1904.

Kimbrell, Gayle. "The Religious Ideas of Harriet Beecher Stowe: Her Gospel of Womanhood." *Studies in Women and Religion.* Vol. 8. New York: Edwin Mellen, 1982.

Klingberg, Frank J. "Harriet Beecher Stowe and Social Reform in England." *American Historical Review.* 43 (1938): 542–552.

Klunder, Willard Carl. *Lewis Cass and the Politics of Moderation.* Kent, OH: Kent State UP, 1996.

Knight, William G. *A Major London "Minor": The Surrey Theatre, 1805–1865*. London: Society for Theatre Research, 1997.

Kolchin, Peter. *Unfree Labor: American Slavery and Russian Serfdom*. Cambridge: Belknap P of Harvard UP, 1987.

Kristeva, Julia. "Women's Time." *The Kristeva Reader*. Ed. Toril Moi. New York: Columbia UP, 187–213.

Krueger, Christine. *The Reader's Repentance: Women Preachers, Women Writers, and Nineteenth-Century Social Discourse*. Chicago: U of Chicago P, 1992.

"The Lady Abolitionists." *Spectator* (London), 4 December 1852, 1164; *Times* (London), 1 December 1852, 4, 8.

Lang, Cecil. "Swinburne and American Literature: With Six Hitherto Unpublished Letters." *American Literature* 19.4 (1948): 336–350.

Lapsansky, Phillip S. "Afro-Americana: Frank J. Webb and His Friends." *The Annual Report of the Library Company of Philadelphia for 1990* (1991): 27–43.

Lebedun, Jean. "Harriet Beecher Stowe's Interest in Sojourner Truth, Black Feminist." *American Literature* 46.3 (1974): 359–363.

Leerssen, Joep. *Remembrance and Imagination: Patterns in the Literary and Historical Representation of Ireland in the Nineteenth Century*. Cork: Cork UP, 1996.

Lemke, Mikhail. "Emigrant Ivan Golovin: Po neizdannym materialam." *Byloe*. 5 (1907): 39.

Lenard, Mary. *Preaching Pity: Dickens, Gaskell, and Sentimentalism in Victorian Culture*. New York: Peter Lang, 1999.

Levine, Lawrence W. *Highbrow/Lowbrow. The Emergence of Cultural Hierarchy in America*. Cambridge, MA: Harvard UP, 1988.

Levine, Robert S. *Martin Delany, Frederick Douglass, and the Politics of Representative Identity*. Chapel Hill: U of North Carolina P, 1997.

Longfellow, Henry Wadsworth. *Poems on Slavery*. Boston: New England Anti-Slavery Tract Association, 1842.

Lorimer, Douglas A. *Colour, Class, and the Victorians: English Attitudes to the Negro in the Mid-Nineteenth Century*. Leicester: Leicester UP, 1978.

Lounsbury, Richard, ed. *Louisa S. McCord: Political and Social Essays*. Charlottesville: UP of Virginia, 1995.

Mackay, Charles. *Medora Leigh: A History and an Autobiography, with an Introduction and a Commentary on the Charges Brought against Lord Byron by Mrs. Beecher Stowe*. London: Richard Bentley, 1869.

Manning, Susan. *Fragments of Union: Making Connections in Scottish and American Writing*. Basingstoke: Palgrave, 2002.

———. *The Puritan Provincial Vision: Scottish and American Literature in the Nineteenth Century*. Cambridge: U of Cambridge P, 1990.

Martineau, Harriet. "The Achievements of the Genius of Scott." *Miscellanies*. Vol. 1. Boston: Hilliard, Gray and Company, 1836.

Mather, Cotton. *On Witchcraft: Being the Wonders of the Invisible World*. 1692. Whitefish, MT: Kessinger, 2004.

McConachie, Bruce. "Out of the Kitchen and into the Marketplace: Normalizing *Uncle Tom's Cabin* for the Antebellum Stage." *Journal of American Drama and Theatre* 3.1 (Winter 1991): 5–28.

McFadden, Margaret H. *Golden Cables of Sympathy: The Transatlantic Sources of Nineteenth-Century Feminism*. Lexington: UP of Kentucky, 1999.

McFeely, William S. *Frederick Douglass*. New York: W. W. Norton, 1991.

McPherson, Susan. "Opening the Open Secret: The Stowe-Byron Controversy." *Victorian Review* 27.1 (2001): 86–101.

Meer, Sarah. *Uncle Tom Mania: Slavery, Minstrelsy, and Transatlantic Culture in the 1850s*. Athens: U of Georgia P, 2005.

Mesick, Jane Louise. *The English Traveller in America, 1785–1885*. New York: Columbia UP, 1922.

"Metropolitan Theatres." *Theatrical Journal*. 8 December 1852: 307.

Meyer, Susan. "'Safely to Their Own Borders': Proto-Zionism, Feminism, and Nationalism in *Daniel Deronda*." *ELH* 60 (1993): 733–758.

Midgley, Clare. *Women Against Slavery: The British Campaigns, 1780–1870*. London: Routledge, 1992.

Miles, Margaret Ruth. *Carnal Knowing: Female Nakedness and Religious Meaning in the Christian West*. Boston: Beacon, 1989.

Mills, Sara. *Discourses of Difference*. London: Routledge, 1991.

Moers, Ellen. "Mrs. Stowe's Vengeance." *New York Review of Books*. 3 September 1970: 25–32.

Monga, Luigi. "Harriet Beecher Stowe's European Journeys, and the Journal of Her Stay in Naples (1860)," in Luigi Monga, ed. "Americans in Italy," special edition of *Bolletino Del Centro Interuniversitario di Recherche sul "Viaggio in Italia,"* Vol 11–16, 1987. 117–143.

Moon, David. *The Abolition of Serfdom in Russia*. Edinburgh: Longman, 2001.

Morgan, David. *Protestants and Pictures: Religion, Visual Culture, and the Age of American Mass Production*. New York: Oxford UP, 1999.

Nead, Linda. *The Female Nude: Art, Obscenity, and Sexuality*. London: Routledge, 1992.

Newman, Judie. Introduction. *Dred: A Tale of the Great Dismal Swamp*. By Harriet Beecher Stowe. Ed. Judie Newman. Halifax, England: Ryburn, 1992. 9–25.

———. "Staging Black Insurrection: *Dred* on Stage." Weinstein 113–130.

———. "Stowe's Sunny Memories of Highland Slavery." Beer and Bennett 28–41.

———. "Was Tom White? Stowe's *Dred* and Twain's *Pudd'nhead Wilson*." *Slavery and Abolition* 20.2 (August 1999): 125–136.

Nikoljukin, Alexander, ed. *A Russian Discovery of America*. Trans. Cynthia Carlile and Julius Katzer. Moscow: Progress, 1986.

Nolan, Charles J. *Aaron Burr and the American Literary Imagination*. London: Greenwood, 1980.

"North American Slavery." *New York Daily Times*. 10 November 1852: 3.

O'Brien, Michael. *Conjectures of Order: Intellectual Life and the American South, 1810–1860.* Chapel Hill: U of North Carolina P, 2004.

———. *Rethinking the South: Essays in Intellectual History.* Baltimore: Johns Hopkins UP, 1988.

Ó Gallchoir, Clíona. *Maria Edgeworth: Women, Enlightenment, and Nation.* Dublin: U College Dublin P, 2005.

———. "'The Whole Fabric Must Be Perfect:' Maria Edgeworth's *Literary Ladies* and the Representation of Ireland." *Gender and Nineteenth Century Ireland: Public and Private Spheres?* Ed. James H. Murphy and Margaret Kelleher. Dublin: Irish Academic P, 1997. 104–115.

O'Connell, Catherine E. "'The Magic of the Real Presence of Distress': Sentimentality and Competing Rhetorics of Authority." *The Stowe Debate: Rhetorical Strategies in Uncle Tom's Cabin.* Ed. Mason I. Lowance, Jr., Ellen E. Westbrook, and R. C. De Prospo. Amherst: U of Massachusetts P, 1994. 13–36.

Olien, Diana Davids. *Morpeth: A Victorian Public Career.* n.p.: UP of America, 1963.

"Opinions of the British Press." *The Travels of William Wells Brown.* Ed. Paul Jefferson New York: Markus Wiener, 1991. 229–232.

Orlova, Raisa D. *Khizhina, ustoiavshaia stoletie.* Moscow: Kniga, 1975.

Owenson, Sydney (Lady Morgan). *The Wild Irish Girl.* 1806. Ed. Claire Connolly and Stephen Copley. London: Pickering and Chatto, 2000.

P. E. "Pomeshchiki i Krest'iane." *Russkii Vestnik* (Sovremennaia letopis') 19.2 (1859): 219–230.

Parker, Pamela Corpron. "Constructing Female Public Identity: Gaskell on Bronte." *Literature and the Renewal of the Public Sphere.* Ed. Susan VanZanten Gallagher and M. D. Walhout. New York: St. Martin's, 2000. 68–82.

———. "Fictional Philanthropy in Elizabeth Gaskell's *Mary Barton* and *North and South.*" *Victorian Literature and Culture* 25 (1997): 321–31.

Parrington, Vernon Louis. "Harriet Beecher Stowe: A Daughter of Puritanism." Ammons 212–218.

Paskoff, Paul F., and Daniel J. Wilson, eds. *The Cause of the South: Selections from De Bow's Review, 1846–1867.* Baton Rouge: Louisiana State UP, 1982.

Pettinger, Alasdair. "'Send Back the Money': Douglass and the Free Church of Scotland." Rice and Crawford. 31–55.

Pickering, Michael. "'A Jet Ornament to Society': Black Music in Nineteenth-Century Britain." *Black Music in Britain: Essays on the Afro-Asian Contribution to Popular Music.* Ed. Paul Oliver. Milton Keynes, England: Open UP, 1990. 16–33.

Pinion, F. B. *A Brontë Companion: Literary Assessment, Background, and Reference.* Houndmills, Basingstoke: Macmillan, 1975.

Pitcock, Jennifer Workman. "Imaginary Bonds: Antislavery Dramas on the New York Stage, 1853–1861." Diss. U of Kentucky, 2002.

Pointon, Marcia. *Naked Authority: The Body in Western Painting, 1830–1908.* Cambridge: Cambridge UP, 1990.

Poovey, Mary. *Uneven Developments: The Ideological Work of Gender in Mid-Victorian England.* Chicago: U of Chicago P, 1988.

Porter, Dennis. "Orientalism and Its Problems." *Colonial Discourse and Post-Colonial Theory: A Reader.* Ed. Patrick Williams and Laura Chrisman. Hemel Hempstead: Harvester Wheatsheaf, 1993. 150–161.

Prokhorov, A. M, *et al.*, eds. *Bol'shaia Sovetskaia Entsiklopediia.* 3rd ed. Vol. 3. Moscow: Sovetskaia Entsiklopediia, 1970.

Pryse, Marjorie. "Stowe and Regionalism." Weinstein 131–53.

Pugh, Evelyn. "Women and Slavery: Julia Gardiner Tyler and the Duchess of Sutherland." *Virginia Magazine of History and Biography* 188 (1980): 186–202.

Pushchin, I. I. *Sochineniia i pis'ma.* Ed. M. P. and S. V. Mironenko. Vol. 2. Moscow: Nauka, 2001.

Reed, James. *Sir Walter Scott: Landscape and Locality.* London: Athlone, 1980.

Reiser, S., *et al.*, eds. "Gonorarnye vedomosti *Sovremennika*." *Literaturnoe Nasledstvo* Vol. 3.53–54. Moscow: Izdatel'stvo Akademii Nauk SSSR, 1949.

Review of *Uncle Tom's Cabin. Times* (London). 3 September 1852. Rpt. in *Uncle Tom's Cabin.* By Harriet Beecher Stowe. Ed. Elizabeth Ammons. New York: Norton, 1994. 478–483.

Rice, Alan J., and Martin Crawford, eds. *Liberating Sojourn: Frederick Douglass and Transatlantic Reform.* Athens: U of Georgia P, 1999.

Rice, Alan J., and Martin Crawford. "Triumphant Exile: Frederick Douglass in Britain, 1845–1847." Rice and Crawford. 1–14.

Richards, Eric. *A History of the Highland Clearances: Agrarian Transformation and the Evictions, 1746–1886.* 2 vols. London: Croom Helm, 1982.

Ripley, C. Peter, ed. *The Black Abolitionist Papers.* Vol 1. Chapel Hill: U of North Carolina P, 1985.

Robertson, Fiona. *Legitimate Histories: Scott, Gothic, and the Authorities of Fiction.* New York: Oxford UP, 1994.

Rohrbach, Augusta. "'Truth Strange and Stronger than Fiction': Reexamining William Lloyd Garrison's *Liberator.*" *American Literature* 73.4 (2001): 727–755.

Romero, Lora. *Home Fronts: Domesticity and Its Critics in the Antebellum United States.* Durham: Duke UP, 1997.

Ross, Marlon B. "Romancing the Nation-State: The Poetics of Romantic Nationalism." *Macropolitics of Nineteenth-Century Literature: Nationalism, Exoticism, Imperialism.* Ed. Jonathan Arac and Harriet Ritvo. Philadelphia: U of Pennsylvania P, 1991. 56–85.

Ryan, Mary P. *The Empire of the Mother: American Writing About Domesticity, 1830–1860.* New York: Haworth P, 1982.

Sabiston, Elizabeth Jean. "Anglo-American Connections: Elizabeth Gaskell, Harriet Beecher Stowe, and the 'Iron of Slavery.'" *The Discourse of Slavery: Aphra Behn to Toni Morrison.* Ed. Carl Plasa and Betty J. Ring. London: Routledge, 1994. 94–117.

Sánchez-Eppler, Karen. *Touching Liberty: Abolition, Feminism, and the Politics of the Body.* Berkeley: U of California P, 1993.

Saul, Norman. *Distant Friends: The United States and Russia, 1763–1867*. Lawrence: UP of Kansas, 1991.

Schachner, Nathan. *Aaron Burr: A Biography*. New York: Frederick A. Stokes Co., 1937.

Scott, Walter. *The Bride of Lammermoor*. 1819. New York: Dutton, 1979.

———. *Letters on Demonology and Witchcraft*. 1830. Whitefish, MT: Kessinger, 1884.

Seager, Robert II. *And Tyler Too: A Biography of John and Julia Gardiner Tyler*. New York: McGraw-Hill, 1963.

Sedgwick, Catharine Maria. *Letters from Abroad to Kindred at Home*. 2 vols. 1841. New York: Harper, 1855.

———. *Life and Letters*. Ed. Mary E. Dewey. New York: Harper, 1871.

———. *The Linwoods; or, "Sixty Years Since" in America*. New York: Harper, 1835.

———. *A New-England Tale*. 1822. Ed. Victoria Clements. New York: Oxford UP, 1995.

———. *Redwood*. 2 vols. New York: E. Bliss and E. White, 1824.

Semevskii, V. I. *Krest'ianskii Vopros v Rossii v XVIII i Pervoi Polovine XIX Veka*. Vol. 2. St. Petersburg: Obshchestvennaia Pol'za, 1888.

Semmel, Bernard. *George Eliot and the Politics of National Inheritance*. New York: Oxford UP, 1994.

Shebunin, A. N. *Nikolai Ivanovich Turgenev*. Moscow: Gosudarstvennoe Izdatel'stvo, 1925.

Sheets, Robin. "History and Romance: Harriet Beecher Stowe's *Agnes of Sorrento* and George Eliot's *Romola*." *CLIO* 26 (1997): 323–346.

Shepperson, George. "Harriet Beecher Stowe and Scotland." *Scottish Historical Review* 32 (1953): 40–46.

Sherman, Sarah Way. *Sarah Orne Jewett: An American Persephone*. Hanover, NH: UP of New England, 1989.

Skabichevskii, A. M. *Ocherki Istorii Tsenzury (1700–1836 g.)*. St. Petersburg: Obshchestvennaia Pol'za, 1892.

Sklar, Kathryn Kish. *Catharine Beecher: A Study in American Domesticity*. New Haven: Yale UP, 1973.

"Slavery and Slave Power in the United States of America." *Blackwood's Edinburgh Magazine* January 1853: 1–20.

Soth, Lauren. "Vincent van Gogh Reads Harriet Beecher Stowe." *Word and Image* 10.2 (1994): 156–162.

Southwood, Marian. *Tit for Tat*. New York: Garrett, 1856.

Starnes, Ebenezer. *The Slaveholder Abroad*. Philadelphia: Lippincott, 1860.

Steele, Thomas J. "Tom and Eva: Mrs. Stowe's Two Dying Christs." *Negro American Literature Forum* 6 (1972): 85–90.

Stephens, J. R. *The Censorship of English Drama, 1824–1901*. Cambridge: Cambridge UP, 1980.

Stirling, William. Letter to William Hickling Prescott. 8 November 1852. Prescott Papers. Massachusetts Historical Society, Boston.

Stone, Rev. A. L. Introduction. *Mothers of the Bible.* Ed. Mrs. S. G. Ashton. Boston: John P. Jewett, 1855. v–viii.

Stone, Harry. "Charles Dickens and Harriet Beecher Stowe." *Nineteenth-Century Fiction* 12 (1957): 188–203.

Stoneman, Patsy. *Elizabeth Gaskell.* Bloomington: Indiana UP, 1987.

Stowe, Calvin E. Letter to Harriet Beecher Stowe. 24 and 25 June 1848. Acquisitions. Harriet Beecher Stowe Center, Hartford, CT.

Stowe, Charles Edward. *The Life of Harriet Beecher Stowe.* London: Sampson Low, 1889.

Stowe, Harriet Beecher. *Agnes of Sorrento.* Boston: 1862.

———. "An Appeal to the Women of the Free States of America, on the Present Crisis in Our Country." *Independent* 23 February 1854: 1.

———. "Bodily Religion." *Household Papers and Stories. The Writings of Harriet Beecher Stowe.* Vol. 8. Boston: Houghton Mifflin, 1896. 330–346.

———. *La Cabane de l'Oncle Tom ou Les Noirs en Amérique.* 2nd ed. Trans. Leon de Wailly and Edmond Texier. Paris: Perrotin, 1853.

———. *Dred: A Tale of the Great Dismal Swamp.* 2 vols. Boston: Phillips, Sampson, 1856.

———. *Dred: A Tale of the Great Dismal Swamp.* 1856. Ed. Judie Newman. Krumlin, Halifax, England: Ryburn, 1992.

———. *Dred: A Tale of the Great Dismal Swamp.* 1856. Ed. Judie Newman. Edinburgh: Edinburgh UP, 1999.

———. *The Footsteps of the Master.* New York: J. B. Ford, 1877.

———. Introduction. *The Works of Charlotte Elizabeth.* 2nd ed. New York: M. W. Dodd, 1845.

———. Introductory essay. *The Incarnation: Or, Pictures of the Virgin and Her Son.* By Charles Beecher. New York: 1849.

———. *A Key to Uncle Tom's Cabin.* 1853. Bedford, MA: Applewood, 1998.

———. "Khízhina Diádi Tóma." *Russkii Vestnik.* 13.2 (1858): 304.

———. *Khízhina Diádi Tóma.* Trans. P. Novosil'skii et al. St. Petersburg: Tipografiia Glavnogo Shtaba Ego Imperatorskago Velichestva po Voenno-Uchebnym Zavedeniiam, 1858.

———. *Khízhina Diádi Tóma.* Trans. Z. N. Zhuravskaia. St. Petersburg: O. N. Popova, 1898.

———. *Lady Byron Vindicated: A History of the Byron Controversy.* Boston: Fields, Osgood, 1870.

———. *Lady Byron Vindicated: A History of the Byron Controversy.* London: Sampson Low, 1870.

———. Letter from Mrs. Stowe. *Frederick Douglass' Paper.* 20 January 1854.

———. Letter to Calvin E. Stowe. [July, August 1853?]. Beecher-Stowe Family Papers. Schlesinger Library, Radcliffe Institute for Advanced Study, Harvard University, Cambridge, MA.

————. Letter to Charles Beecher. [November 1856]. Acquisitions. Harriet Beecher Stowe Center, Hartford, CT.

————. Letter to Elizabeth Gaskell. 10 July 1860. Harriet Beecher Stowe Center, Hartford, CT.

————. Letters to George Eliot. The Henry W. and Albert A. Berg Collection of English and American Literature. The New York Public Library, Astor, Lenox, and Tilden Foundations, NY.

————. Letter to Henry Ward Beecher. 4 September n.y. Beecher Family Papers, Manuscripts and Archives, Yale University Library, New Haven, CT.

————. Letter to James T. Fields. 16 January 1861. FI 4010. Henry Huntington Library, San Marino, CA.

————. List of paintings owned by HBS. [1862 or later]. Katharine S. Day Collection, bound ms. Harriet Beecher Stowe Center, Hartford, CT.

————. *The Minister's Wooing.* 1859. Harmondsworth: Penguin, 1999.

————. *The Minister's Wooing.* In *Three Novels: Uncle Tom's Cabin, The Minister's Wooing, Oldtown Folks.* Ed. Katherine Kish Sklar, New York: Library of America, 1982.

————. "Modern Uses of Language." *The Oxford Harriet Beecher Stowe Reader.* Ed. and intr. Joan D. Hedrick. Oxford: Oxford UP, 1998. 23–26.

————. "The Old Oak of Andover: A Reverie." *Independent* 7 (1853): 33.

————. *Oldtown Folks.* 1869. In *Three Novels: Uncle Tom's Cabin, The Minister's Wooing, Oldtown Folks.* Ed. Katherine Kish Sklar. New York: Library of America, 1982.

————. *The Oxford Harriet Beecher Stowe Reader.* Ed. Joan D. Hedrick. New York: Oxford, 1999.

————. *The Pearl of Orr's Island: A Story of the Coast of Maine.* 1862. Foreword by Joan D. Hedrick. New York: Houghton Mifflin, 2001.

————. *Poganuc People: Their Loves and Lives.* New York: Howard & Hulbert, 1878.

————. Preface. *Dred: A Tale of the Great Dismal Swamp.* Vol. 1. London: Sampson Low, 1856. 1: iii–x.

————. Preface. *Uncle Tom's Cabin or Life Among the Lowly.* London: Thomas Bosworth, 1852. vii–xiv.

————. *Sketchbook from 1859–1887.* Sketchbooks. Stowe-Day Foundation Library, Hartford, CT.

————. "Sojourner Truth, the Libyan Sibyl." *A Narrative of Sojourner Truth; A Bondswoman of Olden Time, With a History of Her Labors and Correspondence Drawn from Her* Book of Life. 1878. Oxford; Oxford UP, 1991. 151–172.

————. *Sunny Memories of Foreign Lands.* 2 vols. Boston: Phillips, Sampson, 1854.

————. "The True Story of Lady Byron's Life." *Atlantic Monthly* 24 (September 1869): 295–313.

————. *Uncle Tom's Cabin.* London: J. Cassell, 1852.

————. *Uncle Tom's Cabin.* 1852. Ed. Elizabeth Ammons. New York: Norton, 1994.

————. *Uncle Tom's Cabin.* 1852. Intro. Alfred Kazin. New York: Bantam, 1981.

————. *Uncle Tom's Cabin.* 1852. Ed. Jean Fagan Yellin. Oxford: Oxford UP, 1998.

————. *Uncle Tom's Cabin, or Life among the Lowly.* London: Thomas Bosworth, 1852.

————. *Uncle Tom's Cabin; Or, Life among the Lowly. A Tale of Slave Life in America.* London: Nathaniel Cooke, 1853.

————. *Uncle Tom's Cabin or, Life Among the Lowly.* Harmondsworth: Penguin, 1987.

————. *Uncle Tom's Cabin: Or, Negro Life in the Slave States of America.* The People's Illustrated Edition. London: Clarke & Co, 1852.

————. *Uncle Tom's Cabin: Or, Negro Life in the Slave States of America.* 1st edition. London: Routledge; C. H. Clarke and Co., 1852.

————. *Uncle Tom's Cabin: A Tale of Life Among the Lowly; Or, Pictures of Slavery in the United States of America.* 3rd ed. London: Ingram, Cooke, & Co., 1852.

————. *Uncle Tom's Cabin; Or Negro Life in the Slave States of America.* 6th edition. London: George Routledge & Co., 1852.

————. *Woman in Sacred History: A Series of Sketches Drawn from Scriptural, Historical, and Legendary Sources.* 1873. New York: Portland House, 1990.

Stowe, Lyman Beecher. *Saints, Sinners, and Beechers.* 1834. Indianapolis: Bobbs-Merrill, 1983.

Stowe, William W. *Going Abroad: European Travel in Nineteenth-Century American Culture.* Princeton: Princeton UP, 1993.

Sundquist, Eric J. *New Essays on Uncle Tom's Cabin.* Cambridge: Cambridge UP, 1986.

Surwillo, Lisa. "Representing the Slave Trader: *Haley* and the Slave Ship; or, Spain's *Uncle Tom's Cabin.*" *PMLA* 120 (2005): 768–782.

Sussman, Charlotte. *Consuming Anxieties: Consumer Protest, Gender, and British Slavery.* Stanford: Stanford UP, 2000.

Taft, Lorado. *The History of American Sculpture.* New ed. New York: Macmillan, 1924.

Tang, Edward. "Making Declarations of Her Own: Harriet Beecher Stowe as New England Historian." *New England Quarterly* 71.1 (1998): 77–96.

Taylor, Clare, ed. *British and American Abolitionists: An Episode in Transatlantic Understanding.* Edinburgh: Edinburgh UP, 1974.

Taylor, Helen. Letters 21 November 1856–2 January 1857. Mill-Taylor collection, Vol. 51. British Library of Political and Economic Science, London School of Economics.

Taylor, William R. *Cavalier and Yankee: The Old South and American National Character.* New York: Anchor, 1963.

Thistlethwaite, Frank. *The Anglo-American Connection in the Early Nineteenth Century.* Philadelphia: U of Pennsylvania P, 1959.

Thomson, Rosemarie Garland. "Benevolent Maternalism and Physically Disabled Figures: Dilemmas and Female Embodiment in Stowe, Davis, and Phelps." *American Literature* 68 (1996): 555–586.

"To the Duchess of Sutherland and the Ladies of England." *Southern Literary Messenger* 19 (February 1853): 120–126.

"To the Earl of Shaftesbury," *Times* (London), 1 December 1852, 8b.

"To the Editor of *The Times*," *Times* (London), 1 December 1852, 8c.

Tol'stoi, L. N. *Polnoe Sobranie Sochinenii.* Ed. V. G. Chertkov, *et al.* Vol. 47. Moscow: Khudozhestvennaia Literatura, 1937.

Tompkins, Jane. *Sensational Designs: The Cultural Work of American Fiction, 1790–1860*. New York: Oxford UP, 1985.

————. "Sentimental Power: *Uncle Tom's Cabin* and the Politics of Literary History." *The New Feminist Criticism: Essays on Women, Literature, and Theory*. Ed. Elaine Showalter. London: Virago, 1986. 81–104

Trotter, James M. *Music and Some Highly Musical People*. 1878. Chicago: Afro-American P, 1969.

Trumpener, Katie. *Bardic Nationalism: The Romantic Novel and the British Empire*. Princeton, NJ: Princeton UP, 1997.

Turgenev [Tourgueneff], Nikolai. *La Russie et les Russes*. 3 Vols. Paris: Comptoir des Imprimeurs-unis, 1847.

————. "Russia and the Russians." *The Liberty Bell: By Friends of Freedom*. Boston: National Anti-Slavery Bazaar, 1853. 210–225.

The Tyrant! The Slave!! The Victim!!! & The Tar!!!! London: Thomas Hailes Lacy, 1864.

Tyrrell, Alex. *Joseph Sturge and the Moral Radical Party in Early Victorian Britain*. London: Christopher Helm, 1987.

Uglow, Jenny. *Elizabeth Gaskell: A Habit of Stories*. 1993. London: Faber and Faber, 1999.

————. *Elizabeth Gaskell: A Habit of Stories*. New York: Farrar, Straus, Giroux, 1993.

"Uncle Tom's Cabin—or the Negro Slave." MS. Lord Chamberlain's Collection, British Library. 2.3.

"*Uncle Tom's Cabin*." *Blackwood's Edinburgh Magazine*. October 1853: 393–423.

Van Hook, Bailey. *Angels of Art: Women and Art in American Society, 1876–1914*. University Park, PA: Penn State UP, 1996.

Vance, William L. *America's Rome*. 2 vols. New Haven: Yale UP, 1989.

Vasilieva, M. E. "Notes of a Serf-Woman." 1911. Ed. and trans. John MacKay. *Slavery and Abolition*. 21.1 (2000). 146–158.

"Vnutrennie partii v Soedinennykh shtatkh." *Russkii Vestnik* (Sovremennaia letopis') 3.1 (1859): 1–17.

Wagenknecht, Edward. *Harriet Beecher Stowe: The Known and the Unknown*. New York: Oxford UP, 1965.

Waller, Ross D. *Letters Addressed to Mrs. Gaskell by Celebrated Contemporaries*. Manchester: Manchester UP, 1935.

Warhol, Robyn. *Gendered Interventions: Narrative Discourse in the Victorian Novel*. New Brunswick, NJ: Rutgers UP, 1989.

Warner, Charles Dudley. "The Story of *Uncle Tom's Cabin*." *Atlantic* 78 (1896): 311–321.

Warner, Susan. *The Wide, Wide World*. 1850. New York: Feminist P, 1987.

Waters, Hazel. "How Oroonoko Became Jim Crow: The Black Presence on the English Stage from the Late Eighteenth to the Mid-Nineteenth Century." Diss. U of London 2002.

Weinstein, Cindy, ed. *The Cambridge Companion to Harriet Beecher Stowe*. Cambridge: Cambridge UP, 2004

Weisbuch, Robert. *Atlantic Double-Cross: American Literature and British Influence in the Age of Emerson*. Chicago: U of Chicago P, 1986.

Weld, Rev. H. Hastings, ed. *The Women of the Scriptures*. Philadelphia: Lindsay and Blakiston, 1848.

Whitley, John S., and Arnold Goldman. Introduction. *American Notes for General Circulation*. By Charles Dickens. 1842. Harmondsworth: Penguin, 1985.

Williams, Raymond. *Culture and Society, 1780–1950*. New York: Columbia UP, 1960.

Wilson, C. P. "Tempests and Teapots: Harriet Beecher Stowe's *The Minister's Wooing*." *New England Quarterly* 58.4 (1985): 554–577.

Wilson, Forrest. *Crusader in Crinoline: The Life of Harriet Beecher Stowe*. Philadelphia: J. B. Lippincott, 1941.

Winks, Robin W. "The Making of a Fugitive Slave Narrative: Josiah Henson and Uncle Tom: A Case Study." *The Slave's Narrative*. Ed. Charles T. Davis and Henry Louis Gates, Jr. Oxford: Oxford UP, 1985. 112–147.

Winship, Michael. "The Transatlantic Book Trade and Anglo-American Literary Culture in the Nineteenth Century." *Reciprocal Influences: Literary Production, Distribution, and Consumption in America*. Ed. Steven Fink and Susan S. Williams. Columbus: Ohio State UP, 1999. 98–122.

Wise, Thomas James, and John Alexander Symington, eds. *The Shakespeare Head Brontë. The Brontës: Their Lives, Friendships, and Correspondence*. 2 vols. Oxford: Blackwell, 1933.

Wolstenholme, Susan. "Voice of the Voiceless: Harriet Beecher Stowe and the Byron Controversy." *American Literary Realism* 19.2 (1987): 48–65.

Wood, Marcus. *Slavery, Empathy, and Pornography*. Oxford: Oxford UP, 2002.

———. "Uncle Tom in England: The Publishing, Piracy, and Influence of *Uncle Tom's Cabin* in Britain, 1852–1900." *Publishing History* 32 (1992): 83–84.

Wright, Nathalia. *American Novelists in Italy: The Discoverers, Allston to James*. Philadelphia: U of Pennsylvania P, 1965.

Yellin, Jean Fagan. "Doing It Herself: *Uncle Tom's Cabin* and the Women's Role in the Slavery Crisis." *New Essays on* Uncle Tom's Cabin. Sundquist 85–105.

———. *Women and Sisters: The Antislavery Feminists in American Culture*. New Haven: Yale UP, 1989.

———, and John C. Van Horne, eds. *The Abolitionist Sisterhood: Women's Political Culture in Antebellum America*. Ithaca: Cornell UP, 1994.

Zaeske, Susan. *Signatures of Citizenship: Petitioning, Antislavery, and Women's Political Identity*. Chapel Hill: U of North Carolina P, 2003.

Zagarell, Sandra A. "Narrative of Community: The Identification of a Genre." *Signs* 13 (1988): 498–527.

"Zagranichnye izvestiia." *Sovremennik*. 61.1 (1857): 140–142.

INDEX

abolitionist movement. *See* antislavery movement

"The Achievement of the Genius of Scott" (Martineau), 113

Adams, Charles, 199–200, 206n16

Address to the Women of America, 132

advice literature, 197–98

"An Affectionate and Christian Address of the Many Thousands of Women of Great Britain and Ireland to Their Sisters" (Shaftesbury), 137

Agnes of Sorrento (Stowe), xv, xxvi, xxvii, 168–74, 175, 182–85; art as sacrament, 173–74, 175; blending of paganism and Christian moral purity, 171–73; body as art, 182–83; and female body, 180–82, 183–84; as international art novel, 168–69; and womanhood, 169–71, 185

Alcott, Louisa May, xiv

Alton Locke (Kingsley), 129

American and Foreign Anti-Slavery Society (AFASS), 138–39, 144n3

American Anti-Slavery Society (AASS), 138–39

American Notes for General Circulation (Dickens), xix

The American Woman's Home (Beecher and Stowe), 96, 197, 198

Ammons, Elizabeth, 17, 93

Angelico, Fra, 186n3

anti-Semitism, 124–25

antislavery movement: American-British relations, xxixn21; revitalization by *Uncle Tom's Cabin*, xxii; split within, 134–35, 136–37, 138–39

An Appeal to the Christian Women of the South (Grimké), 109n6

"An Appeal to the Women of the Free States of America" (Stowe), 93

Atlantic Monthly, xxvii, 3, 169

Augustinianism, 15

auto-exoticism: American women's literature, 30–31, 32–34; Irish women's literature, 24–25, 28–30, 33; *Uncle Tom's Cabin*, 26, 28, 32–34

Baender, Paul, 23n28

Bailey, Gamaliel, 135, 144n3

Baker, Dorothy Z., 22n16, 62n7

Baker, William, 129–30n6

Baldwin, George C., 199

Barker, Kathleen, 217–18

Barry, Thomas, 216

Barrymore, Maurice, 221

Batoni, Pompeo Girolamo, 178, 204

Baym, Nina, xiii, xxviiin4, 24, 35–36

Beecher, Catharine, 7, 15, 23n26, 100, 109n6; *American Women's Home*, 96, 197, 198

Beecher, Charles, 133, 140, 167, 177, 185;

travel journal, 153–55, 165n3, 165n5, 192, 193

Beecher, George, 153

Beecher, Henry Ward, 139, 174

Beecher, Lyman, xv, 5, 188, 189, 206n10, 206n13

Beecher, Sarah Buckingham, 153

Belinda (Edgeworth), 41

"Belles Lettres" (Eliot), 120

Belloc, M., 191, 192

Bentley, Richard, xviii

Berkson, Dorothy, 14, 63–64n16

Bhabha, Homi, 150–51

biblical female biographies, 199–201, 206–7n18. *See also Woman in Sacred History*

Biddles, Adelaide, 216

Bingham, J. A., 195–96, 197

Binney, Reverend, 139

Birmingham City Archives, 220

The Birth of Venus (Botticelli), 195

Blackwood's Edinburgh Magazine, xiv, xx, 117, 140, 142

Blake (Delaney), 129n3

Bludova, A. D., 74

Bodenheimer, Rosemarie, 104, 105

"Bodily Religion" (Stowe), 178

Boggs, Colleen Glenney, 208, 209

Bolton, H. Philip, 210, 216

Booth, Michael, 211

Borgstrom, Michael, 100

Botticelli, Sandro, 195

Bratton, J. S., 213

The Bride of Lammermoor (Scott): historical landscape of, 53–54; merging of Paganism and spirituality, 60; oracular women of, 49, 51–53; and *The Pearl of Orr's Island*, 46, 49, 56–57, 59, 61–62; and women's time, 59

Bright, John, 140–41

"Britannia, Hoxton" (*Era*), 211

British and Foreign Anti-Slavery Society (BFASS), 144n3

British Industrial Reform novel, 92–93

British stage productions, 210–12; censorship of, 215, 216, 220–21; influence of, 222; tar dramas, 213; *Uncle Tom's Cabin*, xi, xxi, 217–18. *See also Dred* (Stowe)

Brochart, Charles, 203

Brontë, Anne, 4–5, 21

Brontë, Charlotte, 21n4, 89

Brontë, Reverend, 5, 21n4

Brown, Gillian, 32–33, 96, 208–9

Brown, William Wells, 140–41

Browning, Elizabeth Barrett, xvi, xxvi

Browning, Robert, xxvi

Buckingham, William, 153

Burchard, S. D., 200, 206n16

Burr, Aaron, 11–12, 23n27

Burritt, Elihu, 137, 144n11

Byron, Lady, xxvii, 4, 8, 21n7; Stowe's defense of, 5, 18–19

Byron, Lord, xxvii, 3–9; *Don Juan*, 4, 6–7, 8–9, 23n21; eternal damnation theme, 5–6, 7–8; women conservative writers and, 3–4, 6–7, 21

Cain (Byron), 7

Calvinism, 188–89; Stowe's disenchantment with, 21, 63n16, 189

Campbell, Lord Chief Justice, 142

Carlisle, Earl of, 138, 144n12

Caskey, Marie, 186n1

Cass, Lewis, 87n10

Cassell, John, xx

Catholicism, 190

Chapman, Maria Weston, 72, 139

Le Charivari, xviii, xix, xxiv, xxv

Chase, Lucien, xxii

Christian Examiner, 93

Chute, J. H., 218

Cincinnati Journal, 155

Clark, H. Savile, 19, 20

Clarke and Company, xvii, xix

Clarkson, Thomas, 139

Claxton, Francis, 70

Cleon (Stowe), 21n6

Cleopatra (Story), xxvi, 177

Cobden, Richard, 140
Coelebs in Search of a Wife (More), 22n10
Coleman, John, 218
Committee of the Law and Order Party, 144n4
conduct literature, 197–98
Congregationalists, 205n5, 206n10
Coningsby (Disraeli), 125
"Constructing Female Public Identity" (Parker), 100
Contemporary, 70, 81, 86–87n6; *Uncle Tom's Cabin* in, 81–82, 83–85
Cooke, Nathaniel, xix
Cooper, Harwood, 221
Corinne (Staël), 3
Cornhill Magazine, 169
Cotugno, Clare, xvi
courtesy literature, 197–98
Crawford, Martin, xii
Crawford, Thomas, xxvi
Creswick, William, 216
Cropper, Edmund, 135
Crozier, Alice C., 5, 20–21, 62n1, 186n1
Crumpacker, Laurie, 63n7

Daily News (London), 125
Daily Times (New York), xxi, 18, 139
Daniel Deronda (Eliot), xvi, 112, 113, 121–24, 125–28; author's intent, 123–24; criticism of, 122–23, 130n7; and Jewish question, 125–26; separateness with communication theme, 126–28
David, Deirdre, 130n7
Davidson, Cathy, xiii, 198
Davis, Alfred, 219
Davis, Edward Dean, 218
Davis, Jim, 211
De Jong, Mary, 199, 200–1
Dead Souls (Gogol), 72
Deane, Seamus, 27
Decembrists, 87n11
"De Profundis" (Barrett Browning), xvi, xxvii
Delaney, Martin, 129n3

Delaroche, Paul, 203
Denvil, Mrs., 213
Deutsch, Emmanuel, 126
Dewey, Orville, 178–79
Diary in America (Marryat), xix
Dicey, Edward, 93
Dickens, Charles, xv, xix, xxi, 93
Disraeli, Benjamin, 125
Domestic Manners of the Americans (Trollope), xix
Don Juan (Byron), 4, 6–7, 8–9, 23n21
Douglass, Frederick, xxii, 139
Dred (Stowe), xiv, xvi, xxiv, 113, 116–20, 168; British stage adaptations, 210–21; censorship of, 220–21; criticism of, 117, 119–20; influence of, 222; melodrama in, 211–12; "Penny Pictorial," 214; playbills for, 219–20; popularity of, 217–18; provincial performances, 217–21; publication of, xxvi
Dubufe, Edouard, 203
Dunlap, William, 180

Eakins, Thomas, 179
Edgeworth, Maria, xv–xvi, 24, 25, 41, 44; education emphasis, 34–35; *Ennui*, 29–30, 32, 33, 35; Gothic influence, 29–30, 43; Irish and British identity, 27
Edinburgh Review, 101
Edwards, Jonathan, 12, 15
Egeria (nymph), 60
Elbert, Monika, xv
Eliot, George, 7; anti-Semitism of, 125–26, 130n7; *Dred*, critique of, 119–20; literary reform credo, 111–12, 115–16, 128; and spiritualism, 114–15; and Stowe, xvi–xvii, 111, 112, 114, 115, 119–20, 123–24. See also *Daniel Deronda*
Elliot, Dorice Williams, 102, 103
Elmore, Jenifer, 25
Elwin, Malcolm, 6
Emeljanow, Victor, 211
Emerson, Ralph Waldo, 49–51, 63n10
Emmons, Nathaniel, 23n26

engaging narrator, 94
Engel'son, Vladimir Aristovich, 71–72
English Notebooks (Hawthorne), 179–80
English Serfdom and American Slavery
    (Chase), xxii
Era, 211, 215, 216
An Essay on Slavery and Abolition
    (Beecher), 109n6
Evans, Augusta Jane, xiv
Eve, 190
"Eve of St. Agnes" (Keats), 181

"Fate" (Emerson), 63n10
Fedorov, D. D., 88n30
Feldman, David, 124, 125
Felix Holt (Eliot), 7
female divinity, 189–90
Fern, Fanny, xiv
Fetterley, Judith, 62n6
Field, Daniel, 81, 86n5
Fielder, Leslie, 27
Fields, Annie, 156, 163, 164
Fisch, Audrey, xxixn12, xxixn16, xxixn20,
    89, 90
Fladeland, Betty, 135, 140, 141
The Footsteps of the Master (Stowe), 189,
    194, 199
Formichella, Annamaria, 186n1
Foster, Charles H., 5, 22n13, 186n1
Foster, Shirley, xxiv–xxv
Franchot, Jenny, 179, 186n1
Franklin, Caroline, xvi, xxvii
Frederick Douglass' Paper, 142, 143
Freeman, Joanne B., 12
French and Italian Notebooks (Hawthorne),
    179, 180
Fuller, Margaret, 63n14
Fun Magazine, 18–19

Gallagher, Catherine, xxiii, 106
Gardella, Peter, 186n1
Gardner, Albert TenEyck, 179
Garrison, William Lloyd, xxii, 134–35,
    144n3

Gaskell, Elizabeth, xvi, xxvi, 90, 93, 100;
    and Stowe, 89, 90–91. *See also Mary
    Barton; North and South*
Gatta, John, 63n7, 63n16, 186n1
Gay, Peter, 179
Gertds, William H., 178
Gertsen, Aleksandr, 71, 72, 77–78, 79
Giles, Paul, xii, 91
Gilroy, Paul, xii, xxiv, 129n3
Glasgow Ladies' Anti-Slavery Society, 89,
    134
Glasgow New Association for the Aboli-
    tion of Slavery, 89, 134
Gogol, Nikolai, 72
Golovin, Ivan Gavrilovich, 79–80
Goodall, Frederick, 202, 203
Gravil, Richard, 91
The Greek Slave (Powers), 178–79
Greenfield, Elizabeth, xxiv
Greg, W. R., 101
Grimké, Angelina, 109n6
Grimsted, David, 211–12
Guiccioli, Teresa, xxvii, 23n21
Guy, Josephine, 110n9

Hadley, Elaine, 105
Haight, Gordon, 111, 114–15, 124, 125, 127
Hale, Sarah Josepha, 29, 30
Hall, Basil, xix
Halttunen, Karen, 62n1, 198
Hamilton, Alexander, 12
Harman, Barbara Leah, 104, 105, 106
Harris, Neil, 174
Harris, Susan K., 22n16
Harsh, Constance, 92, 104
Hawthorne, Nathaniel, xiii, xxvi, 177,
    179–80, 186n7
Heaven and Earth (Byron), 7
Hedrick, Joan D., xxii, 25, 31, 39, 92, 100,
    110n8, 117, 151, 152, 155, 162, 168, 177,
    185, 186n1, 188, 191, 206n13
Helen Fleetwood (Tonna), 92
Helsinger, Elizabeth, 129n5
Herzen, Alexander, 71, 72, 77–78, 79

The Hidden Hand (Southworth), xiv
Highland clearances, 164
"History" (Emerson), 49–51, 63n10
Holy Family Dell Divino, 195
Hood, Thomas, 216–17
Hosmer, Harriet, xxvi
Household Words (Dickens), xxi
Howard, William George Frederick, xvii
Humboldt, Alexander von, 80, 88n25

Ida of Athens (Owenson), 3
Imlay, Gilbert, 17
The Incarnation (Beecher), 22n11, 185
Ingram, Cooke and Company, xix
Innocents Abroad (Twain), 156
"The Internal Parties in the United
    States" (*Russian Messenger*), 76–77
international art novel, 168
Irish National Tale, 24, 25–26; education
    discourse, 34–35
Irish women's literature: and American
    women's literature, 24–25; auto-exoti-
    cism of, 28–30, 33; criticism of, 27;
    politicization of, 24, 25
Irving, Henry, 219
Italy (Owenson), 3

Jameson, Anna, 167, 171, 174, 175, 182,
    186n3
Jehenne, Paris, 202
Jewett, Sarah Orne, 48, 62n5
Judeo-Christianity, diminution of female
    divinity, 189–90

Karcher, Carolyn L., 36, 44n3
Kasson, Joy, 178, 179
Keats, John, 181
Kestner, Joseph, 92
A Key to Uncle Tom's Cabin (Stowe), xxiv,
    133, 137
Khomyakov, Alexei Stepanovich, 74–76
Kimbrell, Gayle, 23n26
Kingsley, Charles, vii, xv, 129
Kolchin, Peter, 75

Kossuth, Louis, 139
Kowhler, Christian, 203
Kristeva, Julia, 51
Krueger, Christine, 107

Lacy, Thomas Hailes, xi
Lady Byron Vindicated (Stowe), xv, xxvii,
    3, 4, 8, 9, 21n2, 21n7
Lamb, Caroline, 3, 23n21
Landelle, Charles, 204
Lander, Maria Louise, xxvi
"Landowners and Peasants" (*Russian Mes-
    senger*), 78–79
Lane, Sarah, 213
Lang, Cecil, 3, 19
Lansbury, Marquis of, 138
Leah and Rachel (Portael), 203
Lebedun, Jean, 22n19
Leerssen, Joep, 27, 28
Legends of the Madonna (Jameson), 171,
    174, 175–76
Leigh, Medora, 19
Lemke, Mikhail, 79
Lemon, Mark, 217
Lenard, Mary, 107
Letters from Abroad to Kindred at Home
    (Sedgwick), 166n8
Letters of Mrs. Gaskell, 89
letter-writing, 152–53
Levine, Robert S., 117, 129n3
Liberating Sojourn (Crawford and Rice),
    xii
Liberator, 137
The Liberty Bell, 72
The Libyan Sibyl (Story), xxvi–xxvii, 177
Life and Letters (Sedgwick), 24
Life of Byron (Moore), 4
The Life of Charlotte Brontë (Gaskell), 89
Lincoln, Abraham, xiii
The Linwoods (Sedgwick), 35, 36, 37, 45n8
London *Daily News*, 125
London *Spectator*, 89
London *Times*, 90, 142, 210, 216
Lord Byron's Defence (Clark), 19, 20

Low, Sampson, xxvi, 133
Lowell, James Russell, 191

Mackay, Charles, 19
MacKay, John, xxiv, 209
Macmillan's Magazine, 3
Madonna del Cardellino (Raphael), 195
Madonna del Gran Duca (Raphael), 194
Magnalia Christi Americana (Mather), 190
Manning, Charles Henry, xxvi, 28
Manning, Susan, 25–26
The Marble Faun (Hawthorne), xxvi, 177, 186n7
Marryat, Captain, xix
Martineau, Harriet, 7, 113–14, 116
Mary Barton (Gaskell), 91–96, 110n9; criticism of, 101; engaged narration, 94; and middle-class women, 95; and *Uncle Tom's Cabin*, 93–96
Mary the Mother of Jesus (Goodall), 202
Mather, Cotton, 62n7, 190
McCord, Louisa, xxiii
Meyer, Susan, 130n7
Middlemarch (Eliot), 115
Midgley, Clare, 96, 135, 217
Milbanke, Annabella, 6. See also Byron, Lady
Mill, John Stuart, 3
Mills, Sara, 150
Mills, T. E., 220
The Minister's Wooing (Stowe), xiv, xvi, 12–13, 22n18, 22–23n20, 168; and New England theology, 10–11
mir (traditional village community), 75
Miriam and Moses (Delaroche), 203
"Modern Uses of Language" (Stowe), 39
Moers, Ellen, 117
Moncrieffe, Margaret, 14
Moon, David, 70, 86n3
Moore, Thomas, 4
More, Hannah, 6, 7, 8, 22n10
Morgan, Lady. *See* Owenson, Sydney
Morpeth, Lord. *See* Carlisle, Earl of
My Recollections of Lord Byron and Those

of Eyewitnesses of His Life (Guiccioli), 23n21

The Nation, 18
National Anti-Slavery Standard, 142
National Era, 144n3
"The Natural History of German Life" (Eliot), 115, 120
Nazarenes, 186n3
Nekrasov, Nikolai, 81, 88n26
New Association for the Abolition of Slavery, 89, 134
New York Daily Times, xxi, 18, 139
New York Herald, xxi–xxii
Newman, Judie, xxvi
Nicholas II, 86n3
Nikoljukin, Alexander, 81
North American Review, 142, 145n19
North and South (Gaskell), 91–92; and women in public sphere, 100–8
North Star, xxii
Northern Ensign, xxiii–xxiv
Northwood (Hale), 29, 30
Norton, Charles Edward, 109n1
The Nottingham Weekly Journal, 218
Novosil'skii, P. M., 81–82
nudes in art, 174–80

Ó Gallchoir, Clíona, xv–xvi
O'Brien, Michael, 28
O'Connell, Catherine, 94, 98
"Old Oak" (Stowe), 174, 184–85
Oldtown Folks (Stowe), xiv, xvi, 13–18
Olien, Diana Davids, 144n12
Orlova, Raisa D., 81
Ormond (Edgeworth), 35
"The Over-Soul" (Emerson), 63n10
Owenson, Sydney, 3, 24, 25, 44; Gothic influence on, 29, 43; Irish and British identity, 27; *The Wild Irish Girl*, 27, 29

Parker, Pamela Corpron, 95, 100, 107
Parrington, Vernon Louis, 63n16
Paul, 206n6

Pavilion Theatre, 221

The Pearl of Orr's Island (Stowe), xiv, 46–49, 54–62, 63n8; and *The Bride of Lammermoor*, 46, 49, 56–57, 59, 61–62; conflation of magical and mundane, 48; merging of paganism and spirituality, 60; mysticism of, 47–48; oracular women of, 48–49, 54–59, 60; and women's time, 59–60

"Penny Pictorial" (Seaman), 214

Phelps, Elizabeth Stuart, xiv

Phillips, Frederick, 215, 220

Pictures of the Virgin and Her Son (Beecher), 22n11, 185

Pinion, F. B., 5

Poganuc People: Their Lives and Loves (Stowe), 199

Pointon, Marcia, 180, 185

Pollack, Lord Chief Justice, 137–38

Portael, Jean François, 203

Porter, Dennis, 150

Powers, Hiram, xxvi, 178–79, 186n6

print media, 187–88

prophecy, 48

proslavery movement, xxiii

Pryse, Marjorie, 26, 28, 34

Punch (Hood), 217

Puschin, I. I., 71, 82

Putnam's Monthly, 143

Raphael Sanzio, 194–95, 202

Redwood (Sedgwick), 30–31, 36–37

Reed, James, 52

reform aesthetic, 112–13, 128–29, 129n2. *See also Daniel Deronda; Dred*

Reform Bill (1867), 124–25

religious iconography: Calvinist objection to, 188–89. *See also* Stowe, Harriet Beecher

Religious Training of Children in the School, the Family, and the Church (Beecher), 15

Reynold's Newspaper, xxiii–xxiv

Rice, Alan, xii

Riehl, Wilhelm, 115

Rineer, Carla, xxvi

Romantics, 63n11

Romero, Lora, 7

Ross, Donald, xxii, xxv

Rovira (Golovin), 79–80

Ruskin, John, xvi, 186n3

Russell, Lord John and Lady, 139

Russia: censorship of *Uncle Tom's Cabin*, 69–70, 81, 82–85; *mir* (traditional village community), 75; press censorship, 69, 86n5; publication of *Uncle Tom's Cabin*, 67, 69, 81–82; resonance of *Uncle Tom's Cabin*, 71–73, 75; responses to *Uncle Tom's Cabin*, 68, 71–79; serfdom, 67, 68–69, 75, 77–79

Russian Messenger , 76–77, 78–79, 86n6; version of *Uncle Tom's Cabin,* 81, 82, 83, 85

"Russian Serfdom" (Herzen), 77–78, 79

La Russie et les Russes (Turgenev), 72

Ruth Hall (Fern), xiv

Ryan, Mary P., 198

Sabiston, Elizabeth Jean, 94

Sacred and Legendary Art (Jameson), 182

Sand, George, 70

Sanzio, Raphael, 194–95, 202

Sara the Princess (Brochart), 203

Saul, Norman, 70

Scott, Walter, xv, 46–48, 50. *See also The Bride of Lammermoor*

Scottish National Penny Offering, 132

Seaman, William, 214

Sedgwick, Catharine Maria, 24, 25, 44, 166n8; Gothic influence, 43; *The Linwoods*, 35, 36, 37, 45n8; narrative strategies, 44n3; *Redwood*, 30–31, 36–37

Semevskii, V. I., 74, 87n15

Semmel, Bernard, 129–30n6

The Sempstress (Lemon), 217

Senior, Nassau William, xx

sentimental novel, 45n8

serfdom, 67, 68–69, 75, 77–79

Shaftesbury, Earl of, xxiii, xxiv, 132, 137, 138, 139, 140
Shakespearean plays, 209
Shelley, Mary, 3
Shepherd, Richard, 216
Sherman, Sarah Way, 64n16, 64n18
"A Short Story" (Winthrop), 190
"Silly Novels by Lady Novelists" (Eliot), 112
Simpson, Mercer Hampson, 220–21
Sistine Madonna (Raphael), 195, 202
The Slaveholder Abroad (Starnes), xxii
"Slavery" (*Blackwood's Edinburgh Magazine*), xiv
Slavophile thinkers, 74
Smith, Gail K., xxvi
Smith, Sidney, xvii
Smith, Whitney Womack, xvi
"The Song of the Shirt" (Hood), 216–17
Son of the Fatherland, 81
Soth, Lauren, 205
Southwood, Marian, xxii
Southworth, E. D. E. N., xiv
Soviet Union, 67
Spectator (London), 89
St. Elmo (Evans), xiv
Staël, Germaine de, 3
Star of Freedom, xxiii–xxiv
Star Papers (Beecher), 174
Starnes, Ebenezer, xxii
Stars and Stripes (Golovin), 79
Steele, Thomas J., 38
Stone, A. L., 200
Stone, Lucy, 139
The Stones of Venice (Ruskin), xvi
The Story of Avis (Phelps), xiv
Story, William Wetmore, xxvi–xxvii, 90, 177
Stowe, Calvin, vii, 110n8, 153, 178; antislavery speeches, 131, 134, 135, 141
Stowe, Charles, 150
Stowe, Harriet Beecher, xiii, xiv–xv, xxiv–xxv, 90, 109n1, 149–50; and Anglicanism, 62–63n7; and biblical women, 190–92, 199, 201–4; British Industrial Reform novel, 92–93; British popular culture and, 209–10; and fictional portrayals of Burr, 12, 14–15; Byron and, 5, 8, 9–10, 11, 12, 21, 21n7; and Calvinism, 21, 63n16, 189; conservatism *vs.* radical vision, 8–9; and *Daniel Deronda*, 122–23; and Edgeworth, 25; and Eliot, xvi–xvii, 111, 112, 114, 115, 123–24; exaltation of Venus, 193–94; and Gaskell, 89, 90–91, 93–94; and Lady Byron, 5, 18–19; literary influences, xv; literary reform credo, 111, 115, 128; Mariolatry, 194–95, 202; nudes and, 177–78; public persona, 149, 151–52; publishing savvy, xxvi, 133; reasoning, 39–40; religious iconography, 188; and Scott, 46–48; and Sedgwick, 37, 44n3; spiritualism, 114; theology, 10–11, 12, 14–16; transatlantic exchanges, xi–xii, xvi–xvii, xxvi–xxvii; and true womanhood, 17, 18, 22n17, 100; vision of female divinity, 194–97. *See also specific works*
Stowe, William, 151
Sturge, Joseph, 132, 135–37, 144n3, 144nn9–11, 154
The Subjection of Women (Mill), 3
Sunny Memories of Foreign Lands (Stowe), xv, xvi, xxiv–xxv, 166n10, 188; American republicanism, 162–64; Anglo-American connectedness, 151; antislavery movement and, 133–34, 136; on art, 170, 173, 174, 178, 192, 204, 207n22; British aristocracy and, 137–39, 140, 164; Calvin Stowe's antislavery speeches, 131, 134, 135, 141; and Charles Beecher's journal, 153–55; criticism of, 142–43; epistolary form, 152, 155; iconoclasm, 161–62; intent of, 132–33, 153, 167; Mariolatry, 202; mix of travel and political content, 131–32, 133; narrative voices, 153–65; and pacifism, 137; and religion, 192–93; self-referential irony, 149, 154–55, 158–61, 165n6; sentimental tourism,

156–58; and social ills, 139–40, 145n18; temperance message, 141–42; and Venus, 194

"Surrey Theatre" (*Times*), 210

Sussman, Charlotte, 96, 98

Suter, W. E., 214–15

Sutherland, Duchess of, 132, 163, 164

Sutherland, Duke of, 163, 164

Swinburne, Algernon, 19

Talfourd, Justice, xvi

Tancred (Disraeli), 125

Tappan, Lewis, 144n3, 144n11

tar dramas, 213

Taylor, Helen, 218–19, 220

Taylor, Nathaniel, 5

Taylor, William R., 28, 29, 30, 31

The Tenant of Wildfell Hall (Brontë), 4–5

Theatres Act (1843), 215

"The Thieving Magpie" (Herzen), 72

Thompson, George, 139

Thomson, Rosemarie Garland, 100

Times (London), 90, 142, 210, 216

Tit for Tat (Southwood), xxii

Tolstoy, Leo, 71

Tompkins, Jane, xiii, 38, 45n8, 96, 99

Tonna, Charlotte Elizabeth, xv, 92

A Tramp Abroad (Twain), 156

transatlantic literary scholarship, xii, 209

transcendentalism, 50

travel writing, 150–51

Travels in America (Hall), xix

A Treatise on Domestic Economy (Beecher), 7

Trimmer, Sarah, 6

Trollope, Frances, xix

true womanhood: cult of, 4–5, 7; biblical biographers and, 201; fictional antitype, 63n9; fictional examples, 63n8; Stowe and, 17, 18, 22n17, 100; *The Wide, Wide World*, 187–88

"The True Story of Lady Byron's Life" (Stowe), xxvii, 3, 7

Turgenev, Ivan, 71

Turgenev, Nikolai Ivanovich, 72–73, 74, 87n14

Twain, Mark, 23n28, 156

Tyler, Julia Gardiner, xxiii, 141

The Tyrant! The Slave!! The Victim!!! & The Tar!!!! (Lacy), xi

Uglow, Jenny, 101

Uncle Tom Penny Offering, xxii, xxxixn20

"Uncle Tom's" (*Blackwood's Edinburgh Magazine*), xx

Uncle Tom's Cabin (Stowe), xiv; agency of characters, 38–39, 40–41, 96–98; antislavery movement and, xxii, xxiii, 34; auto-exoticism of, 26, 28, 32–34; censorship of, 69–70, 81, 82–85, 86n2; contrastive structure, 31–34; criticism of, vii–viii; domestic benefactress theme, 96–99; domesticity as gauge of moral character, 97, 109–10n7; education theme, 34, 40–43; engaged narration of, 94; and Enlightenment thought, 38–40; European critiques of U.S., xx–xxii; foreign publications, xviii–xx, 67, 69, 81–82; Gothic influence, 43–44; instability of interpretation, 209; and *Mary Barton*, 93–96; and middle-class women, 96–99; Russian intelligentsia's response to, 68, 71–79; savior theme, 37–38, 42–43, 99; stage adaptations, xi, xxi, 217–18; success of, vii, xvii–xviii, 69, 90

Van Gogh, Vincent, 204–5, 207n23

Van Hook, Bailey, 169

Vance, William L., 179, 186n1

Vindication of the Rights of Woman (Wollstonecraft), 4

The Vision of Judgment (Byron), 7

Waller, Ross D., 93

Ward, Samuel, 141

Warhol, Robyn, 94

Warner, Susan, xiv, 187–88, 205nn1–2

Waters, Hazel, 222–23n3
Webb, Mary, xxiv
Weisbuch, Robert, xii
Weld, H. Hastings, 200
West Indies, emancipation of, 144n9
Westminster Review, 112, 119
white slave debate, xxiii–xxiv
The Wide, Wide World (Warner), xiv,
    187–88, 205nn1–2
Widow of Nain (Goodall), 203
The Widow's Mite (Dubufe), 203
Wigham, Eliza, 135
The Wild Irish Girl (Owenson), 27, 29
Wilkinson, James, 12
Williams, Arthur, 221
Williams, Raymond, 95, 101
Wilson, C. P., 23n21
Wilson, Forrest, 138, 167, 177, 185

Winship, Michael, 91
Winthrop, John, 190
Wollstonecraft, Mary, 4, 17
Wolstenholme, Susan, 18
"Woman" (Emerson), 63n10
Woman in Sacred History (Stowe), xv,
    64n17, 178, 199, 201–4, 206n12; repro-
    duction of religious iconography,
    205n2, 207n21
Woman's Fiction (Baym), xxviiin4, 24
The Women of the Scriptures (Weld), 200
women's movement, 4
Work (Alcott), xiv
The Works of Charlotte Elizabeth (Gaskell),
    92
The Wrongs of Women (Tonna), 92

Yellin, Jean Fagan, 96